NOW URBANISM

After more than a century of heroic urban visions, urban dwellers today live in suburban subdivisions, gated communities, edge cities, apartment towers, and slums. The contemporary cities we know are more often the embodiment of unexpected outcomes and unintended consequences rather than visionary planning.

As an alternative approach for rethinking and remaking today's cities and regions, this book explores the intersections of critical inquiry and immediate, substantive actions. The contributions inside recognize the rich complexities of the present city not as barriers or obstacles but as grounds for uncovering opportunity and unleashing potential. *Now Urbanism* asserts that the future city is already here. It views city making as grounded in the imperfect, messy, yet rich reality of the existing city and the everyday purposeful agency of its dwellers.

Through a framework of *situating, grounding, performing, distributing, instigating,* and *enduring,* these contributions—written by a multidisciplinary group of practitioners and scholars—illustrate specificity, context, agency, and networks of actors and actions in the remaking of the contemporary city.

Jeffrey Hou is Professor and Chair of Landscape Architecture at the University of Washington. His work focuses on critical urbanism, design activism, and democratic placemaking. His previous books include *Greening Cities, Growing Communities: Learning from Seattle's urban community gardens* (2009), *Insurgent Public Space: Guerrilla urbanism and the remaking of contemporary cities* (2010) and *Transcultural Cities: Border-crossing and placemaking* (2013).

Benjamin Spencer is Assistant Professor in the Department of Landscape Architecture and Adjunct Assistant Professor in the Department of Global Health at the University of Washington. His research engages design as a catalyst for sustainable, community-driven development and technology and its cultural integration.

Thaisa Way is a landscape historian teaching history, theory, and design in the Department of Landscape Architecture at the University of Washington. Her work focuses on feminist and alternative histories of landscape architecture in the US, including *Unbounded Practice: Women and landscape architecture in the early twentieth century* (2009) and *The Landscape Architecture of Richard Haag: From modern to urban ecological design* (forthcoming).

Ken Yocom is Associate Professor in the Department of Landscape Architecture at the University of Washington. His work focuses on the functional convergence of urban design and ecological processes, specifically examining design responses to the impact of development on urban water systems. He is a co-author of *Basics Landscape Architecture 02: Ecological design* (2011).

Now Urbanism is a landmark for students and practitioners of contemporary urban planning, design, and scholarship. Its provocative subtitle, "the future city is [already] here," insists that it is time to stop being distracted by utopias. There's no perfect urban model waiting for us just around the bend, its editors argue, adding that we'd do better to stop, listen, and learn about the future city in the present, from the informal settlements of Caracas to the streets of Mumbai, to the glass and green of Silicon Valley. This volume makes the case that if we fail to understand the reality and richness of contemporary urban experience, cities will be at risk repeating the mistakes of the mid-20th century—swinging urban renewal's wrecking ball through functioning, sustainable socioeconomic networks. Here is a 21st-century case for an alternative approach, structured into themes of analysis and action including "performing," "distributing," and "instigating." Through case studies, histories, and speculative projects grounded in place, Now Urbanism cuts a section through the "thick" city. There's no panacea here, yet there's enough breadth, fervor, and evidence to show that engagement with community is fundamental for planning a sustainable future that includes 2 billion new city dwellers by 2050.

Ray Gastil, AICP, City Planning Director, Pittsburgh, USA

This thoughtful, thought-provoking collection examines—and questions—the forms, mechanisms, practices and ethics of contemporary urbanism. Using case studies from across the developed and developing worlds to track the significance of cultural context, historical process, political agency, grassroots activism and ecological transformation, *Now Urbanism* makes a compelling argument for the power of tactical intervention to catalyze meaningful change.

Jane Wolff, Associate Professor, University of Toronto, Canada,
Daniels Faculty of Architecture, Landscape, and Design

NOW URBANISM

The Future City is Here

*Edited by Jeffrey Hou, Benjamin Spencer,
Thaisa Way, and Ken Yocom*

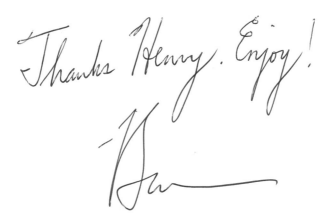

Routledge
Taylor & Francis Group

LONDON AND NEW YORK

First published 2015
by Routledge
2 Park Square, Milton Park, Abingdon, Oxon OX14 4RN

and by Routledge
711 Third Avenue, New York, NY 10017

Routledge is an imprint of the Taylor & Francis Group, an informa business

British Library Cataloguing-in-Publication Data
A catalogue record for this book is available from the British Library

Library of Congress Cataloging-in-Publication Data
Now urbanism : the future city is here / edited by Jeff Hou, Benjamin Spencer, Thaisa Way and Ken Yocom
    pages cm
  Includes bibliographical references and index.
  1. City planning. 2. Cities and towns. I. Hou, Jeffrey, 1967–
HT165.5.N69 2014
  307.1'216–dc23   2014013320

ISBN: 978-0-415-71785-4 (hbk)
ISBN: 978-0-415-71786-1 (pbk)
ISBN: 978-1-315-75306-5 (ebk)

Typeset in Bembo
by Keystroke, Station Road, Codsall, Wolverhampton

Printed and bound in India by Replika Press Pvt. Ltd.

CONTENTS

Enduring   **241**

Afterword   **287**

NOTES ON CONTRIBUTORS

Jorge Alarcon is a practicing architect and the on-site coordinator for the Informal Urban Communities Initiative. His recent work has focused on architectural research and design projects with positive social and ecological impacts in the slums surrounding Lima, Peru.

Martin Joseph Barry is a Fulbright Scholar and Associate at W Architecture in New York. He is the founder of reSITE, a non-profit think-tank based in Prague, and is currently a Fellow with the Design Trust for Public Space. He lectures in the US and Europe about landscape and urbanism.

John Bela is an urbanist and artist focused on public space design. He co-founded Rebar Group and created some of the firm's most ground-breaking work, including Park(ing) Day and the Victory Garden. He is currently a lead urban designer with Gehl Studio, and a Distinguished Lecturer at the University of California, Berkeley.

Susan Bolton is a Professor in the School of Environmental and Forest Sciences, an Adjunct Professor in Civil and Environmental Engineering, and an Adjunct Professor in Global Health at the University of Washington. Her current research focuses on international sustainable development in Costa Rica, Bolivia, Peru, and Guatemala.

Viren Brahmbhatt (Principal | de.Sign) is an architect and urban designer based in New York. In addition to his practice, he is Adjunct Associate Professor of Architecture at Columbia University and Visiting Professor at Pratt Institute. His work strives to achieve small but implementable change in cities like New York and Mumbai.

Joshua Brevoort is Chief Scientist and co-founder of zeroplus, an architectural practice that has been building projects and questioning the future of architecture and building construction since 1999. His work at zeroplus has been awarded, published, and exhibited widely and he has taught and lectured at the University of Washington.

Alfredo Brillembourg was trained as an architect at Columbia University, where he remains a Guest Professor. He founded the award-winning interdisciplinary design firm Urban-Think Tank with Hubert Klumpner in Caracas. Since 2010, the two have held a Chair of Architecture and Urban Design at the Swiss Institute of Technology in Zürich.

Jon Christensen is an Adjunct Assistant Professor, journalist-in-residence and senior fellow in the Institute of the Environment and Sustainability, the California Center for Sustainable Communities, the Department of History, the Center for Digital Humanities, and cityLAB at UCLA. He has been an environmental journalist and science writer for over 30 years.

Lisa Chun is co-founding partner of zeroplus, an architectural practice that brings together innovative thinkers as collaborators and clients. With co-founder Joshua Brevoort, she creates a wide range of built projects and research-based investigations exploring the thresholds of current design possibilities. She has also taught design studios at the University of Washington.

Thomas Fisher is Professor and Dean of the College of Design at the University of Minnesota. His books include *In the Scheme of Things: Alternative thinking on the practice of architecture* (2006), *Ethics for Architects: 50 dilemmas of professional practice* (2010), and *Designing to Avoid Disaster: The nature of fracture-critical design* (2012).

Denise Hoffman Brandt is Director and Associate Professor of Landscape Architecture at the City College of New York and Principal of Hoffman Brandt Projects, LLC. Her work focuses on landscape as ecological infrastructure, the social, cultural, and environmental systems that generate urban form and sustain urban life.

Jeffrey Hou is Professor and Chair of Landscape Architecture at the University of Washington. His work focuses on critical urbanism, design activism, and democratic placemaking. His previous books include *Greening Cities, Growing Communities: Learning from Seattle's urban community gardens* (2009), *Insurgent Public Space: Guerrilla urbanism and the remaking of contemporary cities* (2010) and *Transcultural Cities: Border-crossing and placemaking* (2013).

Andrew Karvonen is a Lecturer in Architecture and Urbanism in the School of Environment, Education and Development at the University of Manchester, UK. He studies the politics and practice of sustainable urban development with a particular focus on the role of infrastructure networks in the production of cities.

Hubert Klumpner was trained as an architect at the University of Applied Arts in Vienna and Columbia University. He founded the award-winning interdisciplinary design firm Urban-Think Tank with Alfredo Brillembourg in Caracas. He is currently serving as the Dean of the Architecture Department at the Swiss Institute of Technology in Zürich.

Laura Kozak is a designer, curator, and educator. She has contributed to projects at 221A Artist Run Centre, AICAD, ASIR Studio, CityStudio Vancouver, Helen Pitt Gallery, and Spacing Vancouver. A core interest in collaborative design of the urban environment informs her research and teaching practice at Emily Carr University of Art + Design.

William Morrish is Professor of Urban Ecologies at Parsons The New School for Design, author of *Civilizing Terrains* (1996), and co-author of *Building for the Arts* (1984), *Planning To Stay* (2000), and *Growing Urban Habitats* (2009). He is a nationally recognized urban designer whose interdisciplinary research and practice is applied to innovative community-based city projects.

Joseph Mulligan is a Chartered Civil Engineer and Associate Director of Kounkuey Design Initiative. He specializes in the design and implementation of sustainable infrastructure systems and innovative water management strategies, in both rural and urban contexts. He has extensive field experience in Asia, Africa, Latin America, Europe, and the US.

Arisa Nakamura is a graduate student in Landscape Architecture at University of Washington. She studied Social Engineering and Community Design at Tokyo Institute of Technology from 2010 until 2013. Her recent research focuses on community and art.

Osamu Nishida founded ON Design Partners, a practice based in Yokohama, Japan. The recipient of many awards including the JIA Young Architect Award, and the JCD Design Award silver prize for Roppongi Nouen Farm, he teaches at the University of Tokyo, Tokyo University of Science, and Kyoto University of Art and Design.

Chelina Odbert is co-founder and Executive Director of the award-winning design and community development firm, Kounkuey Design Initiative. She leads urban and rural development projects throughout Africa, Latin American, and the US. Her research, writing, and practice focus on the intersection of participatory planning and design, and economic development.

Margaret O'Mara is Associate Professor of History at the University of Washington. She is the author of *Cities of Knowledge: Cold War science and the search for the next Silicon Valley* (2005). Her current research explores high technology's impact on American politics and culture since the 1970s.

Daniel H. Ortega is an Associate Professor of Landscape Architecture at the University of Nevada Las Vegas. He currently holds the appointment of Landscape Architecture and Planning Program Coordinator. His interests lie in the cultural interpretations of place and the role(s) that those interpretations play in crafting urban landscapes.

Gundula Proksch is a scholar, registered architect, and Assistant Professor of Architecture at the University of Washington. Her research investigates sustainable infrastructures and the design with living systems, such as urban agriculture. Over the past 18 years, she has practiced and taught architecture in New York, London, Vienna, and Seattle.

Irma Ramirez is Professor of Architecture at California State Polytechnic University Pomona and teaches housing and urban design. Her degrees are a B.S. in Architecture from UCBerkeley, and an M.Arch. and M.URP. from UCLA. Among other awards, she has received the National Lynton Citation Award for Distinguished Scholarship, and has been co-awarded the NCARB Grand Prize for work in Mexico and the EDRA Planning Research Award for work in China.

Deni Ruggeri is Assistant Professor of Landscape Architecture at the University of Oregon. His research and teaching focus on promoting livability and place identity in master-planned communities. He participates in EU-funded international cooperation programs for the promotion of landscape-based urbanism. His most recent community-based effort, *Zingonia 3.0*, employs urban and landscape design to shift the public narrative of an Italian New Town from decline to resilience.

Benjamin Spencer is Assistant Professor in the Department of Landscape Architecture and Adjunct Assistant Professor in the Department of Global Health at the University of Washington. His research engages design as a catalyst for sustainable, community-driven development and technology and its cultural integration.

Judith Stilgenbauer is an Associate Professor of Landscape Architecture at the University of Hawaii's School of Architecture. In her creative work in teaching, applied research, and professional practice, she examines the role of placemaking, process, performance, and production in the designed urban landscape across spatial and temporal scales.

Thaisa Way is a landscape historian teaching history, theory, and design in the Department of Landscape Architecture at the University of Washington. Her work focuses on feminist and alternative histories of landscape architecture in the US, including *Unbounded Practice: Women and landscape architecture in the early twentieth century* (2009) and *The Landscape Architecture of Richard Haag: From modern to urban ecological design* (forthcoming).

Ken Yocom is Associate Professor in the Department of Landscape Architecture at the University of Washington. His work focuses on the functional convergence of urban design and ecological processes, specifically examining design responses to the impact of development on urban water systems. He is a co-author of *Basics Landscape Architecture 02: Ecological design* (2011).

ACKNOWLEDGMENTS

This book represents the culmination of intersecting inquiries by faculty members at the University of Washington (UW) since 2009. The term "Now Urbanism" first arose out of a faculty retreat of the College of Built Environments in May of that year. The retreat was arranged around a series of self-organized, cross-disciplinary faculty groups to develop a set of "schematic agenda" for the future development of the College. Now Urbanism was a concept developed by one faculty group that included Jennifer Dee, Robert Mugerauer, Ken Tadashi Oshima, and Vikramāditya Prakāsh, in addition to the editors of this book. With "Situated Urbanism," "Porous Urbanism," and "Performative Urbanism" as specific facets, Now Urbanism represents a focus on cities as-is, and the urgency of actions to address the environmental, social, spatial, and political challenges and opportunities facing the planet today. We are indebted to the collegiality, camaraderie, and collective wisdom of our co-conspirators.

Over the next few months after the faculty retreat, there were several discussions on ways to turn the concept into actual initiatives. One initiative was in response to an invitation to propose a 2010–2012 John E. Sawyer Seminar at the University of Washington with funding from the Andrew W. Mellon Foundation. With Thaisa Way and Margaret O'Mara as the principal investigators, lead collaborators included Susan Bolton, Kim England, Ray Gastil, Deborah Guenther, Jeffrey Hou, Susan Kemp, Anne Vernez Moudon, Gina Neff, Ben Spencer, Peter Steinbrueck, Barbara Swift, James Tweedie, Kathleen Woodward, Ken Yocom, and Joseph R. Zunt. Titled "Now Urbanism: City-Making in the Twenty-First Century," the two-year-long series of lectures, symposia, and seminars eventually involved over 125 faculty members from across every college at UW and at least 1,500 members of the public, to discuss issues ranging from informal settlements and global health to the roles of universities in cities. We are grateful to the Andrew W. Mellon Foundation for funding the initiative and to the College of Built Environments, the College of Arts & Sciences, the Simpson Center for the Humanities, UW Alumni Foundation, and the Graduate School of the University of Washington for supporting the long list of activities. In addition, Now Urbanism was a central component of NEXT CITY, a two-year special initiative of the UW Office of the Provost that focused on the challenges and opportunities of urbanization in the twenty-first century.

While the planning for the Now Urbanism initiative was under way, a separate effort to organize a symposium titled "Next Eco-City: Emergent Urbanism" was initiated by the UW Department of Landscape Architecture. Intended as a critique of the recent Eco-City development in developing economies, the symposium eventually became a component of the Now Urbanism initiative. Featuring speakers including Kongjian Yu, Jane Wolff, Andrew Karvonen, Kristina Hill, Chelina Odbert, Jennifer Toy, Viren Brahmbhatt, Alfredo Brillembourg, John Bela, Nicholas de Monchaux, and Denise Hoffman Brandt, the event provided the impetus for this book. We would like to thank Daniel Friedman, the former Dean of the UW College of Built Environments for providing the intellectual and financial support for the symposium, and to Anchor QEA, Gustafson Guthrie Nichol, and SvR Design Company for co-sponsoring the event that took place at the Seattle Central Library. We are also grateful to Kelley Pagano, who provided key staff support for the symposium, and to Tera Hatfield, who contributed the visual design.

With the presentations from the symposium as the initial materials and as a blueprint, we invited additional contributors to enrich the diverse perspectives embodied in this project. As co-editors, we would like to thank all the contributors to this book who take us on a collective journey to Caracas, Las Vegas, Lima, Manchester, Mumbai, Nairobi, the New Towns of Harlow (United Kingdom), Marne-la-Vallée (France), and Irvine (California), New York City, Prague, San Francisco, Seattle, Silicon Valley, Tijuana, Tokyo, Vancouver, and other present cities of the Global South and North. In bringing this project to a larger audience, we would also like to thank Louise Fox, the Landscape Editor at Routledge, for recognizing the value of this work, and to our assistant Nancy Chan, whose impeccable organizational and editorial skills were instrumental in bringing the project to completion. This book is dedicated to urban dwellers, researchers, and thinkers around the world whose everyday ingenuity and perseverance are the foundation for the urbanism of Now.

Introduction

1

THICK CITY, NOW URBANISM

Jeffrey Hou, Benjamin Spencer, Thaisa Way, and Ken Yocom

This is a book of consilience. On the surface, it reveals juxtaposition: a divergence of perspectives on urbanism and cities—then, now, and into the future. And yet within the essays a synergy of approaches and readings emerges that unites the generation of knowledge with its application in the making of cities. The emerging consilience connects the contextual contingencies of local conditions with systems operating at global scales. Building upon recent discourses on the design of cities, *Now Urbanism* opens new avenues of critical inquiry while calling for the integration of rigorous theory with action. The book recognizes the rich complexities of the present city not as barriers or obstacles but as the foundational conditions of our work and as grounds for uncovering opportunity and unleashing potential.

Collectively, the book's chapters argue that knowledge of contemporary urbanism emerges from a complex interaction between cultural structures, social values, individual and collective actions, and observations of the material arrangements and processes of the physical environment. Efforts to catalyze social, political, and environmental change are furthered by means of the processes of city making through multiple theoretical views constructed across the boundaries of science, history, and design. The chapters seek to explore and understand how current intellectual claims about contemporary urbanism "are created, legitimated, and contested" (Hannigan 1995: 3). They attempt to pry the lid from the "black box"[1] of contemporary urban theory by simultaneously clarifying and thoroughly questioning the objectives and values that lie inside its making (Latour 1987: 129–131).

As Leonardo da Vinci is said to have written, "When you put your hand in a flowing stream, you touch the last that has gone before and the first of what is still to come." While the physical presence of the hand alters the flow, it does not stop it. It represents the present, the now, the immediate lens through which we comprehend the past and speculate on the future. Arguably some 8,000–10,000 years old, the "flow" of the urban age has become a torrent within the last 100 years as urbanization has increased at an unprecedented rate. At the start of the twentieth century, only 16 cities in the world had populations of one million people or more. By the year 2000, this number had swelled to 417. In 1950, only one city in the world had a population of over ten million people. Today, there are at least 20 such mega-cities (UN-DESA 2005). Most rapid urbanization is occurring in societies quickly transitioning from small-scale agrarian to large-scale industrial economies, resulting in profound economic polarization, social dislocation, and cultural change. The twenty-first century promises a magnification of these trends.

In this context, cities are no longer considered as isolated places, but rather as metropolitan regions comprised of multiple cities and developments, ranging from the inner city to suburban and exurban developments. These are not merely distinct parts, but a dynamic and complex whole, networked at regional and global scales. As we turn our attention to that whole, scientists, policy-makers, and academics increasingly acknowledge the interdependent nature of built and natural environments and the consequent challenges such relationships suggest in the advancement of urban sustainability, social equity, and political empowerment. Professionals, scholars, and political leaders are tasked with the collective description of these complex challenges and the definition of possible interventions and responses.

Much as our understanding of ecological systems has evolved over the last century to engage dynamic environmental processes, our understanding of cities has become increasingly nuanced along similar lines of thought, leading us to question whether it is possible to engage the processes of city making in new ways. How can we harness the evolving notion of ecology as a correlate for the complexity and interdependence of social and ecological systems in the urban built environment? Rather than proposing another utopian vision of cities, can we envision a different approach that responds to the ecological, economic, political, and social complexity of our present city? How might an understanding of such thickness fuel the transformation of cities NOW? How might immediate and tactical actions lead to strategic and organized change with long-term trajectories and ramifications?

System Entropy: Towards an Alternative Urban Praxis

Today, the city represents one element in the expanding landscape of the metropolis, what we label the urban. Cities worldwide face a multiplicity of new realities including growth and outward expansion, population diversification, uneven educational accessibility, income polarization, food shortages, political instability, and financial crisis (World Bank 2012). Urban environmental problems are coupled with social and economic inequality in the wake of political turmoil. While cities are characterized by distinct conditions of location, governance, populace, and economies, they engage a porosity of place that connects local and global forces, public and private realms, micro and macro scales, natural and constructed environments. This is not a simple increase in the consumption of space, but rather a complex transformation of the conditions of community, production, and place (UN-Habitat 2004: 2–6).

The challenges of today's global cities stand in sharp contrast to the rather limited concepts and toolkits available to designers and planners in the past. Urban planning emerged as a prevalent profession early in the twentieth century. During preceding decades, leaders of the Sanitary Movement articulated concerns over urban environmental pollution and addressed a diverse range of community health problems through the provision of sanitary water supply, sewerage, and garbage collection systems. The design, implementation, and operation of these systems fostered the rise of increasingly top-down urban administrations establishing the conceptual foundations of the city as a machine composed of centralized infrastructural networks. Building upon this conceptual foundation, Le Corbusier and other modernists of the early twentieth century sought to systematize urban form and function based on advances in technology and Fordist economic efficiencies.

FIGURE 1.1 Vernacular cityscapes are often discarded in contemporary urbanization in cities like Shanghai.

Urban planning in the twentieth century evolved into an increasingly elite profession and, in most cities worldwide, remains so today. As described by Nabeel Hamdi and Reinhard Goethert, planners are

> grounded in the high ground of monumental civic design, borrowed from colonial planners and modernists alike, with their rewards measured in civic design awards and more jobs, and their prestige in the acclamations of fellow professionals, public lectures and professional journals . . . Their spatial plans are behaviorally deterministic and, in compliance with the orthodox development patterns, represent end states. In other words they are determined by pre-set goals with targets and deadlines rather than development processes.
>
> *(Hamdi and Goethert 1997: 18)*

Despite the prevalence of deterministic planning practices, dissenting voices have emerged and gained increasing currency in debates of city making. In the 1960s, urban theorists such as Lewis Mumford and Jane Jacobs claimed urban and suburban patterns of sprawl were the result of a political emphasis on economic efficiencies and were detrimental to the long-term viability of city cores as centers of community development. Around the same time, in Europe, architects from the Team 10 group rejected the modernist doctrines and sought to create architecture and places that could be appropriated by their users (van den Heuvel and Risselada n.d.). Simultaneously, the environmental movement, focused on wilderness, conservation, and preservation, emerged across the US. Environmental pollution came onto the radar with labor unions pressing demands to address the exceptional levels of exposure in city factories. Rachel Carson's book, *Silent Spring* (1962), brought these issues to the American public as well as to those in the design and planning professions.

More recently, social ecologist Murray Bookchin has argued that "Ecology . . . is more a societal project than a biological one. It should be conceived in terms that explore how notions of domination and the historical development of hierarchy have led to the social as well as natural problems we face today." He advances a programmatic agenda for recovering not only the ecological concept of the city and an active citizenry but the "creation of a new politics that combines the high ideal of participatory citizenship with a recognition of what the city or town can be in a rational, free and ecological society" (Bookchin 1992: xxv). Extending these thoughts, Dipesh Chakrabarty (2009) has argued for an intersecting of natural and human histories in which people are described as critical agents for comprehending and assessing the catalytic components that have increased the rate and potential severity of global climate change.

Drawing on these bodies of knowledge, contemporary theorists suggest that we need a wholesale reconfiguration of how urbanity is conceived and configured. This is what Rem Koolhaas (1998: 969) refers to as the "irrigation of territories of potential," the development of new frameworks and conditions for comprehending the complex and dynamic qualities of contemporary urbanism and projecting new advancements where certainty plays a far lesser role in the outcome. These alternative approaches must accommodate the processes of urbanization driven by interconnected flows of capital, people, ecology, and resources at local, regional, and global scales.

A THICK City Framework

"The shapes of knowledge are always ineluctably local, indivisible from their instruments and their encasements," is the argument of anthropologist Clifford Geertz. He suggests that to gain meaningful insight into the complex relationships between knowledge, action, and local culture requires replacing "thin descriptions" that focus on the narrowly empirical approach for deriving knowledge with "thick descriptions" that offer explorations and explanations of local contexts looking across a "multiplicity of complex conceptual stories, many of them superimposed upon or knotted into one another, which are at once strange, irregular, inexplicit" (Geertz 1993: 4).

Similar to Geertz, Donna Haraway (1995: 175–194) uses the term "situated knowledges" to describe the means by which people engage in an action or event from particular vantage points. Although a group of people participating in an event may have similar intentions, each individual engages in the action from his or her own particular vantage point shaped by individual values and experiences. Thus, participants provide individual perspectives on how the action or event was developed, proceeded, experienced, and came to conclusion. Our approach in this book is complementary to those proposed by Geertz and Haraway. The intent is to explore the "strange, irregular, inexplicit" ways in which people interpret, make, and inhabit their surroundings, grounding in the past, performing in the present, and instigating the future.

Building upon Douglas Hofstadter's (1999) classic description of the ant colony as the metaphor of agent-based emergence, we propose the idea of "Now Urbanism" as a means of challenging Modernists' reliance on master planning the future and the tools of deterministic design and planning. For this exploration, we build on the concept of emergence as a means for understanding how designers and planners might intervene in a city or urban landscape so as to catalyze nascent urban responses or performances. This approach suggests that, in the design of the city, we do not believe we can determine the product, but rather we must carefully consider the scenarios that might arise out of a multitude of possible interventions, selecting those interventions that suggest a path towards the increased health of coupled human and natural environments. What emerges is an understanding of the city as lived, experiential, and thick.

Drawing upon these concepts, many urban scholars and practitioners have recently begun to focus less on creating visions of urban components and structure and more on the processes (both active and latent) that support the potential performance of urban environments. Working across disciplines, they are developing integrated frameworks that shed light on the complexity of coupled human–environment interactions. We share this interest in the depolarization of humans and nature as distinct entities. Framing our discussion within broader global trends that range from rising consumption to burgeoning informal cities to insurgent community activism means thinking and knowing differently. It means engaging the interplay of political, cultural, and environmental dynamics in urban planning and design and re-imagining how we assess and respond to the realities of cities and their critical role in the global landscape of the twenty-first century.

We have to come to comprehend cities and their larger metropolitan areas of influence as complex and adaptive systems characterized by hierarchical associations and hybrid responses. In this manner, large-scale patterns evolve from the dynamics and interactions of local agents with the surrounding environment. These patterns are not cast in place, but emergent in their qualities and conditions. They are autonomous agents of the city, adapting and responding to changing conditions and stimuli through time. This conception of the city acknowledges that urban interventions must appeal to our basic human instincts: to connect with nature, to socialize, to feel safe and healthy, and to prosper both economically and emotionally. Rather than pursuing social and environmental reforms as sacrifices or restrictions, it promises to transcend ingrained ideological divides, revealing the richness of urban living wherein critical services and cultural offerings are never far from the front doorstep and nature is a stewarded property of daily life.

Next City, Now

Now Urbanism asserts that the future city is here and works to reconstruct contemporary urbanism as a critical and complex practice that is simultaneously local, regional, and global. It examines the diversity, richness and potential of the present city through the framework of *situating*, *grounding*, *performing*, *distributing*, *instigating*, and *enduring*. Presented by a multidisciplinary group of practitioners and scholars, the chapters here illustrate specificity, context, agency, networks, and vision in the remaking of the contemporary city. For some, it is a matter of re-describing the city, its slums, and its experience. For others, it is the proposition of an alternative language of response. And for others, it is a critical revealing of what has been made invisible. *Now Urbanism* views city making as grounded in the imperfect, messy, yet rich reality of the present city and the everyday purposeful agency of its dwellers.

FIGURE 1.2 Parents and teachers work together to build a terraced garden and stair at the Pitagoras School in the informal urban settlement of Lomas de Zapallal, Lima, Peru.

Within this complex discourse, consilience emerges alongside a growing resilience. We envision the processes and forms that shape a city to be not merely responsive, but adaptive to shifts and perturbations of ecological and social consequence. We envision the functional design of the city as scientifically informed, culturally generated, and democratically organized. As such, the rubric of Now Urbanism serves less as a model than as a reminder of the dynamic complexity and interconnectedness of our actions, settings, and processes. No longer is the coarse separation between human and nature a dividing post, but more a rallying point to engage in the complex and multi-faceted conditions that support coupled realities of our urban environments.

Now Urbanism seeks alternatives to the common perceptions of urbanism as a singular entity and challenges the reader to embrace the positive influences of contemporary urbanity, stretching the purlieu of urban theorists to develop new modes of understanding and initiate the practices necessary for emerging urbanisms to suggest new futures. It is a call for catalyzing changes in the systems within contemporary urban environments. The specific focus on "NOW" refers to the urgent need for action in the face of today's grand challenges, as well as the opportunities and possibilities that already exist in today's urban environments. We believe that the knowledge needed to catalyze socially equitable, ecologically resilient, prosperous cities is well within our grasp. The cities of the future are the cities we now inhabit. Their evolution will be defined by our actions today.

Note

1   The phrase "black box" comes from Royal Air Force slang for a navigational instrument in an airplane; later the meaning was extended to denote any automatic apparatus performing intricate functions (Ayto 1999: 31). Latour uses the phrase in the latter context, arguing that modern approaches to science and technology have packaged understanding and distilled knowledge into a format that inhibits comprehension of complex actions, events, or artifacts.

References

Ayto, J. (ed.) (1999). *Oxford Dictionary of English Idioms*. Oxford: Oxford University Press.

Bookchin, M. (1992). *Urbanization without Cities: The rise and decline of citizenship*. Montreal: Black Rose Books.

Carson, R. (1962). *Silent Spring*. New York: Fawcett Crest.

Chakrabarty, D. (2009). The climate of history: four theses. *Critical Inquiry*, 35(2), 197–222.

Geertz, C. (1993). *Local Knowledge*. London: Fontana Press.

Hamdi, N. and Goethert, R. (1997). *Action Planning for Cities: A guide to community practice*. Chichester: John Wiley & Sons.

Hannigan, J. (1995). *Environmental Sociology: A social constructivist perspective*. London: Routledge.

Haraway, D. (1995). Situated knowledges: the science question in feminism and the privilege of partial perspective. In Feenberg, A. and Hannay, A. (eds), *Technology and the Politics of Knowledge*. Bloomington, IN: Indiana University Press, 175–194.

Hofstadter, D. R. (1999) [1979]. *Gödel, Escher, Bach: An eternal golden braid*. New York: Basic Books.

Koolhaas, R. (1998). Whatever happened to urbanism? In Koolhaas, R., Mau, B., and Werlemann, H. (eds), *S, M, L, XL*. New York: Monacelli Press, 958–971.

Latour, B. (1987). *Science in Action: How to follow scientists and engineers through society*. Cambridge, MA: Harvard University Press.

UN-DESA (2005). *"Fact Sheet 7: Mega-cities" World Urbanization Prospects: The 2005 Revision*. Working Paper No. ESA/P/WP/200. [Online]. Available: www.un.org/esa/population/publications/WUP 2005/2005WUP_FS7.pdf [September 13, 2013].

UN-Habitat (2004). *Second Session of the World Urban Forum, Barcelona, 13–17 September, 2004, Executive Summary.* [Online]. Available: http://ww2.unhabitat.org/wuf/2004/documents/wuf_exec_summary.pdf [March 6, 2014].

van den Heuvel, D. and Risselada, M. (n.d.) *Introduction: Looking into the Mirror of Team 10.* [Online]. Available: www.team10online.org/team10/introduction.html [February 1, 2014].

World Bank (2012). *World Bank Database.* [Online] Available: http://data.worldbank.org/ [November 17, 2012].

SITUATING

Since the Middle Ages, city dreamers have constructed heroic visions of utopia, idealized cities built nowhere for unknown cultures. These visions unwittingly aggregate urban layers and systems, dulling the sharp complexities that comprise cities. The grey-washed urban visions, whether centralized or decentralized, of Le Corbusier, Ebenezer Howard, or Frank Lloyd Wright have been critiqued and debunked by the likes of Jane Jacobs and Henri Lefebvre as authoritarian and ignorant of the rational and social process of planning and designing space—generators of dystopia rather than utopia. And yet the ideal remains in urban renewal projects that seek to rid the city of slums, in the suburban nation, and in the development of new towns.

To challenge the construct of these thin utopian futures, we begin with the following collection of chapters to firmly establish and interrogate a place, by situating our discourse in the messiness and complexities of existing geographies, cultures, and ideas. The chapters dig beneath the surface of utopian visions to identify the urban as a complex, integrated coalescence of often tremendous diversity and deep stratification. We begin with a polemic on slums and what they contribute to urban thinking in the twenty-first century, then move to the suburbs of high technology, and finally revisit the legacy and lessons of New Towns as they age.

A situation represents the intersection of historic movements and processes, the present dynamic, and opportunities for the future. To situate is to construct a critical understanding of the complexities of the present city and to act on those complexities as opportunities.

2

MESSY URBANISM

Transformation and Transmutation of Cities under Globalization

Viren Brahmbhatt

Emerging large cities of the world today are grappling with the conflicting logic of globalization and localization. Propelled by the infusion of international investment, finance, technology, and services, these cities are at a crossroads in terms of growth, development, diversity, income, and social divide. Developer-friendly policy, planning, and financial incentives are appropriating contemporary discourses about new cultural alternatives and identities in such mega-cities, while producing hitherto unknown urban forms that blur cultural boundaries. In Beijing, Shenzhen, Mumbai, Rio, Medellín, and many other large cities, social and cultural limits are being renegotiated as emerging networks of global trade and finance create new opportunity spaces. Under globalization, the question about "culture" hangs in the balance . . . The flattening of cultural geographies and its assumed effects are pushing towards creating a more homogenized world culture.

These issues are both distinct and unfamiliar, lacking historical precedent. The politics of urban transmutations along with the issue of identity and self-representation of cultures within such cities remains to be analyzed in light of globalization, transnational technology transfers, and exchanges in terms of professional practice. From this perspective, there is a need to explore and generate discourse on potentially new, reflexive frameworks to understand how we see "culture" in the present context—and what role, if any, architecture and urban design may play in defining a new kind of urbanism for the twenty-first century that is both socio-economically and environmentally sustainable. In this sense, the practice of architectural homogenization and disregard for specificity or identity are problems that have yet to be fully explored.

Although globalization and its influence have been transforming the physical as well as the social and cultural spaces of the city, in many instances the economic growth does not extend to its numerous poor in such rapidly growing cities. On the other hand, mass migration from villages and rural areas to these urban agglomerations is overwhelming their already overburdened and underdeveloped infrastructures, making these cities increasingly dysfunctional. It is estimated that there are almost a billion people in the world living in poverty, with the highest percentage in Asian cities; of this number, over 750 million live in urban areas without adequate shelter and basic services (UN 2013).

More than half of the world's population lives in cities. In developing regions, more than 45 percent of the urban population lives in informal settlements or "transient cities" constituting a major part of our living environment (UN-Habitat 2013). These are staggering statistics that barely describe the crises and challenges faced by emergent, albeit ill-prepared, global cities. Insufficient and inadequate housing, deficient infrastructure, poverty, inequality, and encroachment are among the most pressing challenges facing the world's emerging cities, making such precarious urbanization a global issue.

Under this overarching premise, this chapter outlines the difficulties and unique predicament these locales face in defining urbanization in the mega-cities of the Global South. Through observations and thoughts on Mumbai as a case study, the premises, processes, and pedagogies shaping urban futures and future urbanisms in these cities are described and explored.

Cities in India: Between Dystopia and Dysfunction

In India, massive urbanization on an unprecedented scale will sweep through the nation's current (and potentially new) cities. For example, the city of Mumbai grew by more than two million residents between 2010 and 2012. Recent projections suggest that a staggering 350 million people will move into urban areas from rural communities by 2030, a number expected to double by 2050 (Sankhe et al. 2010). Imagine having less than 20 years to develop existing cities and plan new ones, equipped with infrastructure, housing, transportation, and civic amenities to accommodate the size of the current US population by 2030, and more than twice that by 2050. This will be the largest mass migration of people the world has ever experienced. It will require a few hundred new cities, in addition to revitalizing and retrofitting many existing cities in a hurry. This is a Herculean task, even if resources were readily available. The socio-economic and political problems in regards to retrofitting and reprogramming existing cities would be quite a long and arduous process—notwithstanding difficulties associated with upgrading and reworking the infrastructure from within existing fabrics. This latter challenge may need to be addressed through vertical expansion and planning higher densities within the perimeters of existing cities, rather than expanding exponentially.

As in most densely populated areas, the most contested commodity in existing Indian cities is space. However, what distinguishes Indian cities from the rest is their capacity to absorb and celebrate density, crowdedness, chaos, and messiness the way people would in a carnival. Jostling is pretty much a way of life, and a high level of tolerance, acceptance, and adjustment is required; this enables cities to do more with less and to share more of every little resource available even when, more often than not, it means sacrificing personal needs for the greater good of the community. In many ways, scarcity coupled with density, underscored by a cultural attitude towards maximal gain through shared resources, is an intriguing urban paradox that defines the "messy urbanism" of Indian cities, and distinguishes urban growth in many Asian cities.

Density is destiny amongst the city-dwellers and particularly for the incoming migrant workers. The traditional concepts of density are, however, easily defied by cities like Mumbai, as at any given time of the day there are more people outdoors than indoors (on streets, in parks, on sidewalks, in public spaces, in leftover pockets of infrastructure like railways and flyovers). The sheer magnitude of human density overwhelms the city's already stressed infrastructure, placing it under inexorable strain as it struggles to balance, on the one hand, the needs of the current population and, on the other, the inflow of urban migrants arriving every day with their dreams of a better life. These emerging cities are dynamic places—poised between dystopia and dysfunction, exile and arrival, memory and loss, as they reshape themselves in response to the aspirations of the current local residents and in the imaginations of the incoming migrants. The manner in which they will inhabit and occupy marginal spaces of the city will shape future urbanisms in these parts of the world.

While many challenges lie ahead, there are also many opportunities. Emerging cities like Mumbai are among some of the most exciting places to explore the twenty-first-century city and emerging new urbanisms, because they are at once loved and loathed, messy and modern, chaotic and lyrical, rich and poor, old and new, vigorous and corrupt. Above all, they are naively energetic in their insatiable hunger for growth. Unlike Western cities, Indian cities are rural in spirit, shaped by the slow linking of towns and villages. They have retained their rural character and spirit, as well as overlapping hierarchies of public and private spaces where distinctions are easily blurred, and where "contamination" is an accepted norm generating, altering, and constantly modifying the urban landscape, creating transitory urbanism(s) with not-so-clearly defined boundaries, formalities, or territories. Every space is a contested territory, ephemeral yet rooted, and perpetually dynamic. In some ways, the contamination and messy urbanism of the "informal" are traits closely related to poverty, a lack of resources, and the need for sustenance that have translated into historic urban patterns stigmatizing Indian cities.

Mumbai: A Liminal City

Mumbai can be variously described as a city in transition, a city of slums, a city of rich ghettos, a city of dreams, a city of islands, a crowded city, a "maximum city" (Mehta 2004), a colonial city, and a city of villages, but above all, it is a liminal city (Turner 1969: 95)—a city on the verge of a massive change.

Mumbai is a liminal city in both a temporal and a spatial sense. Poised to experience a massive makeover and urbanization, it is a city defined by its diversity and multiplicity. Mumbai's liminality is also framed through the interactions of its people, the spaces they inhabit, the multiple cultures that coexist and perpetually collide in daily lives, the social divides and inherent inequalities, the marginal spaces that are home to close to half of Mumbai's population, and a constantly changing urban landscape bringing temporal liminality through its interchangeable uses of the public realm and peripheral fissures creating overlapping transitional conditions within the city. It is a city on the threshold, in every sense of the word, characterized by dynamic ambiguity and perpetual transition where borders and boundaries are blurred, erased, and constantly negotiated while various intersecting zones of interactions and exchange are preserved intact. Mumbai is not a city but rather a site for reinvention, rejuvenation, and redefinition through a series of flows—of shifting morphologies and juxtaposed heterogeneity, continual change, ephemerality, and flux.

The city's liminality is also defined by the socio-economic disparities between its inhabitants, their cultural and political conditions, their inequalities of income and social status, their divisions, and other incongruities that barely describe the unmapped geographies of difference. While Mumbai is looking to position itself on the global stage as the next

FIGURE 2.1 (clockwise from top left) Architecture in response to culture and climate; liminal spaces; Marine Drive, Mumbai; Ban-Ganga Village, Mumbai; JJ Flyover, Mumbai; informal street, Bandra W.

emergent mega-city, it confronts rapid urbanization, selective erasures, and a loss of collective memory—an emerging disconnect between its past, present, and future.

Mumbai's rapid expansion is predominantly horizontal, in the form of urban sprawl. The lack of adequate infrastructure in inner-city areas prompts outward growth into the suburbs, with densities that compete with or surpass those in the old city—South Mumbai. While the older areas of the city, with limited availability of developable land, restrict density, the outlying communities have no clear development policies or regulations in place for growth. Here, newer development is taking place without appropriate infrastructure planning, zoning, or land-use laws, further dividing the fabric into gated communities and rich ghettos, while much of the existing building stock within Mumbai City is underbuilt, old, and in disrepair, including precious "housing societies" that sell out to developers in return for higher-density, newer replacement housing, and improved amenities. This could be viewed positively if done in unison with a progressive urban design vision and planning strategies for the city at large. Perpetuating the problem is the use of Transfer of Development Rights (TDR) policies both within and outside of the old city, creating a discontinuous urban tissue dotted by disjointed developments and engendering urban morphologies that are incompatible with context and climate. Improperly adopted building typologies in the name of contemporary lifestyles characterize these new developments with utter disregard for the surrounding communities comprised of low-density slums or older villages now engulfed by the ever-growing city.

An aging and decaying building stock, inadequate infrastructure, and a culture of encroachment place undue stress on the public realm, including streets and the limited public space that exists. Compounding that, there are more than eight million people living in informal settlements with poorly built shanties, improper sanitation, a lack of differentiation between living and production spaces, and overcrowding adding to the complexity and woes of urban form in Mumbai. Every occupied space is used for more than one activity, making it a most efficient land-use strategy. These marginal ecologies are treasures that in fact provide a model for sustainable urban living, though with issues of poor hygiene and associated health risks. Furthermore, in addition to the large populations living in the slums, Mumbai does not provide any shelters for the population of approximately 180,000 homeless people who inhabit the city streets. Compelled to sleep in the streets in pouring rain and heat, and on littered sidewalks, this floating population of the city lives mostly outdoors, injecting the concept of liminality with yet another dimension.

Mumbai is not a city—at least not in the strictest sense of what defines and makes any urban agglomerate truly a city. Understandably, as usually is the case with most emerging cities, urbanism is an afterthought in Mumbai. It is more about retrofitting Mumbai to reach its destiny as a mega-city. While the slow linking of multiple villages within the city and on the peripheries has historically defined Mumbai, there is a continuous influx of rural migrants that requires the city to absorb growth, modernize, and expand. Mumbai is confronted with a choice: either apply the traditional notions of urbanism and adopt existing comparable international models, or embrace this complexity and exploit the unique opportunity to define its own kind of urbanity with new or alternate forms of urbanism rooted in the peculiar and particular reality of its culture, locale, context, and climate. There

FIGURE 2.2 Density/urban morphologies: a comparative study of the historical medieval cities of India. (from left to right) Jaisalmer, Jaipur, Ahmedabad. Density is also a function of culture and climate. The dense physical fabrics of the historical city provide shelter from sweltering heat for cooler streets and public spaces. However, in the contemporary city, density (of both population and built form) is governed by a more complex set of criteria.

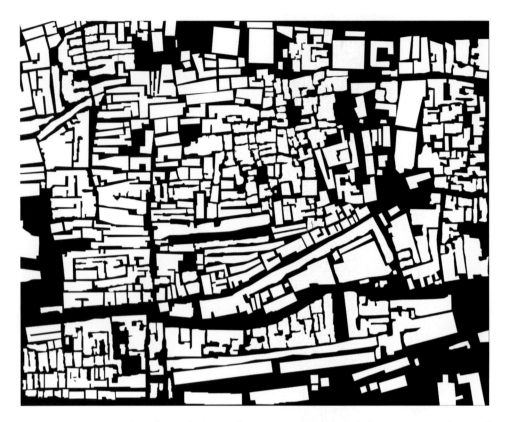

FIGURE 2.3 Density/informal morphology: Dharavi, Mumbai. Though dense in terms of physical form, Dharavi's current level of density is incompatible with the surrounding city fabric and puts added pressure on the site for growth and more efficient land use.

is a sense of euphoria in Mumbai's desire to become the next major, global mega-city. Phrases like "the next Shanghai," "the next Tokyo," or "the next New York" are in wide use by the media, politicians, and developers to further promote the aspirations of vested interests. However, the realities of its current quandary will likely be a part of slowing the rhetoric down and allowing for a slow, incremental evolution of a sense of urbanity, engaging other forms of urbanism in order to flourish and guide the city into the future.

In that sense, the political quagmire and blurred boundaries between public and private, and between property and community could be a blessing in disguise, making Mumbai a "reluctant city" in embracing rapid urbanization. Mumbai also needs to take into account the difficulties in implementing any significant infrastructure projects and plans within its hugely contested bounds. On the one hand, a functioning democracy allows for public participation and a much-desired slowness; however, on the other hand, there are complex and often draconian property development and zoning laws that restrict some types of development and challenge any changes that might foster effective and efficient land use and sustainable zoning. Instead, the existing system allows development where existing land-use patterns are conveniently appropriated by the developer-friendly market for large high-end rich ghettos (gated communities for which Mumbai is now notoriously known) surrounded by poorly planned and constructed low-rise housing societies and slums. Inevitably, the

FIGURE 2.4
Informal settlements,
Mumbai.

developers' sights are now set on these old cooperative housing societies that are in utter disrepair, and on slum areas that are underbuilt on high-value land and occupied by the poor, sometimes with or without any legal rights (a claim that gets murky very quickly in many instances for which there is no space in this chapter).

Large areas in Mumbai City and its outer suburbs (now within the city limits and jurisdiction) are carpeted by such low-rise housing societies and slums earmarked to undergo redevelopment. This is an opportunity, both for the city's regeneration, and for reimagining and reshaping its urban future and for the city to plan for inclusive sustainable growth. However, in practice, building typologies similar to those already in place are implemented; density is the cry of the hour and is met by the much-maligned tower-in-the-park approach with ineffective land use and planning and a fractured (unshared) city fabric. High-end residential and mixed-use buildings (shops at grade levels and offices above) are in huge demand, prompting the city and state governments to pursue plans for the wholesale erasure of existing neighborhood fabrics to make room for large-scale development in their place. The marginalized areas and populations of the city (the slums) in close proximity to business districts of South Mumbai and other satellite nodes in the northern suburbs like Bandra,

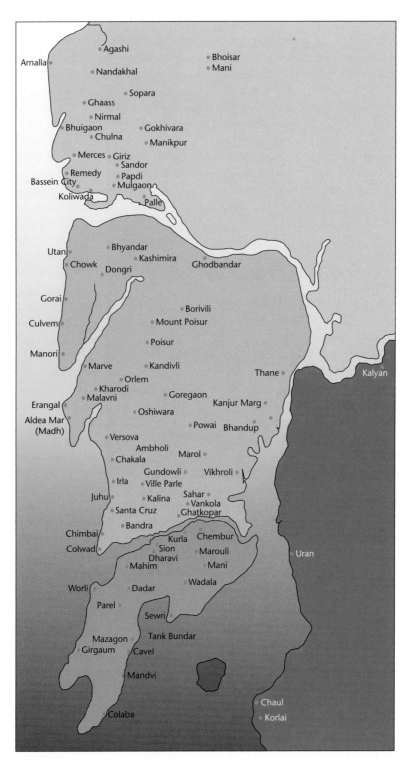

FIGURE 2.5 Mumbai: city of villages.

Juhu, and Andheri are being pushed further out as a result of these redevelopment schemes and the associated rise in land values. There are no clear planning guidelines regulating such growth. Haphazard urbanization is further complicated by the lack of comprehensive housing and transportation policies, and of good governance.

And yet, a lot can be achieved through innovative urban design, community participation, and smart design-thinking that may allow for the retention of some of these productive neighborhoods and the coexistence of diverse scales to ensure the "city of slums" remains a vibrant, viable, and sustainable metropolis. There is an opportunity for Mumbai to see its own urbanity and development in light of its uniqueness as a city of fishing villages and slums. Both are places where a live/work lifestyle and entrepreneurial spirit are integral to the culture of their inhabitants. Both exemplify a symbiotic relationship with the land and landscape they occupy as a shared resource. Both put into question the traditional notions of property and community—as they merge into a unified field of shared resources and needs that could provide lessons in sustainability, performative zoning, and land use. As local and central governments have failed to provide adequate, equitable and affordable housing, these informal communities have developed self-sustaining economies and systems that generate both housing and jobs.

However, with the rising real estate prices and market pressures, these thriving communities are now under tremendous stress. These areas are underbuilt, occupy high-value land, and are easy targets for real estate development. Nevertheless, with effective social activism in these areas and renewed global attention to the problem of slums, these communities are coming together to find ways to ensure planned, equitable development that is inclusive while fostering growth. This is a great opportunity for the city, and for urban thinkers to carry out careful analyses, research, and innovation as they seek to develop a responsive urbanism that is unique to its place. Implementing lasting policies with purpose—for urban design, transportation, accessibility, housing, and infrastructure—should be a priority.

While there is an opportunity to plan a state-of-the-art physical infrastructure—essential for fostering growth in an increasingly competitive world system—it must be done in conjunction with overall planning strategies that include policies for fair housing, transportation, and public space. Density and tall buildings with glittering architecture may stir the imagination of a lot of people but, paradoxically, they also highlight the simultaneous need for small, incremental, and sustainable change. Current planning premises, projects, and pedagogies fall short of these expectations, revealing systemic failures in addressing complex urban needs that require imagination and innovation to go beyond the traditional, outdated planning methodologies that only produce tried and tired solutions leading to the repetition of failed urban experiments.

Architecture of Disjuncture: Informal Cities

The urbanization of Indian cities like Mumbai is marred, and also characterized, by three basic factors:

1   low-density, decaying, and outdated existing building fabrics pitted against high population density further complicated by the continuous influx of rural migrants;

2   lack of good governance and national or local urban policies, prompting ad hoc urbanization, unplanned growth, and misguided planning, resulting in inefficient urbanism; and

3   inadequate infrastructure, coupled with the politics of the "informal": street encroach-
    ments, street markets, informal settlements, and slums with high populations.

These factors add to the woes of cities such as Mumbai and make urban regeneration and
redevelopment a slow process and an uphill task. Positively, it may allow for rethinking
strategies, adaptation, and innovation through frugality—a cultural hallmark of India's
people to do more with less and turn mess into more: more sustainable lifestyles, and
maximizing the potential of scarce and shared resources.
    As Robert Neuwirth claims:

> one in seven people on the planet live in squatter communities or shantytowns. More
> than half the workers of the world earn their living off the books. These markets and
> neighborhoods provide housing and jobs where governments and the formal private
> sector fail to. Governments need to work with these communities rather than neglect
> or suppress them.
>
> *(Neuwirth 2011: 56)*

Asia's plate is full as far as global risks are concerned: from population growth, rapid
urbanization, inadequate infrastructure, deficient housing, and urban poverty to climate
crisis, ecological hazards, contaminated land, air and water, and a million people flocking to
the cities every day. Urbanists across the world are unanimous in acknowledging that the
city is a solution to the problems of our age in addressing many of the challenges the world
faces. The best that cities like Mumbai can do to meet these challenges is to tap into their
largest resource—people—and the informal economies provide one avenue. The broad
majority of the workforce at the bottom of the economic pyramid is also the largest consumer base—a fact that multinational companies cannot ignore. These populations are
consumers as well as vendors of their products; they consume and, in many instances, produce the very same goods these companies are seeking to sell.
    Global Urban Development Magazine states:

> India has 433 million people living on less than $1 a day, which is 36 percent of the total
> number of poor in the world. Out of the 290 million (28 percent of the total popu-
> lation of the country) that live in urban areas, 62 million live in slums. This represents
> over 21 percent of the urban population in India.
>
> *(Buckley et al. 2007: 2)*

The face of emerging India is much more scarred than the painted faces in the *National
Geographic* pages.
    Urbanization and growth in this sense is a global issue and not merely a local condition
considering the total population of the world living in informal settlements or slums, which
is approaching a billion people; that is one in seven people. According to the United
Nations, this population could more than double by 2030 (UN Millennium Project 2005:
12). Insufficient and inadequate housing, deficient infrastructure, poverty, inequality, and
encroachment are among the most pressing challenges facing the world's cities, making
India's precarious urbanization a global issue. As the Urban Age Conference in Mumbai
concluded, India's slums draw attention to the difficulties of improving the quality of urban

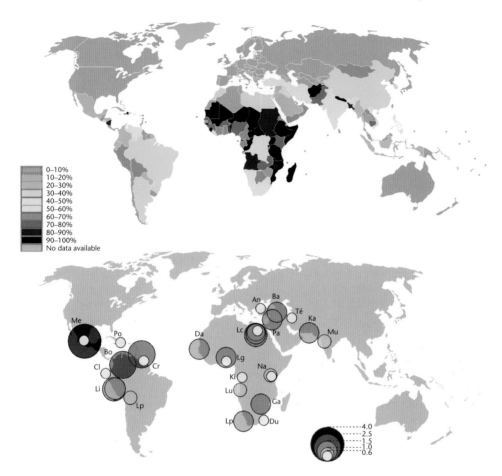

FIGURE 2.6 (top) Urban populations living in slums. (bottom) Map representing the locations of the 30 largest "mega-slums" in the world, according to Mike Davis (2006). Data compiled from various sources, taking average values. The circles' size and color indicate the number of inhabitants in millions, while the letters indicate the name of the city. Note that some cities have several mega-slums, while other cities (particularly in South Asia) may have more inhabitants living in slums, but scattered in many small slums rather than in a few mega-slums. This map therefore does not show all cities with slums, rather only those with well-known, large slums.

life in rapidly growing, densely populated areas. The extent of informal settlements in India and the scale of encroachment make its cities ideal sites for reflecting on strategies to better accommodate the growing number of urban residents and their multiple needs while exploring new modes of thinking.

Urbanity is an attitude, a cultural trait in response to the context and climate it inhabits. If Mumbai fails to exploit its unique position as a rapidly growing metropolis supported by economic growth, globalization, and foreign investment, it will tread similar paths to other global cities like New York, Chicago, Tokyo, and Shanghai, which are now looking for ways to reverse previous practices in order to identify a more sustainable urbanism, reducing environmental footprints and inequities while increasing livability for residents. Mumbai's asset in the struggle to avoid these pitfalls lies in its ability to constantly adjust, adapt, and appropriate minimal resources for maximum gain—doing more with less is a way of life for the majority of its people who live on less than a dollar per day. The availability of a large workforce in the formal and informal sectors, and the existence of interdependent economies that establish a symbiotic relationship between the two, make Mumbai's place on the global urban scene unique. However, much remains to be done not only for the affluent few who control the city's formal sector, but also for its many urban poor who fuel Mumbai's economy with their hard work. Economists the world over have been debating the difficulties that informal economies present and the benefits that they can offer; however, their counterparts in India—the politicians, policy-makers, urban planners, and real estate developers, who are governed by short-term gains—do not tap such potential. Globalization countered by strong local culture(s), harnessing local labor as an immense resource that supports informal economies, adjustable thinking, and innovation, may pave the path to a more sustainable approach to Indian urbanism. This may be achieved by developing and implementing a city-making and managing approach that is more inclusive of the urban poor and the welfare of migrant workers without perpetuating the problems of slums and squatter settlements. There is sufficient argument to emphasize the need for seriously considering socially and culturally inclusive planning strategies. Under the current scenario of shared global risks we have inherited and may face, there is a strong consensus to develop planning premises and pedagogies that underscore and prioritize social issues such as the welfare, skills development and well-being of the urban poor and migrant workers, and to examine how this will directly shape and affect our urban environments.

For cities like Mumbai, the problem lies in failing to understand the vitality that arises from its multitude of contradictions: the urban elite pitted against the rural migrants; rich versus poor; high-end mansions and apartment blocks within a backdrop of slums; and squatter settlements dotting its streets, sidewalks, and commuter rail lines. As Mumbai undergoes population growth, urbanization, and economic development, it is poised between being a failed experiment, not unlike the cities of the West in the mid-twentieth century, and an opportunity for defining the twenty-first-century model for sustainable urbanism and architecture. With more than half of the world's population living in cities—a third of whom live in the informal settlements or slums—these "transient cities" are real and constitute a major part of our living environment. Places like Dharavi, the largest slum in India, have a unique opportunity to become models for sustainable living and redefine the city for the new millennium. As with informal cities around the globe, Dharavi not only illustrates how risks can be transformed into assets that support more sustainable living, but also epitomizes the dichotomies between cultures of less and those of excess. There are lessons to be learnt from such functioning slum societies that may lead twenty-first-century urbanism towards building more sustainable cities and communities; but, more importantly, these lessons can help them rebuild their own communities in the face of market pressures while also addressing contemporary needs and improving living conditions for the millions without adequate representation or voice.

Reflexive Urbanism: Towards a New Urban Paradigm

Emerging mega-cities of the Global South collectively face enormous challenges, but they also offer opportunities to rethink urbanism(s) and critique the socio-economic theories of the late nineteenth- and twentieth-century city. With their large populations, emerging markets, and pressing urbanization, they also present immense possibilities for growth, innovation, and cultural contributions in developing alternate urbanisms that could radically challenge our conceptions of urban design and the design of cities. Cities like Mumbai, São Paulo, Shanghai, and Lagos are ideal locations that provide opportunities for redefining new urban paradigms in the wake of current crises and risks faced by the global community at large.

Many of today's global risks are the result of the processes of modernization, including urbanization, economic growth (or decline), and social inequalities. There are others that scientists describe as manufactured risks, produced by human activity—risks that have transformed the modernization process itself (Giddens 1999). Social relations have changed with the introduction of manufactured risks owing to increased public awareness, media, and information technologies. With the influx of tele-technologies and the internet, social and physical urban networks are being replaced by flows—together with, and produced by, the interdependent nexus of formal–informal economies and social interactions.

Risks are also culturally relative, and are perceived differently depending on what interests, contexts, ideologies, and politics are at stake in determining their nature. Much like resources, risks are distributed unevenly in terms of geography, location, and population density. Global space is now defined more by shared risks rather than by shared resources. Hence, a case for a more reflexive approach towards managing collective risks to avoid collective catastrophes is not unfounded. Sustainability and sharing have become synonymous keywords in defining reflexive frameworks for minimizing risks or turning them into resources. In the age of reuse and recycling, the design of the next generation of cities calls for a re-evaluation of what is already being used by society and works, to engender new urban paradigms.

References

Buckley, R., Singh, M., and Kalarickal, J. (2007, November). Strategizing slum improvement in India: a method to monitor and refocus slum development programs. *Global Urban Development Magazine*, 1–24. [Online]. Available: www.globalurban.org/GUDMag07Vol3Iss1/Buckley.htm [March 8, 2014].

Davis, M. (2006). *Planet of Slums*. London: Verso.

Giddens, A. (1999). Risk and responsibility. *Modern Law Review*, 62(1), 1–10.

Mehta, S. (2004). *Maximum City: Bombay lost and found*. New York: Knopf.

Neuwirth, R. (2011, August 16). Global bazaar. *Scientific American*, 305(3), 56–63.

Sankhe, S., Vittal, I., Dobbs, R., Mohan, A., Gulati, A., Ablett, J., Gupta, S., Kim, A., Paul, S., Sanghavi, A., and Sethy, G. (2010). *India's Urban Awakening: Building inclusive cities, sustaining economic growth*. New York: McKinsey & Company. [Online]. Available: www.mckinsey.com/insights/urbanization/urban_awakening_in_india [June 10, 2014].

Turner, V. (1969). *The Ritual Process: Structure and anti-structure*. Chicago, IL: Aldine Publishing.

UN (2013). *The Millennium Development Goals Report*. New York: UN.

UN-Habitat (2013). *State of the World's Cities 2012/2013: Prosperity of cities*. London: Earthscan.

UN Millennium Project (2005). *A Home in the City: Achieving the Millennium Development Goals*. London: Earthscan.

3

THE ENVIRONMENTAL CONTRADICTIONS OF HIGH-TECH URBANISM

Margaret O'Mara

Few urban spaces receive more hyperbolic treatment in the early twenty-first century than places that are the command and control centers of the high-tech economy. Often, these spaces' verdant surroundings and their industries' ability to create astounding levels of wealth become a self-reinforcing virtuous circle. Their denizens get wealthier, and the surroundings get progressively more pleasant—and unattainable. Places like Northern California's Silicon Valley and its international analogues are subjects of high-flying rhetoric within the business press, in halls of political power, and in business school classrooms and campus computer labs. The global economic crisis of 2008–09 did little to dull their luster. Landscapes of office parks and campuses that rarely are considered "cities" have become some of the most alluring sorts of urbanism, and are widely imitated.

The transposition of some of these activities to denser, older, central-city neighborhoods in the Web 2.0 era—not to mention digital technologies designed to create seamless interactions with urban environments—have further burnished the reputation of high-tech places. They are marquee locations for what Leslie Sklair (2005) terms "the transnational capitalist class." Not only has the technology industry become the Holy Grail of post-industrial urban economic development, but software itself also has come to be seen as the panacea for all kinds of urban ills, from potholes to community health care to a slow taxi service (Packer 2013). Need to fix the city? There's an app for that.

Moreover, in an era of increased concern about environmental sustainability, the marketing of flagship urban high-tech districts has become drenched in green. "Welcome to a neighborhood for people who care about the future," went one pitch by Vulcan Real Estate, a major developer of Seattle's South Lake Union neighborhood, home to the headquarters of Amazon.com as well as other new-economy standouts. "Be green here" (Vulcan 2012). "We embrace being green, going green, living green!" exclaims the Singaporean real estate enterprise Ascendas, a leading developer of high-end technology parks throughout Asia. As proof of its commitment, Ascendas cites among other amenities the parks' "lushly landscaped grounds that create an ideal green ambience that motivate innovation and creativity" (Ascendas 2013).

It might be easy to dismiss this glossy hyperbole as mere greenwashing, but the reality of contemporary high-tech spaces is more messy and contingent. High-density and transit-oriented, filled with bikes, pedestrians, and electric-car charging stations, South Lake Union has successfully attracted not simply those who "care about the future" but those who are willing to change their habits to make that future more sustainable. Amid the hype and cynicism about "smart cities" run by software rather than by paper-pushing bureaucrats, digital technologies are proving to have positive environmental impacts as well as profoundly democratic possibilities, allowing more flexible patterns of work as well as empowering individuals with information and helping build social capital and social movements. Yet technology atomizes urban environments, segregating people according to education level and Twitter feeds, and the hardware that makes it all possible—from smart phones to server farms—comes with a high environmental price of its own.

Although all things digital are often construed to be "new," the creation of high-tech urbanism has been decades in the making. Its makers have not only been planners and politicians, but tech titans and futurists and real estate developers as well. Throughout its construction, a key facet of this high-tech urban mythos is that these places are environmentally "cleaner" than other spaces of production. This chapter considers this history and traces the environmental discourses embedded within it by sketching short portraits of technological spaces over time and place, from early twentieth-century Cleveland to semiconductor-era Silicon Valley to twenty-first-century Bangalore. Situating ourselves in this history allows us to separate out the urban imaginary from the messy reality of these landscapes of technology, knowledge, and wealth—and to start to plan where these cities might go next.

Escaping the Smokestacks

The conflations of greenery with sustainability, and the presumption that green spaces encourage deep thought, are familiar tropes to scholars and students of urbanism. Residential suburbanization since the early nineteenth century was in part a response to the noxious environment of the industrial city, and its proponents presented decentralization as beneficial to both physical and mental health (Jackson 1985; Fishman 1987; Hayden 2002). Similarly, the movement of white-collar industry to the suburbs from the early twentieth century forward drew its energy and rationale from the presumption that more pleasant surroundings would attract and retain the best class of workers as well as create more productive and healthier working conditions (Fishman 1987; O'Mara 2005; Mozingo 2011).

The remediation of industrial environments was a theme running throughout seminal urban decentralization visions of the prewar period, from Ebenezer Howard's Garden City to the garden suburbs of the Regional Planning Association of America (Light 2009). It won national policy imprimatur in the United States with the urban ecological vision of the National Resources Planning Board and the greenbelt towns of the New Deal's Resettlement Administration. To these reformers, the solution to the pollution problem involved not simply the clean-up of industrial facilities, but also the rearrangement and removal of these facilities from the center of the city.

Urbanists also are familiar with the degree to which metropolitan realities diverged from the environmental utopianism of some of these planning visions, particularly in the era of North American mass suburbanization after World War II. Suburbs ate up agricultural land and open spaces, polluted rivers and lakes with sewage outflows, vastly increased the number of trips taken by car, and took a measurable toll on human health (Rome 2001; Frumkin et al. 2004; Acevedo et al. 2006; Duany et al. 2010). As less industrialized nations like China and India evolved into economic superpowers at the end of the twentieth century, similar suburban developments sprung up there, exhibiting many comparable patterns of land consumption and carbon footprint (O'Mara and Seto 2013). The development of what James Kunstler (1994) famously called "the geography of nowhere" featured plenty of greenery, but came at a profound environmental cost.

High-tech landscapes followed a similar discursive and spatial trajectory, in good part because the rise of industrial research and scientific-based industry occurred at the same time that cities were decentralizing rapidly. In new multi-storied office buildings that sprouted in American cities from the 1870s forward, clerks and stenographers had to battle with the smells, dust, and constant noise that accompanied life in the big city. The ascendance of scientific management and other forms of organizational science framed such nuisances as not simply discomfiting to the individual, but as detrimental to worker productivity (Taylor 1911; Duffy 1980).

As companies vertically integrated and developed sophisticated organizational hierarchies, they began to establish physically separate facilities for the different stages of production, and different activities (and personnel) began to occupy separate facilities and landscapes (Chandler 1977; Adams and Butler 1999). Among those spinning off far from traditional industrial districts were corporate research and development facilities, as well as what was becoming known as "light manufacturing" that involved smaller machines, fewer energy demands, and more specially skilled workers. Within this stratum were the technologically sophisticated fields of electrical and telecommunications equipment.

The burgeoning field of electric lighting was one sector where these trends became visible. By the end of the nineteenth century, the spread of electrification had given rise to a number of smaller companies engaged in the development and manufacture of incandescent light bulbs. Seeking greater market share and enhanced research capacities, several Midwest-based firms consolidated their operations to become the Cleveland-based National Electric Lamp Association. In 1907, the electric behemoth General Electric (GE)—itself the product of an earlier merger—quietly bought a controlling interest in National. By 1910, a prosperous National was making about a million dollars each month and it had outgrown its original factory in the city of Cleveland. It employed hundreds of engineers and laboratory technicians as well as white-collar managers, salesmen, and secretaries. Flush and ambitious, the firm began casting about for a more spacious location.

National was about as high-tech as an American company could be at the turn of the last century, and its executives had the iconoclastic qualities that have marked many a technology titan since. Prompted by the chief engineer's plea that the firm move its laboratories "away from the smoke, gaseous fumes, mechanical and electrical disturbances" in the city, National's chief officers, Franklin Terry and Burton Tremaine, decided to pursue the rather quixotic idea of building the new facility in the outer suburbs of Cleveland. General Electric executives discovered to their distress that Terry and Tremaine not only wanted to build "way out in the country" but to create a highly-landscaped campus that would be more than twice as expensive as building anything in the city. Appropriating the National Electric Lamp Association acronym, the executives named the development "Nela Park" and commissioned New York-based architect Frank Wallis to design a series of imposing neo-Georgian buildings, all deep-red brick and granite columns, housing various laboratories and sales and marketing offices (Townsend 1960: 12).

Terry and Tremaine's stated rationale reflected a blend of pragmatism and environmental determinism that marked later high-tech landscapes as well. Land was cheaper in the countryside, and in an era of rapid lateral urban growth it seemed easy to bring streetcar lines further out of the city to bring employees and customers to the campus. However, a pleasant, suburban location would also create "an atmosphere for more effective work and much more pleasant working conditions with the absence of smoke, dirt, dust, noise, overcrowding and other distractions" (Townsend 1960: 14). This was environmental improvement in the name of enhanced worker productivity, rather than ecological health.

Once in operation, Nela Park became the focus of extensive company-generated mythology that trumpeted its many extraordinary features and its distinctive qualities as a high-end workplace. The company began to call the facility "The University of Light" and to frame its profit-making activities as a search for broader social good (Woods 1923). National newspapers and periodicals echoed GE's framing of its lighting research as a selfless pursuit rather than a profit-making enterprise, describing in rhapsodic language "the remarkable laboratories which the National Lamp Works maintain at Nela Park in East Cleveland" (*Washington Herald* 1915).

Ten years into its existence, Nela Park had become not only a jewel in General Electric's crown but also a community institution in Cleveland. Starting in 1925, it began an annual Christmas light display that showcased both its advanced lighting technologies and the landscape design and architecture of the facility. Thousands of Clevelanders flocked each year to the light show, and corporate publications, brochures, and national press stories shared dramatic photographs of the annual festival with a wider audience. In these illustrations,

FIGURE 3.1 The "University of Light" at GE's research facility outside Cleveland featured a popular evening water and light show. Nela Park, Cleveland, Ohio, 1951.

elaborate light displays and illuminated plumes of water shooting from Nela's fountains dwarf tiny human figures; the park becomes a nocturnal, man-made Yosemite (Maedje 1951; Townsend 1960).

GE's presentation of Nela Park as a higher-order type of industrial development remained consistent over successive decades. By the middle of the century, corporate histories noted with satisfaction the prescience of Terry and Tremaine in moving National's facilities to a suburban campus setting, paving the way for thousands of suburban industrial parks to come (Townsend 1960). The research park was now the default setting for corporate research activity, and particular campuses—like Bell Laboratories and Johnson & Johnson in New Jersey, and IBM in suburban New York—became high-modernist showplaces (Graf and Voorhees 1944; Knowles and Leslie 2001; Mozingo 2011). Such developments fed into a broader, global phenomenon of what Kargon and Molella (2008) have termed "techno-cities": self-contained urban environments of technological production that ranged from the secret nuclear cities of the wartime Manhattan Project to postwar European company towns.[1]

Corporate development continued to emphasize the particular importance of a clean and restful setting for research, hinged on the idea that scientists and engineers were a special, privileged class who were serving the greater good of society. Through its many decades of concerted public relations, General Electric conveniently forgot to mention that underneath the fountains, the greenswards, and the Georgian buildings, Nela Park remained a facility of industrial production—and pollution. The business of researching, developing, and manufacturing light bulbs could be a dirty one. Chemicals and heavy metals, particularly mercury, were an unavoidable byproduct; more than nine decades of production left a large contaminated footprint in and around the campus, and within the bodies of those who worked there.

By the 1990s, Nela Park had won the dubious distinction of being listed as a federal Superfund site by the Environmental Protection Agency (EPA). Successful remediation brought Nela Park off the Superfund priority list by the early 2000s, although the EPA calculated in 2008 that the facility continued to produce over 74 tons of mercury waste annually. Nela Park was not alone. The parks and campuses that emerged in its wake also eventually had to grapple with pollution and public health problems that flew in the face of corporate assertions that these were, at last, factories without smokestacks.

The Postwar High-Tech Suburb

Mass suburbanization after World War II, precipitated by a complex bundle of political, economic, and cultural catalysts, accelerated the process of industrial decentralization at the same time that the Cold War military-industrial complex began to funnel extraordinary amounts of money into research and development, boosting the nascent high-tech industry as well as turning the American research university into a powerful social and economic force (Geiger 1993; Leslie 1993; Lowen 1997; O'Mara 2005). Rising incomes and consumer demand enriched the bottom lines of American corporations and corporate research budgets. The results were burgeoning and largely suburban districts of technologically focused white-collar industry that Robert Fishman (1987) calls "technoburbs" and that I call "cities of knowledge" (O'Mara 2005), the most prominent of which were along Route 128 outside Boston and in the San Francisco Peninsula of Northern California.

The latter region, which by the turn of the 1970s had come to be known as Silicon Valley, came to be the pre-eminent embodiment of high-tech urbanism, and its evolution demonstrates the environmental contradictions embedded within. A sleepy agricultural area lauded as "a veritable Paradise" by one local poet in the 1920s (Lawrence 1927), the Valley was transformed over the passage of only a few decades into a busy landscape of low-slung factories and research laboratories, residential subdivisions, shopping malls, and freeways. By the turn of the twenty-first century, little evidence of the Valley's agricultural past remained (Seto and O'Mara 2006). Yet the mythos of the largely lost "Valley of Heart's Delight" (Lawrence 1927: 32) provided the underpinning for Silicon Valley to market itself throughout its history as a different type of productive space, whose industries were clean and non-polluting, and where workers could enjoy an unparalleled standard of living. The businessmen and land developers of Silicon Valley took the ideas behind Nela Park, Bell Laboratories, and other high-end corporate research campuses and used them as a rationale for introducing industry into places it had not been before, and for recruiting and retaining a high-skilled workforce. The landscape they created provided a model city that regions across the globe tried to emulate. Over time, however, the Valley's own promise of growth without pollution proved impossible to deliver.

While industry had been present in various forms in the Valley prior to World War II, the origins of the Valley's high-tech transformation came with the end of the war, when an influx of population and defense-related activity fundamentally changed the complexion of the region. The expansion of defense spending during the early Cold War period brought huge new streams of money to the region and its institutions. Stanford University, located in the heart of the Valley, embarked on an ambitious program to strengthen its science and engineering capacities, and in rather short order became one of the largest university recipients of federal research monies (Lowen 1997; O'Mara 2005). The spillover effects of this research activity proved significant, not only because of the high-tech entrepreneurs who emerged from Stanford's programs (William Hewlett and David Packard were among the first wave of them), but also because Stanford decided to develop some of its considerable Valley landholdings into an industrial park explicitly designed for "advanced" and research-intensive industries. The park welcomed its first tenant in 1951 (Findlay 1992; O'Mara 2005).

With setbacks and building restrictions that far exceeded the requirements of local zoning, and the promise of regular interaction with Stanford scientists, the University lured a range of corporate tenants who were willing to pay a premium for admission to this technological garden. "We didn't know what the hell we were doing," Stanford business manager Alf Brandin admitted to a group of real estate developers in 1958. "If we knew how hard it was to get industry, that you've got to give tax exemptions, cheap labor, and free buildings, we probably wouldn't have tried" (Wax 1958). However, Brandin and his colleagues knew enough about economic development to take pains to emphasize to the public—particularly community residents anxious about the introduction of industry in their midst—that the inhabitants of what became known as the Stanford Research Park had "no smoke, no heavy manufacturing" and were "clean and electronic" (Stanford Oral History Project 1980: 42).

The lush grounds and discreet architecture of the research park reinforced this idea, creating a productive space that echoed and complimented adjoining suburban residential neighborhoods and the university campus itself. The disguise was so thorough that Palo Alto residents mistook one newly constructed industrial facility for an elementary school, calling

FIGURE 3.2 The Stanford Industrial Park set the standard for many university-anchored parks that followed, and featured low-slung buildings and ample setbacks that allowed it to blend into the surrounding suburban landscape. Houghton Mifflin Building, Stanford Industrial Park (later Stanford Research Park), mid-1950s.

the school district to complain that the lights were being left on in the building all hours of the night.[2]

The persistence of agricultural landscapes and open spaces further masked the true extent of industrialization in the Valley, as did accounts of the burgeoning technology scene in the popular press. The great pop-culture chronicler Tom Wolfe described the transitional landscape in a later *Esquire Magazine* profile of Intel co-founder Robert Noyce: "From the work bays of the light-industry sheds that the speculators were beginning to build in the valley, you could look out and see the raggedy little apricot trees they had never bothered to bulldoze after they bought the land from the farmers" (Wolfe 1983: 356).

The classified nature and scope of the military projects on which the nascent tech economy depended, however, left Valley neighbors with unanswered questions about the possible contaminants to the surrounding environment. As one resident who lived adjacent to defense contractor Lockheed's Palo Alto facility wrote in the local paper in 1960, "it is disconcerting . . . to have a federal agent pick leaves from our shrubs once a month, to test them for radioactivity" (Steers 1963). Another group of homeowners complained to Stanford's president that one industrial park tenant was not living up to the university's clean-industry promises. "The noise and fumes from their stack continues unabated 24 hours a day," they wrote. "On certain days the acid odor is very strong and the acid fumes has [sic] damaged many of our trees and shrubs, our cars and much of our patio furniture" (Petition 1962). As the decade progressed, such plaintive complaints were growing in frequency. Yet the potential hazards in high-tech production remained oddly unpublicized.

Instead, the wealth-generating reputation of the region began to spread. Although the defense cuts of the late Vietnam era decimated the region's defense economy, there now were growing commercial markets for mainframe computers and the chips that powered them. National and international press coverage of the Valley and its denizens in the 1970s and early 1980s focused on its innovations, its entrepreneurs, and its high quality of life. One breezy account in *Esquire* was typical: "No smokestacks, no railroad sidings, no noise, only 'the world's most beautiful freeway' and high-tech industries with sales in the billions" (Smith 1981: 13). Some other articles of the period noted details like "the opaque veil of pink-brown smog" that hung low over the Valley, and observed the loss of agricultural lands, but these were colorful footnotes to the main story of the marvelous microchips, and the men who made them (Johnston 1982: 463).

Toxic Tech

The story changed in January 1982. San Jose residents sitting down to read the morning newspaper were alarmed to discover that, six weeks earlier, the city had found chemical contaminants in the local drinking-water supply—and had identified local computer-industry manufacturing as the culprit. The problem centered on the working-class neighborhood of Los Paseos, which seven years earlier had become home to a fabrication plant run by the semiconductor pioneer Fairchild Camera and Instrument Corporation. One resident likened the problem to "a chemical bomb" coming through her household faucets (Cummings 1982: A22). For Los Paseos residents, the presence of high levels of toxins in an underground holding facility only 2,000 feet from the source of the community's water supply provided an answer to what had been a mysterious and devastating spike in premature deaths, stillbirths and miscarriages, and birth defects (Cummings 1982; Siegel and Markoff 1985).

The local news story soon became a national one, and as publicity around the Fairchild story grew, more questions began to be asked about the scope and toxicity of high-tech production across the region. Residents and local activists began to raise questions not only about the possible pollution in the Valley's air and water but also in the bodies of those who worked there, particularly the blue-collar stratum in the assembly lines and "clean rooms" of the chipmakers. Concerned environmentalists, labor union leaders, and local politicians formed the Silicon Valley Toxics Coalition (SVTC) in 1982 to push for stricter industry standards within and around factories, as well as to agitate for broader environmental clean-up efforts around the region (Dooley 2002).

By 1983, the U.S. Environmental Protection Agency had become involved, tracking the extent of contamination and mobilizing government action at the state and local levels. In an article the following year in the *EPA Journal*, Regional Administrator Judith Ayres acknowledged, "it has become obvious that the absence of smokestacks does not mean an absence of environmental problems" (1984: 14). However, she also warned, the situation had "led to some elements of the press and the community to overstate the magnitude of the environmental health problem: 'high-tech toxics' make best-selling headlines." Not all areas of the Valley were equally affected, wrote Ayres. Remediation was possible with governmental partnership. She concluded evenly, "with the help of our state and local partners, we can ensure environmental health here in Silicon Valley, and in other Silicon Valleys not yet built" (1984: 15).

Fairchild paid a large price for its pollution, incurring at least $15 million in clean-up costs and an unquantifiable amount of public relations damage. Within a few years, it closed the Los Paseos plant entirely, making it what technology journalists Lenny Siegel and John Markoff termed "a monument to the dying myth of high tech as a clean, light industry" (1985: 165).

The Fairchild case was also a monument to the environmental side effects of rapid regional growth. In a rush to build new plants anywhere they could—and with a diminishing supply of buildable, flat land—the Valley's computer and chip manufacturers built heavy manufacturing facilities next door to people's homes. With policy-makers convinced that this growth was "clean," and desirous of new economic activity, few rules or regulations stood in the chipmakers' way. Rapid growth also created communities with inadequate infrastructure—particularly working-class areas like Los Paseos, whose dependence on a local well rather than a central urban water system allowed leaks from the Fairchild tanks to make their way quickly into home water supplies.

The case also exposed the class and racial fault lines that had emerged in this archetypal landscape without smokestacks. The Valley's early industrial landscape had been premised on the idea that green spaces and smart people went together. It presented an image of a high-tech world populated almost entirely by highly educated workers who were almost always white and male. Yet the economic success of the rarified environs of the Stanford Research Park and other places like it depended on the fabrication plants that dotted the flatlands—

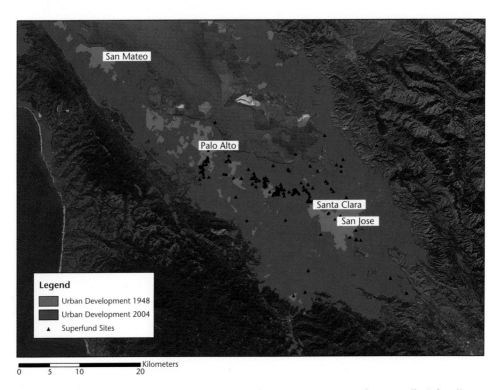

FIGURE 3.3 One measure of the environmental toxicity of generations of supposedly "clean" industrial activity in Silicon Valley is the high density of sites in the region marked for Superfund clean-up by the U.S. Environmental Protection Agency.

and whose workers were often minorities and women with a high-school education or less. Those most likely to be exposed to the environmental contaminants of the local high-tech industry—either by working in the factories or living near them—were working-class people and people of color (Matthews 2003; Smith et al. 2006). As EPA official Judith Ayres admitted, the pollution problem was not distributed equally across the Valley; as she left unsaid, those with fewer resources and less political power were far more gravely affected (Ayres 1984).

The EPA proceeded to conduct a study of the matter, whose findings distressed environmental activists and pleased the embattled semiconductor industry. Air pollution and chemicals in imported drinking water were in fact bigger health hazards in the region than groundwater contamination, the agency concluded. Semiconductor Industry Association official Jim Dufour commented happily, "if [pollution] were a big problem it would have come out in spades in this study . . . [i]t was the toughest test that could have been devised, and industry passed with an 'A'" (Benson and Kutzmann 1985). The SVTC disagreed, arguing that the EPA had based its findings on incomplete data (Benson and Kutzmann 1985).

Ironically, both activists and business interests overlooked the relationship of high-tech activity to another source of pollution the EPA cited as an even greater threat to human health: decreased air quality. The research-park model that so much of the Valley's development followed had, by the early 1980s, created a vast, car-dependent urban ecosystem of exurban workplaces, high-priced real estate, and grinding highway commutes (Reilly, O'Mara, and Seto 2009). As later scholarship has demonstrated, air pollution was merely one of multiple ways in which this type of built environment profoundly affected human and ecological health (Jackson 1985; Wachs and Crawford 1992; Frumkin 2003).

The environmental scandals of the early 1980s did not rupture the connection between "tech" and "green." In fact, the subsequent history of the Valley helped strengthen it. Starting in the mid-1980s, Valley firms began to move their manufacturing activities out of the United States, tapping into cheaper labor pools in East Asia and Latin America. Although Japanese competition was a major factor, looser environmental regulations in these new markets also were a powerful lure, and in some cases played as much if not more of a role in the offshoring and outsourcing of the dirtier parts of the high-tech business (Smith et al. 2006).

Despite continued environmental and labor activism, the winners in the public relations battle about the environmental impact of high-tech were the corporations and entrepreneurs themselves. By moving the most polluting parts of the technology supply chain overseas, and reframing technological production as an intellectual pursuit whose raw ingredients were smart people and good ideas, this iconic high-tech capital was able to reinvent itself once again as a clean, green playground.

The Globalization of High-Tech Urbanism

Silicon Valley's half-century-long track record of attracting the best and brightest entrepreneurs and generating immense wealth inspired countless regions around the world to build Silicon Valleys of their own. While replicating the Valley's ability to spur innovation and develop disruptive new products proved tremendously difficult, imitation of its built environment was relatively easy. The "if you build a research park, they will come" approach to tech-driven economic development undergirded the growth of countless regional initiatives from the 1950s forward.

Although Silicon Valley was not alone in locating postindustrial production in a low-rise, car-dependent environment, the economic success of the Valley helped to promulgate the form globally, and made it the *de rigueur* vehicle for tech-driven economic development from Beijing to Buffalo. The "clean" appearance of this type of landscape was a critical part of its allure, and the global spread of the Silicon Valley model further reinforced the conventional wisdom that postindustrial production was inherently non-polluting.

In India, for example, national and provincial technology policies from the 1970s forward took an intensively place-based approach to high-tech economic development centering upon the construction of new exurban industrial parks. The southern Indian state of Karnataka was an early and aggressive entrant into this arena, establishing an independent state corporation in 1976 to encourage the growth of the electronics industry. In the following year, Karnataka broke ground on a large new research park, Electronic City, about 18 kilometers south of the city of Bangalore (Heitzman 2004: 188).

In 1991, the national government of India jumped on the high-tech park bandwagon in major fashion with the Software Technology Parks of India (STPI) initiative, designed to attract multinationals and export-oriented firms. The policy established self-contained industrial park developments around the country that—in a spirit similar to that of the Stanford Research Park—offered their tenants a unique and enticing set of amenities. Along with tax and tariff relief that freed companies from the onerous restrictions of the Indian "License Raj," the parks provided robust infrastructure that contrasted sharply with the public utility woes that plagued the rest of urban India, where severely limited tele-communications capacity and regular power cuts were the norm. Inside the software parks, firms and workers were literally "off the grid" and enjoyed self-sustained electric power and broadband communication networks.

By the turn of the millennium, India was a growing high-tech superpower that offered firms a range of incentives to locate in low-density, self-contained environments. Karnataka's IT policy of 1999 contained provisions waiving conventional floor-to-area ratios that might constrain the size and shape of high-tech facilities. It allowed firms to consume electricity and other resources at industrial, rather than commercial rates, freeing up space for the energy-gobbling server rooms and 24-hour telecommunications facilities needed by India's burgeoning software industry (State of Karnataka 1999).

In Bangalore, the IT boom between 1990 and 2000 resulted in the loss of thousands of acres of farmland and sharply declining population density even as the city's overall population grew threefold (O'Mara and Seto 2013). While public transit remained the way the over-whelming majority of Bangaloreans traveled from home to work, car ownership and private transportation (e.g., company-provided shuttle buses) rose (Reilly, O'Mara, and Seto 2009).

The loss of open space and tree cover, the disruption of natural ecological processes, and the displacement of poor people have spurred grassroots conservation and environmental justice movements in a city that already had a robust tradition of such activism (Shiva 1994). Yet local protests tend to focus on piecemeal disruptions and corruptions at the urban core rather than the self-contained IT islands at the outskirts. The built environment and pro-ductive processes of the technology industry—and the government sanction of the exurban software park as the preferred site of such activity—receive less attention, particularly among the educated globe-trotting techies who live and work there.

FIGURE 3.4 As the technology industry globalized, its pastoral aesthetic and suburban setting globalized along with it. Infosys Headquarters, Electronic City, Bangalore, 2006.

Throughout India's high-tech urban archipelago, a green glow pervades the marketing and self-presentation of both industrial and residential developments. These latter-day factories without smokestacks published glossy brochures featuring broad swaths of green lawn and sparkling glass-clad buildings, more spa than office.

This percolated into the consciousness of the people who inhabited technological spaces. When asked about environmental issues in a series of interviews conducted at the height of the Indian technology boom in the mid-2000s, technology executives, property managers, planners, and real estate developers seemed to have given the question little to no consideration. "Of course, IT industry is non-polluting, so there's no big issue" with environmental concerns, one property manager remarked, with a wave of his hand. The bigger issue was coping with India's bureaucracy and convoluted property laws so that firms and developers could assemble a large and self-sufficient land package on which to build.[3]

The adaptation of the low-density research-park model, and the perpetuation of high-tech activity as "clean," is evident in other emerging economic superpowers as well. Across pollution-choked urban China, government officials embarked on a variety of software and technology park schemes designed to attract "smokeless" industry and move up the manufacturing value chain. In an extraordinarily crowded nation, some of these were striking in their isolation, such as the University Town development built outside the southern Chinese manufacturing hub of Shenzhen, where graduate engineering campuses of Tsinghua and Peking Universities anchored an emergent cluster of home-grown high-tech firms (O'Mara

FIGURE 3.5 New knowledge landscapes around the world replicate the "green" campus landscapes of Anglo-American universities. University Town, Shenzhen, China, 2007.

2011). In lightly settled farmland outside Moscow, a high-profile government-sponsored effort to create a "Russian Silicon Valley" announced in 2010 featured striking buildings designed by name-brand architects, set amid landscaped grounds, with Californian-style suburban housing developments. The overall intent was to provide the educated scientific workforce a reason to stay in Russia. In the words of the development's publicist, "they should be isolated from our reality" (Kramer 2010: BU1).

Even when located in relatively denser locations, separation and segregation from the urban norm characterized such developments. In Singapore, extraordinary density and a lack of buildable land have prompted more urban reinterpretations of the Silicon Valley model, financed by huge amounts of government resources. The developments have high-rise laboratories and denser floor-to-area ratios, but nonetheless market themselves as entirely self-contained communities offering a special set of amenities for scientists and technologists (Agency for Science, Technology, and Research 2011).

Tech and the Green City

Back in the United States, the urban economic comeback of the 1990s forward and an emerging cultural preference for denser, diverse environments catalyzed the growth of urban knowledge-economy districts from New York to Chicago to San Francisco and Seattle. While different in look and location from the suburban technology campuses of an earlier era, however, these neighborhoods also operated as self-contained, high-amenity units designed to appeal to an educated white-collar class. As the bike-riding and transit-loving millennial generation comes of age, an increasing number of consumers of such spaces are often those to whom environmental sustainability has strong appeal (Urban Land Institute 2011).

The "green" promises of emergent neighborhoods like Seattle's South Lake Union are in some respects little different from those of Nela Park more than a century ago. What's more, just as the pollution of Nela lurked beneath its greenswards, the steep environmental costs of technology dependence lie hidden, offshore and out of the city. Amazon.com's multiple South Lake Union buildings may not have smokestacks, but its business depends on giant electric-powered data centers located in remote areas of the American West and scattered across the globe. The kinds of consumer electronics sold with such efficiency on the Amazon website are now responsible for 15 percent of household energy consumption in the United States, and this number is expected to rise over time (Mouawad and Galbraith 2009). The less green elements of high-tech production—and the blue-collar workers who staff call centers and warehouse facilities—are removed once again from the landscape of high technology.

And yet: Amazon.com's thousands of employees are working—and often living—in a dense and lively urban environment that is a stark departure from the car-dependent suburban landscape that has dominated North America—and its high-tech spaces—for more than seven decades. The South Lake Union neighborhood bristles with LEED-certified buildings and green infrastructure, and more is on the way. And little of this would have been possible without the wealth and innovative resources of the technology industry, which not only built the fortune of the neighborhood's main property owner and developer, Microsoft co-founder Paul Allen, but also its anchor tenant, Amazon.com.

The environmental contradictions evident in South Lake Union circa 2014 present both a challenge and an opportunity for those concerned about the present and future of cities. With a globe-trotting managerial workforce, offshore production, gargantuan server farms, and astounding quantities of e-waste, the technology industry has a carbon footprint like few other smoke-belching industries before it. Yet technology companies and the real estate interests who serve them increasingly are finding that sustainable urbanism positively affects their bottom line, helping attract and retain workers and—like the industrial capitalists of a century ago—helping brand them as new-era, innovative enterprises.

History indicates that these industrial enterprises might have helped fuel the problems of high-tech urbanism, but that they by necessity must be part of the solution. Unlike some other kinds of cityscapes, high-tech urbanism owes its distinct spatiality and aesthetics—not to mention its ubiquity—to market forces (and policies governing markets) more than formal planning. The planner and the architect have been minor players in the urban evolution of Silicon Valley, and places like it. When they appear, it is in service to the lead actors: corporations, and large institutions like universities and government agencies. This power structure has replicated itself in denser central-city settings, where the desire to bring in technology companies and their workers has spurred local officials to build new infrastructure, change zoning, suspend regulations, and create a cornucopia of tax breaks for these kinds of firms and associated activities. Amid cries of gentrification and corporatization, however, these strategies have created the sorts of lively, walkable, transit-oriented neighborhoods that urbanists have been advocating for decades. The future of high-tech

FIGURE 3.6 Home to Amazon.com and other fast-growing technology companies, Seattle's South Lake Union markets itself as both environmentally sustainable and economically dynamic.

urbanism thus not only will entail grappling with its environmental contradictions, but in engaging the private-sector players who have built and inhabited these landscapes past, present, and future.

Notes

1   Purpose-built and often government-sponsored, these techno-cities did not have the broader and lasting influence on other kinds of urbanism later seen with Silicon Valley, nor did many of these places have a great deal of staying power.
2   Audience comments to author (2004, January 22) during a presentation to the Stanford Historical Society, Stanford, CA.
3   Interview conducted by author, (2006, October 6), Bangalore, India. All interviews were conducted in confidentiality, and the names of interviewees are withheld by mutual agreement. Interviewees in both India and China gave similar responses to our questions about environmental impact.

References

Acevedo, W., Taylor, J. L., Hester, D. J., Mladinich, C. S., and Glavac, S. (eds) (2006). *Rates, Trends, Causes, and Consequences of Urban Land-Use Change in the United States.* U.S. Geological Survey: Professional Paper 1726.
Adams, S. B. and Butler, O. R. (1999). *Manufacturing the Future: A history of Western Electric.* Cambridge; New York: Cambridge University Press.

Agency for Science, Technology, and Research [Government of Singapore] (2011). *A World-class Research Hub.* [Online]. Available: www.a-star.edu.sg/tabid/863/default.aspx [December 7, 2011].

Ascendas (2013). *Our Green Efforts.* [Online]. Available: www.ascendas.com/greenmonth/green_efforts.asp [August 21, 2013].

Ayres, J. E. (1984). Controlling the dangers from high-tech pollution. *EPA Journal,* 10, 14–15.

Benson, M. and Kutzmann, D. (1985, October 12). EPA calls valley water treatment, air pollution the chief cancer risks. *San Jose Mercury News* (CA), A1.

Chandler, A. D. (1977). *The Visible Hand: The managerial revolution in American business.* Cambridge, MA: Belknap Press of the Harvard University Press.

Cummings, J. (1982, May 20). Leaking chemicals in California's "Silicon Valley" alarm neighbors. *The New York Times,* A22.

Dooley, E. E. (2002). Silicon Valley Toxics Coalition. *Environmental Health Perspectives,* 110(4), 183.

Duany, A., Plater-Zyberk, E., and Speck, J. (2010). *Suburban Nation: The rise of sprawl and the decline of the American dream.* New York: North Point Press.

Duffy, F. (1980). Office buildings and organisational change. In King, A. (ed.), *Buildings and Society: Essays on the social development of the built environment.* London: Routledge & Kegan Paul, 255–280.

Findlay, J. (1992). *Magic Lands: Western cityscapes and American culture after 1940.* Berkeley, CA: University of California Press.

Fishman, R. (1987). *Bourgeois Utopias: The rise and fall of suburbia.* New York: Basic Books.

Frumkin, H. (2003, May–June). Urban sprawl and public health. *Public Health Reports,* 117, 201–217.

Frumkin, H., Frank, L., and Jackson, R. (2004). *Urban Sprawl and Public Health: Designing, planning, and building for healthy communities.* Washington, DC: Island Press.

Geiger, R. (1993). *Research and Relevant Knowledge: American research universities since World War II.* New York: Oxford University Press.

Graf, D. and Voorhees, W. (1944). *Convenience for Research: Buildings for the Bell Telephone Laboratory, Inc., Murray Hill, New Jersey.* New York: Foley & Smith.

Hayden, D. (2002). *Building Suburbia: Green fields and urban growth, 1820–2000.* New York: Pantheon Books.

Heitzman, J. (2004). *Network City: Planning the information society in Bangalore.* New Delhi; New York: Oxford University Press.

Jackson, K. T. (1985). *Crabgrass Frontier: The suburbanization of the United States.* New York: Oxford University Press.

Johnston, M. (1982). High tech, high risk, and high life in Silicon Valley. *National Geographic,* 162(10), 459–477.

Kargon, R. H. and Molella, A. P. (2008). *Invented Edens: Techno-cities of the twentieth century.* Cambridge, MA: MIT Press.

Knowles, S. G. and Leslie, S. W. (2001). Industrial Versailles: Eero Saarinen's corporate campuses for GM, IBM, and AT&T. *Isis,* 92(1), 1–33.

Kramer, A. E. (2010, April 9). Innovation, by order of the Kremlin. *The New York Times.* [Online]. Available: www.nytimes.com/2010/04/11/business/global/11russia.html?fta=y [June 15, 2010].

Kunstler, J. (1994). *The Geography of Nowhere: The rise and decline of America's man-made landscape.* New York: Free Press.

Lawrence, C. L. (1927). *Poems Along the Way.* San Jose, CA: Tucker Printing Company.

Leslie, S. W. (1993). *The Cold War and American Science: The military-industrial-academic complex at MIT and Stanford.* New York: Columbia University Press.

Light, J. (2009). *The Nature of Cities: Ecological visions and the American urban professions, 1920–1960.* Baltimore, MD: Johns Hopkins University Press.

Lowen, R. (1997). *Creating the Cold War University: The transformation of Stanford.* Berkeley, CA: University of California Press.

Maedje, C. W. (1951). General Electric's Nela Park, U.S.A. holds worldwide reputation as being the "University of Light." Cleveland, OH: Lamp News Bureau, General Electric.

Matthews, G. (2003). *Silicon Valley, Women, and the California Dream: Gender, class, and opportunity in the twentieth century.* Stanford, CA: Stanford University Press.

Mouawad, J. and Galbraith, K. (2009, September 20). Plugged-in age feeds a hunger for electricity. *The New York Times*, A1.

Mozingo, L. A. (2011). *Pastoral Capitalism: A history of suburban corporate landscapes*. Cambridge, MA: MIT Press.

O'Mara, M. P. (2005). *Cities of Knowledge: Cold War science and the search for the next Silicon Valley*. Princeton, NJ: Princeton University Press.

O'Mara, M. P. (2011). Silicon Valleys. *BOOM: A Journal of California*, 1(2), 74–81.

O'Mara, M. P. and Seto, K. C. (2013). The influence of foreign direct investment on land use changes and regional planning in developing-world megacities: a Bangalore case study. In Kraas, F., Aggarwar, S., Coy, M., and Mertins, G. (eds), *Megacities: Our global urban future*. New York: Springer, 81–97.

Packer, G. (2013). Change the world. *The New Yorker*, 89(15), 44–55.

Petition (Palo Alto Residents to Stanford University) (1962, December 2). File Folder 5, Box A16, SC 216, Stanford University Archives. Stanford, CA.

Reilly, M. K., O'Mara, M., and Seto, K. C. (2009). From Bangalore to the Bay Area: comparing transportation and activity accessibility as drivers of urban growth. *Landscape and Urban Planning*, 92(1), 24–33.

Rome, A. (2001). *The Bulldozer in the Countryside: Suburban sprawl and the rise of American environmentalism*. Cambridge; New York: Cambridge University Press.

Seigel, L. and Markoff, J. (1985). *The High Cost of High Tech: The dark side of the chip* (1st ed.). New York: Harper & Row.

Shiva, V. (1994). Conflicts of global ecology: environmental activism in a period of global reach. *Alternatives: Global, Local, Political*, 19(2), 195–207.

Sklair, L. (2005). The transnational capitalist class and contemporary architecture in globalizing cities. *International Journal of Urban and Regional Research*, 29(3), 485–500.

Smith, A. (1981). Silicon Valley spirit. *Esquire*, 96(11), 13–14.

Smith, T., Sonnenfeld, D. A., and Pellow, D. N. (eds) (2006). *Challenging the Chip: Labor rights and environmental justice in the global electronics industry*. Philadelphia, PA: Temple University Press.

Stanford Oral History Project (1980). *Interview with Alf Brandin*. Stanford University Archives. Stanford, CA.

State of Karnataka (1999). The Millennium IT Policy.

Steers, M. G. (1963). Letter to the editor. *Palo Alto Times*. File Folder 8, Box A29, SC 216, Stanford University Archives. Stanford, CA.

Taylor, F. W. (1911). *The Principles of Scientific Management*. New York: Harper & Row.

Townsend, H. (1960). *A History of Nela Park*. Cleveland, OH: National Electric Lamp Association.

Urban Land Institute (2011). *What's Next? Real estate in the new economy*. Washington, DC: ULI Press.

Vulcan Real Estate (2012). *Discover South Lake Union*. [Online]. Available: www.discoverslu.com/be-green-here [February 14, 2012].

Wachs, M. and Crawford, M. (1992). *The Car and the City: The automobile, the built environment, and daily urban life*. Ann Arbor, MI: University of Michigan Press.

Washington Herald (1915). Artificial daylight discovered, three kinds of it. *Chronicling America: Historic American Newspapers*. Washington, DC: Library of Congress.

Wax, M. (1958, November 16). Stanford Park: weird success. *San Francisco Chronicle*. Stanford Lands Scrapbook V, 1960–1961, Subject File 1300/9, Stanford University Archives, Stanford, CA.

Wolfe, T. (1983, December). The tinkerings of Robert Noyce. *Esquire*, 346–374.

Woods, K. (1923, May). An ideal that proved practical. *Light*, 31.

4

FROM BLUES TO GREEN

The Future of New Towns Worldwide

Deni Ruggeri

For hundreds of years, planners and designers have been experimenting with the design of the ideal community and its component parts. However, it was not until the end of World War II that some of these visions became a reality through the construction of modernist New Towns. At the foundation of the New Town movement were Le Corbusier's obsession with efficiency and functionality and Ebenezer Howard's Garden City model, which was predicated upon a need for cities and their inhabitants to be in close contact with nature. England, France, and the US were among the few countries to establish government programs for the creation of New Towns. Architects embraced the challenge, producing a variety of solutions ranging from highly architectural to landscape-driven New Towns. While most New Towns struggled in establishing a place identity, those organized around a strong landscape framework seemed to have an edge.

This chapter investigates the design, development, and subsequent growth of three New Towns, which have become case studies for a landscape-driven solution to urban development: Harlow (England), Marne-la-Vallée (France), and Irvine (US). While differing in many ways, all embraced their landscape with pride and enthusiasm. In return, the landscape gave them imageability (Lynch 1960)—i.e., the distinctiveness and memorability needed for a unique *genius loci* to emerge (Norberg Schultz 1980). Irvine residents marveled at the imageable village edges that bordered their neighborhood—renamed "villages" to further stress its past rural identity—from the outside world. In Harlow, green wedges separated each neighborhood and provided a memorable backdrop for its architecture. In Marne-la-Vallée, nature and transportation came together to create a linear *trame verte* of forests, meadows, and artificial ponds.

Decades after their completion, New Towns continue to be deeply committed to the landscape, which has become integral to the place identity of their residents. This place identity is reflected in the NIMBY attitude of some communities, but also in their efforts to increase and enrich their habitat through the reuse of obsolete infrastructure, the redevelopment of old industrial sites, and a land management process that seeks to balance growth and ecological integrity. Seen from the landscape perspective, New Towns appear much "thicker" and emerging than many designers and planners give them credit for. Far from being a thing of the past, New Towns remain relevant. As developing countries worldwide are searching for models of sustainable and livable communities, New Towns have the experience necessary to lead them there. Now Urbanism will not be effective unless it learns from and builds on their legacy.

The New Town Movement

At the end of World War II, as a result of the reconstruction efforts, many countries sought to accommodate the growing number of urban residents by building New Towns. The New Town movement in the UK originated in 1943, when the Abercrombie Plan laid the foundations for a comprehensive strategy to house new urban dwellers in well-planned communities of 50,000 people located 30 miles from the capital (Merlin 1971; Evans 1972). Thirty-four New Towns were planned as a result of these efforts, but the original goal to stop the expansion of existing large cities was never fully achieved.

French New Towns developed in the late 1960s in support of the centrality of Paris, booming under the pressures of postwar reconstruction and the end of colonialism. Fast RER (*Réseau Express Régional*) trains connected the New Towns to the city center, which continued to provide the majority of jobs. While the "concentrated deconcentration" policy that led to the construction of five New Towns did provide some relief to the sprawl that was engulfing metropolitan Paris, the creation of Cergy Pontoise to the west and Marne-la-Vallée to the east helped focus Paris' metropolitan development in these critical directions (Orillard and Picon 2012: 26).

Title 7 of the Housing Act Urban Growth and New Community Development Act of 1970 began a relatively timid US engagement in the creation of satellite cities by promoting public support to those involved in New Town planning, and by offering federal loan guarantees to development companies in exchange for the creation of new communities that would emphasize comprehensive planning, a diversity of affordable housing, and jobs, and that would serve as economic boosts for the surrounding regions. Only a few of the 13 communities originally planned were actually constructed, and several of these decided to disconnect from the federal program, realizing the rigid and often unnecessarily detailed control overseen by the Department of Housing and Urban Development (Watson 2005).

Yet, at the core of the New Town movement was an optimistic belief that communities could be designed from scratch, thanks to the careful integration of uses and activities needed for human life. In the minds of their planners, design would provide the distinctiveness and imageability needed for people to move in, identify with their image, and develop a strong sense of belonging (Ruggeri 2009). While some environmental designers were enthusiastic about working on such a challenging task, others warned that cities could not be seen as the simple assemblage of functional parts and that strict oversight, leaving nothing to chance, would lead to dysfunctional places (Alexander 1965). Yet in the successful New Towns, it was the landscape—both the contextual settings and the integrated systems of established parks and trails—that provided residents with relief from the uniformity and blandness of the built form.

A History of New Towns

Generally inspired by Ebenezer Howard's Garden City model and by the modern movement in architecture, the New Town concept has varied in terms of aesthetics, conceptual framework, and relationship with the surrounding landscape. The idiosyncratic, context-driven interpretation of their shared ideals has defied a common definition and begun to suggest a more flexible and inclusive view of New Towns as the gestalt of *core* characteristics and the unique *genius loci* of the places in which they were installed (Table 4.1) (Forsyth and Crewe 2009; Ruggeri 2013).

At the heart of all early New Town experiments was a reliance on efficiency, a fundamental tenet of the modern movement, which translated into the application of strict zoning and the emphasis on efficient transportation. Though hardly a modernist discovery, the concept of efficiency is embedded in Ebenezer Howard's Garden City model (1902), which called for a regional planning policy for the organization, location, and sizing of self-contained, satellite urban centers of 32,000 residents enjoying the best of country living, yet well connected to a central city. These communities would be established on land held in public trust, thus limiting the effects of real estate speculation. A productive ecological greenbelt surrounding the city core would prevent subsequent sprawl and provide every resident easy access to nature in both its pristine and cultivated forms.

Because they required large tracts of land and collaboration across the various agencies, New Towns required the establishment of public development companies charged with the land acquisition, master planning, construction, and sale of the new neighborhoods. These development companies were given unprecedented powers to exercise eminent domain, negotiate regional planning decisions, and engage in a dialog with local municipalities. In France, this led to the creation of a new quasi-governmental agency called *Syndicat Communautaire d'Aménagement* (SCA) that could more easily engage in a dialogue between local and government interests (Orillard and Picon 2012).

New Towns' aesthetics were often "brutalist," inspired and modeled after Le Corbusier's sketches for a "radiant city" (Le Corbusier 1986) (Figure 4.1). Whereas in traditional cities many of the functions usually associated with living and working were dispersed within the urban fabric, modernist New Towns would assemble them in superblocks of "towers in the park" efficiently linked by arterial roads and grade-separated pedestrian paths (Trancik

TABLE 4.1 The author's working definition of a New Town

Core Characteristics	Contextual Characteristics
1) Master planning and coordination	10) Regional planning orientation
2) Diversity of housing supply	11) Reliance on mass transit or high-speed road infrastructure
3) Self-containment/mixed use	
4) Maximum size/scale	12) Complete to partial limitation to car access within neighborhoods
5) Emphasis on leisure and recreation	
6) Balance of jobs and residents	13) Imageability (memorability, distinctiveness, and wayfinding)
7) Careful phasing	
8) Greenfield development	14) Emphasis on affordable housing and inclusion
9) Policy and land-use strategies to limit real estate speculation	15) Engagement/partnership with local municipalities
	16) Technological innovation
	17) Presence of university and higher education institutions

Source: Ruggeri (2013)

FIGURE 4.1 Modernism's influence on New Town design is clearly reflected in Harlow's Market Square.

1986). Designed to be experienced from the car, the modernist city employed architecture and landscape architecture as wayfinding and place identity shapers, while newly invented closed-circuit television channels, local museums, and weekly newsletters would educate residents about the virtues of New Town living and build a sense of social cohesion and shared values (Gibberd 1952; Merlin 1971; Ruggeri 2014).

Built in record time, New Towns were often critiqued for their utter placelessness and monotony. Critics used the term "New Town Blues" to describe the homogeneity and overall dullness of life in a new community (Williamson 1983). The female residents of New Towns were to suffer most from this isolation. While their husbands and children found social outlets in the workplace and at school, women felt alienated and underwhelmed, and regretted leaving the intense social life of their neighborhoods of origin (Carruthers 1996).

In contrast to the monotony and placelessness of the built form, the landscape played a key role in the construction of place identity in the young communities. New Town planners adopted an iconographic stance toward the landscape, for example, often orienting the urban fabric to align with views and vistas. In the English New Town of Harlow, chief planner Sir Frederick Gibberd scrutinized the landscape in search of specimen trees, iconic views, and unique topographical features, which could help residents find their way around the New Town. Existing canals, footpaths, and agricultural landscapes were preserved to remind residents of their shared history. In Irvine, California, an extensive system of eucalyptus windbreaks created to protect the cultivations of lima beans, strawberries, and orange groves was preserved and integrated into the transportation system of the city through the creation of pedestrian *paseos* (Ruggeri 2014).

Within neighborhoods, a landscape framework of small parks and playgrounds offered young mothers and children places to socialize and play sports within easy reach of each resident's home. Leisure activities once only available to the rich were now open to every resident, regardless of income. Major emphasis was placed in the establishment of state-of-the-art schools and other cultural amenities. Many New Towns implemented extensive public art programs to inspire civic pride in the residents and remind them of their community's urban ambitions. In Harlow, Gibberd hired successful contemporary artists like Henry Moore and Auguste Rodin to produce 79 public art installations, which were embedded into the New Town's urban fabric. At his death, his rural estate and associated sculpture garden was also donated to the municipality for the enjoyment of Harlow residents.

Early on, the public landscapes of New Towns like Harlow, Marne-la-Vallée, and Irvine offered residents an escape from the rigidity and uniformity of their built environments. Today, they offer an element of continuity in the context of their changing communities. New Towns have discovered that landscapes, far from being a liability, can become sources of revenue and renewal. The result has been the proposal to create new residential infill in order to capitalize on the presence of this well-established green infrastructure and illustrates the central role the landscape will play in the sustainable growth, evolution, and long-term resilience of New Towns.

The following case studies are emblematic of a deliberate effort on the part of their planners to embed the landscape with artistic, ecological, infrastructural, or sociological value. Years before the emergence of discourses of landscape infrastructure, ecosystem services, and Landscape Urbanism, Gibberd conceived of a city where green wedges would function as eco-tones. Marne-la-Vallée structured its entire master plan on the centrality of a blue and green infrastructure corridor where urban run-off would be collected, cleansed, and allowed to re-enter naturally into the water cycle. In Irvine, the landscape edges and neighborhood parks offered a framework for socio-economic development, giving the villages a marketability that has allowed it to withstand the boom-and-bust real estate cycles of the past half a century. As a whole, these case studies shed important light on the "thick" nature of the New Town landscape, its processes, and future ambitions.

Irvine: Landscape as Infrastructure

The city of Irvine dates back to the 1960s, when the Irvine family, owners of a 90,000-acre ranch in Southern California, decided to hire architect William Pereira to plan a New Town in direct opposition to the undifferentiated sprawl of Los Angeles. They planned a New Town centered on a new university campus surrounded by self-contained residential neighborhoods or villages; each with a village center, schools, public swimming pools, and other amenities. A grid of heavily landscaped arterial roads, each aligned to a particular vista or landmark, would help drivers navigate the city. Within each village, pedestrian *paseos* were integrated into a hierarchical circulation of streets and boulevards (Watson 2005; Ruggeri 2009). Surrounding the villages was a productive, pastoral landscape so tranquil that "you can hear the asparagus grow" (Ruggeri 2009: 22).

Today, Irvine has grown into a city of 230,000 residents, and is a center of attraction for many of the suburban communities of the Los Angeles region. Irvine has expanded its claim to include the majority of the agricultural land at the center of the Irvine Ranch, and is now investing in the creation of new habitat and the preservation of what currently exists. Ken Smith's recent master plan for the former El Toro base known as Orange County Great Park is envisioned as an integration of restored nature and urban agriculture reminiscent of the ranch's productive past.

Yet, even the early Irvine villages were surrounded by greenbelts, linear landscapes that buffered each village, projected its landscape identity to the outside world, and enhanced the city's imageability (Lynch 1960). Although quite popular with runners and walkers, village edges were mainly designed for the aesthetic appreciation of those driving at high speed along six-lane arterial roads. Limited in size and acreage, and seldom accessible from the inside, these landscapes did not offer landscape architects much room for imagination and design experimentation, save the opportunities of added visibility at the village entries.

In 1995, the Municipality of Irvine and the Irvine Company, owner of the ranch and heir to the Irvine family fortunes, began long negotiations to set aside a 325-foot-wide and 3.5-mile-long linear corridor along Jeffrey Road, one of Irvine's east–west arterials. This 76-acre park, accounting for 15 percent of Irvine's total park acreage, would connect its downtown to the Natural Community Conservation Preserve (NCCP), a 50,000-acre nature preserve established in the 1980s in response to citizen concerns over projected growth (Figure 4.2). The park would be structured along a grade-separated bike and pedestrian trail and serve as the backbone for the Irvine villages of Woodbury, Stonegate, and Portola Hills. The trail

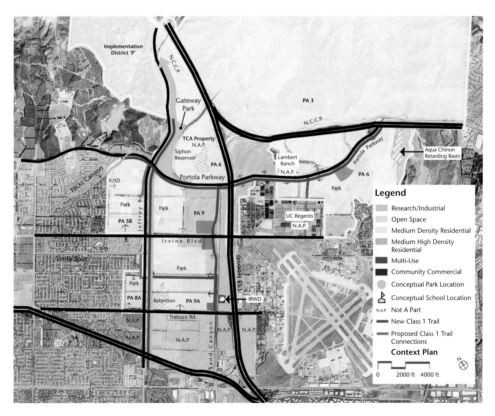

FIGURE 4.2 Context map showing the backbone-like function of the Jeffrey Open Space Trail (in bright green).

would meander through a series of landscape habitats designed to mimic the landscapes that pre-existed the Ranch.

The multi-year community consensus process that resulted in the design of the Jeffrey Open Space Trail (Figure 4.3) was the first of its kind in the history of the New Town, and a successful example of public–private partnership. Irvine residents, planning officials, landscape architects, and the developer participated in a series of collaborative workshops and public events through which a vision and set of guiding principles emerged; these included a focus on the pedestrian experience, opportunities for active and passive recreation, a predominant use of native plantings for the creation of habitat, and an "improvement credits" financing mechanism to counter higher development densities in the village cores.

Although the public process was responsible for many design choices, the use of a material palette, and an architectural vocabulary reminiscent of Frederick Law Olmsted's work, it was the responsibility of the designer to ensure that these decisions be integrated into a cohesive vision that complemented the neo-traditional image of the nearby village of Woodbury. Today, the Jeffrey Open Space Trail has become an integral component to Irvine's landscape infrastructure. Due to the improvement credits financing mechanism, densities in the surrounding neighborhoods have been increased and transit lines extended, turning the trail into a true multimodal transportation corridor. Most of all, the park has become integral to the place identity of North Irvine, earning of the moniker "the community backyard" (Irvine Company 2013).

Harlow: A Landscape of Continuity

Designed in 1947 to accommodate 60,000 people, Harlow is the second and best-known English New Town. Its plan was the work of Sir Frederick Gibberd, an architect, planner, and landscape enthusiast who—like Camillo Sitte and Raymond Unwin—believed that buildings and landscapes should be arranged to form memorable pictorial compositions (Gibberd 1980). Nowhere was the picturesque approach more visible than in Harlow's downtown:

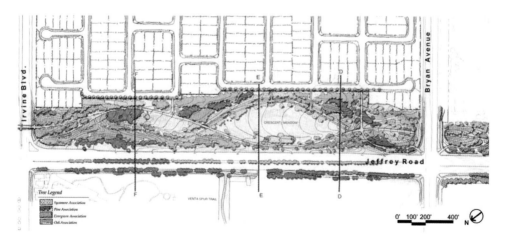

FIGURE 4.3 Plan of Segment 2 of the Jeffrey Open Space Trail, showing the variety of habitats being created.

> The town center is a composition in its own right, and for that composition to have unity it will require a dominant element or crown . . . As a first principle, it may be said that the major civic buildings must be in themselves the most impressive in scale.
>
> *(Gibberd 1953: 96)*

The town center was divided into two districts, each focusing on a public square. To the north was the market square, surrounded with retail and offices. To the south, the Civic Square complex included a church, a hotel, and the Town Hall building. The town center was framed to the south by the Water Gardens, a sculpture garden/eco-tone of lawns, shrubs, and hedges seeking to create transition between the hard surfaces of the town center and the soft textures of the green wedges (Figure 4.4).

North of the town center was the Town Park, a large open space occupying the gently sloping Stort River valley. By setting aside and preserving some the most imageable land, Gibbert gave the landscape a central role in his vision. By increasing densities, he was able to preserve the large tracts of open space he needed to accentuate the transition between city and nature, a condition usually found in small UK villages. Gibberd used the landscape to both separate and integrate neighborhoods. The placement of homes within walking distance of open space gave Harlow residents respite within nature, because "no one can be stimulated by bricks and mortar alone" (Gibberd 1953: 30).

Rather than assigning these spaces with specific uses, Gibberd conceived of them as adaptable open spaces, serving as riparian corridors, recreational trails, or allotment gardens. While in many New Towns landscapes tended to be highly programmed and manicured, Gibberd saw Harlow's open space as a dynamic, constantly emerging, and evolving mosaic

| other |
| agricultural land |
| metropolitan green belt |
| wildlife sites |
| green wedges |
| buildings |

1: 100 000

FIGURE 4.4 Map showing the rich mosaic of Harlow's green infrastructure.

of recreational spaces for both active and passive enjoyment, new and old habitats, community gardens, and family farms.

After more than a half century, and despite the shrinking municipal budgets of the post-Thatcher era, Harlow's landscape continues to thrive. A 2012 study documenting the state of parks and gardens, amenity green spaces (playgrounds), natural and semi-natural spaces, and green corridors and links has found evidence of a system that is well used, cherished, and healthy, supporting a rich habitat of natural areas, wetlands, forests, and meadows (Land Use Consultants 2012). Within Harlow's neighborhoods, parks and playgrounds are being managed as green infrastructure, an interconnected network of open spaces and green linkages providing environmental, social, and economic benefits to the community (Benedict and McMahon 2006). A recent study by Harlow Council suggests that its landscape continues to be used and appreciated by citizens. One out of two residents visits a park on weekends, while one out of four visits a park once a day. And most importantly, 83 percent of all users get there on foot, just as Gibberd had intended.

On the edge of town, Harlow's agricultural greenbelt continues to thrive as well, but there have been many attempts to attack its integrity. A 2011 law has given municipalities permission to develop parts of their greenbelt to boost their finances. Like other municipalities, Harlow has indeed rezoned some of its agricultural land to allow for the development of new neighborhoods, but other redevelopment areas have been sought closer to the town center, on sites once occupied by factories, outdated sports facilities, or schools. The construction of new housing has aimed at expanding the current population, maintaining a fairly young demographic profile, ensuring positive economic growth, and attracting new businesses and services (Harlow Council 2013).

Newhall is Harlow's most recent residential neighborhood, yet its design reflects Gibberd's original vision, reinterpreting some of the original forms and functional solutions found in the 1960s neighborhoods. The neighborhood features districts of dense urban fabric of apartments, villas, and row houses centered on a neighborhood park separated by means of green wedges (Figure 4.5). Like the original Harlow neighborhoods, Newhall must be experienced on foot, as a sequence of carefully composed scenes tested and refined to perfection as only a visual artist would do (Gibberd 1953; Cullen 1963). The picturesque approach used by Gibberd redefined the street as the resulting space between architectural volumes, and resulted in a cellular, non-linear, and visually stimulating urban pattern (Gibberd 1953).

The neighborhood's picturesque forms do not go unnoticed. Writing about Newhall's urban design, an architectural critic has written: "the scale is that typically found where a Victorian residential inner city gives way to lower-rise twentieth-century suburbs. It is as if the branch of an older place has been ripped from its trunk and transplanted into a rural setting" (ArchDaily 2013) (Figure 4.6). By reinterpreting in contemporary form the urban design strategies used in the planning of the original Harlow neighborhoods, Newhall designers have chosen to respect Gibberd's vision:

> however small or apparently trivial the new work may be, it must always respect existing work of character . . . All great designers have a sense of tradition, a historical sense which involves "a perception not only of the pastness of the past, but also of its presence".
>
> *(Gibberd 1953: 19, quoting T. S. Eliot's 1919 essay*
> *"Tradition and the Individual Talent")*

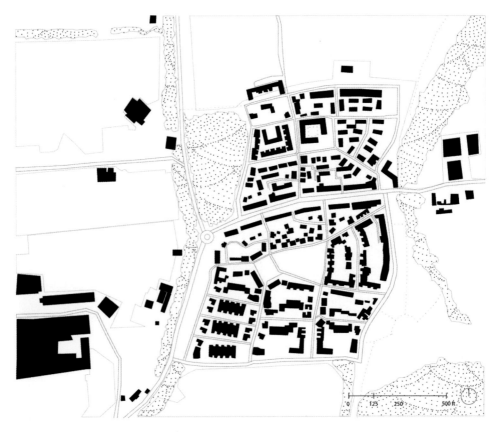

FIGURE 4.5 The Newhall neighborhood in Harlow, a contemporary reinterpretation of the original planning ideals set forth by Gibberd.

Marne-la-Vallée: Landscape as Habitat

Planned in 1969, the New Town of Marne-la-Vallée was the result of a national policy aimed at managing the urban growth of Paris through the creation of transit-oriented satellite cities. Its plan featured a 20-kilometer-long polycentric city divided into four administrative sectors encompassing 25 pre-existing villages. The site chosen for the New Town was the valley of the River Marne, populated with farms, chateaus, and one of France's most important industrial archaeological sites, the nineteenth-century Menier Chocolate Factory. This mosaic of historic and natural sites was carefully preserved and integrated within the planning schemes, becoming an integral part of the identity of Marne-la-Vallée and its specialized districts: Val d'Europe as the center of commerce, Disneyland Paris as a prime tourism and leisure destination, the Cité Descartes as a university town, and Noisy-le-Grand as the main administrative center. Overall, the plan of Marne-la-Vallée resembles a greenway—or *trame verte*—of agricultural fields, wooded areas, and riparian landscapes also known as Marne-la-Vallée's "Blue and Green Necklace" (Orillard and Picon 2012; Laborde 2013).

The *trame verte* landscape framework serves to separate the districts into smaller, more manageable sectors while also providing function as a recreational amenity for nature-thirsty

FIGURE 4.6 Like other Harlow neighborhood centers, Newhall's features stores, offices, a pub, a community room, and public art.

Parisians. The original scheme (Figure 4.7) revealed a network of green spaces layered with ecological and transportation functions, as the open space also housed the RER train line to Paris. While the quantity and variety of open space present in Marne-la-Vallée contributed to its reputation as a place for leisure, its green areas proved to be too large and intimidating and did not succeed in attracting the multitude of users for which they had been designed (Merlin 1971; Laborde 2013).

Marne-la-Vallée's planners were aware of the deleterious consequences urban development would have on the local hydrological cycle. First among many French municipalities, Marne-la-Vallée recognized the importance of separate stormwater and sewer systems, and of the design of open spaces to accommodate numerous artificial ponds and wetlands functioning as water detention and filtering systems (Orillard and Picon 2012). Also innovative was the design of naturalistic ponds, with articulated landscape edges that would maximize their ecological performance as eco-tones.

Four decades later, the size and diversity of Marne-la-Vallée's landscape presents both challenge and opportunity, as it provides an immense reservoir of potential green infrastructure and important ecosystem services. Similarly, the coarse development pattern visible on the territory of Marne-la-Vallée should offer plenty of future opportunity for infill development. Plans for the densification of the Cité Descartes have already been set in motion and will hopefully contribute to the city's objective of becoming a university town (Orillard and Picot 2012). More infill will become possible as street right-of-ways are narrowed and new developable space is created where the RER train tracks and stations used to be.

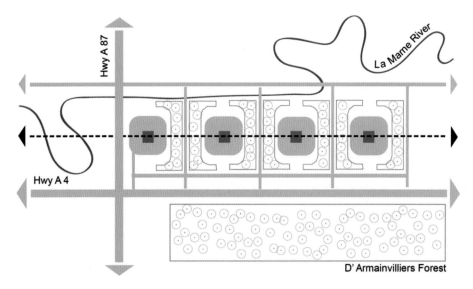

FIGURE 4.7 Diagram showing the *trame verte*, the "Blue and Green Necklace", and its integration with automobile and rapid transit transportation.

Predicated on a vision of innovation in transportation, housing, urban design, and landscape architecture, Marne-la-Vallée's plan carefully balanced two seemingly opposing goals: the diversification required by the polycentric urban form and the need to create a *gestalt* that would provide a strong and unified identity. The solution was the introduction of a "Blue and Green Necklace" of natural and cultural landscapes, from stormwater ponds to industrial canals, from farms to castles, from wetlands to beech forests, all within a relatively short distance of the densely populated residential areas. This approach has had a profound impact on Marne-la-Vallée's identity, and earned the city a reputation as a leader in sustainability.

Indeed, the original *parti* of a blue and green system of ecological sites linked by high-speed rail transportation continues to affect the evolution of the New Town and generate both conflicts and opportunities. Merging two of Marne-la-Vallée's unique vocations, the city has recently launched "Village Nature," a one-of-a-kind sustainable tourism destination adjacent to the already popular tourist hub of Disneyland Paris. Similarly, the link between Université Paris-Est Marne-la-Vallée and EPAMARNE, the New Town's business development office, has led to creation of the Montévrain eco-neighborhoods, the first of a number of new sustainable neighborhoods being retrofitted into the existing urban fabric (EPAMARNE 2012).

The ecological identity of Marne-la-Vallée is reflected in the plans and visions for its future as well as in the everyday landscape management practices. The recently concluded EUROSCAPES Project—an EU-funded effort to develop a shared methodology for the valuation, preservation, and management of urban and suburban landscapes—showcased the city's new *Schéma de Cohérence et d'Orientation Paysagère* (Plan for the Coherence and Orientation of the Landscape), which has implemented a citizen-science approach committed to the assessment, preservation, and maintenance of open space areas. The community-based process has involved numerous engagement efforts, including a Photovoice campaign, which has used photography as a source of information about residents' landscape preferences (Ruggeri 2014). Through participation, community members and city officials are reminded of the richness of their landscape, and of its value to the health and resilience of individuals and families alike.

Lessons

Despite the undeniable uniqueness of each of the three case studies, there is an element of consilience in the way New Towns have approached the task of preserving and enriching the health and diversity of their landscape infrastructure (Figure 4.8). The following discussion takes the individual lessons learned and attempts to synthesize them into a set of axioms for the future of Now Urbanism.

Change is Good

Change has been a challenge for many New Towns, which have struggled to shed their "New Town Blues" image and attract new residents and investors. Meanwhile, severe budget cuts are taking a toll on their ability to successfully manage an immense landscape infrastructure of parks, nature preserves, and neighborhood gardens (Scott and Ben-Joseph 2012). Other New Towns have been more fortunate in attracting new residents and business, but struggle to reconcile the necessity to grow the local economy with the residents' natural resistance to physical and social changes.

New infill is a common sighting in the contemporary New Town landscape. Low-density office parks, obsolete schools, and even former military bases have become sites of innovation and change. While lost space continues to remain the prime candidate for infill, greenfield development may continue to be developed strategically and for the benefit of all, but only if its design is sensitive to context and fits into the existing ethos. In the words of Sir Frederick Gibberd, planner of Harlow:

> A town is never a completed structure . . . Any proposal for town redevelopment . . . must be so broad and flexible that it may be re-cast by future generations. Time is the fourth dimension of town design.
>
> *(Gibberd 1953: 20)*

Designed with time in mind, Harlow's landscape maintained a level of flexibility and variety in terms of function, cultural significance, and ecological value. Gibberd's intuition proved instrumental to strengthening the town's resilience to future environmental, economic, and cultural change, and may be the reason why the city is now moving from blues to green.

Participation is Key to Resilience

The European Landscape Convention of 2006 officially recognized the need to engage residents in identifying culturally and ecologically significant landscapes as a fundamental civil rights issue (Déjeant-Pons 2006). Once again, New Towns have been leading the way in community engagement and participation, remaining true to their original mission to innovate. In Irvine, Harlow, and Marne-la-Vallée, public participation has been essential to achieving landscape sustainability and in sending residents a clear message about the need for stewardship and direct engagement.

Marne-la-Vallée has authored one of the most extensive community-based habitat and landscape assessments, educating residents about biodiversity and plant maintenance, and has even disseminated its expertise to other communities around Europe by taking a leading role in many projects aimed at fostering cooperation between New Towns (Gaborit 2013).

FIGURE 4.8 Diagrams comparing the landscape mosaics in the case studies of Harlow, Marne, and Irvine.

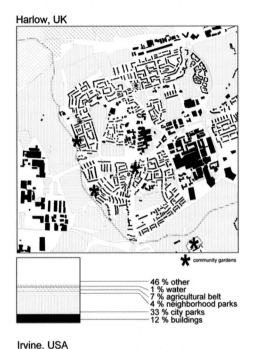

Harlow, UK

✱ community gardens

46 % other
1 % water
7 % agricultural belt
4 % neighborhood parks
33 % city parks
12 % buildings

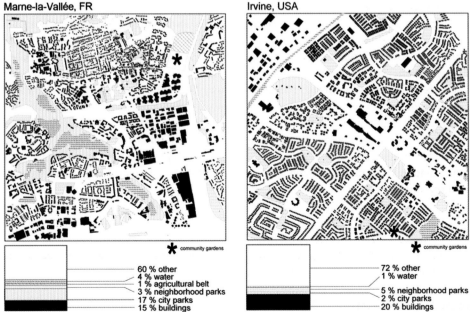

Marne-la-Vallée, FR

✱ community gardens

60 % other
4 % water
1 % agricultural belt
3 % neighborhood parks
17 % city parks
15 % buildings

Irvine, USA

✱ community gardens

72 % other
1 % water

5 % neighborhood parks
2 % city parks
20 % buildings

Harlow has been proactive in developing a comprehensive landscape inventory and in quantifying the benefits of its landscape infrastructure to its residents. Irvine has taken its own steps toward sustainability by implementing a gray water recycling system and in the implementation of other green infrastructure projects, including the Jeffrey Open Space Trail. Much more is to be done, and New Towns can continue to lead the way by example.

Less is More, When It Comes to Landscape Design

The strict land-use separation and extreme efficiency that characterized the building of many modernist New Towns may have prevented them from achieving the kind of dynamism and resilience found in traditional urbanism. Architects and landscape architects have certainly played a role, designing and embedding into design guidelines and maintenance regulations a static view of the landscape as an image to preserve at all costs. In Irvine, a large part of the public landscape is devoted to signage, entryways, and green buffers that leave little room for improvement.

Sir Frederick Gibberd's goal to limit programming of many of the city's landscapes and the use of community gardens and agriculture to allow the landscape to produce, change, and adapt to the changes in the community should serve as lesson to landscape architects and planners—a lesson that, when it comes to landscapes, less is indeed more. The opposite lesson may be drawn from Marne-la-Vallée, where the embedding of train stations within the *trame verte* is in conflict with the sustainable goal of concentrating development around transit nodes for increased walkability.

Conclusion

Half a century has passed since the implementation of the New Town policies and theories that led to the creation of post-World War II new communities. Meanwhile, developing countries like China, India, Egypt, Algeria, and Morocco, under the pressure of rural to urban migrations, are seeking to learn from the past to initiate urban development processes that are capable of facing the growing number of uncertainties: climate change, volatile economics, poverty, social unrest, and the retreat of many into personal and virtual spaces. Having experienced the consequences of rigid modernist planning and developed a rich repertoire of innovative solutions, twentieth-century New Towns are poised to take the lead in helping the rest of the world envision a new future for cities, one in which the landscape will continue to play a central role.

The 50-year-long vicissitudes of Irvine, Harlow, and Marne-la-Vallée are stories of consilience in that they speak of a shared awareness and appreciation for the social, economic, and environmental benefits the landscape provides. A double imperative emerges from this observation:

1   to identify, manage, and preserve the most valuable and ecologically sensitive landscapes of our cities for the benefit of future generations;
2   to understand these places as evolving organisms for which growth and regeneration are as essential to long-term resilience as preservation.

Might the path toward Now Urbanism indeed pass through the New Towns of yesterday?

References

Alexander, C. (1965). A city is not a tree. *Architectural Forum*, 122(1), 58–62.

ArchDaily (2013, August 9). Newhall South Chase/Alison Brooks Architects. [Online]. Available: www.archdaily.com/?p=412945 [January 25, 2014].

Benedict, M. A. and McMahon, E. T. (2006). *Green Infrastructure: Linking landscapes and communities*. Washington, DC: Island Press.

Carruthers, J. (ed.) (1996). *Brave New World: Early memories of Stevenage New Town*. Stevenage Museum: Stevenage Borough Council, Herts.

Cullen, G. (1963). *Townscape*. London: Architectural Press.

Déjeant-Pons, M. (2006). The European landscape convention. *Landscape Research*, 31(4), 363–384.

EPAMARNE (2012). *Marne-la-Vallée: 40 years' worth of projects for a sustainable future*. Paris: EPAMARNE-EPAFRANCE.

Evans, H. (ed.) (1972). *New Towns: The British experience*. New York: Wiley & Sons.

Forsyth, A. and Crewe, K. (2009). A typology of comprehensive designed communities since the Second World War. *Landscape Journal*, 28(1), 56–78.

Gaborit, P. (ed.) (2013). *New Medinas: Towards sustainable New Towns?* Brussels: Peter Lang.

Gibberd, F. (1952). *Harlow New Town*. Harlow: Harlow Development Corporation.

Gibberd, F. (1953). *Town Design*. London: Architectural Press.

Gibberd, F. (1980). *The Design of Harlow*. Information Services Department: Harlow Council.

Harlow Council (2013). *Harlow Future Prospects Study: Linking regeneration and growth*. Harlow: Nathaniel Lichfield and Partners. [Online]. Available: www.harlow.gov.uk/sites/harlow.gov.uk/files/documents/files/Harlow%20Future%20Prospects%20Study%20–%202013.pdf [December 13, 2013].

Howard, E. (1902). *Garden Cities of To-Morrow: A peaceful path to real reform*. London: Swan Sonnenschein.

Irvine Company (2013). *Experience the Jeffrey Open Space Trail* [brochure]. Irvine, CA: Irvine Company LLC.

Laborde, J. (2013). Les villes nouvelles à l'épreuve du temps. L'exemple de Marne-la-Vallée. *Project du Paysage*. [Online]. Available: www.projetsdepaysage.fr [July 3, 2014].

Land Use Consultants (2012). *Harlow Open Space and Green Infrastructure Study*. Harlow: Harlow Council. [Online]. Available: www.harlow.gov.uk/sites/harlow.gov.uk/files/Harlow%20Open%20Space%20and%20Green%20Infrastructure%20Study%20Part%201%20-%20Chapter%201%20to%205.pdf [July 3, 2014].

Le Corbusier (1986). *Towards a New Architecture*. New York: Dover Publications.

Lynch K. (1960). *The Image of the City*. Cambridge, MA: MIT Press.

Merlin, P. (1971). *New Towns: Regional planning and development*. London: Taylor & Francis.

Norberg-Schulz, C. (1980). *Genius Loci: Towards a phenomenology of architecture*. New York: Rizzoli.

Orillard, C. and Picon, A. (2012). *De la ville nouvelle à la ville durable: Marne-la-Vallée*. Paris: Editions Parenthèses.

Ruggeri, D. (2009). Place-identity, attachment and community attitudes in suburbia: the Irvine Ranch case. Dissertation. Berkeley, CA: University of California.

Ruggeri, D. (2013). A traveling concept: the New Town ideal from Howard's Garden City to today's ecocity. In Gaborit, P. (ed.), *New Medinas: Towards sustainable New Towns?* Brussels: Peter Lang, 73–104.

Ruggeri, D. (2014). My Mission Viejo: A photovoice investigation of place identity and attachment in master planned suburbia. *Journal of Urban Design*, 19(1), 119–139.

Scott, A. and Ben-Joseph, E. (eds) (2012). *ReNew Town: Adaptive urbanism and the low carbon community*. New York: Routledge.

Trancik, R. (1986). *Finding Lost Space: Theories of urban design*. New York: Van Nostrand Reinhold.

Watson, R. (2005). *Planning and Developing the New Town of Irvine, California, 1960–2003: Irvine Company President, 1973–1977; Walt Disney Company Chairman, 1983–1984, an oral history conducted in 2003 by Ann Lage*. Regional Oral History Office. Bancroft Library at the University of California, Berkeley.

Williamson, J. D. (1983). "New Town blues": planning versus mutual. *International Journal of Social Psychiatry*, 29(2), 147–152.

GROUNDING

Grounding acknowledges that there is no tabula rasa; every moment builds on the prior, the layers of place synergistically generating narratives across time. It builds on Situating, in that as once located, we are able to ground ourselves in the knowledge of place. We can no longer waste time, space, or resources dreaming up utopian cities that build on new, as-yet undiscovered ground, but rather must identify the power of what exists, of the narratives, places, and time of now. In this way we challenge the new as "not existing before" replacing it with "now" as "in the present time." This displacement of "e" by "o" radically broadens our inquiry, both in its rhetorical and grammatical provocation. Now Urbanism effectively sets all assumptions into abeyance, clearing fresh space for other ways to think about cities. Obvious though this distinction may be, each word suggests a discrete polemical compass and orientation to the future—"new" is prescriptive, "now" is projective.

Grounding in now insists that we understand what we have, what exists, where, why, and how. It is about how cities and urban landscapes become, in the language of Gilles Deleuze and Felix Guattari. Such a process of becoming describes the relationships between discrete elements of the assemblage or, in this case, the city as assemblage. In "becoming," one element or space or experience or time is drawn into the territory of another, changing its value and bringing about a transformed assemblage. Thus we must not only ground our work in what exists but in the relationships between these parts and times.

The chapters in this section investigate the complexity of the social and ecological histories of cities embedded in urban narratives. Specifically, they investigate the power of now narratives to conceptualize metropolitan nature as more complex than any constituent part, suggesting that urban landscapes are collective consequences of time, form, and behavior.

5

13,001 A WASTE ODYSSEY

William Morrish

> In analyzing socio-ecological systems or simulating their behavior into the future, biophysical laws that govern aspects of nature can give an "envelope of regularities" in projections or analyses (but complex natural systems also have strong nonlinearities). The broad envelope of regularities can define the "environmental space" within which human societies operate. But contingent events, which may be difficult to impossible to predict, often determine the trajectories of socio-ecological systems within that space and are thus crucially important to how the future will actually unfold. As we continue to create the future, we need to know more about the range of possibilities.
>
> *(Costanza et al. 2007a: 526)*

In the last 100,000 years, civilizations have been geological agents through acts of wasting, wastefulness, and wastedness, urbanizing the non-linear forces of earth, wind, fire, and water. The earth's crust is strewn with stone foundations, boundary lines, landforms, and open pits symbolizing epic civilizations. Our global oceans, ecologies, and atmospheres are filled with the accumulation of residual particles tossed aside from daily human activity. As this chapter will show, historians, scientists, and others are producing very clear maps and pictures of how waste generated from the last 100,000 years of political and technological innovation creating human settlements and growing civilizations has pushed today's global society into what can be described as a next "envelope of regularity" of social, economic, and ecological reality, where waste is no longer out of sight, but very much in view and in mind. It is an urban ecology defined by its vast material scale, motility, and virtual or ether-like omnipresence.

Waste's antonym is conservation. Before we can conserve our global human and natural resources and make cities of hope, we need to explore the term "waste" in greater depth. To visualize its multi-dimensional usage as a term to describe the wide range of human activities at work, I have attached a diagram from Visual Thesaurus 3 software developed by Thinkmap, Inc. (Figure 5.1). It has a constellation of 43 synonyms used as nouns, verbs, and adjectives, representing daily urban political, economic, social, and ecological acts.

Waste as known by the word "garbage" has three key synonyms: "refuse," "scraps," and "food waste." Words such as "desolate," "squander," "liquidate," "ravage," "barren," "rot,"

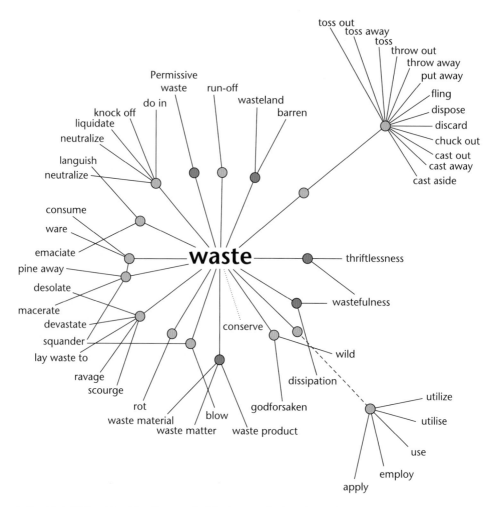

FIGURE 5.1 This spider-like diagram (a 2D picture of a 3D chart—hence the overlapping terms) reveals that the simple word "waste" is a congested intersection in a complex web of individuals competing with each other over resources in an act of trying to live and work as an urban society. It is both a picture of coexistence and of blatant aggression. Waste is not garbage, waste is a picture of human values.

"godforsaken," "consume," "languish," "knock-off," "fling," and "run-off" populate a constellation of nouns, verbs, and adjectives representing a wide range of daily societal activities that define what is wasted, who is wasted, and how we value our resources. They can be organized into three categories of waste activities: wasting, wasteful, and wasted.

1 Wasting: daily processes of decay laying down historic footings for the next generation and its basic elements and atmospheres of existence within which citizens will breathe life. All human and natural material decay. The prefix "eco-" in the words "economy" and "ecology" recognizes a common theme embedded in the making of an urban household or, as the Greeks called it, *oikos*. In other words, constructing a home or a city requires constant management (or economy), and maintenance (or ecology). Economy

and ecology reflect the interdependent relationship between the dynamic "natural" flows, stock accumulation, and decaying processes of urban and natural habitation that cannot be hidden or thrown away.

2   Wasteful: daily internal and external impacts emanating from new technological inventions, social living patterns, and civil society organization. Wasteful is about the norms of collective living, the design terms by which we name and frame the urban spaces, systems, and rules that form our cities. This is an ethical question of negligence and human failure even, as it reveals unanticipated consequences stemming from technological invention and social innovation, or unpredictable events.

3   Wasted represents the conscious act of destruction—demolition by bulldozing, bombing, human genocide, or economic dispossession—of an existing living urban habitat. To waste is to kill a place, through shock, to enact swift acts of aggression, killing an occupied space and thus rendering it empty land. The goal is to end history and start a new future on the wasted land. The journalist Naomi Klein (2008) describes neo-liberal capitalist development dispossessing *barrios* in global cities for "sustainable urban enclaves" as the "Shock Doctrine." The collective psychiatrist Mindy Fullilove (2005) describes the ecological, cultural, and spiritual purge of predominately ethnic and lower-income neighborhoods in US cites as "root shock." In the second War on Iraq, the United States and its allies sought to convert a whole country's urban landscape from one political regime to a "democracy" through "shock and awe" bombing of its civil society infrastructure into a vast wasted landscape. No one speaks about the local and global impacts of these wasted landscapes—the long-term social, economic, and health impacts of the displacement of governmental social budgets, health care costs, or low economic productivity, to name a few of the residual flows that seep into our everyday climate. Nor have we sampled the air after the bombing of Iraq, or forecast climatic and cultural impacts of the Chinese government's massive displacement of 250 million farmers from their productive land into new urban centers composed of thousands of grey vertical residential towers, in the hope that they will become consumers. This is a massive increase in carbon production that cannot be easily relocated or "traded away" through tree-planting credits since it is global in nature. Nor is there little conversion of forest land to grow the food necessary to support these former farmers, who are working in service jobs and now rely on the food supply chain from distant countries.

Together, these three forms of waste are now primary components of our global atmosphere, waters, social matrices, flora, fauna, and cultural histories. They circumscribe the envelope of social, economic, technological, and ecological regularity, our concept of normal climate, common wealth resources, and baseline metrics for anticipating future cities. We are not merely in a period of recession, nor of climate adjustment, nor at a point of technological intelligence and ubiquity that we can transcend past waste residues and project ourselves into a new sustainable future. There is no going back, as we will see in the following section; the processes of wasting away have produced in the last 100 years a very different context.

The Envelope of Regularity

Modern society is obsessed with tracking weather and making future predictions on how local and global climates will occur and operate. Weather soothsaying is basic to human survival, defining when to grow food for an ever-increasing population and when to protect cities and citizens from harm. Today, meteorologists are writing more than farmers' almanacs. Weather tracking is integral to economic, social, and environment "supply chain" logistics with millions of sensors dispersed around the globe measuring minute changes in climate, soil and water temperatures, and flow dynamics. The new data is combined with historic patterns and used to navigate container ships and airplanes around storms on their routes delivering products from industry to showroom. They set insurance rates for giant companies covering residents in regions prone to significant climate change. Everything seems to be connected to weather predictions in the hope that everyday life can be woven in and around climate rhythms in favor of commerce, mobility, and a sustainable city. What does it mean if the historic patterns are no longer relevant to today's weather prediction?

Over the last ten years, a team of interdisciplinary professionals and academics have been working on a research project called Integrated History and Future of People on Earth (IHOPE) that illustrates how humans have been directly and indirectly over a long period of time actively "doing something about it." This team of ecologists, natural historians, anthropologists, geographers, and climate, biological, environmental systems analysts, and terrestrial scientists are involved in an epic quest to "develop a new integrated analytical modeling paradigm that reveals the complex web of causation across multiple spatial and temporal scales" (Costanza et al. 2007a: 522).

Using today's cultural, scientific, and sustainable design thinking regarding the inter-dependency of human and natural processes in the shaping of our city's urban landscapes and global nature, IHOPE has created a chart or prism to re-evaluate historical flows (Figure 5.2). It is a picture of interactions between changing political settlement patterns, technological invention, and the flows of water supplies, forestation decline, carbon gas increases, and even the radical changes to the cyclical nature of monsoon cycles that have defined the cultures of India and Southeast Asia for thousands of years. It suggests that up until the last 150 years, changes in the region had little effect on the entire global system. IHOPE's research illustrates that the earth can no longer absorb such waste and that waste-ful and wasted development has a universal impact. This team published an article on the Encyclopedia of Earth website entitled "Evolution of the Human–Environment Relationship," which describes the limits of the existing view of historical, ecological, and social analysis and their interactions based on epic events. They argue for a more robust reading of the many different macro, meso, and micro interactive flows between the natural and the human together with an understanding of how different geographic situations and socio-technical and political organizations have the capacity to respond to changes. In their opening paragraphs, they write:

> The present nature and complexity of socio-ecological systems are heavily contingent on the past; we cannot fully appreciate the present condition without going back decades, centuries or even millennia. As we are witnessing today with global warming, current societal actions may reverberate, in climatic and many other ways, for centuries into the future. As such there is a real danger that our visions of the future are becoming unconstrained by knowledge of what has already occurred, at least in part because information about human–environment interactions in the historical past has not been well organized for this purpose or properly utilized.
>
> *(Costanza et al. 2007b: 7)*

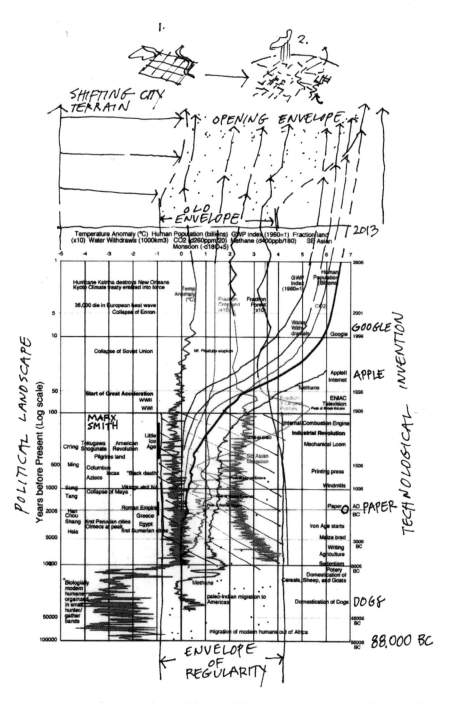

FIGURE 5.2 Integrating human and natural history. This chart is composed of selected indicators of environmental and human history. While this depiction of past events is integrative and suggestive of major patterns and developments in the human–environment interaction, it plots only coincidence. In this graph, time is plotted on the vertical axis on a long scale running from 100,000 years before present until now. Technological events are listed on the right side and cultural/political events are listed on the left.

Figure 5.2 makes this point even more vividly. The chart is a product of a trans-relational integration of disciplinary research methods and technological advances in digital tools that offers the capacity to organize large volumes of data across centuries and at different global scales. Their plots are represented by a set of interweaving lines covering the last 100,000 years, revealing points of coincidence and interaction between political regimes, environmental change, and technological innovation. The chart is defined by three parallel lines plotting information points across a chronological framework of dates starting from 88,000 BC to 2006 AD. This chart is a rare science and social science collaborative production; by synthesizing diverse research inquiries and databases, the compelling graphic frames time and the undulating lines define space, thereby visualizing the hidden dimensions of our present-day envelope of regularity.

On the left side of the chart is a line dedicated to the evolution of cultural/political events. The line documents key moments in the evolution of human polity and the constant quest to organize forms of civil order, forms of government, and administrative systems to run cities reflective of certain forms of civilization. Each polity revealed a distinct city pattern, a distinct political ordering of space, a physical manifestation of each form of governance carved into the earth's crust, stones stacked, land subdivided, rivers straightened, forests harvested, land contoured, seas and air filled with the miasma of human industry and creativity. They also produced spatial patterns of destruction such as wars, disease, and conquest.

The opposing line is the progression of technological inventions from the domestication of the dog, to grains and animals, through the Industrial Revolution, and into the digital age where each technological innovation has expanded our environment and ability to see and reach across the global landscape expanse. Each has had an environmental consequence that has destroyed certain ecologies and promoted others and the chart shows the effects upon natural processes.

The colored lines in the middle undulate through time and season, representing natural processes such as air quality, water degradation, forest cover, and the cycles of the monsoon. The chart illustrates how our desire to make human settlements and cities through political and social organizations interacting with technological inventions "throw off" external impacts upon natural systems—a constant dialogue on our changing concept of humanity, city, and nature. It is an ironic picture of humans seeking to build safe and supporting urban landscapes through planning strategies, technological invention, and scientific research to tame nature, or at least be able to predict a stable future. In actual fact, our acts have produced a wilder and more unpredictable nature, throwing past environmental rhythms out of sync into new trajectories, thereby producing a new history and envelope of regularity that is very different to the one we have studied and used to set our contemporary urban knowledge upon.

For example, in the middle of the chart, an undulating green line plots the annual cycle of the Southeast Asian monsoon season. Like clockwork, it has been reappearing every six months until the mid-twentieth century, when it loses its regularity and charts a different course. The city of Bangkok, Thailand, was built two meters above sea level with canal-based, hydrologic drainage systems based on this past "known and predictable" environmental pattern. Bangkok now exists in the midst of a radical shift in the monsoon seasonal hydrologic rhythms. In 2011, rain fell at different times and in larger volumes, producing massive countrywide flooding and overwhelming a city built for a different environmental regime.

The researchers describe the basic contradiction of human–environment interaction. Engulfed by the currents of the planet's non-linear and dynamic natural systems, humans seek the safety and surety of a predictable environment, an envelope of regularity, within which to set the foundations and infrastructure of their civilizations and cities. This term is used to describe a frame of general agreement or average in data from which scientists and other experts seek to analyze socio-natural processes and make projections for human–environment systems that are inherently non-linear. The researchers write:

> In analyzing socio-ecological systems or simulating their behavior into the future, biophysical laws that govern aspects of nature can give an "envelope of regularities" in projections or analyses (but natural systems have strong nonlinearities). This broad envelope of regularities can define the "environmental space" within which human societies operate.
>
> *(Costanza et al. 2007a: 526)*

Cities rely upon this perceived governance of nature, where the design of the political landscape and technological invention can, we assume, turn the envelope of regularity into an annual set of urban growth predictions and social stability. We have constructed this envelope of regularity to function in three ways:

1   It is a "clearing," a safe haven within a rough wilderness. Waste is taken away by the vastness of the environment, in the hopes of absorbing our byproducts.
2   It is a "scene," a beautiful, sublime, or picturesque visual environment created for the re-creation of the human soul through the act of being "in nature." All infrastructure and waste produced to support these environmental sceneries are hidden in the "back yard," out of sight.
3   It is the ecological networks and process flows, underfoot and in the air, that we rely upon as the infrastructure of our coexistences and the horizon of our future.

This has been the envelope of regularity of the past, where waste is out of sight and out of mind.

Sketching over the envelope of regularity chart (Figure 5.2) and speculating about where we are now and where we are heading, a different "envelope" or atmosphere whose currents, chemistry, and cycles begin to reveal these environmental lines should be seen in the frame of converging political and technological landscape flotsam and jetsam, forming three intersecting waste streams called material (inescapable ecologies), motile (drifting cities), and ether (congested public interfaces). Like massive ocean currents, these waste streams collide and upwell, shaping global and regional environments. Counter-flows produce social and political turbulence that undercuts economic productivity, civil society ties, and cultural identity.

Material Waste Streams: Inescapable Ecologies

Looking down from an airplane on a city below, you can see the boundaries, mobility channels, lot patterns, and objects of a city's civic identity and daily function. Hidden behind and beneath this picture are hidden lines of past political regimes, structures of rule, and

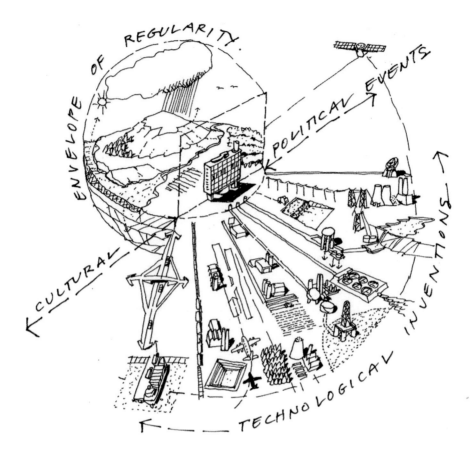

W. MORRISH 2013

FIGURE 5.3 The traditional envelope of regularity view of waste is that the waste streams out of sight, therefore out of mind. We divide our environmental space into two landscapes, the back yard where we place our waste and the front yard where we mitigate the negative flows through technological innovation of back-yard waste streams from our view outward into a benevolent and endless supply of nature.

methods of mentorship or civic leadership that continue to shape a particular city. The American geographer J. B. Jackson (1986) calls it a city's "political landscape." As a native of Southern California, I was intrigued by the urban historian Phillip Ethington's research on Los Angeles and his article, "*Ab Urbe Condita*: Regional Regimes since 13,000 Before Present." He opens with the following paragraph:

> Los Angeles is a very old work-in-progress, retaining the shapes of power by genera-
> tions since the first human settlements of the late Pleistecene Era. I begin with the
> first Angelenos to identify those features of rulership that can be recognized in later
> epochs (the remnants). My goal is to explain why Los Angeles became a global city and
> identify the political-cultural forms of its rulerships. Those are traced as they spread

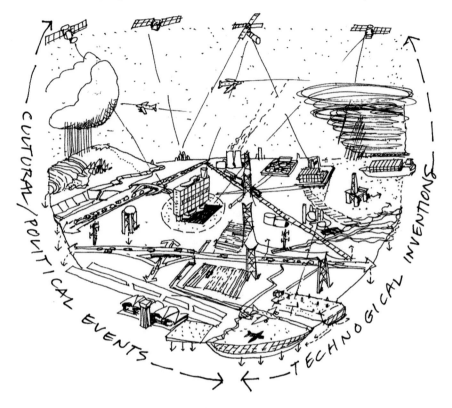

NEXT ENVELOPE OF REGULARITY

W. MORRISH 2013

FIGURE 5.4 The next envelope of regularity is one socio-ecological nature, where the bifurcated world of back-yard and front-yard environments operates as a single planetary urban ecology, where waste streams intertwine with the everyday channels of economic vitality, social civility, and ecological sustenance.

through time and space. This method divides the region's history into nine "regional regimes."

(Ethington 2010: 177)

Ethington's essay is a radically different history of Los Angeles than the many urban histories that start with a picture of the Hollywood sign as a trope representing a city without a true urban history, rather the poster child of post-modern urban sprawl. To many other urban historians, Los Angeles is a city without history, unlike traditional European cities.

Ethington's deep reading of natural and human patterns and long hours overlaying images and dates has produced a rulership cartography. The pictures he has embedded with rich data sets and cultural narratives reveal the flotsam and jetsam of a long history organized into nine historical epochs, each a complex fragmented mosaic of political/cultural/ecological/regional regimes and interwoven by traces of governing mentorship. Each of these epochs has left a trace of its operation in the landscape. Assembling these "leftovers" from past regimes, Ethington's work has pieced together a cartographic picture of Los Angeles' "terrain" on which the history of a city can be apprehended as a vast "landscape of the present, strewn with artifacts" accumulated from countless "past moments of human labor." He continues:

> My story is a narrative of inscription and mentorship: of the durable attachment of human institutions to the terrestrial landscape: or generations that entered this institutional landscape; of how they shaped it, and how they were in turn shaped by it. Every new ruling cadre assumed command, not merely of people and location, but of the pre-existing rules of production and exchange; and of the norms of command and obedience: of standards of justice, and other human binds. The thickness and endurance of these institutional ways of life are precisely what I mean by "region" and "place." To enter the Los Angeles Basin in any given calendar year was to enter a network of power relations. Every person and material object was already spoken for.
>
> *(Ibid.: 179)*

The phrase "landscape of the present, strewn with artifacts" conjures an image of a nineteenth-century painting of adventurers climbing around Aztec pyramids covered in tropical vegetation or someone finding a buried arrowhead in their back yard along the Santa Monica headlands. Today the landscape is not as romantic or sublime, but filled with painful human memories, such as graves and scarred land left behind by Khmer Rouge "killing fields," toxic swirling chemical outflows of past labor practices drifting in the soil and air of the San Joaquin Valley of California, and blocks of economically and racially secluded city residents who are tossed aside by assumed progress.

Ethington's maps expand such a perspective to include individuals, plants, animals, and political rulership and regime changes leaving behind a collective residue, adding up to a very different urban terrain than is pictured in city brochures and even official planning documents. In other words, each epoch remixes the local and global terrain to underpin itself; how it mixes the political and ecological regimes will determine what futures the next generation will be facing: opportunity or an "inescapable ecology." It is a local toxic cocktail of deferred negative waste from this regime rulership narrative; a historic "plume" that continues to flow underfoot. We try to cover it up in our dumps with soil and methane gas-lit reclamation parks. It is now part of our regular envelope. In our local narrative, we tend to focus on the positive elements, the successes, never on the waste left behind as a way to read some future options.

Our urban history books focus on origin stories, golden ages, and collapse. Rarely do we look at the resultant waste of those evolutionary epochs as the foundations for the next phase of urban building. What was seen as waste? This is not a history of negative actions, but one of how natural and human resources were utilized towards a rulership narrative on society and nature. It is a different urban map than one would find in an urban design history book or travel map.

The historian Linda Nash has articulated in great detail in her recent book, *Inescapable Ecologies: A History of Environment, Disease and Knowledge*, a more dynamic picture of

Ethington's terrain cartography of a landscape strewn with artifacts. Her research reveals a different historical map in which a landscape is composed of active memories and labors, turning the present ground from a static map into a layered cultural ecology that she calls an "inescapable ecology." In the concluding chapter she writes:

> It is not simply that what we think of as "nature" is really a complex mixture of nature and culture: what we call "human" is similarly mixed. Not only have humans mixed their labor with nature to create hybrid landscapes; nature—already a mixture of human and nonhuman elements—has intermixed with human bodies, without anyone's consent or control, without anyone's knowledge.
>
> *(Nash 2006: 209)*

Most citizens do not realize that human settlements, cities, towns, and rural communities are founded and operate continually upon dynamic terrains—changing natural and human ecologies. How and what is defined as waste is central to designing and sustaining the dynamic foundation terrain of any city. In her work, Nash clearly reveals that change in the medical understanding of the origins of disease, and in views on how the open environment influences the human body, had a profound impact on the shape of the San Joaquin Valley, more influential than any city planner in producing today's toxic industrial-scale agricultural landscape.

Nash's study of the San Joaquin Valley, the fruit and produce capital of the world, reveals the hidden interactions between humans and natural systems that we need to appreciate in our daily lives. She writes:

> The Central Valley, like all of North America, is now a complicated mixture of human and nonhuman elements, a hybrid landscape: aquifers and aqueducts, soils and chemicals, native plants and commercial crops. But change did not occur in only one direction. As people have shaped the landscape, the landscape has shaped the bodies of its inhabitants.
>
> *(Ibid.: 209)*

This is a critical fact of which few city residents are aware until they are shocked into reality by devastating earthquakes, monster hurricanes, or toxic chemical plumes from agricultural fields filtering into city water aquifers. Knowledge of this dynamic state may be withheld by corporations seeking maximum profits, or cities avoiding litigation, or the current lack of scientific urban research on the interactions between urban settlements and natural ecologies. To me, the primary reason is that we do not realize that our urban landscapes start as a political fiction about creating a city that will sustain a given society within a specific geographic and ecological situation. To turn this hope into a living physical fact requires the creation of a civil terrain, a constructed platform, supported by a multilayered infrastructure that underpins a city's history and its everyday operations and sets the terms by which any urban future will be defined. As Ethington shows in his work, this requires the creation of a governance regime and technological superstructure that has the capacity to combine the existing non-linear natural systems flows into a public infrastructure supporting an urban landscape that we inhabit. It requires not only the wealth to set up this framework, but also a continued creative and inventive management system that makes constant adjustments and changes to this artificial terrain. Nash's work reminds us that these civil terrains define the dialogue between the human body, society, and the natural habitat. This civil terrain is an "inescapable ecology" that sets city components into context with its local geography, establishes a community's basic relationships of inclusion and exclusion, and determines if the future has been wasted in the present. In other words, this civil terrain or ecology is inescapable because you cannot hide from toxic behaviors or, more importantly, it is inescapable because those behaviors are fundamental to our existence and central to societal cultural pursuits and aspirations while we live on the planet.

Motile Waste Streams: Drifting Cities

Lives are filled daily with high-speed texting, a full schedule of meetings, and social activities that do not allow us to slow down and take measure of where we are, to see and read the slow-moving streams of an aging built environment, spent systems, biological transformations, and global economic and ecological currents at work undermining the perceived stability of our urban landscape. Today's digital telecommunications-driven socio-technical infrastructure produces a public perception that we all live on solid ground. Slow down and you can see that our cities are like ships on a journey, drifting like earth's continents, the crust composed of the waste from the heat and molten material of our planet's core and mantle.

When hurricanes, such as Sandy, surge into the city of New York or Katrina floods the city of New Orleans, we are awakened to the turbulent terrain that we have built our cities upon. Disaster's historic forces both reveal deferred acceptance of the need to constantly maintain the dynamic foundation that our cities stand on, and accelerate radical shifts in economic, social, and ecological streams that constitute the stock of the city's infrastructure.

For example, long before Katrina arrived, another storm had been quietly brewing—out of sight, out of mind, and mostly underground. New Orleans' basic public infrastructure had been on a steady starvation diet, wasting away for decades. A declining tax base, erratic lines of authority among public agencies, and a rich legacy of corruption all conspired to deprive the system of critically needed maintenance and investment capital. The city could barely keep up with emergency repairs and court-ordered environmental upgrades, much less respond to the steady demands for ad hoc improvements to lure new development and jobs. In a nutshell, the city tried to squeeze as much service out of ragged outdated networks for as long as it could without taking stock of more strategic capital needs and investment priorities or the heavy odds that its piecemeal actions—to avert crises or cater to powerful private interests—merely accelerated overall system decline. In the end, New Orleans was the first city in modern US history to suffer a sweeping catastrophe due in large measure to public sector myopia and basic human denial.

After any disaster, the common desire of civic leaders and citizens is to quickly restore their city back to its familiar precondition map. This might be possible after a big storm that merely knocks down power lines or rips shingles from houses' roofs, but in the aftermath of historic events such as Hurricane Katrina or 9/11, the cultural and physical landscape fundamentally and irrevocably alters the dynamic flows of the economic and ecological realities of everyday life, resulting in two challenges: hindering rebuilding efforts and reducing a city's capacity to address future needs.

The waste from these storms has not only changed the city for the short term of rebuilding, it has altered the history and future of the place. Ecologists call this type of change "succession": the transformation of the existing ecology into a radically different ecology, such as when an open grassy field changes into a young forest, or when the ocean reclaims the sand bar beach into the ocean. Many understand the idea of ecological succession as a slow process of natural change. In fact, we are leading agents in these motile streams, channeling processes to suit our needs as long as we have time to manage and accommodate the progressive changes. The new landscape demands an entirely different operating system to support its future vitality.

In contrast, disasters are swift and decisive in their impact on the local cultural and physical ecology. They leave behind a huge list of "change" issues that can overwhelm local governance capacity and paralyze residents. In the case of New Orleans, the power of Hurricane Katrina and the weakness of the city's protective systems nearly undermined its landmark institutions and clearly upended the norms of everyday life.

Metropolitan New Orleans is a mosaic of five different drainage basins that are urbanized sub-watersheds (Eskew, Schwartz, and Morrish 2007). Katrina demonstrated that each of these basins has unique flood exposure conditions and that the city's topography is more complex and dynamic than previously assumed; in fact, the city is floating on a wet urban landscape surrounded by a massive wet Mississippi River delta landscape. Hence, the basis for New Orleans' stability, safety, and survival does not rest on high ground—instead, it depends entirely on the continuous gardening and tending of both landscapes. The silt, mud, and water that pour through the bayous, underground conduits, canals along curb gutters, and main channel of the Mississippi River are all part of the same gigantic watershed that drains off all the fluids of the nation's vast mid-section. On the river, change is the only constant.

We take for granted that our cities are rooted on solid economic foundations and supported by benevolent environments, yet many float on conditions as fragile and uncertain as those in New Orleans. They may not have abundant blue water nearby to remind them of their vulnerability, but the basic circumstances are often the same—faltering infrastructure, aging and/or diminishing population, waning tax base, severe weather events, declining resources, and the growing realization that time is not on their side. Cities that neglect the care of their basic economic and ecological footings set themselves up for swift and radical changes like those witnessed in the aftermath of Katrina.

Ether Waste Stream: Congested Public Interfaces

In 2012, 2.5 quintillion bytes of data (2.5 followed by 18 zeros) were created every day, with 90 percent of the world's existing data mine created since 2010. As a society, we are producing and capturing more data each day than has been seen by everyone since civilization began. Is all this data creation and internet connectivity enhancing research and public and ecological interactions, or has it become an atmosphere of contested waste?

The ancients used the word "ether" to describe the fifth and highest element after air, earth, fire, and water. It was believed to be the substance composing all heavenly bodies. Today, the word "ether" has conjoined with the word "network" to form the term "ethernet," which refers to a family of computer networking technologies for local area networks or LANs.

The ethernet, the internet, and ambient computing are just a few of the evolving steps that set today's reality, where the information "waste" that is generated from such devices as RFIDs, nano-sensors, and other data-monitoring micro-devices is turning the air around us into a digital waste ether. This ether is open for mining by anyone who has the economic horsepower to buy and maintain the hardware to crunch all of this "ambient" data emanating unseen from our daily interactions and feed it to some unknown corporate, personal, or government mining actor. The void between buildings, the open space of the park, and the sky above is a congested virtual ocean of information flows and currents that become the "occupied ether" of today's envelope of regularity.

In the IHOPE chart (Figure 5.2), the evolution of computer technology from a processing machine, through a virtual computing network, to a hybridizing social/corporate omnipresent telecommunication can be seen as interacting with the natural system, which reacts to the development of such fast systems to activate the growth of more and more urban places and stimulate existing and new production industries. What is not seen in the chart is what I call the ether waste stream, also called ubiquitous computing, producing ambient technology where the space between our bodies, the air, becomes an ether, crowded with massive volumes of digital data.

Rob Van Kranenburg, a Belgian philosopher and internet activist, has been on the frontline for the last ten years, working and writing about the forces shaping our basic ideas of civil society norms of control and trust. He has experienced these changes as author, consultant, and community activist and documented them in an essay entitled, "The Internet of Things: A Critique of Ambient Technology and the All-Seeing Network of RFID." Van Kranenburg's essay is a wake-up call to explosive, Wild West-like growth in scale and diversity, the battle for power over who controls the space that defines our freedom to act in public, and how the private world is an open mine to be quarried by anyone with the money and computer capacity to harvest random data at a mega-bit scale. Given the rapid expansion of the interconnected use of RFIDs, cell phones, sensors, and cameras in the quest by corporations to connect everything to everything, this vast waste mine of information thrown off by our everyday commercial and social transactions is being captured seemingly out of thin air, the ether space between us. Von Kranenburg writes:

> We are entering a land where the environment has become the interface. We must learn a know-how to make sense. Making sense is the ability to read data and not noise . . . Reading this local slowing down of flowing reality has never been easy, in fact it has never been possible. The challenge we are facing is now reading the flowing reality of our surface when the environment is increasingly the interface.
>
> *(Van Kranenburg 2008: 15)*

Van Kranenburg is describing a massive expansion of the public realm from being more than a park, a plaza, and a sidewalk. Today, the sidewalks are filled with pedestrians talking on cell phones to distant friends, walking into stores, and purchasing clothes or food. These fields of public movement, words, and buying habits are captured and converted into digital bits of information channeled through fiber optic cables, credit and debit card transactions, and RFID tags embedded in a product, a sensor in the ground, or a camera focused on the street. This massed information is dumped into the physical and virtual atmosphere, until it is channeled into secret spying, or corporate high-speed computing and big data storage warehouses churning through this effluent mining for gold. Today, the new reality of this ether waste stream is that few understand what kind of envelope of regularity is becoming contested out in the streets of São Paulo, Brazil, Istanbul, Turkey, Zuccotti Park in New

York City, and Tahrir Square in Cairo, Egypt. This, added to new such public protests appearing daily in the news and on the streets of our cities, is a reflection of a very real battle for control of this ether or fifth element by a powerful and wealthy few. Both the public and the wealthy powerful few recognize the critical alchemy involved in harvesting and

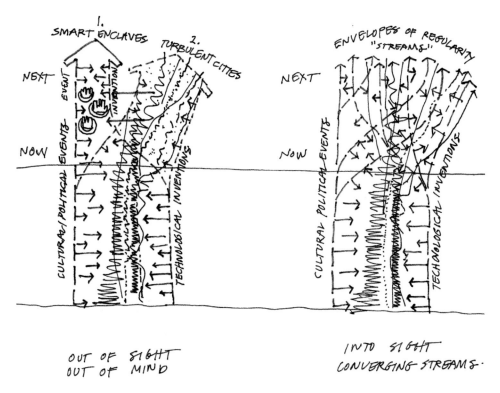

FIGURE 5.5 (left) Segregating the next envelope into the regular and the irregular. Continuing with the "out of sight, out of mind" approach to integrating waste streams into our socio-ecological envelope of regularity is starting to produce a bifurcated future. One city is what corporations and developers call the SMART City, an urban enclave of wealthy residents supported and secured from the negative effects of waste streams through heavily capitalized and sophisticated digital technology systems. The other envelope of regularity is an expansive meshwork of cities surrounding these political and technological safe havens. The majority of global urban residents who live in civil societies are over-stressed by waste streams with little capacity for innovation and governance, struggling to negotiate their turbulent cities. To maintain the two separate and unequal envelope systems narrows the range of cultural, political, and technological solutions open to the diverse social and geographic global city situations that "reveal the waste" and capture the value. (right) Co-constructing the next envelope of regularity from material, motile, and ether waste streams. Two separate envelopes of regularity are wasted energy. Gathering and channeling waste streams into sight and therefore into our collective cultural, political, and technological creative minds provides the material resources of shared common wealth of our next envelope of regularity. Adopting the "into sight, into mind" approach is to project a future envelope of regularity in which the socio-ecological relationship is not one of confrontation pitting politics, technology, and ecology against each other. Rather, the waste streams illustrate that that it is a story about coexistence, a shared and highly congested civil terrain filled with complicated situations and flows. The challenge is to capture these waste streams past and future and to turn inescapable ecologies into urban alchemy supporting civil society, drifting cities, the discovery of human and non-human "ties" that strengthen city stability, and public interfaces that expand our capacity to see the complexity of our shared lives.

fermenting digital waste. The battle lines are drawn between those few who seek control for power and money and citizens who see that their digital information is not waste but the food for an open "know-how" platform of collective trust to help citizens build and maintain a civil society, and a sustainable city through a productive interface with the emerging envelope of regularity.

Beginning at 13,001

For urban designers like myself, there is much to be mined, drawn out, and projected from the research work of these historians, scientists, and social scientists seeking to articulate in great detail the human and environmental interactions and how they have and might have informed the construction of the envelope of regularity or everyday environment that we all inhabit and count upon for making decisions. Translating this information into a language that can be understood by the many different actors who design and develop policies or make objects, spaces, and buildings is necessary if we seek to engage in change rather than merely to document it.

I began this process with the word "waste," because in the urban development game these climate and human dynamics are seen as "negative externalities," the side effects of urbanization as either pollutions or system failures that result in unintentional impacts and/or piles of refuse or wasted energy.

To me, this body of research reverses this line of thinking from an outcome, and translates it into a proactive protocol seeking to attract many different social and ecological activities into the waste discourse, working to reveal a wider range of inherent values and outputs. The noted sustainable architect, William McDonough, would at this point quote a seminal message that "waste equals food." I agree, but waste is more than food and/or converted energy, not to be lost through wasteful practices. This important design and industrial/manufacturing axiom applied to the research discussed in the essay opened my imagination to see that there might be three very specific human and environmental interactions throughout history that are important to planning any futures. Waste as a process of life wasting away, a multiplicity of wasteful outdated knowledge, and human economic habit and explicit acts of violence of war and displacement rendering a city into wasted space, begins to show a more detailed urban landscape from these research data bundles, chart lines, and historic map overlays.

The urban landscape upon which our cities and communities stand and in which we breathe and look upon is a hybrid terrain underpinned by the confluence of material, motile, and ether waste streams. These streams, which started in past envelopes and continue to flow into uncertain futures, contour the land, shape our cities, and alter our urban and public bodies. This has resulted in today's envelope of regularity, an urban landscape of inescapable ecologies, drifting cities, and congested public interfaces.

The question at hand is whether we will construct a segregated envelope for the "regular" society, which lives in a SMART enclave divided from the "irregular" society struggling in the turbulent world? Or will we co-construct an envelope of material, motile, and ether waste streams within sight and fuel our creative imagination to grow an equitable civil terrain (Figure 5.5)?

The waste odyssey continues—only this time waste is in sight and in our everyday minds.

References

Costanza, R., Graumlich, L., Steffen, W., Crumley, C., Dearing, J., Hibbard, K., Leemans, R., Redman, C., and Schimel, D. (2007a). Sustainability or collapse: what can we learn from integrating the history of humans and the rest of nature? *Ambio*, 36(7), 522–527.

Costanza, R., Graumilch, L., Steffen, W., Crumley, C., Dearing, J., Hibbard, K., Leemans, R., Redman, C., and Schimel, D. (2007b). Evolution of the human–environment relationship. *Encyclopedia of Earth*. [Online]. Available: http://www.eoearth.org/view/article/152703/ [September 15, 2013].

Eskew, A., Schwartz, F., and Morrish, W. (2007). *District 3 Recovery Plan, Unified New Orleans Plan (UNOP) Report*. New Orleans, LA: Unified New Orleans Plan.

Ethington, P. J. (2010). *Ab urbe condita*: regional regimes since 13,000 before present. In Deverell, W. and Hise, G. (eds), *The Companion To Los Angeles*. Cambridge, MA: Blackwell, 177–215.

Fullilove, M. T. (2005). *Root Shock: How tearing up city neighborhoods hurts America, and what we can do about it*. New York: One World Ballantine Books.

Jackson, J. B. (1986). *Discovering the Vernacular Landscape: A pair of idea landscapes*. New Haven, CT: Yale University Press.

Klein, N. (2008). *Shock Doctrine: The rise of disaster capitalism*. New York: Macmillan, Picador.

Nash, L. (2006). *Inescapable Ecologies: A history of environment, disease, and knowledge*. Berkeley, Los Angeles, London: University of California Press.

Van Kranenburg, R. (2008). The Internet of things: a critique of ambient technology and the all-seeing network RFID. *Institute of Network Cultures*, Network Notebooks 2. [Online]. Available: www.networkcultures.org/_uploads/notebook2_theinternetofthings.pdf [January 15, 2009].

6

CONTINGENT ECOLOGICAL URBANISMS

Jon Christensen

Geoffrey West stood in front of a crowded auditorium at the Long Now Foundation in Fort Mason on a pier jutting out into the San Francisco Bay and told the story of how he had found the secret key to the city (West 2011). Cities, West said, are much like organisms, except they rarely die. A physicist at the Santa Fe Institute, West is famous for having discovered, with biologist James Brown, fundamental laws about the scale of organisms, from tiny mice to giant blue whales (West, Brown, and Enquist 1997). A human being is just a blown-up version of the mouse, says West, and the blue whale is just a blown-up version of a human being. Their metabolisms, their circulatory systems, and their life spans scale at a constant rate. The mouse just lives faster than the human being, who lives faster than the whale. The whale reveals a great economy of scale—its metabolism is slower, its circulatory system more efficient than mouse or human being. But they all have roughly the same number of heartbeats in one lifetime.

Astonishingly, West said, cities also scale at constant rates. As they grow in population size, they add new roads, electric lines, and gas stations, and they produce more wealth, file more patents, and even spawn more disease and crime. Infrastructure achieves the same economies of scale in cities as the circulatory system of the blue whale does. It scales at a "sub-linear" rate. As the city gets bigger, its infrastructure can handle increasing increments of population. It becomes more efficient. However, consumption increases at a one-to-one rate. It is linear. Each additional person requires an additional increment of energy, water, and food. Meanwhile, wealth, patents, disease, and crime all benefit from social network effects that expand with growth. Cities produce more as they add more people. They are "superlinear" effects. And these are the kinds of descriptions that many urbanists celebrate (Bettencourt et al. 2007; Bettencourt and West 2010; Glaeser 2011).

"But what about nature?" I asked West after his talk. "Parks, open spaces, other species?" "There is no correlation," he said. Although his urban model was inspired by nature, the model cannot explain nature in the city. If we consider open space and nature as essential contributors to the quality of life in cities, then a closer analysis of why such places do not increase in accordance with growth is critical. Following a case in San Francisco Bay, one can trace the reasons and begin to formulate alternative responses.

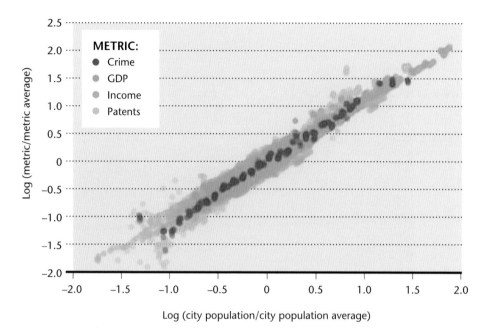

FIGURE 6.1 Predictable cities: data from 360 US metropolitan areas show that metrics such as wages and crime scale in the same way with population size.

The star architect Peter Calthorpe's plan could not have been more retro and, yet, futuristic at the same time: take some of the last remaining salt ponds on the fringe of the San Francisco Bay—prime targets for restoration of vanished marshes; fill them in to create new land—as if the 50-year-old effort to "save the bay" from being filled were simply history; and build a "new urbanist," "transit-oriented" village called Saltworks to house nearly 23,000 residents on the bayside shore of Silicon Valley (Redwood City Saltworks n.d.).

For many, it seemed hard to believe that Peter Calthorpe, one of California's—indeed, the nation's—most widely recognized advocates for environmental planning and green architecture, would be on the opposite side of this battle from Save the Bay, the organization and movement that symbolized more than any other the struggles and successes of a generation of environmental activists and planners in the region. Calthorpe's version of new urbanism is not without controversy, particularly as many of his projects have been on open land rather than previously developed or disturbed sites, unlike Saltworks which would be carved out of an industrialized wetland, a massively altered landscape.

Calthorpe's Saltworks plan marvelously represents the contingent nature of emergent urbanisms—particularly ecological urbanisms—in what is one of the foremost historical hotbeds for environmental visions of metropolitan futures, the San Francisco Bay Area. Even if it is never built—and it never will be built in exactly the form that Calthrope first proposed—Saltworks will occupy a special place in the history of emergent urbanisms.

For Saltworks is in many ways a perfect example of a newly emergent form of ecological urbanism in the twenty-first century. Calthorpe's proposal envisioned that half of the 1,433-acre site—where salt has been harvested in shallow ponds in an industrial process for more than a century—would be restored as tidal wetlands. On the remaining landfill, his proposed

FIGURE 6.2
The
Redwood
City
Saltworks
site.

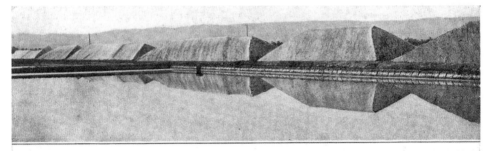

SALT WORKS, REDWOOD CITY, CAL.

FIGURE 6.3 Historical salt works in Redwood City.

village was to be a dense mix of single-family homes and multi-family units gathered around walking and biking paths within easy reach of a million square feet of shops and restaurants, as well as schools and 200 acres of parks and recreational playing fields. Calthorpe was working with the developer DMB Associates, an Arizona-based company that specializes in master-planned, mixed-use communities in the western United States, and whose slogan is "a passion for great places" (DMB Associates n.d.). DMB argued that Saltworks would go a long way toward providing housing for the 40,000 workers who currently commute to Redwood City from around the bay and beyond, thereby diminishing carbon emissions contributing to global warming and sea level rise, and, in some measure, ameliorating Silicon Valley's legendary housing and commuting problems.

Given these glaring contradictions between a model planned development claiming green values and a site that may well be among the worst possible sites to develop in this day and age, one can see Saltworks as either the apotheosis or apogee of new urbanism, as advocates and opponents respectively have contended. Or perhaps it is both at the same time, as skeptics about new urbanism might conclude. On the other hand, perhaps it is more

FIGURE 6.4 The Saltworks plan for the development and restoration of the Redwood City salt ponds.

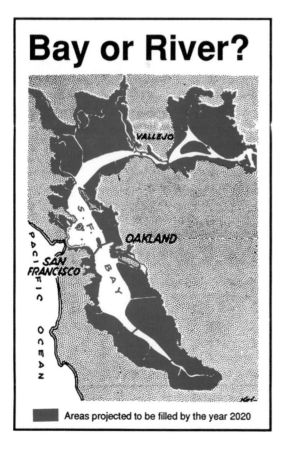

FIGURE 6.5 Projections for filling the San Francisco Bay with development spurred the creation of Save the Bay.

fair to see it simply as another in a long history of contingent developments (whether they are ultimately developed or not) that have shaped the always uneasy, if often spectacularly beautiful, mix of nature and urbanism for which the San Francisco Bay Area is justly famous.

Saltworks ran into predictable opposition. Save the Bay, the region's environmental watchdog, turned it into a poster child of the bad old days of filling the bay come back to life, despite the fact that the vast majority of salt ponds owned by Cargill, the owner of the Saltworks site, have been purchased and are being restored as marshes around the bay. Redwood City was deeply divided. Dueling polls asserted support for the project's approach to providing badly needed housing, on the one hand, and NIMBY opposition to any development, especially bayside, on the other. Several years into the project, DMB withdrew Calthorpe's plan and said it would go back to the drawing board, focusing development only on a smaller core industrial parcel on the site, leaving the salt ponds to be restored. At the same time, discussions quietly continued about restoring the entire site by adding it to the vast salt marsh restoration projects already taking place around the bay.

Contingency

Saltworks is a starting point for exploring the contingent emergence of historical strands of environmental urbanism that have shaped and been shaped by the San Francisco Bay Area, up to and including the latest arguments over ecological urbanism and new urbanism embodied in the controversy. While this chapter looks back, providing a brief historical review of ecological urbanisms in the context of the San Francisco Bay Area, it also looks forward to the possibilities and perils alive today in the recombinations of ideas, practices, and disciplines implicated in emergent ecological urbanisms that are engaged in challenges old and new, here and around the world.

This chapter also takes issue with the rise of a new urban triumphalism, which asserts that cities are the best answer to the world's environmental problems, and at the same time that making room for nature in the city is at cross purposes with urban efficiencies. Edward Glaeser is the most prominent proponent of this view in his book, *Triumph of the City: How Our Greatest Invention Makes Us Richer, Smarter, Greener, Healthier, and Happier* (2011). Here Glaeser stands in for a much wider circle of contemporary urban triumphalism, which privileges density above all else. Glaeser is also a particularly useful foil for this chapter because much of his argument hinges on using the San Francisco Bay Area, where I have done my own research, as his primary example of a place where conservation or preservation of nature has been an obstacle to the rational development of the metropolis. This is an argument also favored by developers and opponents of conservation. In the case of Silicon Valley, where colleagues and I studied the effect of conservation on housing stock, this argument is simply wrong, as I will explain below.

However, although Glaeser is the foil in this chapter, and his argument is a powerful and dangerous one to have loose in a world of rapidly growing cities, proving him wrong is not the only point here. Another key point is the importance of the historical emergence of what we might call a variety of ecological urbanisms, but since that useful shorthand is a new and anachronistic term, it might be more accurately thought of as different conceptions of nature in the city over time.

The underlying reason that nature and the city do not correlate in Geoffrey West's model, and that the conservation of nature cannot function usefully as a simple negative factor in Edward Glaeser's economic model of urban development, is that the relationship between the city and nature is historically contingent and emergent. The relationship is grounded in space and time. Site specifics matter. So do ideas that circulate and sometimes dominate in particular times. Urbanism is always emergent and always in a complicated conversation with society, culture, and nature. And so, any urbanism of the moment—and particularly any urbanism that combines nature and the city—is always contingent upon this emergence, grounded in particular times and in particular places. Spatially specific historical narratives can help us understand critically how cities developed, but also the possibilities not pursued, paved over, or lingering underground. And understanding the possibilities of contingency and emergence through historical narratives could provide important keys to the next eco-cities around the world.

The Trouble with Urban Triumphalism

"There is nothing greener than blacktop," Edward Glaeser provocatively asserts in *The Triumph of the City*. "If you love nature, stay away from it," he admonishes (2011: 210). Among the mountains of books and articles published in recent years celebrating the city and the great global demographic transition that finds a majority of the world's population now living in cities, Glaeser's book stands out as the most challenging for urbanists who aim to reconcile nature and the city.[1]

What concerns me here is the use to which Glaeser puts the San Francisco Bay Area— and what I will argue is its contingent history—in building a general argument, a model even, about cities and nature. He then uses the model to launch an extended attack on two contingent historical tools that have proved crucial for shaping nature in the city: zoning, on the one hand, and, on the other, the conservation or preservation of nature in the city in parks and open space. Glaeser sees the city and nature through a narrow economic lens. While his analysis of the economic life of cities is sophisticated, he is naive about nature, assuming that culture and nature are separate, when several generations of scholars have shown just how intertwined human cultural and environmental history are.[2]

The argument that dense, compact cities produce social and economic benefits for residents is not new and needs no rehearsing here. Likewise, there is little need to recapitulate in detail the bandwagon of urbanists that Glaeser has joined, asserting that energy efficiencies gained through the shared walls of apartments and increased use of public transportation result in reduced carbon emissions per capita for residents of cities, compared to suburbanites and exurban and rural residents. The increased benefits and reduced carbon costs of density have become the new gospel of urbanism. And I will not quarrel with them here, except to remark that suburbs, exurbs, and even rural areas still hold out benefits valued by many people for different reasons, and, as Glaeser acknowledges, per capita carbon emissions depend a great deal on latitude and weather in addition to population density.[3]

The San Francisco Bay Area plays a key role in Glaeser's argument. Glaeser has lived in the Bay Area, and lauds it as one of the most desirable places in the world to live and work, a creative, global, economic engine, and an environmental success story. At the same time, however, he also derides the region for pushing problems it has caused farther out into the Central Valley of California and the world beyond.

"The environmentalists of coastal California may have made their own region more pleasant," Glaeser argues, "but they are harming the environment by pushing new building away from the Berkeley suburbs, which have a temperate climate and ready access to public transportation, to suburban Las Vegas, which is all about cars and air-conditioning" (ibid.: 14). Glaeser pulls no rhetorical punches in this critique of Bay Area environmentalists. "The advocates of California's growth limitations are often put forward as ecological heroes. But they're not," he declares (ibid.: 211).

"Coastal California is by far the greenest part of the country," Glaeser writes (ibid.: 210). However, by "green," Glaeser is not praising the region's protection of parks and open space. Instead, he defines "green" much more narrowly, in terms of per capita carbon emissions. "The five greenest metropolitan areas in the country are San Diego, San Francisco, Los Angles, San Jose and Sacramento," he writes. "A household in San Francisco emits 60 percent less carbon than its equivalent in Memphis" (ibid.: 210).

And conservationists are preventing more people from living in this "greenest part of America," Glaeser asserts (ibid.: 221). "By using ecological arguments to oppose growth, California environmentalists are actually ensuring that America's carbon footprint will rise, by pushing new housing to less temperate climates" (ibid.: 212). If only more people lived in the Bay Area, Glaeser assumes, there would be fewer people living in cold places that force them to heat their homes in the winter, like Boston, or run air conditioning in the summer, like Las Vegas. "The path of America's future is being determined by the whims of local zoning boards that don't want more people living in their highly productive, pleasant communities," Glaeser complains (ibid.: 193).

Here Glaeser exhibits a common trope in *The Triumph of the City*, in which he conflates zoning restrictions with the protection of parks and open spaces and historical preservation. All are evil, but none more so, it seems, than the protections that have resulted in the iconic landscape of the San Francisco Bay Area. Glaeser writes:

> In the beautiful landscape of the San Francisco region there are endless miles of open mountain ranges and protected seascape. The computer magnates of Silicon Valley live in a region blessed not only by an extraordinary climate, but also by a beautiful setting protected from development by some of the world's most restrictive land-use controls.
>
> *(ibid.: 205)*

These protections and restrictions have resulted in a shortage of land available for housing construction, Glaeser asserts. "But that shortage is the handiwork of regulation, not nature," he writes. "There's plenty of land; it just isn't available for construction" (ibid.: 191). Glaeser argues that shortage of land has reduced the amount of new construction and pushed prices up. He states:

> Prices in California are kept high by draconian limits on new construction . . . These rules are joined with a policy of pulling more and more land off the market as protected parks and wildlife areas. By 2000, one quarter of the land in the Bay Area has become permanently protected, that is, off limits to building.
>
> *(ibid.: 211)*

In Silicon Valley's Santa Clara County, Glaeser writes, only about 16,000 new homes were permitted between 2000 and 2008. If, instead, Santa Clara had built 200,000 homes, he asserts, housing prices would have dropped 40 percent. That would have resulted in a

50 percent increase in housing in the county. But where would those houses have been built?

That, of course, is a counterfactual question. Those houses were not built. And it is the kind of question at the heart of thinking historically. By exploring that question in more depth, rather than just asserting that those houses should have been built, we can learn a lot about why those houses were not built, and what, in fact, would be likely to have happened if the land that Glaeser wants to open to development had, indeed, been left open to development. The answer is not as simple as he supposes.

Glaeser's is a common claim, particularly among homebuilders, and particularly in the Bay Area. So my colleagues and I decided to investigate whether conservation has led to a reduction in housing stock and higher home prices. The importance of contingency in history is manifest even in the best models of nature and the city. So we developed a model that has history embedded within it. In our model, we created a counterfactual map, or a map that hypothesizes what might have happened had history unraveled differently, to predict the nature of development on currently protected lands had they historically been left available to developers, estimating the probability of development and predicted housing density for every conserved parcel in Silicon Valley (Denning, McDonald, and Christensen 2010).

If all the parks and open space in the area had been developed, the housing stock would have increased by only about 6 percent. We found little evidence that parks and protected areas significantly reduced the housing stock in Silicon Valley. Most of that housing would

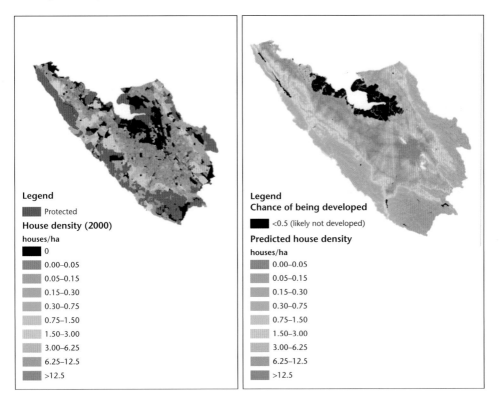

FIGURE 6.6 Mapping housing density in the existing landscape and the counterfactual likelihood of development in parks had they not been protected in Silicon Valley.

be very expensive houses on relatively large lots. Very few of these units would be affordable by any standard, and those would entail buildings on all of the pocket parks and playing fields created precisely as amenities within the metropolitan fabric.

Our research indicated that about 51,000 additional homes would likely have been built if all of the areas that have been conserved in the Silicon Valley over more than a century had instead been developed during that period. This is a much different proposition than Glaeser's vision of building 200,000 additional houses in just eight years. Glaeser's dream floats free of history, carried aloft on pure economic abstractions. But, to rework a famous old saw, it might behoove those seeking to defy history to first understand it.

In our model, we first sampled the historically produced landscape to tease out variables that explain the probability that any given parcel would be developed and the likely density of that development. The six variables that best explained the historical variation were slope, wetland status, distance to streams, distance to highways, distance to railroads, and distance to historical urban centers. Areas close to the bay, with low slope and close to streams, are the places in this landscape most likely not to be developed, probably because they are more likely to be wetlands. Areas with intermediate distance to streams and intermediate slope are most likely to be developed, while sites with high slope are somewhat less likely to be developed, likely due to the difficulty and risk of building on steep slopes.

Housing density on sites that are developed is also a function of topography, hydrology, and transportation variables. All else being equal, sites farther from streams tend to have higher housing density, likely because they are on safer ground. Generally, the highest housing densities are on flat sites near historical centers and close to highways. Steep slopes significantly decrease housing density.

We then used the factors that produced this observed probability of development and likely density to predict how many housing units would have been built on similar conserved parcels. We found that large parcels at lower elevation would have seen most of the new development, an additional 33,000 housing units at a density of about one house per acre, although there is substantial variation within this category, with some sites likely to have been built at a higher density of on average seven housing units per acre. We found that the many small urban and suburban parks in the existing metropolitan matrix would support housing densities similar to land-use patterns in the immediate vicinity. These parcels also varied in their predicted density, but on average these parks could have contained close to two houses per acre, resulting in 5,400 expected housing units in these areas. Our final category of high-elevation parcels larger than three acres would have provided an additional 13,000 houses at a relatively low predicted density of more than an acre per housing unit.

Of the 51,000 counterfactual housing units that we predict would have been constructed in parks and open space in the Silicon Valley, 41 percent would have been equivalent to single-family detached homes on more than an acre of land. Fewer than one out of ten of these new units—3,400 housing units—would be in the highest-density class of housing in the area, a lot size of a fifth of an acre or around 8,000 square feet. Of the 33,000 housing units that would have been developed if all of the 30,448 acres of low-elevation protected areas near the bay had been developed, only about 3,378 of those would have been built at the new urbanist densities proposed by Peter Calthorpe for Saltworks.

Areas such as Saltworks historically have been developed at an average density of only about one housing unit per acre. If Calthorpe's proposal for Saltworks had been successful, it would have bucked the trend with an average density of five to eight units per acre. That, of course, is one of the project's big selling points. Saltworks' proponents aimed to defy history. Our model shows that even without any land protection, Silicon Valley's housing stock would not be substantially larger and it would still be a very expensive housing market. Our model shows how people probably would have organized space under prevailing conditions but absent open space. However, the fact remains that people decided to organize their city with conservation embedded in it.

Contingent History

Cities have historically been dynamic engines of the conservation of nature, as well as the engines of economic growth and innovation celebrated by Glaeser and other urbanists. Urban environmental historians who embrace this dynamic relationship have produced some of the best environmental history in recent years.[4] The meaning of conservation in cities has changed over time, ranging from protecting watersheds for clean drinking water, to the City Beautiful movement and the creation of parks and open space for scenic beauty, recreation, spiritual renewal, and, lately, as habitat for other species, as space for ecosystem processes to unfold and evolve, and to provide ecosystem services for people. Geographer Richard Walker celebrates the San Francisco Bay Area as a case study of such historically constructed metropolitan landscapes in his book *The Country in the City: The Greening of the San Francisco Bay Area* (2007). Our own research in the San Francisco Bay Area has also attempted to tease out this complicated interplay between urban development and open space conservation over time in order to understand the changing motivations and consequences of conservation in a metropolitan setting.

In Walker's account, this history took place in three acts. The first act set the scene after the Gold Rush, when, fresh from exploiting the bounty of the city's hinterlands, Progressive Era reformers in San Francisco and the East Bay embraced the city beautiful and parks for people. Initially, conservationists in the Bay Area were concerned with protecting valuable drinking water reservoirs and watersheds in the late nineteenth and early twentieth centuries. However, by the early twentieth century, the City Beautiful movement was in full swing, championing parks as a way to preserve human vitality and bucolic peacefulness amidst urban chaos. Golden Gate Park was a result, inspired by Frederick Law Olmsted's design for Central Park in New York City. Olmsted's philosophical case for parks was based on three moral imperatives: improving public health by planting trees and creating clean spaces free of air and water pollution, providing a place of recreation for the urban poor, and democratizing open spaces for all. This mission is still familiar, though the method of creating the open space of Golden Gate Park—converting miles of sand dunes into manicured lawns, lakes, and groves—may be alien to us today.

Walker marks the start of the second act with the end of World War II. Residents of booming Silicon Valley and Marin County suburbs turned on developers, often soon after they moved into their new homes, and created successful campaigns to save foothill and bay views. Smaller cities like Oakland and San Jose rapidly grew, and small towns steadily sprawled into an interconnected suburban and urban matrix throughout the nine-county Bay Area. This development was spurred by a robust highway system and cheap land, enabling businesses and housing developments to spread out from the area's historical urban centers. Urban and suburban parks became essential elements throughout this matrix, providing a natural respite from an expanding paved maze.

Though much of this suburbanization was a result of flight from urban centers, Walker points out that rapid suburban growth shocked even the suburban residents who were its cause. They lamented the loss of orchards, ranchlands, and mountain and bay vistas, and their complaints sparked an open space movement in the Bay Area. Like the City Beautiful activists decades earlier, these new crusaders' arguments were couched in a human need for outdoor experiences and aesthetic beauty, as well as a revulsion against crowded development. It was during this time that many communities in the Bay Area enacted urban growth limits and zoning restrictions as a way to protect communities from additional development and exploding populations. By the 1980s, the open space movement began adopting new arguments about biodiversity and habitat preservation. And while this shift is often criticized as a move to separate humanity from nature for the sake of preserving nature, ultimately these policies were driven by people's very human desire for a connection with the environment and nature around them.

In the third act, as a new millennium approached, the reach of a new generation of ambitious "metrotopians" had exceeded its hold. Walker describes how a modernist environmental vision of top-down regional planning and growth control was roundly rejected in favor of a balkanized politics that kept planning and growth control local. However, instead of skulking off with their tails between their legs, conservationists and urbanists melted into this balkanized landscape, and a thousand flowers bloomed in local growth control measures, efforts to encourage in-fill development, build transportation hubs, and protect greenbelts and open space around the Bay Area.

This latest phase—which is still ongoing—raises important questions. First, after the "metrotopians" failed, much of the effort and money that had been going into public conservation and environmental planning went into more private conservation work, including using public money for conservation easements to pay private landowners not to develop their lands, while sometimes not making those open spaces open to the people. This was especially true when conservation easements preserved productive agricultural lands, ranches, and vineyards, as has been increasingly the case. Finally, when the growing environmental justice movement is included in this history, as Walker writes, it becomes very clear that "it is not quite true that we all drink the same water, breathe the same air, or enjoy the same bay views" (2007: 230). Quite the contrary.

Despite knowing that we do not all experience life around the San Francisco Bay in the same way, one could still come away from Walker's book—and living in or just visiting the Bay Area—feeling that its residents really do live in the best of all possible places on the planet. Certainly, the Bay Area has got some problems, but it is hard to imagine a better natural setting for a sophisticated metropolis that incorporates the country in the city. However, what Walker does is to show that this seemingly natural setting is itself the result of history. The natural setting is not the other to the city's self. It is not an impediment to the development of the metropolis. It is a product of the development of the metropolis, just like the city itself.

The San Francisco Bay Area encourages a special kind of exceptionalism. It is hard not to succumb. And if by exceptional we may mean contingent, then so be it. Every city has its own unique, exceptional history. However, before we turn our back on models completely, are there any similar patterns that emerge across cities in their relationships with nature?

A rich historical literature suggests some fundamental patterns that result in protecting, producing, and reproducing nature in cities: the need for clean water and sewage treatment, the enclosing of commons, the creation of parks for the recreation of citizens, the production and protection of aesthetic landscapes, the preservation of open space for people and for habitat for other species, and now, again, the protection and production of nature or "natural capital" for the "ecosystem services" provided for people. The literature of parks planning also suggests that the historical period of a city's development, geography, leadership, funding, politics, and culture all play a role in the creation and success of parks and other nature in the city (Harnik 2000). However, despite these similar patterns, the existence of nature in the city is highly variable and difficult to theorize, because it is so contingent.

"Cities that are superficially quite different in form and location are in fact, on the average, scaled versions of one another, in a very specific but universal fashion described by the scaling laws," Geoffrey West and his colleagues claim (Bettencourt et al. 2007: 7303). But not when it comes to nature. In our most recent research on "city nature," which compares parks, open space, and nature in 40 cities and 2,661 neighborhoods around the United States, we were unable to find a single set of variables that explains the tremendous variation in nature among cities and neighborhoods within cities (City Nature 2013).

On the one hand, this could suggest that, "nature is irrelevant to the city," as Stewart Brand (2011) suggested after West's talk at the Long Now Foundation. However, on the

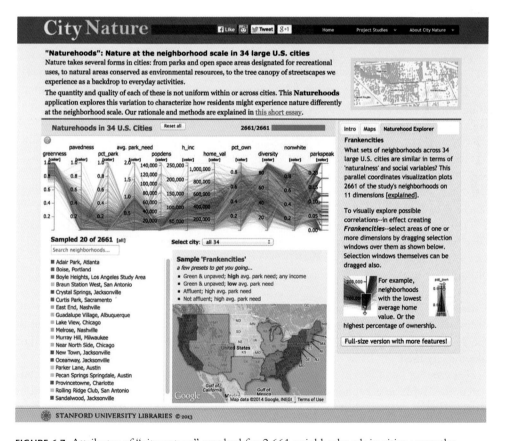

FIGURE 6.7 Attributes of "city nature" graphed for 2,661 neighborhoods in cities across the United States

other hand, this also suggests that Edward Glaeser and urbanists who see conservation in the city as an impediment to the development of the city are wrong. Indeed, cities and neighborhoods seem to develop regardless of how much nature they contain, protect, or produce within their ambit. So protecting and producing nature in the city is a contingent choice. There is also a large literature that suggests that these choices have real effects on the city, its residents, their sense of identity and place, and, quite likely, their health and well-being.[5]

Historians like myself are quite comfortable with contingency as an explanatory variable. However, are there ways to get beyond contingency, or to embed contingency within larger explanatory patterns? We think there may well be. Using an interdisciplinary approach, we are currently studying the patterns of parks, open space, and nature across several large, diverse sets of cities around the world.

Historical contingency will remain powerful, however. Consider the example of Saltworks again for a moment. If the site for the proposed new urbanist development had never been made into salt ponds—quite literally salt works—in the nineteenth century, there might never have been the possibility of Saltworks, nor, quite possibly, the potential of restoring salt marshes on the site. And what the site becomes could, in turn, continue to shape emergent urbanism in the San Francisco Bay Area and perhaps beyond. History matters.

To be sure, the history of conservation in the Bay Area is very much a product of the region's particular politics and environment. Yet this history is also, in many ways, not exceptional. While the histories of all cities and regions are contingent on many factors—including geography, their historical period of development, regional, national, and global forces, culture, and ideas—the urban foundations of conservation and its changing meanings have been important throughout the United States and the world. Conservationists and policy-makers around the world need to better understand the historical range of desires behind conservation—from protecting resources essential to human health, to valuing parks for recreation and fitness, to valuing open space for its aesthetic value and as habitat for species. This variety of human needs for nature provides us with a toolkit to help shape rapidly developing cities of the twenty-first century, during which the urban built environment on earth will double in size. How that emergent ecological urbanism takes place will fundamentally shape how human beings live with each other and with nature in the future.

Notes

1 These books range from those written for a popular audience, such as Owen (2009), to those written for academic and professional audiences, such as Mostafavi and Doherty (2010).
2 For one important example, see Williams (1973).
3 See also Owen (2009).
4 See Gandy (2002), Orsi (2004), Klingle (2007), and Rawson (2010).
5 See Louv (2011).

References

Bettencourt, L. and West, G. (2010, October 21) A unified theory of urban living. *Nature*, 912–913.
Bettencourt, L. M. A., Lobo, J., Helbing, D., Kühnert, C., and West, G. (2007, April 24). Growth, innovation, scaling, and the pace of life in cities. *PNAS*, 7301–7306.

Brand, S. (2011, July 25). Personal communication.

City Nature (2013). [Online]. Available: http://citynature.stanford.edu [January 30, 2014].

Denning, C. A., McDonald, R. I., and Christensen, J. (2010). Did land protection in Silicon Valley reduce the housing stock? *Biological Conservation, 143,* 1087–1093.

DMB Associates (n.d.). *Our Unique Approach.* [Online]. Available: www.dmbinc.com/communities [February 5, 2012].

Gandy, M. (2002). *Concrete and Clay: Reworking nature in New York City.* Cambridge, MA: MIT Press.

Glaeser, E. (2011). *Triumph of the City: How our greatest invention makes us richer, smarter, greener, healthier, and happier.* New York: Penguin Press.

Harnik, P. (2000). *Inside City Parks.* Washington, DC: Urban Land Institute.

Klingle, M. (2007). *Emerald City: An environmental history of Seattle.* New Haven, CT: Yale University Press.

Louv, R. (2011). *The Nature Principle: Human restoration and the end of nature-deficit disorder.* Chapel Hill, NC: Algonquin Books.

Mostafavi, M. and Doherty, G. (eds) (2010). *Ecological Urbanism.* Baden, Switzerland: Lars Müller Publishers.

Orsi, J. (2004). *Hazardous Metropolis: Flooding and urban ecology in Los Angeles.* Berkeley, CA: University of California Press.

Owen, D. (2009). *Green Metropolis: Why living smaller, living closer, and driving less are the keys to sustainability.* New York: Riverhead Books.

Rawson, M. (2010). *Eden on the Charles: The making of Boston.* Cambridge, MA: Harvard University Press.

Redwood City Saltworks (n.d.). [Online]. Available: www.rcsaltworks.com [February 5, 2012].

Walker, R. A. (2007). *The Country in the City: The greening of the San Francisco Bay Area.* Seattle, WA: University of Washington.

West, G. (2011, July 25). *Why Cities Keep On Growing, Corporations Always Die, and Life Gets Faster.* Lecture given at Cowell Theatre in Fort Mason Center in San Francisco, California.

West, G., Brown, J. H., and Enquist, B. J. (1997). A general model for the origin of allometric scaling laws in biology. *Science,* 276, 122–126.

Williams, R. (1973). *The Country and the City.* New York: Oxford University Press.

7

PROCESSCAPES

Dynamic Placemaking

Judith Stilgenbauer

The temporal aspects of natural processes distinguish landscape from architectural form. Landscapes and their phenomena are dynamic; they are in flux; they flow, develop, and change. Processes in natural landscapes occur at various speeds. Some take millions of years, others minutes. Plant life, for example, reacts to the annual pattern of seasons and the cyclical rhythm of night and day. Natural ecosystems and elements of the designed landscape evolve over the course of their lives—they go through successional processes and cycles of decay, regeneration, growth, maturity, and destruction (Stilgenbauer 2008) (Figure 7.1). Accordingly, landscape architects and environmental designers throughout history have been concerned with the dimensions of time and space. The degree, however, to which the design of landscapes has focused on the temporal on the one hand and the visual-spatial on the other has varied dramatically throughout the centuries.

Traditionally, for example in French formal gardens of the Baroque era, landscape architects intended to control and tame nature or to enhance its beauty by manipulating temporal qualities and slowing change. In contrast, in the nineteenth century, as Frederick Law Olmsted and H. W. S. Cleveland were defining the emerging practice of landscape architecture, they often took a different stance, acknowledging and working with characteristics of time and change. This work was furthered by designers into the early twentieth century. However, by the mid-century, such approaches were viewed with less enthusiasm as modernism and issues of professionalism sought to read landscape design as a form of architectural design. This approach discounted the ephemeral and dynamic nature of the landscape medium, instead describing projects as formally determined, rigid spatial scenarios. Inflexible, expensive, and maintenance-intensive solutions designed to withstand time resulted. Figure 7.2 shows the Parterre Garden at the Kempinski Airport Hotel in Munich, Germany, designed by Peter Walker and Partners in collaboration with the local Rainer Schmidt Landscape Architecture firm, and built in the mid-1990s. This public garden, characterized by two overlapping orthogonal grid systems and the use of highly manicured elements, represents a contemporary, yet traditionally designed, formally-determined and static high-maintenance project. Such a landscape type, conceived to remain static over time, fails to balance placemaking and the visual-spatial with processuality. Emphasizing a

FIGURE 7.1 Successionary landscape processes, here: European White Birch seedlings at Zollverein Essen, Germany.

common problem with such stable and artistic approaches to landscape design, the landscape architect Anne Whiston Spirn stresses that "[a]rchitects and landscape architects tend to focus not on process, but on form and material; when designs fail to be substantiated in the real world, it is often because designers ignore the processes that shape them during and after construction" (Spirn 1998: 96).

In contrast to the more traditional static models, many recent open-space concepts, as exemplified by the works of Peter Latz, James Corner and Michel Desvigne, foreground regenerative and ecologically and environmentally performative landscape processes. Such contemporary designers' works conceptually embrace a new aesthetic of ephemeral characteristics such as growth, succession, spontaneity, and even decay. A strong focus on indeterminacy and adaptability can work against the creation of well-crafted, usable landscapes. Thus, the key question at hand is: how much process is too much process? How do we as designers strike a project-appropriate balance between the potentially conflicting design goals of process and placemaking?

First, let us briefly examine the dimension of time. Many elements in natural and designed landscapes mark time in space. Sundials are the most literal example of such a materialization of time. Time itself, however, is invisible to humans—we cannot sense it. Since antiquity, philosophers, artists, and scientists have worked to explain the interrelated concepts of space and time. Barbara Adam, a British expert in the area of socio-environmental time, notes that

FIGURE 7.2 Parterre Garden, Kempinski Airport Hotel, Munich, Germany, by Peter Walker and Partners, with Rainer Schmidt Landscape Architecture.

"[n]ature, the environment and sustainability ... are not merely matters of space but fundamentally temporal realms, processes and concepts. Their temporality ... is far from simple and singular" (Adam 1998: 8). Similarly, in "The Temporality of the Landscape," social anthropologist Tim Ingold reminds us of a key characteristic of the medium we work with. He insists that "the landscape is never complete: neither 'built' nor 'unbuilt,' it is perpetually under construction" (Ingold 1993: 162).

The lack of understanding and the difficulty of representing the fourth dimension of existence, time, and change make it challenging to successfully and deliberately incorporate time into complex urban landscape design concepts. In recent years, nevertheless, the importance of the temporal component in landscape architectural work has been widely recognized. For example, discussing temporality and how it relates to the creation of places, Marc Treib emphasizes that "time is the crucial dimension of landscape" and "[c]hange is the direct byproduct of time" (Treib 1999: 37). He further recognizes that "[e]xistence involves change, and change demands time" (ibid.: 41). Landscape architects and environmental designers must acknowledge in their work the fundamental temporality of the landscape and its elements. As a profession, we need to learn how to take advantage of and work *with* time and process rather than against these qualities. The following broad historical overview highlights selected precedents that resonate with the current discussion about process-driven approaches to urbanism and landscape design and that are of significance to the case studies presented later in this chapter.

In the 1950s and 1960s, scientists such as Eugene Odum and colleagues were instrumental in the rise of general and ecosystem ecology (Odum 1953). Landscape architects began to understand that all things and actions are interconnected through dynamic and evolving relationships and that the present is a provisional state, not a final result. Ian McHarg's 1969 book *Design with Nature* was one of the shapers of the environmental movement, building on the work of earlier designers and writers. McHarg raised the profession's awareness of the fragile interdependencies and complexities of natural systems. In 1973 Canadian ecologist Crawford (Buzz) Holling, in his article "Resilience and Stability of Ecological Systems," articulated the influential concepts of resilience, adaptability, and transformability and the trade-offs between constancy and change as well as between predictability and unpredictability. Since then, Holling (1986), Brian Walker et al. (2004) and other ecologists have furthered the understanding of resilient systems and their role in sustainability science. We now recognize that in nature, ecosystems do not normally reach one optimal, stable equilibrium state but rather fluctuate and develop multiple stable conditions as the result of non-linear patterns such as adaptive cycles. In the 1980s, Richard Forman's work was instrumental in developing the landscape ecology field (Forman and Godron 1986). Forman's view of the landscape as a mosaic consisting of a matrix, patches (as the basic units that evolve and fluctuate), and corridors forming networks (Forman 1995), has strongly influenced the contemporary process-driven landscape design discourse.

Similar in impact to the scholarship of ecologists, the twentieth-century works of cultural geographers have influenced the way we understand landscape processes. In his article "The Morphology of Landscape," Carl Sauer discusses how time relates to the development of a culture, claiming that "[w]e cannot form an idea of landscape except in terms of its time relations as well as of its space relations. It is in continuous process of development or of dissolution and replacement" (Sauer 1925: 36). Beginning in the 1950s, cultural geographers such as J. B. Jackson emphasized the role of human and cultural processes in attaching meaning to places. In *Discovering the Vernacular Landscape*, Jackson finds that "[a] landscape is . . . a space deliberately created to speed up or slow down the process of nature. As Eliade expresses it, it represents man taking upon himself the role of time" (Jackson 1984: 8).

In the designed landscape, depending on the task at hand, the scale, and the site context, temporal processes can range from the phenomenological and visual to the productively performative. The landscape architecture field draws on a tradition of working with the phenomenological and artistic aspects of process. The early to mid-twentieth-century landscapes of Jens Jensen, Warren Manning, Herbert Bayer, and later Garret Eckbo, Ian McHarg, Richard Haag, and others incorporated time components. From the 1960s on, landscape architect Lawrence Halprin in his projects used design elements that were meant to reflect natural processes—for example, land forms shaped by water and wind erosion. Halprin's original landscape design for The Sea Ranch on northern California's coast (1961–1967) reflected a thorough understanding of flows and changes over time (Meyer 2000). With their strong phenomenological focus, the ephemeral and process-driven works of land artists such as Michael Heizer, Robert Smithson, Alan Sonfist, Richard Long, and Walter De Maria in the 1960s and 1970s, as well as later temporal landscape installations by Andy Goldsworthy and others, had a profound impact on the landscape architectural process discussion of the late twentieth century. Robert Smithson's famous *Spiral Jetty* (1970), located on the shore of the Great Salt Lake in Utah, is a process-heavy earthwork sculpture built of mud, salt, rocks, and water. The 1,500-foot-long dam in the shape of a coil is visible only when the level of the lake falls below a certain elevation, and thus is an example of a large-scale project that makes natural phenomena experienceable. Temporary ice sculptures and other ephemeral works by Andy Goldsworthy provide additional examples of a strong phenomenological focus in land art.

Inspired by such approaches to making art as well as the experiments of landscape architects in the use of land to shape space, landscape architects created dynamic small-scale landscape design projects with a focus on the phenomenological and artistic aspects of process. Landscape architect A. E. Bye was using earthen mounds to shape space but also to guide water through the site and to form abstract patterns of melting snow in the early 1960s. Halprin's interactive and playable civic fountains, most common in the 1970s, as exemplified by the Ira Keller Fountain in downtown Portland, Oregon (1971), contributed alternative material languages. Other examples are Michael Van Valkenburgh's famous ice walls, such as the 1990 Krakow Ice Garden. This 38-foot-diameter circular steel mesh structure located in a residential setting at Martha's Vineyard, Massachusetts, celebrates the change of seasons. In the winter, drip irrigation and below-freezing temperatures turn the fence-like structure into an ice wall. The rest of the year, it provides support for various deciduous and flowering vines (Hodge 1994). This project exemplifies a small-scale process-oriented landscape with a strong phenomenological focus. Similarly, Peter Walker created an experience of process as art or decoration with his 1987 Tanner Fountain at Harvard. Less well known is German landscape architect Peter Latz's experimental, temporal project for a spiral mist garden at the Festival des Jardins de Chaumont-sur-Loire (1998). In this project, vertical limestone slabs, ferns, and spray mist were used to create an artistic, phenomenological process experience for the visitor. These types of installations make a clear statement about the ephemeral character of natural phenomena. By making processes visible, they provide a sense of action and time.

Marking another key moment in the landscape architectural process discussion, Latz & Partners' Hafeninsel Saarbrücken (1985–1989), the conversion of a former coal harbor into a public urban park, indicated the beginnings of a series of process-driven postindustrial reclamation projects in Germany.[1] The best-documented and most well-known of these is Latz's Landschaftspark Duisburg Nord (1991–2000), created in the context of the IBA (International Building Exposition) Emscher Park on the site of a former steel-manufacturing plant. Building on the work of Richard Haag at Gas Works Park and Bloedel Reserve, both in Seattle, Washington (1976 and 1984 respectively), this public park epitomizes an innovative type of process-based cultural landscape characterized by an acceptance of industrial heritage and dramatically altered natural conditions. In his concept, Latz embraces qualities of change and spontaneity, as well as creative and adaptive new uses, as an alternative to more traditional, expensive, static, and inflexible open-space and planting solutions. Duisburg Nord is characterized by an aesthetic of reused industrial structures, rusty steel, and subtle interventions in the landscape (Stilgenbauer 2005). Disturbed soils consisting of slag, cinder, and the remains of coal or coke create extreme environmental conditions. Combined with the introduction of seeds from all over the world as a byproduct of the steel industry, they result in a great variety and dynamic mix of native and exotic plant species. Plants appear in various early stages of natural succession and play a key role in in-situ phytoremediation processes. By accepting and showcasing damaged systems and their processes rather than hiding them, these two and other early European postindustrial landscape projects exemplify time and change in the sense of regeneration, clean-up, and awareness-raising. The conceptual focus is on the performative, problem-solving, and systemic aspects of the process spectrum. At Duisburg Nord, stability is sacrificed for the sake of uncertainty. Following these early examples, many brownfield sites in other parts of Europe, in the United States, and around the world have been converted into parks. In many instances, landscape architects decided to ground their concepts in their sites' intrinsic disturbances (rather than camouflaging them), and thus to make the underlying processes experienceable to users.

Around the turn of the new millennium, designers also began to explore the field of biomimicry, defined by Janine Benyus as "a new science that studies nature's models and then imitates or takes inspiration from these designs and processes to solve human problems" (Benyus 1998: preface). When suggesting that we use "nature as measure" at the ecosystem and city level, Benyus asks designers to apply ecological performance standards with the goal of matching the same levels of ecosystem services that were present in the undeveloped, native, local ecosystem (Benyus 2010). Similarly, many of the current process-driven design approaches strive for self-sufficient, net-zero energy, water, waste, and resource systems.

The much discussed adaptive concept, applying systems theory to landscape, now commonly termed "emergent ecologies," originated as a labeled practice in James Corner, Stan Allen and team's entry of the same name to the international competition for Downsview Park in Toronto. Here the designers attempted to address the "apparent dichotomies of specificity vs. open-endedness and human activities vs. natural systems . . . through the development of precise series of forms and pathways that will each support the emergence of self-organizing flows and behaviors in time" (Corner and Allen 2001: 58). In this concept, initial seeding and propagation, continual change, and adaptive, phased management were meant to lead to self-organization and, over the years, the emergence of a diverse and resilient ecosystem. James Corner and his Field Operations team applied similar concepts in their entry to the Fresh Kills design competition on Staten Island. Throughout the past decade, ecologists such as Nina-Marie Lister, a member of Corner and Allen's team for the Downsview Park competition, have been increasingly engaged in conversations with urban landscape design professionals about questions of resilience, biodiversity, and adaptive ecological design in urban environments (Lister 2007).

Additionally, in recent years, process has played a major role in the writings and design concepts of the landscape urbanism movement. One proponent, Charles Waldheim (2006), characterizes indeterminacy and flux as two key qualities explored in works of landscape urbanism. James Corner, in "Terra Fluxus" (2006), also highlights the importance of processes over time as one of four main themes of landscape urbanism. With his dynamic and performative approach, Corner strives for "open-ended strategic models" (Corner 2001: 123) rather than static and finished solutions. He writes that "[t]he promise of landscape urbanism is the development of a space-time ecology that treats all forces and agents working in the urban field and considers them as continuous networks of inter-relationships" (Corner 2006: 30). Some aspects of these ideas go back to strategies popularized by Rem Koolhaas, Bernard Tschumi, Adriaan Geuze, and others, which conceived landscape as a non-static framework that allows for adaptability.

Michel Desvigne's phased poplar and hardwood tree plantation and maintenance concept for the new Central Park on Greenwich Peninsula in London, a process-driven project located on the site of future residential developments, was designed to accommodate events during the millennium celebrations. Desvigne's goal was to create a landscape that would provide an immediately usable spatial framework that could accommodate diverse, flexible, and evolving scenarios. This Central Park concept and the subsequent development strategies for the right bank of the Garonne River in Bordeaux, France (2000–2004), which proposed a process of transformation over time for a vast former industrial site along the river's edge, are exemplary of Desvigne's heavily process-based landscape urbanism practice. Corner describes Desvigne's work as a "form of earth marking that is inevitably provisional, staged and cumulative," creating a condition and "material environment that effects and propels its own development" (Corner 2009: 7). Desvigne himself states that in his work he is drawn to "the play with time: the highlighting of successive phases, the emphasis on early phases, the coexistence of different stages of development that concentrate and condense, in a short period, processes with historical rhythms" (Desvigne 2009: 12).

In *Ecological Urbanism*, Mohsen Mostafavi (2010) advocates for the synthesis of urbanism and ecology in the planning and design of future urban areas. Landscape architect Fritz Steiner suggests the potential of bringing together "ideas from landscape urbanism and urban ecology . . . to create new territories that reflect cultural and natural processes" (Steiner 2011: 333).

At the site scale, the first decade of the twenty-first century has brought to light numerous extreme process-driven landscape design concepts, which, by integrating ecology and design, offer solutions to many of the problems of our time. Putting natural processes to work, these projects focus on heavily performative (problem-solving and/or productive) processual strategies. Examples of such problem-solving landscape elements and techniques include in-situ bio- and phytoremediation applications, living systems designed to treat and retain urban run-off, graywater and blackwater, living roofs and façades, and various other green infrastructure applications. Examples of productive landscape types include systems of local resources, energy (biofuels, etc.), and food production such as hybrid poplar plantations for biomass production and terrestrial carbon sequestration and storage. Urban agriculture-oriented concepts that make productive landscape processes accessible to experience—particularly the idea of integrating local food production into design and maintenance concepts for public parks and urban leftover spaces—are on the rise. Currently, these productively performative and systemic process-based landscapes types and their elements are often engineered with function in mind rather than form, visual-spatial qualities, or placemaking.

The landscape architecture profession's recent intense focus on urban ecology, systems theory, and performance summarized above brings us back to the "how much process is too much process?" question raised earlier in this chapter. How do we balance process and change in the designed landscape with more traditional placemaking? And what does it take to make process-driven concepts implementable, legible, usable, and maintainable? I argue that in an urban environment, the design of successful processual landscapes[2]—what I call Processcapes[3]—is a quest for a condition of balance between dynamic and enduring site elements, with the latter typically forming a project's spatial frameworks, capable of providing permanencies and reference.

Grounded in site processes and adapted to local ecologies, economies, and cultures, the landforms, built structures, and plantings of Processcapes need to be place- and problem-distinctive. In consequence, these types of landscapes are characterized by a multitude of appearances rather than one universal style or consistent formal idiom. Hester (2006) refers to this quality of a landscape as its "particularness." Particularness, however, does not suggest that intentional design, spatial quality, aesthetics, and placemaking do not matter. Thus, while I agree with James Corner's opinion that process-driven projects "may assume any number of formal characteristics, depending on local circumstances and situations" (Corner 1999: 4), I disagree with his conclusion that "recovering landscape is less a matter of appearances and aesthetic categories than an issue of strategic instrumentality. Form is still important, but less as appearance and more as an efficacious disposition of parts" (ibid.). While fascinating in theory, such an extreme process-driven approach in reality risks sacrificing the creation of well-designed places in favor of achieving indeterminacy. Despite our profession's heightened focus on sustainability and the problem-solving and productive capacities of landscapes, first and foremost landscape architects are designers and placemakers. Thus, successful process-driven landscape design must combine dynamic elements with stability. The permanent, spatial parts of a design function as a datum that enables the perception of change over time.

Presenting a similar argument, Anita Berrizbeitia in her 2007 chapter, "Re-Placing Process," also examines the relationship between changing and stable landscape elements. Her finding that "process results in place when it is paired with additional conceptual frameworks, whether cultural, site-specific, or phenomenological, that transform it from mere technique to legible design language" (Berrizbeitia 2007: 189) confirms the need for balance postulated in this chapter. Similarly, Rosenberg (2009), in the context of her reflections on Van Valkenburgh's open-space concept for the Herman Miller Factory, finds that "[t]his tension between the fixed and the dynamic aspects of landscape points to the inherent dilemma of designing a successional landscape. How does the designer strike the balance between creating formal structure and maintaining openness to change?" (Rosenberg 2009: 105).

In my opinion, it is key in process-oriented design not only to find the project-appropriate position on the continuum from process to stasis, but also to balance the two ends of the art–science gradient. It is important to note that in the conceptual balancing act called for in this chapter, art does not always match stability and science does not always match process. The assumption is that, for example, process can be art (e.g., its phenomenological aspects) and/or science (problem-solving and productive capacities). In fact, successful Processcapes balance not only stability and change, but also the performative aspects of process on the one hand with the phenomenological aspects on the other. Doing so allows us to create places that are problem-solving and dynamic, beautiful, usable, and memorable.

The following selected examples of contemporary, built processual design work feature degrees and types of evolving versus rigid design elements at multiple scales. While the projects all combine aspects of time and process, urban ecology, and placemaking, they approach the quest for balance this chapter advocates for in very different yet successful ways.

Westpark Bochum, a 94-acre postindustrial park on a former steel manufacturing site, designed by landscape architects Danielzik & Leuchter in collaboration with S.K.A.T. architects, is one of the lesser-known and more recent postindustrial landscape projects in Germany. It represents an approach that integrates and balances dynamic processes and change with intentionally designed new and enduring site elements in an exemplary way (Figure 7.3). This project incorporates existing industrial structures and emergent pioneer stages of vegetation and, through careful editing, gives form to process and makes change legible. The dynamic and open-ended character of the site's butterfly meadows and birch, willow, and black locust woodlands (which have emerged since the end of steel fabrication) is contrasted with more conventional, park-like hardwood tree plantings in a large, central expanse of manicured lawn. Newly introduced stable elements such as cobblestone and decomposed granite paths lined by custom-designed blue bollard lights not only create a sense of place but also form a clear datum against which the change over time in other, dynamic elements of this park landscape can be perceived.

FIGURE 7.3 Westpark Bochum by Danielzik & Leuchter landscape architects in collaboration with S.K.A.T architects.

At Westpark, the designers address the presumed dichotomy of urban wilderness and places for human activity by spatially separating priority areas through the very deliberate design of recurring site features, edges, and thresholds. Berrizbeitia finds that "[o]ne of the challenges of landscape architecture as a cultural practice is the legibility of the trans-formations in the environment that take place through design" (2001: 123). The processual, dynamic approach at Westpark is so successful because it makes clearly legible what was designed intentionally for human use and what has emerged on its own.

James Corner and team's acclaimed design for the High Line represents a different kind of project that reuses an existing urban infrastructure element, in this case a former elevated rail line in Manhattan. Unlike the systemic and adaptive emergent ecologies concepts developed by Corner et al. for the Downsview Park competition and for Fresh Kills, the High Line design, while inspired by the existing structure and the ruderal vegetation that developed in the 25 years since the rail tracks went out of use, utilizes process in a much more metaphorical and phenomenological way. Piet Oudolf's planting design for the project references successional processes and naturally occurring plant communities of varying moisture regimes, partially using native plants. The perennial plantings—as in many of Oudolf's other projects—showcase seasonal change, growth, and decay rather than constancy. However, while these intensively managed vegetated areas provide habitat, positively influence the local microclimate, and filter and retain run-off, the focus of this inner-city project clearly (and appropriately) lies on placemaking and human activity.

Hugely successful and popular, the High Line constitutes a great example of what Lister refers to as "designer ecology"—a "largely symbolic gesture" rather than true ecological design (Lister 2007: 35). A site's dimensions, context, and program determine whether or not uncertain, adaptive, self-organizing ecological systems can be initiated through design interventions. Lister stresses the singular importance of "largeness" (ibid.: 35) when it comes to establishing resilient and sustainable urban parks. Berrizbeitia remarks that "[w]hen designing landscapes poised for environmental or programmatic change . . . what becomes critical is the degree of design intervention. If the landscape is overly specified, its capacity for adaptability and response to changes in the environment will be limited" (Berrizbeitia 2001: 121). Linear in nature and located in a dense urban context, the High Line project, with its intensive recreational program, required deliberate design interventions and artificially maintained ecosystem stability. Adaptability and emergence here were intentionally relegated to a role secondary to phenomenological processes as well as to placemaking.

The sunken public garden named "Die Plantage" (the Plantation) designed by the Rainer Schmidt Landscape Architecture firm[4] as part of both the larger public Riemer Park (by Gilles Vexlard) and the site of the year-long BUGA Munich 2005 (German National Garden Exposition) event represents an example of a public landscape that features productive processual elements as an integral part of the concept (Figure 7.4). Inspired by the traditional southern German cultural landscape type of the *Streuobstwiese* (meadow orchard), this public park site, about three acres in size, was planted with a regular, gridded orchard of 137 fruit trees instead of more traditional hardwood shade trees. These trees—all old local apple, pear, and cherry cultivars traditionally used in the cultural landscape surrounding Munich—grow in a flat, pervious, multi-purpose, decomposed granite surface. During the exposition, this area was used to showcase old fruit-bearing plant varieties, including shrubs and other trees grown in containers for the year-long event. Since BUGA 2005 closed, the fruit orchard has been accessible to the public. Park visitors and residents of the abutting new, dense, mixed-use development on the site of the former Munich airport harvest the fruit as it ripens. After the event, the decomposed granite surface beneath the fruit trees was partially converted into a lower-maintenance, stabilized, crushed aggregate lawn that can be mown, withstands light maintenance traffic, and leaves possibilities for future programmatic additions (Stilgenbauer 2012). Die Plantage, along with other projects also featured in *Designing Urban Agriculture* (Philips 2013), demonstrates that process orientation (here: performance/food production), human activity, identity, and placemaking can be compatible and in fact mutually beneficial in public spaces. It is to be hoped that in the near future we will overcome bureaucratic hurdles and find design solutions, operational strategies, and maintenance models that allow more cities to convert underutilized ornamental landscapes into site-appropriately productive and at the same time beautiful and usable urban places.

In the case of the 228 National Memorial Park project in Taiwan,[5] the metaphor of dynamic plant growth and the inevitable revelation of historical truths are pivotal to the concept. The objective of this international design competition was to bring to light the memories and historic significance of the "228 Incident," a national tragedy that occurred on February 28, 1947 on the island of Taiwan.[6] In addition, the new 15-acre urban park located in Chiayi City was to become a multi-faceted public open-space amenity for a

FIGURE 7.4 View of fruit trees at Die Plantage, Riemer Park, Munich.

developing, dense, mixed-use neighborhood (Figure 7.5). The commemorative park landscape, which was inaugurated and opened to the public in 2011, is designed to change and grow in meaning over time. The key idea of phenomenological process is expressed in the growing giant bamboo located in a large, sunken outdoor memorial room surrounded by a vast asymmetrical low-rise earth pyramid. Grand in scale, this earth sculpture allows unobstructed views of the distant Memorial Wall and, in time, also the robust bamboo canopy. The bamboo forest, established by planting small individual bamboo shoots in a regular grid pattern at inauguration, will develop into a dense interwoven network and eventually surface above the Memorial Wall; a symbol of realized life and freedom. This process of growth and revelation signifies the national memory of the 228 Incident, which lives on in Taiwan despite so many years of concealment. Its process-oriented, dynamic approach distinguishes the 228 National Memorial Park from other works of similar scope.

In this project, process is used as a powerful design element and metaphor. The growth of the spatially isolated, dynamic planting element in the central part of the site can be read against the surrounding horizon line formed by the uniform, static structure of the Memorial Wall. As Anne Whiston Spirn expresses it: "[w]hen a single process or a single set of processes dominates—water flowing, wheat growing, wind blowing—or when contexts are relatively homogeneous, as in sandy seashores, arid deserts, and grassy prairies, then landscapes reveal process most clearly" (Spirn 1998: 88). The design of the sloped and surrounding flat parts of the site incorporates process in its performative expression. Systems for storm water capture and treatment—a major issue in a near-tropical climate—are

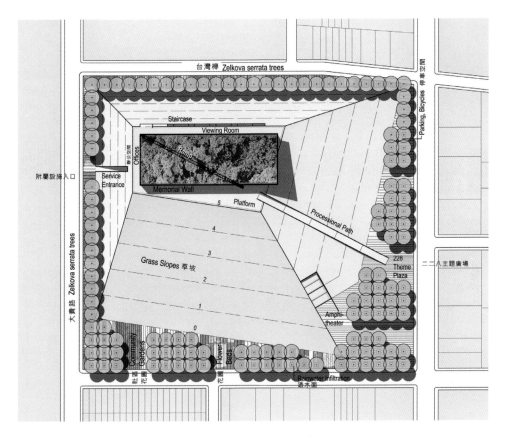

FIGURE 7.5 Schematic site plan, 228 National Memorial Park, Taiwan.

carefully integrated into the plaza design and form the edge of the grass-covered earth pyramid, becoming an integral and visible part of the concept. The design for this new public park and memorial space represents a processual approach that balances change and stability on the one hand and art and science on the other in a problem-specific way. Here the dynamic elements of metaphorical growth processes that are central to the concept are combined with enduring spatial form, which provides the structure and framework and a reference point that enables users to register change over time, and a clear overall focus on phenomenological qualities. While performative landscape processes—for example, the living systems of the green roof above the underground museum and the run-off treatment facilities—are important components of the overall design, in this case they are secondary to the program-born significance of process as phenomenon and metaphor.

As these and many other built examples suggest, process-driven design work can take on a multitude of expressions and forms. Generally, successful post-static landscape design solutions transcend the picturesque and ornamental while emphasizing a sense of space *and* time. Achieving the project-appropriate balance between purely process-driven, dynamic concepts on the one hand and purely visual-spatial and static approaches on the other is a complex problem. It depends on innumerable site- and task-specific factors including project location, context, size, climate, topography, geology, and hydrology, as well as program, use, social context, budget, and maintenance. Identifying and grounding the proper processual design strategy for each site in its time and context must be the premise.

In the second-half of the twentieth century, landscape architects were taught that public landscapes ought to be designed and built for eternity (or at least several decades or a few centuries)—a notion now questioned in the contemporary discussion. Global warming is no longer a matter of debate, sea levels are rising, levees are breaking, infrastructures are crumbling, urban areas are growing, and economies and societies are changing rapidly. Processual landscapes—with their ability to perform and adapt—can provide resilient, dynamic, and flexible real-world solutions to many problems of our time, such as limited public budgets for the installation and maintenance of public urban landscapes, programmatic uncertainties, underutilized brownfield sites and other urban leftover spaces, and the contamination of air, water, and soils. Truly resilient and adaptive ecological systems, able to accommodate both biodiversity and human activity, require large continuous or connected areas, which are rarely found in our dense urban environments. Nevertheless, performative landscape processes can and need to be—to varying degrees—incorporated into the design of any urban site. Underutilized and maintenance-intensive parts of existing public spaces, such as unused irrigated lawns or other purely decorative site elements, should be converted into more dynamic, productive, or problem-solving, yet beautiful systems. Changes in policy, management, and maintenance practices are required to allow for more spatial and programmatic flexibility and a greater degree of uncertainty in our designed urban environment. Landscape architects need to take advantage of the temporality of their medium, the fact that landscapes are dynamic and perpetually changing, without neglecting the underlying objective to create livable places.

Processscapes are landscapes that put the natural site processes they are grounded in to work; they evolve, making changes tangible and experience accessible instead of preventing, slowing, or camouflaging them. I argue that in the city the performative aspects of Processscapes need to be carefully balanced with phenomenological qualities and deliberately designed spatial interventions—what Moore (2010) refers to as "the visual." The resulting landscapes, in which nature and human activity coexist, are complex and able to multi-task in that they are process-driven, yet simultaneously usable, enjoyable, and memorable with a clear focus on the intentionally designed, the structural, and placemaking. If performed carefully, such a conceptual balancing act between ecology and indeterminacy on the one hand and design and stability on the other can lead to landscape architectural solutions in which the seemingly conflicting goals of processuality and placemaking are not only successfully combined, but merged into a mutually beneficial relationship.

Notes

1 The iconic Gas Works Park by Richard Haag, opened to the public in 1975, predates Peter Latz's postindustrial landscapes work. However, this chapter highlights Landschaftspark Duisburg Nord because of its more clearly articulated, strong conceptual focus on site processes, adaptation, and emergence.
2 Processual as in the German word *Prozesshaftigkeit*, literally meaning "tied to process."
3 The term "Processscapes" was first coined by the author as the course title of two graduate-level landscape architecture research seminars taught at UC Berkeley in 2010 and 2011. A 2011 advanced "Processscapes" MLA studio at Berkeley further explored and applied the concept of balancing process-driven design with placemaking. This work resulted in an exhibition of "San Francisco

Processcapes" at the San Francisco Planning and Urban Research Association (SPUR) in 2012, which was conceived and curated by the author.

4   The author served as project manager and lead designer for "Die Plantage" from schematic design through construction documentation during her time as head of the Munich office of the Rainer Schmidt Landscape Architecture firm (2000–2003).

5   228 National Memorial Park, Chiayi City, Taiwan project team: stilgenbauer landschaftsarchitekten—urban landscape design (Judith Stilgenbauer) with Kit Wang and local representatives Progressive Environmental Inc., Taipei and Chen Chien Chou Architect, Taipei.

6   The project is named after an incident that occurred on February 28, 1947, on the island of Taiwan, which after World War II was transferred from Japanese rule to the Chinese Nationalist government under Chiang Kai-shek. What became known as the "228 Incident" started with a confrontation between a black-market cigarette vendor and government soldiers that led to widespread protests and mass killings all over the country. Official estimates of the massacre's death toll range from 10,000 to 40,000. The exact number and fate of many victims are mysteries. The 228 National Memorial Park was the first park and national memorial specially designed and dedicated by the government of Taiwan to commemorating the massacre.

References

Adam, B. (1998). *Timescapes of Modernity: The environment and invisible hazards.* New York: Routledge.

Benyus, J. (1998). *Biomimicry: Innovation inspired by nature.* New York: Perennial.

Benyus, J. (2010, February 24). *Biomimicry in the Built World: Consulting nature as model, measure, and mentor,* lecture UC Berkeley. [Online]. Available: www.youtube.com/watch?v=yVHtAjQoWmg&feature=PlayList&p=9A40EBAA1ED98678&index=7 [August 1, 2011].

Berrizbeitia, A. (2001). Scales of undecidability. In Czerniak, J. (ed.), *Downsview Park Toronto.* Munich, London, New York: Prestel, 116–125.

Berrizbeitia, A. (2007). Re-placing process. In Czerniak, J. and Hargreaves, G. (eds), *Large Parks.* New York: Princeton Architectural Press, 175–197.

Corner, J. (ed.) (1999). *Recovering Landscape: Essays in contemporary landscape architecture.* New York: Princeton Architectural Press.

Corner, J. (2001). Landscraping. In Daskalakis, G., Waldheim, C., and Young, J. (eds), *Stalking Detroit.* Barcelona: Actar, 122–125.

Corner, J. (2006). Terra fluxus. In Waldheim, C. (ed.), *The Landscape Urbanism Reader.* New York: Princeton Architectural Press, 21–33.

Corner J. (2009). Agriculture, texture, and the unfinished. In Tiberghien, G. A. (ed.), *Intermediate Natures: The landscapes of Michel Desvigne.* Basel: Birkhäuser, 7–10.

Corner, J. and Allen, S. (2001). Emergent ecologies. In Czerniak, J. (ed.), *Downsview Park Toronto.* Munich, London, New York: Prestel, 116–125.

Desvigne, M. (2009). Introduction. In Tiberghien, G. A. (ed.), *Intermediate Natures: The landscapes of Michel Desvigne.* Basel: Birkhäuser, 11–13.

Forman, R. T. T. (1995). *Land Mosaics: The ecology of landscapes and regions.* Cambridge/New York: Cambridge University Press.

Forman, R. T. T. and Godron, M. (1986). *Landscape Ecology.* New York: John Wiley.

Hester, R. (2006). *Design for Ecological Democracy.* Cambridge, MA: The MIT Press.

Hodge, B. (ed.) (1994). *Design with the Land: The landscape architecture of Michael Van Valkenburgh.* New York: Princeton Architectural Press.

Holling, C. S. (1973). Resilience and stability of ecological systems. *Annual Review of Ecology and Systematics,* 4, 1–23.

Holling, C. S. (1986). The resilience of terrestrial ecosystems: local surprise and global change. In Clark, W. and Munn, R. E. (eds), *Sustainable Development of the Biosphere.* Cambridge: Cambridge University Press, 292–317.

Ingold, T. (1993). The temporality of the landscape. *World Archaeology,* 25(2), 152–174.

Jackson, J. B. (1984). *Discovering the Vernacular Landscape.* New Haven, CT: Yale University Press.

Lister, N.-M. (2007). Sustainable large parks: ecological design or designer ecology? In Czerniak, J. and Hargreaves, G. (eds), *Large Parks*. New York: Princeton Architectural Press, 34–57.

McHarg, I. L. (1969). *Design with Nature*. American Museum of Natural History: The Natural History Press.

Meyer, E. K. (2000). The post-Earth Day conundrum: translating environmental values. In Conan, M. (ed.), *Environmentalism in Landscape Architecture*. Washington, DC: Dumbarton Oaks Research Library and Collection, 187–244.

Moore, K. (2010). *Overlooking the Visual*. New York: Routledge.

Mostafavi, M. (2010). Why ecological urbanism? Why now? In Mostafavi, M. and Doherty, G. (eds), *Ecological Urbanism*. Baden: Lars Müller Publishers, 12–53.

Odum, E. (1953). *Fundamentals of Ecology*. Philadelphia, PA: W. B. Saunders Company.

Philips, A. (2013). *Designing Urban Agriculture*. Hoboken, NJ: John Wiley & Sons.

Rosenberg, E. (2009). Herman Miller Factory: Suburban sublime. In Berrizbeitia, A. (ed.), *Michael Van Valkenburgh Associates: Reconstructing urban landscapes*. New Haven, CT: Yale University Press, 84–107.

Sauer, C. O. (1925). The morphology of landscape. *University of California Publications in Geography*, 2(2), 19–53.

Spirn, A. W. (1998). *The Language of Landscape*. New Haven, CT: Yale University Press.

Steiner, F. (2011). Landscape ecological urbanism: origins and trajectories. *Landscape and Urban Planning*, 100(4), 333–337.

Stilgenbauer, J. (2005). Landschaftspark Duisburg Nord. *Places, a Forum of Environmental Design*, 17(3), 6–9.

Stilgenbauer, J. (2008). Emergence, progression, procession. *Frameworks*, 7, Spring, 16–19.

Stilgenbauer, J. (2012). CIVIC (agri)CULTURE. *Ground Up*, 1, 64–69.

Treib, M. (1999). Nature recalled. In Corner, J. (ed.), *Recovering Landscape*. New York: Princeton Architectural Press, 29–43.

Waldheim, C. (2006). Landscape as urbanism. In Waldheim, C. (ed.), *The Landscape Urbanism Reader*. New York: Princeton Architectural Press, 35–53.

Walker, B., Holling, C. S., Carpenter, S. R., and Kinzig, A. (2004). Resilience, adaptability and transformability in social–ecological systems. *Ecology and Society*, 9(2), article 5. [Online]. Available: http://www.ecologyandsociety.org/vol9/iss2/art5 [February 1, 2010].

PERFORMING

Performance evokes multiple connotations in planning and design at the current moment. The recent focus on high-performance buildings and landscapes represents a renewed interest in the functional performances of energy systems and ecological processes. Performance, as explored in this section, is associated with a different dimension and process of placemaking in the contemporary city, a more visceral and embodied kind. Performance here refers to the roles of specific actors, actions, and agencies in shaping and reshaping urban spaces, and the political and social relationships as enacted in the built environment.

Performative urbanism through temporary and tactical interventions has been recognized as an innovative strategy of placemaking. These interventions are often conceived with the realization that outcomes of large-scale developments can no longer be planned or predicted and the resources for implementing formal master plans no longer exist. Once considered as outside the legal domain, temporary use is now accepted as a desirable, interim approach for urban development. As everyday spatial practices, temporary, performative urbanism has long been central to the urban vernacular. Such practices encompass a vast array of activities in which ordinary citizens are the main protagonists. Its acts range from those of the street vendors to skateboarders' interventions in transforming urban spaces into unplanned playgrounds. Performances are moments in which the city is enacted, lived, and defined. They are also the medium through which new meanings, identities, and relationships are forged.

This section highlights the performative, an approach executed by a multitude of actors and enacted through the agencies of individuals and collectives. The chapters begin with the everyday performances of car-washers and guerrilla marketers in Las Vegas, to an expanding network of urban workers and rural farmers connected through a restaurant in Tokyo, followed by the enacted and embodied performances of students and community stakeholders in Tijuana, Mexico.

8

NOSOTROS ("WE")[1]

Two Cultures of Sustainability and the "Present City" of Las Vegas

Daniel H. Ortega

The scholarly interest in dynamic urban forces—that is, the physical forms, socio-economic conditions, and cultural identities that combine to form the fabric of the modern city—has resulted in a discursive body of work (Donald 1999; Joyce 2003; Tonkiss 2005; Crinar and Bender 2007). In contrast to the vast majority of the literature focused on institutionalized urban design, this chapter explores alternative processes for city making within the framework of "immediate and substantive actions" that serve as "grounds for uncovering opportunity and unleashing potential" of the already existing city.[2] It is within the context of the "unleashing of potential" that I will examine two disparate cultural interpretations of sustainability and how both of those interpretations have worked to add to the physical and cultural manifestation of the city of Las Vegas, Nevada. Specifically, this chapter will examine the practices employed by specific resort/casino developments, and my observations of two groups of everyday entrepreneurs who are situated within the margins of an "other" Las Vegas; the first being an assemblage of mobile car wash vendors, and the second being represented by a socially anonymous group of guerilla marketers. The observations on these two groups are central to my thesis that the link between the ideology of sustainability as it is prescribed by a technocratic, industrial capitalist power structure, and a more flexibly spatialized "logic of sufficiency," creates a relevant field for investigating the potential impact that "everyday" practices of sustainability can have on an alternative paradigm of city making.

Sustainability in Context

Before going any further, it is probably prudent to offer a working definition of "sustainability" as I mean for it to apply throughout this work. The most widely accepted definition is positioned as "meeting the needs of the present without compromising the ability of future generations to meet their needs" (WCED 1987: 43). However, I am more comfortable with using Princen's assertion that:

> [s]ustainability is a "big idea," a global concept that has arisen to meet a contemporary challenge, one unlike anything humanity has faced in the past: global ecological crisis

> . . . Like "peace," "democracy," "progress," and other "big ideas" of modern times, sustainability is broad, overarching, in some respects, all-encompassing. And like those other big ideas, sustainability is, quite naturally, debated and constantly adjusted to meet new threats and understandings.
>
> *(Princen 2005: 30)*

I prefer to use Princen's description of sustainability precisely because it allows for room to work on and within multiple intellectual frameworks to achieve the goals described in the former more universally accepted definition. Throughout this work, I will attempt to make connections between sustainability and culture, sustainability and ideology, and sustainability and hegemony. I feel that any discussion on sustainability must include a cultural component. More specifically, it must include a cultural component that recognizes the everyday, not just the technocratic version of sustainability that clogs much of the contemporary discussion regarding the subject. As Packalen emphasizes:

> Up until now there has been an overwhelmingly one-sided emphasis on the technical and biological aspects of environmental questions (e.g., energy crises, emissions quotas, fossil fuels, dam-building projects, threatened species, deforestation of rain forests, and melting ice caps). The people involved in the debate about sustainability have often been politicians, environmental activists, forecasters, and experts of various kinds, but not ordinary people. But if the voices of ordinary people are to be heard, and if the ordinary person is to understand what sustainable development is about, then the cultural dimension must be given much more prominence than before.
>
> *(Packalen 2010: 119)*

The Las Vegas Strip in Context

Las Vegas, Nevada is typically identified via its global signifier, the lavishly flamboyant Las Vegas Boulevard, better known as "the Las Vegas Strip," or to local residents and frequent visitors, "the Strip." Within the discourse of architectural design and urban planning, the Strip has been the object of scholarly attention for several decades (see, for instance, Venturi et al. 1972; Hess 1993; Rothman 2002). *Now Urbanism*'s aim to identify "alternative processes for city making" positions Las Vegas as a particularly salient ground for investigation. It can be easily argued that Las Vegas owes its very existence to alternative processes for city making. In his 1993 book, *Viva Las Vegas: After Hours Architecture*, Alan Hess suggests that:

> [t]he Strip has been the perfect medium for creating a new type of city where an old city would have been unable to take root. Possessing few natural resources, little unique scenery, or parks, Las Vegas was a city that had to be invented—with dams, cheap electricity, defense plants, and the imaginary lines that separate bureaucratic jurisdictions. Those lines through trackless deserts turned a crime in one state into a respected industry in the next. Those lines created a unique and robust economy of amusement. And those imaginary lines materialized in the fanciful silhouettes and neon tracery of Las Vegas architecture. A roadway could become a city. A building could become a sign. In no place at all, someplace could be created. That is Las Vegas' genius.
>
> *(Hess 1993: 123)*

In its capacity as a "medium for creating a new type of city," the Strip has embraced an iterative design process like no other global destination. While the physical evidence that can typically be used to trace the paradigmatic urban design shifts found in most cities—that is, historical architecture, cultural landscapes, etc.—are seldom left standing in Las Vegas' obsessive need to physically reinvent itself, the cultural memory of each particular ethos that informed those paradigm shifts has been well documented. In his aforementioned book, Hess identifies six distinct periods of urban design approaches carried out on the Strip from 1855 to the early 1990s.[3] It can easily be argued that the practices employed by those who controlled each of the periodic urban design efforts of the Strip have undergone several more archetypal revisions since the early 1990s. However, it is not my intent to attempt to identify each of those additional approaches. Rather, I intend to focus on one of the more recent shifts in design ideology as it affects the aggregate make-up of the Strip, and, therefore, the popular identity of the city of Las Vegas: the movement toward green, or sustainable, building design.

The Hegemony of Sustainability on the Las Vegas Strip

In 2006, MGM Resorts International released its plans to develop Project CityCenter, a multi-billion-dollar casino-resort, luxury condominium, and shopping development located on the Las Vegas Strip.[4] The project was marketed as the world's largest green development. In true Las Vegas fashion, the ARIA resort, which is just one constituent piece of the Project CityCenter campus, is championed as "The World's Largest Gold-Rated LEED Building," using the U.S. Green Building Council's (USGBC) Leadership in Energy and Environmental Design (LEED) rating system:[5]

> Created with a vision to bring a new level of environmental consciousness to the world-famous Strip, CityCenter is one of the world's largest sustainable developments, from design and construction to operations and guest amenities . . . Using cutting-edge solutions, CityCenter has been able to grow responsibly without sacrificing the quality of materials or guest experience. Due to its size and purchasing power, CityCenter is driving green economies of scale in multiple industry segments, paving the way for other entities to build and operate sustainably.
>
> *(Project CityCenter Press Room 2009)*

The above statement offers a clear indication that the project's developers have embraced a media-savvy marketing plan that aims to illustrate their commitment to sustainability. However, it is my opinion that their commitment is dedicated more to their economic bottom line than to a true commitment to environmental stewardship. It should be noted that MGM Resorts International is not alone in its campaign to use sustainability, and more specifically the LEED rating system, as a mechanism to attract consumers to the city. One only has to visit the website of the Las Vegas Convention and Visitors Authority[6] to learn that:

> [i]n recent years, Las Vegas resorts have turned their attention and focused their efforts on becoming more environmentally conscious. From energy efficiency and water conservation to recycling and implementing greener practices, Las Vegas is doing its

part to contribute to the sustainability of the planet . . . Several Las Vegas projects have even achieved LEED (Leadership in Energy and Environmental Design) certification by the U.S. Green Building Council.

(Las Vegas Convention and Visitors Authority n.d.)

To lend credence to my earlier suggestion that Las Vegas resort developers' main concern is less environmental and more oriented towards corporate profit, I refer to an article in the *Las Vegas Review Journal* from February 22, 2009, in which staff writer Tony Illia states, "gaming's love affair with green construction didn't blossom until the 2005 passage of Assembly Bill 3. The legislation gives projects that achieve a Leadership in Energy and Environmental Design certification up to a decade-long, 50 percent property tax break." In the same article, Illia reports that tax breaks for the $9.1 billion dollar Project CityCenter alone could cost the state of Nevada millions in tax revenue (Figure 8.1).

At this point, I would like to suggest that, in the case of Las Vegas' casino-resort development, the use of the LEED rating system to attract consumers has become a powerful tool that transcends marketing strategies and engages an aggressive ideological hegemony. In its attempt to attract those global consumers who have been taught that behaving more sustainably is a good way to live, this green campaign becomes an ideology in the literal sense, where "[i]deology is any organized set of ideas about the good life and the institutional framework for their realization" (Mark 1973: 247).

It is my position that because of the ideological "goodness" couched within the contemporary cultural understanding of sustainability, there is a lack of willingness to engage in critical debate surrounding the topic. Combine the reticence to engage in a critical inquiry into the culture of sustainability with the ideological/moralistic belief that in the sustainability movement there exists a superior culture that is "[w]ell ensconced in the rationalities

FIGURE 8.1 A portion of the Project CityCenter skyline.

of economic, engineering, and legal thought" (Princen 2005: 341), and the argument that a hegemonic power structure exists begins to take form. For the purposes of this work, I will define hegemony in the Gramscian sense that those who dominate in any given cultural exchange do so by "winning the consent of competing or marginalized groups" (Gledhill 1997: 348).

In fairness, it should be noted that those who help to fuel the "consent" agenda through the media—that is, resort property developers, tourism agencies, etc.—as a way to expedite the ideological hegemony of sustainability are not the only ones guilty of its dissemination. In fact, a larger burden may rest on the shoulders of those who are responsible for designing our cities. The architects, planners, landscape architects, and urban designers who craft our built environment have overwhelmingly embraced the cultural propaganda connected to the USGBC's LEED program to the extent that many practitioners in these fields feel compelled to become certified LEED Accredited Professionals in the hope that it will make them more attractive hires in the competitive design industries. While my use of the terms "propaganda" and "rhetoric" may sound equally declamatory, one only needs to read the USGBC's advertised benefits for becoming a LEED Accredited Professional to see that it is justified:

> If you are looking to show that you have the key technical knowledge, experience and credibility in the exploding green building marketplace, a LEED professional credential is your pathway to success . . . With new jobs specifying the need for expertise in LEED, the LEED professional credential helps you stand out by increasing your opportunity for employment, job stability and promotion.
>
> *(USGBC n.d.)*

The notion that architects and designers embrace a lofty cant in order to lend credence to the ideological nature of their craft is not a new idea. In his *Writings on Cities*, Henri Lefebvre suggests that:

> [a]rchitects seem to have established and dogmatized an ensemble of significations, as such poorly developed and variously labeled as "function," "form," "structure," or rather functionalism, formalism, and structuralism. They elaborate them not from the significations perceived and lived by those who inhabit, but from their interpretation of inhabiting . . . Given that these architects form a social body, they attach themselves to institutions, their system tends to close itself off, impose itself, and elude all criticism.
>
> *(Lefebvre 1996: 152)*

From the perspective of Lefebvre's criticism, and given that in most parts of society, the professionals who have accepted LEED's tokenism en masse are considered to be part of learned groups whose expertise is relied upon to design the cities in which we live, my opinion that a Gramscian type of hegemony has taken root within the culture of sustainable urban design hopefully begins to resonate as a possibility.

Opportunity and Potential in the Mundane

It is within the shadow of Lefebvre's acknowledgement of those who perceive the city by inhabiting it that I will begin to describe two specific non-consent groups, entangled within the hegemony of sustainability. The consent group(s) of inhabitants whose everyday activities (in)form the elementary make-up of the city reside, as in most other cities, in an "other" Las Vegas. In his 2003 essay, "The Mundane and the Spectacular: Everyday Life in Las Vegas," Mark Gottdiener suggests that the majority of the people of the world recognize Las Vegas as a "commodified sign and media driven node in the global tourist industry" (2003: 41). However:

> There is also this "other" Las Vegas—a place of workers in the gigantic gambling/ service economy; a region of private, suburban homes, of schools, of shopping malls, of highways, of churches and synagogues, of hospitals, and of prisons, of drug rehabilitation clinics, emergency rooms, and counseling centers . . . Within this more mundane sphere, problems of urban living and working arise, much as they do everyplace else.
>
> *(Ibid.)*

I use Gottdiener's description of an "other" Las Vegas, because I feel that it is important to show that the city of Las Vegas is a real and tangible place that exists in contrast to the "'astral' Las Vegas established by Hollywood films, television, and celebrity" (ibid.). However, whereas Gottdiener suggests that within this "other Las Vegas . . . problems of urban living and working arise" (ibid.), I choose to embrace *Now Urbanism*'s proposition that "the rich complexities of the present city act not as barriers or obstacles but as grounds for uncovering opportunity and unleashing potential."[7] It is with that same spirit of optimism in mind that, for the remainder of this chapter, I will discontinue the use of the expression "other Las Vegas" when referring to the areas of study presented herein. Instead, I will use the term "present city" to describe the mundane parts of the city which are ripe with future potential (Kaliski 2008: 88). Shortly, I will present the two groups of urban constituents who I feel work counter to the hegemony of sustainability as I have described it, but first it is important to comment that the commonality of each of the sites of my observation is that they took place in "the taken-for-granted everyday that surrounds us" (ibid.) (Figures 8.2(a) and 8.2(b)).

FIGURE 8.2(a) and 8.2(b) The present city of Las Vegas.

The Counter-hegemonic Culture of Sufficiency

An additional common ground found between these counter-hegemonic actors is that each group, in its own way, employs what Princen refers to as a "logic of sufficiency," which he defines as "a 'sense of enoughness' and 'too muchness'" (2005: 18). It is the engaged enactment of this "logic of sufficiency" on the part of the non-consent groups that I will later describe in more detail, which lends itself to my position that these counter-actors have established a culture of sustainability drastically different from that present in the green building hegemony of the Las Vegas Strip. In order to avoid using the term "culture" too loosely, I will refer to Packalen's definition where "culture is an anthropological and sociological concept, i.e., it comprises all that we mean when we talk about norms, values, assumptions, traditions, and practices" (2010: 119).

The first group that is represented within this culture of sufficiency is a local collective of mobile car wash vendors who temporarily occupy the edges of parking lots and strip mall developments. The second is a more socially anonymous but equally visible group that I will refer to as guerilla marketers. The crux of my observations will begin to identify what Michel de Certeau calls a "tactic" (1984: xix). De Certeau's "tactic" refers to a mobile and temporal blend of "opportunities" in everyday life (ibid.). Whereas de Certeau's contentions contemplate the role of the *consumer* in everyday life, I propose that the vernacular assemblage of these two commerce-related activities found in the present city of Las Vegas could be used to invite the "everyday" entrepreneur into his discussion of the "tactical" creation of spaces of consumption. By doing so, I can begin to illustrate how these two specific groups, that stand in contradiction to the hegemonic categorization established by the contemporary ideology of sustainability, present the opportunity to initiate a new understanding of sustainability, one that transcends marketing slogans and technical jargon and begins to initiate "tactics" that foster a milieu of actions that are centered on recognizing the value of what is sufficient versus what is efficient.[8]

By observing specific daily activities and performances that occur in the present city of Las Vegas, I found a positive local cultural infrastructure that exists as a resistant subordinate to the hegemonic structure of the consent ideology of sustainability. The residents who form this resistant cultural infrastructure may offer a less romantic vision of sustainability than the current hegemonic and media-endorsed version. When thoughtfully considered, this deliberate logic of sufficiency becomes equally and fundamentally as important as the all-natural, eco-friendly, green-technology-driven, future healthy environments that the media and mass society, via industrial capitalism, associate with sustainability.[9]

Case Study 1: The Mobile Car Wash Vendors

Throughout history, the public realm has offered sites where individuals can congregate to sell whatever it is they have to sell (McMillan 2002). Within the present city of Las Vegas, there exists a vibrant and relatively new appropriation of the street-vending typology: the mobile car wash (Figure 8.3). This case study looks at four specific mobile car wash vendors who have established their place(s) of business on the east side of Las Vegas, along Tropicana Boulevard, a major arterial road that serves as a transect from one end of the city to the other.

The opportunity for a passing motorist to make a spontaneous decision to patronize any one of the vendors creates a situation where the present city, specifically the parking lot and

FIGURE 8.3
The mobile car
wash vendor.

side streets occupied by these vendors, become reimagined and repurposed as places of both commerce and social activity. This reconstruction of public space into a potentially fluid urban typology essentially begins to initiate a street culture that would typically be negated by the poorly designed streetscapes typically found in the present city. By doing so, the vendors have not only initiated the possibility for a vital and energetic public space, they have also instigated a practice that aids in establishing a unique cultural identity of sufficiency while initiating the potential for economic sovereignty.

Two of the vendors typically set up along the edge of a parking lot owned and operated by an indoor swap meet. The swap meet itself houses independent vendors who mainly sell low-cost clothing and housewares. The other two car wash vendors that I observed are situated directly across the street alongside a strip mall development. Thus, both groups are clearly situated within the present city. By reinterpreting existing spatial conditions—that is, starting a business in a parking lot or along the street-side—the mobile car wash vendors have essentially adopted a tactic of creative entrepreneurialism that employs a logic of sufficiency dependent on visibility and informal networks of communication.

The operational set-up of the vendors is deceptively simplistic: a van, and one or two workers depending on the particular vendor. However, a closer look inside each van reveals a relatively sophisticated system of portable generators, water tanks, and high-pressure water hoses. While the set-up is approximately the same from vendor to vendor, one difference lies in their water-carrying capacity. The two vendors located in the indoor swap meet parking lot each had tanks that held 250 gallons of water, while the two vendors who set up their businesses street-side carried water tanks that held 125 gallons. Based on the size of their water tanks, the vendors are able to service anywhere from 15 to 25 cars per day respectively.

While the basic commercial premise of each vendor is the same—that is, a place where you can easily drive up and get your car washed—there are some differences between the vendors. The most significant one is that the two vendors who occupy the spaces in the swap meet parking lot pay a weekly rent to the swap meet management similar to the vendors located inside the building. When asked whether they had ever considered moving to a public side-street, like the vendors across the street, in order to not have to pay weekly rent, one vendor suggested that he had "tried it about a year ago, but the amount of customers that he gets from the swap meet parking lot make it worth paying the rent."[10] Where he would get 15 cars on a good day parked along a side-street, he almost always has 20 to 25 cars per day in the swap meet parking lot.

On most days, the vendors are able to work until their tanks are nearly empty. Each car wash also has a similar pricing schedule with the typical fee scale being "ten dollars for the outside, ten dollars for the inside, and ten dollars to clean your engine." Each particular vendor was proud to admit that all of their customers become repeat customers, a position that was verified by each of the customers who were interviewed. One, who gave his name as Anthony, stated that he had been coming to the same vendor regularly for the past four years. Ironically, prior to joining the military, Anthony owned and operated an automobile-detailing business. When asked why he chose one vendor over another he said, "I live in the neighborhood and I just pulled in here one day. I know what it takes to do a good job, and these guys do a great job, and the price is good. I used to charge a lot more for the same quality of work that these guys give." Another customer, Albert, was on his second visit to the same vendor. When asked why he decided to come back, he indicated that he also lived in the neighborhood, and that "the drive-thru car washes left scratches [on his car]." He also commented on the high quality of the work and stated, "I feel good about supporting the little guy who's trying to make a decent living."

Despite their differences, the vendors also share several commonalities. The workers are all Latino/immigrants, none of whom actually owns the mobile car wash unit. None of the vendors advertises anywhere other than via the graphic on the side of their van. Rather, each vendor relies on an informal network of word-of-mouth advertising, both from customers as well as from nearby business owners. It is not uncommon for a particular vendor to have a queue of four or five vehicles waiting to be washed. In order to accommodate their waiting customers, each vendor has their own improvised waiting area consisting primarily of plastic lawn chairs and radios tuned into popular Mexican music. In a more traditionally recognized urban design sense, the spaces created by the temporary/improvised waiting areas have the prospect to instigate the urban ideal of the chance to meet others and socialize. It is this type of situation that illustrates the often-overlooked potential that can be found in the present city. Another way in which the car wash vendors work to make their customers' wait time less taxing is by establishing symbiotic relationships with surrounding businesses; they will suggest to their customers that, while they wait, they can get a haircut, have *mariscos* (Mexican seafood) or tacos, or do some shopping or grab a snack at the indoor swap meet. These relationships work well, as the owners of these establishments also typically recommend the car wash services to their clientele.

Case Study 2: The Guerilla Marketers

In an egalitarian society, the street is a powerful emblem of the public domain (Diaz 1995; Millar 2008). It was on the street, or more specifically the sidewalk, where I made my observations of a second group of counter-actors who have initiated a similar change of socio-spatial programming, albeit in a much more ephemeral way. It is a group that I will refer to as "guerilla marketers." For the purposes of this case study, I will draw upon Blakeman's definition of guerilla marketing as an act that employs "tactics that surprise in an unexpected way for less cost than traditional advertising tactics" (2014: 37). The guerilla marketing campaigns observed in this study employ a variety of advertising materials ranging from 8.5″ × 11″ photocopies, to cardboard and ink, to vinyl lettering on plastic backing, to more stylish and sophisticated, presumably self-manufactured stickers (Figure 8.4). This case study examines a portion of Maryland Parkway, a major arterial road that borders the University of Nevada Las Vegas.

Unlike the car wash vendors, who rely on passing motorists to make a conscious decision to stop driving and become a consumer, this group employs a tactic aimed at the pedestrian. The guerilla marketers embrace the conditions and the opportunities available in the present city through their "nontraditional use of space" (Blakeman 2014: 37). While the guerilla marketers employ a non-traditional commercial tactic, it quickly becomes clear that they have the same goal as their more traditional marketplace counterparts: to sell. Based on the sheer quantity of guerilla advertisements in this portion of the present city, one can only assume that a market for their products/services exists.

It should be noted that guerilla marketing is not only a tactic employed by grassroots entrepreneurs. On the contrary, major global brands such as Taco Bell, IKEA, ING, and Volkswagen have successfully incorporated guerilla tactics into their advertising agendas (Blakeman 2014). This is not surprising, as global corporations are becoming increasingly more savvy to the fact that consumers are "overwhelmed by thousands of advertised messages a day [and] that traditional advertising does not reach as many consumers as it once did" (ibid.: 38).

As stated earlier, the actors who carry out the guerilla marketing campaigns are an anonymous group. Admittedly, the difficulty in interviewing them has thus far limited the opportunity to develop a more empirical understanding of their workflow, successes, failures, etc. However, limited though this particular case study might be with regard to primary

FIGURE 8.4
Guerilla
marketing.

empirical corroboration, it is my opinion that the social equity, economic relationships, and spatial constructs initiated by the guerillas arguably constitute a more democratic approach to engaging consumers than traditional advertising. This is because the tactics that they use are reliant upon the present city's most base constituency, the pedestrian, as well as its freely available and abundant physical infrastructure, the streets, sidewalks, and parking spaces.

Conclusion

These two groups—car wash vendors and guerilla marketers—are involved in practices that organize and utilize space in ways that are tactical, progressive, and active. Through the use of unconventional tactics, they have transformed the lackluster sidewalks and parking lots of the present city into vibrant urban "spaces." De Certeau defined space as "the effect produced by the operations that orient it, situate it, temporalize it, and make it function in a polyvalent unity of conflictual programs or contractual proximities . . . In short, space is a practiced place" (1984: 117). As such, I return to my use of the term "logic of sufficiency" and suggest that the car wash vendors and guerilla advertisers have repurposed the present city not only as commercial/advertising zones, but as distinctly identifiable urban spaces that render the possibility for a new speculative cultural grounding of sustainability that differs radically from its current hegemonic position.

It is my position that the tactics described in my two case studies have the potential to resituate the present city as a host where robust opportunities can become critically determinant factors in the construction of space in a direct yet temporal and ephemeral way. It is in such a way that these two groups have transcended the media-endorsed hegemonic ideology of sustainability. By illustrating the unique, tactical performance and formation of space as rendered by the mobile car wash vendors and guerilla marketers, I hope that I have shown that the key practices of these two groups can be drawn upon to foster a future city where it is understood that:

> [a] vital culture and sustainable development go hand in hand. Sustainability can be seen as a constant, ongoing process of searching and self-reflection about our present and our future. The search must consist of a constant review of social norms, values, and practical approaches. The search and reflection need culture as a medium to give shape to the communication that is necessary in order for sustainable development to come about in the economic, ecological, and social spheres.
>
> *(Packalen 2010: 118)*

I am fully aware that a more in-depth construction of a narrative of the practices performed by the members of these counter-hegemonic groups is necessary in order to craft a dialectical reference that can be used to more aptly translate their logic of sufficiency into a culture of sustainability that can be applied at different scales of "everyday" consumerism and city dwelling. However, for now, I will have to be content in knowing that the mobile car wash vendors and guerilla marketers found in the present city of Las Vegas offer a glimpse into a cultural logic of sufficiency that redefines spatial boundaries and traditional consumer– market transaction space(s). I feel that it is their ability to enact this culture of sufficiency that offers the most hope for crafting a more inclusive future/present city where a cultural understanding of sustainability surpasses its current ideological canon.

Notes

1 I have intentionally used the term "we" as homage to Lefebvre's (1996: 150) use of it as a metaphor to mean "those concerned."
2 From the original proposal for this book.
3 The six design paradigms that Hess defines in his book are: Cowboys 'n' Cadillacs, 1855–1940; The Early West in Modern Splendor, 1941–1945; A Place in the Sun, 1946–1957; Mass Market Stardust, 1958–1965; Beyond the Wildest Dreams of Any Roman Emperor, 1966–1980, and The Recent West in Corporate Splendor, 1981–1992.
4 Where I name MGM Resorts International as the Project CityCenter developer, it is important to note that they represent the local interest in the project. Project CityCenter is in actuality a joint venture with Infinity World Development Corp., a subsidiary of Dubai World.
5 The USGBC offers four levels of LEED rated recognition (from lowest to highest): Certified, Silver, Gold, and Platinum.
6 The Las Vegas Convention and Visitors Authority (LVCAV) is the local entity charged with attracting large-scale tourism events such as conventions, trade shows, etc. In addition, it gathers and maintains public access to data on Las Vegas-related commerce, amenities, and tourism.
7 From the original proposal for this book.
8 In order to gain a full understanding of the relationship between sufficiency and efficiency as I use it in the context of this chapter, please see Princen (2005).
9 The irony of the assumedly forward-thinking visioning associated with the contemporary ideology of sustainability is that, despite the popularity of futurist ponderings associated with its current rhetoric, the idealistic vision of a pristine, preserved, natural landscape that often accompanies this way of thinking is deeply rooted in a nineteenth-century romantic notion of aesthetics (Oerlemans 2002).
10 All of the quotes listed in this particular case study were transcribed from on-site field notes. The notes were taken over a span of approximately six weeks, with at least one visit per week.

References

Blakeman, R. (2014). *Nontraditional Media in Marketing and Advertising*. London: Sage.
Crinar, A. and Bender, T. (eds) (2007). *Urban Imaginaries: Locating the modern city*. Minneapolis, MN: University of Minnesota Press.
de Certeau, M. (1984). *The Practice of Everyday Life*, trans. S. Rendall. Berkeley, CA: University of California Press.
Diaz, D. R. (1995) Public space and culture: a critical response to conventional and postmodern visions of city life. In Darder, A. (ed.), *Culture and Difference: Critical perspectives on the bicultural experience in the United States*. Westport, CT: Bergen and Garvey, 123–138.
Donald, J. (1999). *Imagining the Modern City*. Minneapolis, MN: University of Minnesota Press.
Gledhill, C. (1997). Genre and gender: the case of soap opera. In Hall, S. (ed.), *Representation: Cultural representations and signifying practices*. London: Sage, 337–386.
Gottdiener, M. (2003). The mundane and the spectacular: everyday life in Las Vegas. In Jaschke, K. and Olsch, S. (eds), *Stripping Las Vegas: A contextual review of casino resort architecture*. Weimar: Universitätsverlag, Bauhaus-Universität Weimar, 41–50.
Hess, A. (1993). *Viva Las Vegas: After hours architecture*. San Francisco, CA: Chronicle Books.
Illia, T. (2009, February 22). Casinos pursue green practices. *Las Vegas Review Journal*. [Online]. Available: www.reviewjournal.com/business/energy/casinos-pursue-green-practices [March 21, 2010].
Joyce, P. (2003). *The Rule of Freedom: Liberalism and the modern city*. London: Verso.
Kaliski, J. (2008). The present city and the practice of city design. In Chase, J., Crawford, M., and Kaliski, J. (eds), *Everyday Urbanism: Expanded edition*. New York: Monacelli Press, 88–109.
Las Vegas Convention and Visitors Authority (LVCAV) (n.d.) *Green Initiatives*. [Online]. Available: www.lvcva.com/article/green-initiatives/811.html [December 1, 2013].
Lefebvre, H. (1996). *Writings on Cities*. Oxford: Blackwell.
McMillan, J. (2002). *Reinventing the Bazaar: A natural history of markets*. New York: W. W. Norton & Company.

Mark, M. (1973). *Modern Ideologies*. New York: St. Martin's Press.

Millar, N. (2008). Street survival: the plight of the Los Angeles street vendors. In Chase, J., Crawford, M., and Kaliski, J. (eds) *Everyday Urbanism: Expanded edition*. New York: Monacelli Press, 136–148.

Oerlemans, O. (2002). *Romanticism and the Materiality of Nature*. Toronto: University of Toronto Press.

Packalen, S. (2010, March 10). Culture and sustainability. *Corporate Social Responsibility and Environmental Management*, 17(2), 118–121. [Online]. Available: http://onlinelibrary.wiley.com/store/10.1002/csr.236/asset/236_ftp.pdf?v=1&t=hr84z8d3&s=a5f5667d7d8e20db40a7ac3158ed4b7295c14c0f [January 13, 2012].

Princen, T. (2005). *The Logic of Sufficiency*. Cambridge, MA: MIT Press.

Project CityCenter Press Room (2009). *Las Vegas' CityCenter One of the World's Largest Green Developments*. [Online]. Available: www2.citycenter.com/press_room/press_room_items.aspx?ID=845.html [December 1, 2013].

Rothman, H. (2002). *Neon Metropolis: How Las Vegas started the twenty-first century*. New York: Routledge.

Tonkiss, F. (2005). *Space, the City, and Social Theory: Social relations and urban forms*. Cambridge; Malden, MA: Polity.

U.S. Green Building Council (USGBC) (n.d.). *LEED Professional Credentials*. [Online]. Available: www.usgbc.org/credentials.html [December 1, 2013].

Venturi, R., Scott Brown, D., and Izenour, S. (1972). *Learning from Las Vegas*. Cambridge, MA: MIT Press.

World Commission on Environment and Development (WCED) (1987). *Our Common Future*. Oxford: Oxford University Press.

9

MAKING A FARM IN THE HEART OF A CITY

Osamu Nishida and Arisa Nakamura

Japan has faced a serious agriculture problem in recent years. In 2012, according to the Ministry of Agriculture, Forestry, and Fisheries, the nation's food self-sufficiency rate dropped below 40 percent (MAFF 2013). Compared with other industrialized countries, the rate is dismal.[1] The aging farming population and the diminishing number of new farmers are also major issues facing the agrarian future of the nation. Japan's agricultural census in 2010 reported that the total farming population in Japan is about 2.6 million, about only 1 percent of the total national population. In addition, 61.6 percent of the farmers are 65 years old or older (MAFF 2012). In the very near future, Japan will face a drastic decrease in the size of the agricultural labor force. The rural population has already been in decline in recent decades. In the national census conducted from 2005 to 2010, 72 percent of the municipalities had experienced depopulation (MLITT 2013). On the other hand, all 12 cities with populations of more than 100 million had experienced growth. This means the gap between urban and rural populations has been growing.

Roppongi Nouen is a restaurant in the Roppongi district of Tokyo, which was established in response to this growing disparity between the urban and rural communities in Japan (Figure 9.1). Specifically, it was conceived to foster a stronger connection between the city and the country. The main purposes of Roppongi Nouen are first to stimulate the agricultural awareness of business people in Tokyo who are descendants of farming families, and second to serve as a place to enjoy the taste of homegrown food and experience the importance and joy of farming. The restaurant aims to be a place that can nurture various kinds of connections: between children of farmers in the city and farming families in the rural area; between people in different fields in the same rural area; and between urban residents and farmers.

Roppongi Nouen: The Beginning (2008)

Roppongi Nouen was started by a non-profit organization, Children of Farmers, that was founded by a group of business people in Tokyo who are descendants of farming families. The organization had about 200 members and a network of 30 media firms when it was

FIGURE 9.1 Full view of Roppongi Nouen.

formally launched in March 2009. The founders were not farmers themselves, but they aimed to support their parents, who are farmers, and help other young start-up farmers to stand on their own feet, and ultimately cope with the serious social issues facing rural communities in Japan today. Yusuke Miyaji, the representative of the organization and the son of a hog farmer himself, described the activities of the organization as follows: "Our goal is to change the perception of the farming industry from what is currently thought of as the 3K industry—*kitsui* (hard), *kitanai* (dirty), and *kakkowarui* (uncool)—to a new 3K industry— *kakkoii* (cool), *kandou* (touching), and *kasegeru* (profitable)."[2]

Miyaji and other members recognized that the fastest way to change the current situation is to provide the children of farmers with the business experience necessary for them to be able to return to their hometowns and take up farming. Even before the organization was officially founded, members had been engaged in various activities as a way to work toward achieving this goal. By participating in the Hills Marché, for instance, they raised interest in the local farming industry and their production sites by selling locally grown vegetables in Roppongi every weekend. Located near the center of Tokyo, the largest and one of the most developed metropolises in the world, Roppongi district is well known as a place for cutting-edge culture and art—the complete opposite to the image of the farming industry. By choosing such a district as the site for promoting agriculture, the organizers tried to make a big impact by changing the public perception of the farming industry. By 2008, when their activities started to take root in the city, a project was initiated to provide a place where people interested in the act of farming and the vegetables themselves (both growing and eating) could get together on a daily basis. This project materialized into a restaurant where customers can eat vegetables shipped directly from the production sites.

The restaurant is the result of Children of Farmers' aim to sell food crops grown in its members' hometowns, to broaden the market for consumption by developing branding strategies through the voices of customers, and ultimately to help the farmers in its members' hometowns directly. This was a meaningful project in terms of creating a platform to connect the urban and rural areas through a new concept of agriculture. Traditionally, farm products go into distribution without the producers' name, face, and stories of the production sites. The new concept is about establishing a platform to share knowledge between the urban and rural areas and bring forth a deeper understanding of agriculture, the production sites, and the rural communities.

Sharing and Networking (August 2009–)

Roppongi Nouen has been evolving since its establishment in 2009, and will be continuously expanding in the future. In describing how this project has evolved since its establishment, we—ON Design, an architectural firm and a member of the project team for Roppongi Nouen—would like to introduce how the team developed the concept and how they engaged people in this project through various activities.

Experimental Farm Restaurant: Roppongi Nouen

At the end of 2008, the project began with our client, "Team Roppongi Nouen," which consisted of approximately ten members, including Yusuke Miyaji, the representative of Children of Farmers, and a few other restaurant chefs who were all descendants of farming families. The site of the experimental farm restaurant was formerly a French restaurant and was situated on a corner surrounded by commercial buildings located just behind Roppongi Street, in the heart of the dense urban area of Roppongi. The plan was to update the interior while keeping as much of the key functionality remaining from the former French restaurant (Figure 9.2).

The design for the interior renovation was inspired by advice given to us by a local farmer, who said, "earth is an important property for farmers." Inspired by these words, we decided on the concept of "earth" for the interior. To carry out the concept, we asked farmers throughout Japan to offer earth from their land to create earthen interior walls for the restaurant. To make these walls, we organized a series of workshops to have them built by hand by the children of farmers and city people interested in farming. City residents were recruited on the internet using slogans such as, "Recruiting for building earthen wall," and "Participants can eat curry and rice using vegetables from farmers for lunch." Nearly 200 people signed up online. The successful recruitment led us to feel that urbanites were hungry to touch nature since they do not often have the opportunity to do so.

The key idea for the interior design was to share the value of earth, "an important property for farmers," and to draw attention not only to the crops sold in the market but also to the earth and soil that nurture the crops and the spirit of the farmers who provided the earth from the countryside to the city. For this project, the interior walls of the building were covered with earth by hand to the height of the table on the first floor to represent and resemble new ground and to enhance the attractiveness of the vegetables through the texture of the earth. Vegetables delivered from the farm are displayed on the new ground and food is prepared right in front of the customers, which is then served as delicious cuisine. The

FIGURE 9.2 Previous interior of Roppongi Nouen.

walls and floors below the table, as well as the entire basement floor, were also planned to be finished with earth.

The Roppongi Nouen restaurant had a preliminary opening in June 2009. At that time, the interior of the restaurant was still bare; its former interior from the French restaurant was stripped out without additional modifications. During the temporary opening, weekend workshops were held over a period of two months. Earth was used to cover the cold, empty space little by little, under the direction of Naoki Kusumi, a leading expert in plasterwork who is also active abroad. The workshops gave many people opportunities to experience the process of transforming the space step-by-step with earth (Figure 9.3). The process also gave the customers a sense of the evolution of the space. The volunteers engaged in hands-on plasterwork under the supervision of Kusumi. The final touch was entrusted entirely to Kusumi, who also played a role as the general director of this activity. He thought that the formal atmosphere typically seen in a Japanese tearoom would be neither necessary nor appropriate for the space. He saw value in the hand marks created at the workshops, and thus preserved them to express the rusticity of the earth. By the end of the series of workshops, the earth and the spirit of the farmers were molded into a stunning space by the hard work of the farmers' children and the people in the city. This was the moment when the hearts of the farmers, their children, and the people in the city came together as one (Figure 9.4).

Since its completion in 2009, the experimental farm restaurant has become a place not only to enjoy a meal but also to share a vision among people who participate in the many ongoing events. One such event is called Farmers Live, which is held as many as ten times a month. In this event, farmers and their adult children come to the restaurant during a meal and introduce their production site and explain the crops' nutritional values from their

FIGURE 9.3 Workshop for covering the interior wall with earth.

FIGURE 9.4 After the workshop.

FIGURE 9.5 Farmers Live.

perspective as producers. Farmers Live provides an opportunity for direct interaction and communication between consumers and producers, creating a close tie between rural and urban areas. It also helps to raise consciousness towards other issues, such as food safety (Figure 9.5).

Roppongi Nouen Farm (July 2010)

Children of Farmers has also served as part of the executive team for the Hills Marché, which is held on a vacant parking lot right next to Roppongi Nouen. The parking lot is owned by a local developer and is slated for future redevelopment. The owner has been organizing the Marché regularly as part of a regional contribution project.[3] In 2010, an effort was initiated to seek an alternative use of this temporary space.

While the developer acknowledged that the parking lot was the most profitable way to use the temporary space, he also recognized that the Marché has brought a great crowd and liveliness to the community, which has added significant value to the city. Sharing this common view, the developer and Team Roppongi Nouen came up with an idea to use half of the parking lot as an exterior extension of the restaurant.

Inside the restaurant, the customers are able to engage with vegetables, either as-is or through the form of cuisine. With the exterior extension, we looked into expanding this engagement by creating a space in which people can observe vegetables growing (while eating), and satisfy their curiosity in farming beyond processed vegetables. Our aim was to achieve a more realistic experience at both Roppongi Nouen and Roppongi Nouen Farm by putting the production and consumption activities side by side under the theme of agriculture.

To allow for possible relocation in the future, the foundations of the farm greenhouse were built on precast concrete and placed directly on top of the asphalt of the parking lot. The glass units used for the greenhouse are modified versions of those used at temporary construction sites. They were made simply by fitting a glass sash into a common steel frame. These pop-up units can also be rented out to the local authority or farmers in the country-side as an advertisement display for their products, which is much more economical than opening a pilot shop in the city. The seedlings in the units are from the farmers and cared for in the greenhouse by the staff of Roppongi Nouen. A proportion of the vegetables grown in the greenhouse is harvested, cooked, and served to the customers in the restaurant.

This idea of agricultural display has never been attempted before, and it drew a lot of attention from the local citizens. Prior to the opening of the Farm, Roppongi Nouen was functioning as the connection hub between the city and the countryside, but it alone was not providing enough of a visual and spatial intervention to the Roppongi district. Through the subsequent opening of Roppongi Nouen Farm, a connection between the rural and urban was created both visually and spatially. The site has since become a new public space in the city.

Roppongi Nouen Yard (August 2011–)

Building on the success of the temporary use of the vacant lot next door for Roppongi Nouen Farm, Team Roppongi Nouen made a decision to expand this project further in the following year to take advantage of the remaining space in the parking lot. This project was planned with an even smaller budget than Roppongi Nouen Farm, to account for the shorter leasing period of the space and to minimize the cost expected for future relocation. Taking into account these restrictions, the team decided to peel off the asphalt and reveal the earth below so that the design matched with the interior space of Roppongi Nouen and the deck terrace of the Farm. The landscape was constructed by planting trees and by paving the remaining section with earthen materials. The conversion of the pavement from asphalt to dirt reduced the amount of heat reflection, and provided a more pleasant environment for the neighborhood.

The project, called Roppongi Nouen Yard, is arranged as a pocket park, and is open to not only the customers of Roppongi Nouen but also the general public during the day. During business hours, the space can also be used as an outdoor seating and event space for Roppongi Nouen, contributing to the business of the restaurant. Due to the site's location at the dead-end of a road, further expansion of the project would be difficult. To maximize the use of such limited space, the team constructed a deck staircase to allow access to and from the site. The intent of the design was to express the project's active involvement with the surrounding urban environment from both tangible (construction projects) and intangible (workshops and events) points of view.

While the Yard project itself does not strongly reflect the concept of "agriculture" as Roppongi Nouen and Roppongi Nouen Farm do, the Yard does allow its users to take in and share the concept of Roppongi Nouen and the Farm through spatial interaction. Unlike parks that are arranged by the local government under regulation, the Yard is a space shaped by the public, even though it is privately owned.

Rural–Urban Communications

The Roppongi Nouen project began with the concept of connecting urban and rural areas by redefining the image and meaning of "agriculture" for urbanites. The project team has made efforts in getting as many people involved as possible through various activities. More than 80 farmers throughout Japan are currently involved in this project, many of them introduced by Children of Farmers. By removing the barriers between agricultural producers and consumers and enhancing communication between them, we have found that many problems can be solved successfully. Specifically, we believe that a new style of successful urban community can be achieved by engaging people from different positions and backgrounds to communicate with each other. It is becoming more and more important that people communicate strategically with each other on an equal footing, and that everyone can play various roles, sometimes as a student and sometimes as a teacher.

Roppongi Nouen has continued to develop as a place where farm producer and consumer can talk to each other face to face using the restaurant as a platform. We believe that the connection between the city and the production site can be created not only through the need for healthy food for consumers, but also through active engagement between the public and the production site behind the product. The value of agriculture in the city has become increasingly monolithic as the emphasis is put on efficiency, homogeneity, and security. Through close interaction with farmers, Roppongi Nouen engages both consumers and farmers to respect each other's diverse situations, and encourages more heterogeneous social values in the city.

Initiating Cycles

Creating an opportunity for the public to participate in the city is important. However, it is even more important to have many participants who understand the essence and concept of the project. While Roppongi Nouen cannot provide the full experience of farming, our vision is to communicate the key concepts behind the project through an experience, and eventually to provide an opportunity for participants to visit a real farm.

Nippon Travel Restaurant is one attempt to provide such an opportunity. Started in 2010, this program offers a travel package to participants who are interested in learning about the farmers and farming methods from their experience at Roppongi Nouen. The participants travel to a farm in the countryside, experience the production process, and taste the locally grown vegetables. In addition to experiencing the farm and outdoor restaurants, they can also enjoy local recreational activities. Through these activities, the participants are able to get to know the region through the food, come to like it, and hopefully return there again. One of the functions of Roppongi Nouen is to initiate this cycle.

Roppongi Nouen also serves as a starting point of another cycle, from the perspective of the farmers. Yusuke Miyaji of Children of Farmers points out, "Roppongi Nouen can serve as an alternative outlet for their vegetables." In Japan, the traditional distribution of crops is handled by the Japanese Agricultural Group (JA), which involves shipping the crops in standard boxes and obtaining a large amount of stable profit through economies of scale. Due to this shipping process, farmers have focused on the industrial aspect of agriculture to maximize the number of products that meet the standard. The option of private distribution allows farmers to ship products that are outside of those standards. This enables farmers to manage and market their own products. Roppongi Nouen provides farmers with an opportunity to get into private distribution, to have access to customers, and to advertise their products through activities such as Farmers Live.

Ongoing Experiment in the Heart of the City

Roppongi Nouen will continue to evolve and reflect the various values, wills, and strategies of many participants. We expect the project to grow and improve as the participants continue to appreciate, reinterpret, and reflect on the concept. In order for Roppongi Nouen to continue to evolve, it is important to combine new ideas and methods that go beyond urban areas, as put forth by Children of Farmers. This never-ending evolution will help expand our concepts into a wider region and population, and serves as an even grander motivation to sustain and improve the project.

The earthquake that hit the eastern region of Japan in 2011 raised many concerns about the food supply and safety among many people in Japan. This has fueled an increased need for ensuring security in food products and transparency in how food is produced for urban areas. This calls for a tighter connection between the urban and the rural, and a heightened awareness of how they can complement each other. A tighter connection is achieved through people; consumers in urban areas need to recognize that they are paying money to support farmers, not just vegetables.

In an industrialized society, people are inundated with information and countless consumer products. In order to catalyze change in society, it is crucial that people share this concept by participating in its synthesis, and that a new cycle, closely connecting the city and the country, is engendered. As mentioned previously, Roppongi Nouen aims to provide a connection between the city and the rural area in reaction to agricultural and social issues. Not only does it connect consumers to producers, it also helps the children of farmers to broaden the market and return to their hometowns.

Activities such as Farmers Live allow consumers to learn about the production sites and crops. Through Nippon Travel Restaurant, people in the city can visit the production sites in person and get to know the region through the food. In addition, Roppongi Nouen Farm and Yard both provide a new public space for people in the city to observe vegetables growing in front of their eyes. The project also offers a new opportunity for farmers to find alternative distribution networks for their products. As exemplified by the various activities listed above, Roppongi Nouen creates new connections between the city and rural areas at multiple levels. We expect the project to continue its experiments in the heart of the city— experiments that will forge and establish a never-ending connection between the city and the country.

Notes

1 In 2010, the food self-sufficiency rates for the United States, Germany, and the United Kingdom were 124 percent, 80 percent, and 65 percent respectively (MAFF 2011).
2 Interview with Yusuke Miyaji of Children of Farmers in June 2013.
3 Generally, regional contribution projects are operated by land owners and developers. By setting specific rules and adopting specific planning strategies that contribute to solving regional issues, they can receive an incentive in return.

References

Ministry of Agriculture, Forestry, and Fisheries (MAFF) (2011). *FY2010 Annual Report on Food, Agriculture, and Rural Areas in Japan Summary*. [Online]. Available: www.maff.go.jp/e/annual_report/2010/pdf/e_all.pdf [November 29, 2013].

Ministry of Agriculture, Forestry, and Fisheries (MAFF) (2012). *Digest of the Results of the 2010 World Census of Agriculture and Forestry*. [Online]. Available: www.e-stat.go.jp/SG1/estat/ListE.do?bid=000001037762&cycode=0 [November 29, 2013].

Ministry of Agriculture, Forestry, and Fisheries (MAFF) (2013). *FY2012 Annual Report on Food, Agriculture, and Rural Areas in Japan*. [Online]. Available: www.maff.go.jp/j/wpaper/w_maff/h24/pdf/e_all.pdf [November 29, 2013].

Ministry of Land, Infrastructure, Transport, and Tourism (MLITT) (2013). *Evolution of Investments by the Ministry of Land, Infrastructure, Transport and Tourism for Local Revitalization*. [Online]. Available (in Japanese): www.mlit.go.jp/hakusyo/mlit/h18/hakusho/h19/html/i1121000.html [November 29, 2013].

10

BORDER URBANITIES

Embodied and Enacted Performances in a Transnational City

Irma Ramirez

In the testing environment of architectural culture, where constructed images of reality continuously develop in the design studio, and the art of making dwindles in a continuous state of redefinition, the values of a long-standing profession are challenged. Fast-changing technologies rapidly expand the realm of possibility in form making, design representation and construction. These revolutionizing advancements immerse themselves in architectural education and challenge a fundamental notion that the user is of utmost importance. Image replaces functionality, modeling replaces experience, and the learning processes erode. "We live in a world," as the French cultural theorist Jean Baudrillard has postulated, "where there is more and more information and less and less meaning" (Baudrillard 1994: 79). The learning process of architectural education becomes a "remote performance," an isolated process lacking in meaning and existing in its own fabricated realities in which the designer is the author and the user is the audience. In remote performance, the author and the user fail to connect. This essay criticizes remote performance as a means of making cities, and explores architecture as a "live performance" of characters with diverse cultures and values interacting on a common stage to create a meaningful narrative for a multiplicity of audiences and settings.

The location for this experiment in architectural pedagogy is Tijuana, Mexico, itself the theater for a real-life migration drama played out between Mexico and the United States all along their common border. American and Mexican participants work together in this project to test approaches in placemaking. Specifically, we posit a relationship between the structures of the community and the intensity and endurance of people's connections to it. The project, a two-year experimental model, approaches the design studio as a performance in its capacity to reintroduce meaning through the ideas of "embodiment" and "enactment" in product execution. The strategies serve to evaluate the pedagogy of teaching fundamentals; to explore architectural education as an engine of social change; and as a way of reintroducing the audience as a participatory entity that activates and co-creates.

Border Context

Bordering the United States at San Diego, California, the Mexican city of Tijuana has grown in its transnational role fueled by its economic interdependency with the United States. Seen primarily for its illicit entertainment nature, the city's indistinct urban fabric is at first glance devoid of architectural significance. Beyond the tourist gaze, however, exists an unfamiliar urbanity of intense social realism in which architects as screenwriters have played a limited role. The irregular un-urbanized patterns lacking cohesion are rich with intuitive self-help building practices displaying a vivid creation of place with profuse human character. This is a flexible place, a place of hybrid nature, and a place of diverse characters all performing to subsist. The social arena stricken by poverty fuels temporary shelters, resulting in temporal neighborhoods free of precedent and defined identity, yet with a mindset open to experimental solutions. The lack of means is a prompt for resourcefulness and therefore an architectural lesson allowing characters to step outside traditional roles and systems in order to deploy personal narratives. Tijuana serves as a site in which designers as authors must co-write the script with the audience: an educational possibility for designers to develop consciousness and diverse definitions of the value of place through the process of community-led design and construction.

In postmodern thought, Tijuana's rural portrayal as a collage of urban naivety and embattled immigration terrain often comes to light in the academic and professional circles as a hypothetical discussion and an image of inspiration rather than a reality in need of solutions and implementation. Mainstream political and economic discourse incites particular interest for articulating border concepts, making its hypothetical and theoretical interpretations fashionably hyperreal (Baudrillard 1994). Simulated versions of reality are evoked: images of sin city, incivility and chaos, and an immigrant war zone. This much imagined, much theorized, and (un)alluring Tijuana remains a set of sub-urbanities, an isolated human fabric devoid of infrastructure, and constantly in the process of its reinvented survival.

FIGURE 10.1 Informal communities in Tijuana lack basic urban infrastructure and cohesion; however, the informal acquisition and use of the land lends itself to a constantly changing urban landscape primarily shaped by user interaction.

FIGURE 10.2 Mexico–US border fence.

Mexico's border cities have historically experienced accelerated demographic growth resulting from internal migrations fueled by initiatives such as the 1942 Bracero Program and the 1965 Border Industrialization Program. These, among other migration waves, inherently make the urbanization problems of Tijuana a bilateral and transnational issue (Enriquez Acosta, 2009). Many have arrived with the intent of crossing over to the United States in search of promised economic and social advancement. However, many fail to do so and remain in the region, adding to the accelerated growth of the city. Despite their best efforts, local governments have been unable to accommodate and adapt infrastructural growth for these new immigrant communities, leading to a deteriorating urban border environment. More recent years have also seen a new flux of immigrants as millions of people are deported from the United States. Since 2008, more than 461,000 immigrants have been dropped off in Tijuana (Cave 2013). A total of four million people have been deported since 2002, adding even more stress to the city and surrounding informal communities.

Border cities such as Tijuana, with explosive growth patterns and fast changes, are left with the "superimposition and adjacency of incomplete urbanism," and a constant hybrid and "deterritorialized" character (Mendez and Rodriguez 2009: 479). Mendez and Rodriguez (ibid.) describe the border city as the "transitory city," the "passing through city," and the "defensive city," stemming from recorded perceptions of residents. They find that, as a "passing through city," a border city promotes the "anti-encounters" leading to the restriction and constant vigilance of the public space (ibid.). The border is a regulating entity meant to be crossed—an action done legally and illegally, leading to its contentious culture and to the abundance of opportunistic illicit activities constantly reinventing themselves and making the public sphere a heightened space of awareness.

Context Opportunities

Informal communities, quickly and organically growing on the hillsides of Tijuana, clearly pose great challenges as well as opportunities. The organic proliferation has a life of its own.

The government effort, unable to keep up with the added infrastructural need, for the most part, lets the life of the communities self-define the public domain. The private domain expands to the urban arena in scales seemingly beyond the reach of the architect's education—training traditionally confined to the regulated building envelope.

Regulation, an inherent part of architectural education embedded in the culture of safety and urban order, often limits the role of architects in making their work a meaningful public performance beyond the established boundaries. In the context of Tijuana, the potential design interventions have no predefined confines and the public and private realms are fluid with one another. The network of dwellings built up against the US–Mexico border is a live stage constantly changing—an opportunity requiring probing experiments that expand the definition of responsibility beyond the traditional confines of safety and order. The self-help culture of Tijuana opens up the opportunity to bring people together through the process of communal design and collaborative building processes to instill a sense of pride, self-worth, and emotional attachment of residents to the larger place. The success of placemaking lies in the creation of *meaning* and *value* to build ties between people and place.

The InfoStructure Project

The Tijuana Studio is a course at Cal Poly Pomona. In this studio, the development of creative approaches towards making these Mexican communities more livable is explored through a multidisciplinary partnership between the university, faculty, students, community, and non-profit organizations with established social networks in place. The project entails developing urban tactics materialized into urban furniture, artifacts that in this project are referred to as "InfoStructures." The project's name relates to its intent of creating an *infrastructural* network within the local neighborhood dynamics; its role is to disseminate information, a powerful element of making and strengthening community ties in an area where telephone infrastructure is minimally available. Each urban artifact in the public realm of the community becomes a stage of public life. Community documentation, analysis, and assessment performed by students with community input dictate the number of InfoStructures necessary to make successful social communication, clear urban connections, and enriching public performance. Their urban assemblage assists in the creation of a cohesive urban landscape and establishes a more defined community identity. The Tijuana Studio has now built 14 InfoStructures in the communities of Cumbres, Flores Magón, Nuevo Milenio, and Pedregal. The lessons lie in the making of an object that is un-prejudiced by predetermined classification of function or nomenclature, social or cultural. The process attempts to reinstate meaning into making and capitalizes on the specific characteristics of a cross-border culture.

Remote Performance: The Loss of Meaning

Often, architectural education is a model of isolated practices stimulated by technological advancement, supported by the architectural critic as the audience, and diffused by the imagery of graphic media. Working within the boundaries of the design studio, these elements confine architectural students to a permanent state of rehearsal, gaining proficiency in a hyperreal practice and ensuring the accumulation of the student's portfolio of un-built work. Knowledge is limited to the classroom and supported by images; experience is substituted with digital three-dimensional modeling; the art of making is replaced by hypothetical construction details; and product function and feasibility are validated by the architectural critic. Within this closed circle of experts as the exclusive audience, and with the student as the sole author of the narrative, the author is unaware of the user as audience and thereby fails to develop design communication skills for multiple audiences, skills that would in practice ensure the design's public success. The teaching of architectural ideas in a real-life scenario with audience input is a challenge that begins with the commitment to utilize real-world opportunities as stages of performance, a move that breaks down pre-established methods of the profession and calls for shared authorship with the audience.

Another element that has boosted and revolutionized remote performance as the increasing norm, rather than the exception, is technology. Architecture relies on scientific knowledge, a reason for which technical innovation is of the essence. Advancements in drawing techniques, photography, and digital media open up new possibilities for architects, but have also crippled human ability and isolated designers from the people they design for. Measured drawing, for example, makes it possible to detail intent and system mechanics, thus relieving the architect from overseeing construction. Similarly, photography allows us to see a copy of reality, replacing the test of experience. Regularly making its way into the design studio through architectural magazines, the image makes visiting a building a disappointing or life-changing experience, depending on the previewed "saturated image" in architectural media (Leach 1999). Technology additionally allows for design exploration and testing technical performances within the confines of the classroom, no doubt of tremendous value to a profession whose product is expensive to produce. However, so detailed is the delivery of technology that the *model* becomes the testing of itself and the idea. The limitless fluid possibilities in form making today irresponsibly contribute to the further detachment of the designer from the issues of social and local relevance that could make the architect a true force in global problem solving. Finnish architect and Professor of Architecture Juhani Pallasmaa states in his paper "Architecture and the Human Nature: Searching for a Sustainable Metaphor" that:

> in the age of ecology the concept of "form" has to be seen as a temporal process, or emergent situation, rather than a closed and finite aesthetic entity . . . I do not support any romantic bio-morphic architecture. I advocate an architecture that arises from a respect of nature in its complexity . . . and from empathy and loyalty to all forms of life and humility about our own destiny.
>
> *(Pallasmaa 2011: 5)*

Pallasmaa believes that educational reform is necessary; that our "daily practices and education have to be fundamentally re-valuated . . . giv(ing) up the hubris of regarding ourselves as the centre piece of the Universe and as the Homo sapiens who know" (ibid.: 6). He criticizes the "obsessive idea of perpetual growth . . . (and) the suicidal course of industrial civilizations" (ibid.: 9) which does not question our building processes, civil state, and inherent connection to nature. The form and function of our industrial civilizations are greatly perpetuated by the format via context, content via program, and technology via media used in our architectural classrooms. In its different evolutions and iterations, technology has contributed to the isolation of skills from product, the misunderstanding of place as lived experience, and the loss of meaning and inability of built form to enrich the human condition.

Putting into question the remote nature of architectural education is a painful blow to the architect's ego and his specialized studio methodologies and technologies. Schneekloth and Shibley ascertain that "shifting architecture beyond expert culture would require us to love, or at least tolerate, complexity and contradiction by denying architectural expertise a privileged status in the discourse of making" (2000: 130). Instead, such a shift can "affirm the power of architecture to make substantial contributions to the messy vitality of everyday life in service of the promise of lives well lived" (ibid.). Our profession has lost the ability to make meaningful places because we demean the work that maintains our daily lives and value only extraordinary acts of building, an activity delegated to experts (Boyer and Mitang 1996).

Embodied Performance: Ascertaining Meaning

The isolated processes of remote performance threaten the existence of "place" and "human experience" and promote architecture as a commodity rather than a practical and meaningful entity in people's lives. Architecture performs only through human interaction; it formulates a meaningful physical condition and/or psychological state of mind, and as architectural product, it is then "embodied performance," one which satisfies physical necessity and which mounts a psychological influence on the characters. In this sense, embodied performance is capable of public impact, reaching intended and unintended audiences and consequently making its successful meaning based on a state of *awareness* on a common public stage.

In Tijuana, extreme character oppositions force learned and cultured knowledge of human nature, and require thoughtful study of context to ascertain *meaning*. Although this is a complicated responsibility in a field catering to multiple audiences, a structured effort can attain the social sustainability of the architectural performance, even with the complexities and biases of culture and social strata. A starting point is the understanding of *meaning* and *value* in a cross-cultural scenario. Jean Baudrillard discusses four value principles by which people bestow value: "a functional logic of use value" that evaluates the usefulness of an object; "an economic logic of exchange value" assessed by economic or trade worth; "a logic of symbolic exchange" given by the representational meaning of the individual's own experiences and through the manner in which the object is exchanged; and "a logic of sign value" assigned within societal or communally accepted norms (1981: 66). Although the priority of these value systems changes according to context, these fundamentals in the production of architectural performance can serve as a guide for anticipating audience acceptance.

Performance of Functional Value

Ensuring functional value in this project developed from conversations with members of the community and community organizations, and the detailed observations and categorizations of studio research. For the purpose of the community and the non-profit organization, the need was for an effective means of *communication*, a key aspect of community survival, networking, and growth. The primary need to disseminate information in a zone with limited infrastructure opened up the possibility of the InfoStructure, whose main function for the community at large is to serve as a space of expression, a conveyor of community affairs, and a delineator of the public domain.

The lack of traditional urban form, such as the traditional street and the plaza, allows for architecture as performance to take on the roles of these traditional forms in a constantly morphing landscape. The InfoStructures have become "urban markers," generating landmarks and gathering spaces, and making an alternative urban infrastructure within the volatile context.

Programming undergoes two dimensions of co-creation: program intent is established by the studio instructor as director, secondary programming is executed by the student screenwriter, and reprogramming is done by the audience, giving the InfoStructures life as shelters, playgrounds, community gardens, taco stands, bus stops, and, in one instance, the site of a wedding ceremony.

Performance of Exchange Value

A unique quality of the partner organization is its belief in promoting a self-help culture and social pride philosophy, a strategy that sets the basis for a socially sustainable community with prospects for individuals to grow and care for themselves. An individual or family participating in the network is required to perform community work hours that can then be exchanged for any of the services provided by the organization, among those the construction of a compact wood-frame shelter. For the people of Tijuana, participating in projects

FIGURE 10.3 An InfoStructure with planted seating areas and message board. The formal exploration is expressive of the "heart" of the community. Post-project evaluation showed that the structure acquired several nicknames—among them, "the tooth" and "the lungs"—for its formal expression.

FIGURE 10.4 An InfoStructure with a bamboo canopy on a steel structure featuring seating and posting areas became an informal meeting point for community-building activities as well as an informal bus stop.

for the common good ensures an entire community as a support system in times of need. This non-monetary means of assistance eliminates exchange for reasons other than self-improvement. As a means of community building, this is a system that instills social pride as people utilize the value of their work to obtain benefits, and therefore attribute *exchange value* to the benefits received. A different model of non-profit organization provides assistance without anything in exchange, thus promoting a state of poverty in which work is not a necessary means of improving oneself. A person who invests labor in the creation of something is more likely to care for it by association with the exchange value required for its production. People's participation in the construction of the InfoStructures therefore increases the possibilities of the structures' survival in the community and the likelihood of people remaining in the community on a more permanent basis.

Developing trust is a second strategy allowing the community to identify the performance's intentions. Presenting the functional value of the structures was the first step in building exchange value required for a lasting partnership. This was accomplished through the relationship with the non-profit organization, its permanent presence in the community, and its philosophy of individual work for the common good, all elements that ensure exchange value on the part of the community.

Performance of Symbolic Value

Environments with great needs and limited resources lead people to develop attachment to objects beyond their economic or exchange values in search of meaningful lives. This act of

FIGURE 10.5 The family involved in the design and building of this InfoStructure took pride and ownership of it. Known as "la sombrilla" or the umbrella, the structure became a community garden cared for primarily by the family.

self-awareness is important in nurturing relationships with the environment and community at large, and it is this personal experience that ensures social sustainability. In Baudrillard's terms, "what we perceive in the symbolic object is not only the concrete manifestation of a total relationship of desire; but also, through the singularity of an object, the transparency of social relationships in a dual or integrated group relationship" (1981: 65–66). Embodiment occurs as the InfoStructures facilitate micro-performances that empower the audience in its individual or communal form to co-write the script and thereby construct self-awareness. In turn, the architecture's success as embodied performance relies on the symbolic value that people can attribute to it as facilitators of self-identity and place finding.

The audience's participation in the *making process* is equally productive in developing symbolic value. The construction collaboration developed into personal relationships of friendship and gratitude, and a sense of accomplishment between screenwriters and audience. As part of a strategy to enable audience participation, the students organized community workshops. In one of them, the community developed art work in the form of 12″ × 12″ mosaic tiles. The tiles display personal and communal themes, and the medium is a flexible and forgiving aesthetic product appropriate for a variety of skill levels—an important element ensuring the individual's pride. One technique used to initiate the exchange was to present the workshop for its functional value, which is the acquisition of the tile-setting skill. As community members gained trust with the students, the symbolic value developed into a

FIGURE 10.6 A resident from the community makes a personal decorative tile during the project workshop. All tiles made by the community were installed on the InfoStructures.

relationship of trust that allowed personal symbols to emerge in the mosaic tiles. The finished pieces were then installed in the public domain of the InfoStructures. On one level, the tiles provide symbolic value through the personalization of the structure by the individual, and on another level they instill community pride and identity.

Sign Value

The macro-scale of self-awareness can also be measured by "sign value," a measured condition in which the human being relates to the larger society beyond the personal arena and the communal space. Baudrillard argues that, "[t]he object-become-sign no longer gathers its meaning in the concrete relationship between two people. It assumes its meaning in its differential relationship to other signs" (ibid.: 66). Sign value in Baudrillard's terms is a result of comparative observation of other signs functioning in a common mainstream. The planning of Baroque Rome, for example, owed its sign value to the superimposition of the ordained urban plan of Pope Sixtus V onto the chaotic city of Rome. Sixtus' urban plan to reorganize the city with respect to the location of the major churches supported the image of the church as a sign of unity, cohesiveness, and order. The sign value of the urban performance in this respect enabled the city to evolve as an entity.

In Tijuana, the urban chaos of the communities is a result of squatting as a survival mechanism. User attention goes to defining personal space, and human care and identity therefore focus on the home, leaving the public sphere barren, undefined, and unclaimed. A major role of the InfoStructures is to activate this public sphere and to structure urban

FIGURE 10.7 The InfoStructure detail reads "Corazón" (heart) as requested by the community to stand for "Familia Corazón," the name of the local non-profit organization that uses the InfoStructures to post announcements to disseminate information and mobilize the people.

cohesiveness. They network to create urban order by becoming navigational reference points in the absence of street signs.

Enacted Performance: Testing the Model through Implementation

"Enacted performance" in this architectural process is characterized by the implementation of the research, design, and rehearsal leading to the product. The stages of fabrication, use, and post-project evaluation provide a final ground for attaining self-awareness. As a performance of multiple characters, the necessary fundamentals for implementation are communication skills, a flexible mindset, resourcefulness in the art of making, and receptiveness to criticism. The specific language and communication skills vary from site to site; therefore, what is important is to facilitate the learning of resourcefulness and flexibility through the enacted stage of production.

Communication

Tijuana poses the added challenge of language and culture to the collaborative process as a lesson for architecture students. Though English is widely spoken in the border region, in the majority of informal neighborhoods, the primary and often only understood language is

Spanish. However, rather than constituting a problem, the language barrier serves to break down preconceptions and to alleviate cultural tensions. By stripping language from the audience–author relationship, students and residents engage in creative communication at the most fundamental human level. For students as authors, the loss of architectural lingo can be a frustrating and humbling experience as the primary method of understanding is now sensory and experiential. First-hand exposure to the community builds a newly-formed concept of *value* as students understand the people's priorities, which are often different than those valued in the United States.

The first encounter with the community was frustrating but enlightening. In every instance where the community expressed aesthetic interest in the structures, the questions revolved around a dialogue of function and cultural relevance. Students' customary focus on aesthetics quickly took second stage. Breaking down role preconceptions in the dialogues made the student as screenwriter fully aware of his or her audience's needs; for the community, communication with the screenwriter was an empowering self-awareness tool in which their opinion was deemed of revered importance. Another challenge of communication was graphic presentation to an audience not adept in reading architectural drawings. This apparent limitation, however, led to the creative production of hybrid media employing digital, analog, and photographic means. As a teaching tool, the limited means of the communities resulted in a reversal of technical advancement and a reliance on human ability. Without computers on site that could run a digital model, students often experienced frustrating self-awareness at having to pick up a pencil to draw what they are nowadays accustomed to doing with digital media. Similarly, construction problems that arose led to creative solutions, in view of the lack of a hardware store.

Materials and Systems

Equally challenging was the construction process, during which students built the InfoStructures side by side with the community. Unable to communicate through either spoken word or the traditional architectural detail drawing, students resorted to building physical models of details as well as performing on-site demonstrations to their audience through a learn-by-doing approach. In post-project evaluations, students expressed a better understanding of material systems through the building and teaching of the systems to community participants.

Satisfying aesthetic and functional intent combined with budget limitations provides an additional lesson in material research seldom explored in remote performance. Students tested material feasibility and assemblage options, and, with limited funding, they utilized 80 percent recycled or donated materials. Limitations of construction technologies led to creative decisions and fundraising, which in turn led to the adaptation of the designs based on realistic building logistics. One example was the use of concrete, initially thought unfeasible for its technological requirements. However, in Tijuana the lack of technology was compensated for by the abundant number of hands available to help. Concrete is more widely used in Mexico's construction industry, where labor is cheaper than in the United States. The systems, materials, and technologies were adaptive and flexible, and the process turned into a mutual learning collaboration between students and community.

Performance Review

Measuring project performance is an essential part of learning and of project development and evolution. In the case of the InfoStructure project, enacted performance is on one level evaluated through documenting community impressions at completion. On another level, evaluation depends on post-occupancy evaluations performed by the non-profit organization. A third method of evaluation is the process of learning from the adaptations and usage of the InfoStructures through time. One of the structures was found to be appropriated on the weekends as a taco stand. Ironically, during the building process, this particular InfoStructure was relocated when a neighboring resident feared it would block the location of the pre-existing weekend taco stand. Months after the completion of the project, it became the new center of public performance, and the resident who had initially objected to its location now utilizes it as the setting for his food stand.

One feature that particularly stands out in the performance of the InfoStructures and attests to their overall acceptance and care by the community is their resistance to vandalism. Since the first iteration of InfoStructures, the studio has employed more durable and graffiti-resistant construction materials and more solid and complex joints, and pushed towards implementing more playful designs that may appeal to younger people. After two years of experimentation, vandalism to the structures is close to zero. Furthermore, when in the last year the Mexican government paved a major artery in one community, the street was paved carefully around the InfoStructure, allowing it to dictate the width of the street—an acknowledgement of its role in the community by an entity external to the project.

FIGURE 10.8 An announcement for a community meeting. The InfoStructure's design reads "Corazón Cumbres," stating the presence of the non-profit organization in the community of Cumbres.

Conclusion

The InfoStructure project's success is assessed by the value placed on it by its daily users, who are also its co-authors. To the passer-by, an InfoStructure is an oddity fitting comfortably within a disorderly field. An InfoStructure does not have the visual presence of an orderly boulevard with lush trees and the perceived grandness of an urban grid. As a matter of fact, most visitors to Tijuana will never see it; yet, its small presence and local narrative is urbanistically significant to its local audience.

The structures within each community create urban unity and symbolic fraternity among the locals. They are beautiful artifacts whose urban scope grows and changes with use. The project program arose out of conversations with members of the community, who are non-traditional as urban organizers. Though the use of each structure is not categorically a street sign, a bus stop, a bench, a planter, or a pin-up board, each is a hybrid of all and a product of local opportunity. It is an urbanism now, in the absence of formal infrastructure, customized and locally made. The numerous different InfoStructures have led to interaction between neighbors and adjacent communities. The surge of local caretakers signals to the connection developed between people and place. The citizen who previously only cared for his or her own temporary confines now adopts the public domain. Unquestionably, many residents are developing stronger ties to the place and staying rather than continuing on the northward migration. These small products of embodied performance are having an impact on people; therefore, their potential to impact tensions and fluidity between the two countries is also regional.

The InfoStructure project creates local and regional meaning within a conflicted border setting away from the architectural classroom and from cultural comfort. It does so by questioning the sufficiency of *aesthetic value* to endure when devoid of functional, exchange, symbolic, and sign values. The Tijuana communities, forming an alienated sector of society born out of a migration pattern between the United States and its counterparts to the south, create challenges in housing, community building, identity, and infrastructure along the border that invite explorations of values at the most fundamental levels of human necessity. Here, the established architectural processes and the prescribed building typologies do not work, thereby requiring fresh and resourceful solutions to problems that cross borders. International professional collaboration, as in this project, can make for valuable lessons in the making of alternative urbanism. Architecture, along with allied and other diverse fields, can improve circumstances, both physical and psychological, to make meaningful urbanities.

References

Baudrillard, J. (1981 [1972]). The ideological genesis of needs. In Levin, C. (trans.), *For a Critique of the Political Economy of the Sign*. St Louis, MI: Telos Press, 63–87.

Baudrillard, J. (1994). The imposition of meaning in the media. In Glaser, S. F. (trans.), *Simulacra and Simulation*. Ann Arbor, MI: University of Michigan Press, 79–86.

Boyer, E. and Mitang, L. (1996). *Building Community: A new future for architecture education and practice*. Princeton, NJ: The Carnegie Foundation for the Advancement of Teaching.

Cave, D. (2013, May 9). In immigration bill, deportees see hope for second chance in U.S. *The New York Times*. [Online]. Available: www.nytimes.com/2013/05/09/us/politics/in-immigration-bill-deportees-see-hope-for-second-chance.html [June 24, 2014].

Enriquez Acosta, J. A. (2009). Migration and urbanization in northwest Mexico's border cities. *Journal of the Southwest*, 51(4), 445–455.

Leach, N. (1999). *The Anaesthetics of Architecture*. Cambridge, MA: The MIT Press.

Mendez, E. and Rodriguez, I. (2009). Imaginaries and migration. *Journal of the Southwest*, 51(4), 477–490.

Pallasmaa, J. (2011, June 14–17). Architecture and the human nature: searching for a sustainable metaphor. *Ghost 13 Symposium: Ideas in Things*, conducted from Bryan MacKay-Lyons' farm in Nova Scotia. [Online]. Available: www.ads.org.uk/access/features/ghost-13-ideas-in-things-2 [February 12, 2014].

Schneekloth, L. H. and Shibley, R. G. (2000). Implacing architecture into the practice of placemaking. *Journal of Architectural Education*, 53(3), 130–140.

DISTRIBUTING

In the new millennium, an explosion of temporary, tactical, pop-up, and DIY urban interventions has emerged to occupy the over-regulated but often underused urban spaces around the world. In North America, almost every day another parklet is installed or a city parklet program created. In Europe, temporary urbanism serves as a tool for the redevelopment of urban extensions. In 2012, Tactical Urbanism was named by *Planetizens* as one of the top planning trends. Aside from the spontaneous and often light-hearted acts, a perhaps more significant development has been the emergence of distributed networks and platforms that enable and support such actions to take place.

In Christchurch, New Zealand, a group of artists and activists called Gap Filler coordinated efforts to occupy vacant sites in the city with new programs and activities in the aftermath of the recent earthquakes, generating new urban life and building social networks. In Seoul, the non-profit organization Seoul Green Trust has a plan to create 33 million square meters of green space in the city by 2020 by developing a network of parks including the Seoul Forest Park while simultaneously nurturing small-scale community gardens throughout the city. In Vienna, Austria, the Bicycle Self-Help Workshop organizes a monthly Bicycle Flea Market at Werkstätten und Kulturhaus (WUK), to connect people needing affordable bicycles to those interested in selling theirs.

Creating an infrastructure for decentralized yet networked agencies and actions is the theme of this section. The chapters investigate the ongoing evolution of tactical interventions into strategic, organized policy and projects, as well as the development of enabling frameworks and institutions to bring about networked change, from North America to Nairobi, Kenya.

11

USER-GENERATED URBANISM AND THE RIGHT TO THE CITY

John Bela

Rebar created its first urban intervention in 2005, PARK(ing). What began as a two-hour guerilla art intervention was translated and shared with the public as an open-source how-to manual. Over the last eight years, the project has evolved into a global public participatory art and seminal tactical urbanism project: PARK(ing) Day.

Today, tactical urbanism has become commonplace in urban areas across the globe and has expanded in scope and scale. However, the very notion of tactical urbanism versus strategic planning, top down versus bottom up, centralized versus distributed is becoming less useful as a more recent generation of projects blur the boundaries. These initiatives now take place in parking spaces, streets, and large-scale urban sites. Projects span short-term interventions to multi-year experiments. The current lexicon of temporary and permanent is inadequate to account for their indeterminate temporality.

The neat boundaries between technocrats and citizens are changing as new tools and incentives for public participation depose the traditional authority of the professional design community. A current generation of designers embodies a new role in relation to city making processes, either as agents of change or as those who create platforms for partici-pation rather than simply producing design products. New tools for financing urban development that engage citizens not as passive stakeholders but as active investors in development promise the possibility of empowered neighborhoods. The revolution in the music, software, and publishing industries, enhanced by the information-sharing capacity of personal computing, is beginning to occur in planning and design as urban citizens re-engage in shaping the environments they inhabit. Furthermore, the agents of change now range from urban activists to city governments and private developers, in what represents a novel way of thinking about both processes and products of urban development.

In this chapter, I argue that tactical urbanism—once solely the domain of the artist, public-interest designer, and citizen activist—has evolved into a new process for city making called "user-generated urbanism." This emerging field incorporates new processes such as "iterative placemaking," new design products such as "parklets," and new funding mechanisms such as "crowdfunding." Having established the emergence of this new paradigm of city making, I attempt to critically evaluate it against the competing ideals of the "right to the city."

Open-Source Design: PARK(ing)

In 2005, inspired by Gordon Matta Clarke's Fake Estates project to seek out niches of unscripted space in San Francisco's dense urban environment, Rebar investigated the metered parking space as a site for social and spatial innovation. Using a map provided by the San Francisco Planning Department (SFPD), we sought out a metered parking space in an area of the city that was underserved by public open space. On November 16, 2005, we installed a small, temporary public park that provided nature, seating, and shade.

Our goal was to transform a parking spot into a PARK(ing) space, thereby temporarily expanding the public realm and improving the quality of urban human habitat, at least until the meter ran out. By our calculations, we provided 24,000-square-foot minutes of public open space that afternoon.

Conceived primarily as an art piece, we thoroughly documented the piece and posted images on the web. Within a few weeks, we began to receive correspondence from people around the world requesting information about the piece and inquiries about installing PARK(ing) in various locations. In response to this interest and inspired by an IKEA manual's graphic simplicity, we produced *The PARK(ing) Day Manual* and distributed it for free on Rebar's website.

The PARK(ing) Day Manual effectively made the project *open source*, giving both implicit permission and providing cues for anyone interested in creating their own version of the piece. The simple two-hour PARK(ing) intervention thus blossomed into an international event called PARK(ing) Day where people around the globe reclaim the streets for people, for fun, and for play.

Over the last eight years, our understanding of what PARK(ing) represents has evolved as our practice has evolved. What began as an informal art collective is now a multi-partner art studio and design workshop, Rebar Group, Inc. Our earliest conception of PARK(ing) was that it represented sampling and remixing in a niche space. Later, we came to understand the project as a tactical intervention and adopted the role of tacticians versus strategists, bottom up versus top down. We also put the project within the context of the current process of urban remodeling—that is, conceiving of the city as a frozen construct and temporary projects as a way of responding to the slow rate of change of urban infrastructure in an increasingly fast-paced and digitally mediated world.

Guerilla Bureaucracy

However, what we were unprepared for was the degree to which PARK(ing) Day and similar projects would catalyze a revolution in shaping the built environment. Inspired by the flexible, playful approach as modeled by guerilla-style temporary interventions, the SFPD, led by the extraordinarily passionate and dedicated planner and guerilla bureaucrat Andres Power, created an experimental city program meant to repurpose some of the 25 percent of San Francisco's land area dedicated to automobile movement and storage. By adopting the tactical methods of the urban activist, the SFPD sought to "temporarily reclaim these unused swathes and quickly and inexpensively turn them into new public plazas and parks" (SFPD 2010). This program, dubbed Pavement to Parks, was inspired by New York City's Sustainable Streets, piloted by New York's own guerilla bureaucrat, Janette Sadik-Kahn.

The Pavement to Parks program began with the temporary closure of a dangerous intersection in the Castro district, a site with a long history of community concern. After a decade of planning initiatives had resulted in little tangible change, the SFPD used a tactical approach: it directed city workers to install a temporary intervention that would close the intersection to private traffic and establish a new pedestrian space (Figure 11.1). The 72-hour makeover of 17th and Castro Street recalls the bold takeover of Rua XV de Novembro by architect and urban planner Jaime Lerner in 1972.

The first phase of intervention at 17th and Castro Street was used to test ideas at full scale, to engage the community in the process of placemaking, and to circumvent the stagnant planning processes around the site. Public Architecture, the San Francisco-based public-interest architecture group donated their services to the City pro bono and was given an extremely tight timeline to complete the design. The City of San Francisco's Public Works department, the agency in charge of the streets, implemented the project. A local nursery donated the plants and volunteers assisted with the installation. Carefully shepherded through the City's sclerotic bureaucracy by the SFPD with the support of the Mayor's office, the project was a popular success.

Over the course of the first year following the makeover, community residents provided important feedback about the design of the site. Following the evaluation by the SFPD for the year trial period, the Castro Plaza was upgraded using grant funds awarded to the Castro/Upper Market Community Benefit District (CBD). The upgrade to the plaza was

FIGURE 11.1 The first phase of intervention in Castro Commons used low-cost and reclaimed materials such as paint, granite curbs, and plant-filled sono-tubes to claim the space for pedestrian use.

accomplished using the community partnership model common to all Pavement to Parks projects. Much of the labor for the installation was volunteered by people in the community (Figure 11.2). The Castro/Upper Market CBD committed to maintain the new public space and named it Jane Warner Plaza after the beloved San Francisco Patrol Special Police Officer Jane Ellen Warner, who was known as "Officer Jane" around the Castro, surrounding Mission, and Noe Valley neighborhoods.

The Pavement to Parks program utilizes a novel approach. Rather than pursue the more traditional technocratic approach to creating new public space—developing a long-term master plan, engaging a designer, conducting community outreach, implementing a capital campaign, putting the project out to bid, constructing the project, and then conducting a post-occupancy evaluation—the Pavement to Parks program appropriated the site as a new public space. This temporary intervention modeled spatial and social ideas for community members, which allowed the public to experience the project before committing to it. The temporary intervention enabled the City to collect and use data to evaluate the project before investing major resources in a space that may or may not prove to be well used or cared for. Based upon real-time community feedback, the design for the site evolved. The first phase of implementation informed the next phase in an iterative process of design intervention followed by evaluation to shape a place over time in a process we describe as "iterative placemaking."

This process of organic growth and cycle of investment and remodeling is typical of many urban systems and is codified as one of the central processes of the formation of urban landscapes described by Paul Groth, building on the work of J. B. Jackson (Groth and Bressi

FIGURE 11.2 Castro Commons, after a year of evaluation and community feedback. The City of San Francisco upgraded the plaza, an example of iterative placemaking.

1997). Cycles of investment and remodeling are typical of neighborhoods, districts, and entire urban areas. What seems to be novel about the Pavement to Parks program is the scale at which these processes are taking place. Pavement to Parks projects and the iterative placemaking they engage in are at the site design scale and share characteristics of place-making in informal settlements.

Other important characteristics of the Pavement to Parks projects include the coopera-tion between private and public entities and the reliance on generosity in the form of pro bono design, in-kind donations of materials and labor, and private funding. New York City Mayor Bloomberg and Department of Transportation (DOT) commissioner Sadik-Kahn have similarly relied upon public–private partnerships and diverse funding sources in implementing tactical urban interventions under the rubric of "trials" and "pilot programs." The reliance on private funds means that pilots can use government resources without the accountability that comes with the use of taxpayers' money (Chen and Grynbaum 2011). Furthermore, under the framework of a pilot, the DOT's interventions in the public realm circumvented the typical environmental review process that usually lengthens the time for approval of projects in the public realm.

Parklets

Building upon the success of the first round of Pavement to Parks projects in San Francisco, the SFPD decided to explore further tactical interventions at the scale of the parking space. In an innovative evolution of the PARK(ing) Day concept, the SFPD commissioned Rebar and architect Riyad Ghannam of RG-Architecture to develop prototypes of semi-permanent public spaces in the parking lane for two sites in San Francisco, and called them parklets (SFPD 2010).

Rebar designed its first prototype parklet as a modular sidewalk extension system. A set of eight program elements—deep seat, high table, bike rack, etc.—was developed to enable customization of the program for different sites. The modules were designed to clip on to the existing curb and have adjustable feet to accommodate varying curb elevations. Rebar installed 22 modules occupying three parking spaces providing an array of public seating, planting, and bike parking (Figure 11.3).

In debating the shape of both the design and the legal framework for the parklet program, we fought strongly for the notion that parklets should not simply be an expansion of café seating into the parking lane. To turn a parking space into private café seating is to further enclose the commons. We argued that parklets should remain first and foremost public spaces that could also serve the needs of café owners.

Rebar and RG-Architecture's prototype parklets were received warmly by both the public and business owners. Following the success of these early prototypes, the City of San Francisco launched the parklet permit program, which enables any city business or resident to convert parking spaces into mini-parks. Since the inception of the program in 2011, the parklet movement has exploded, with close to 40 parklets created in San Francisco and many more in the planning and regulatory pipeline.

One of the similarities between PARK(ing) Day and parklets is the degree of personal expression in the public realm. As the creators of PARK(ing) Day, we have been stunned by the incredible diversity of interpretations of the concept across the globe. Similarly, each parklet has a unique character that results from the combination of planning guidelines and

FIGURE 11.3 Rebar's walklet, a prototype modular sidewalk extension system to create mini-public parks in the parking lane in the streets.

the personal taste of the project sponsor. Some parklets are nothing more than ordinary café tables and chair seating atop a simple platform. Other parklets are highly expressive and offer unique interpretations of the concept, but still fulfill their function as tiny public parks. The SFPD recently created a *Parklet How-To Manual* that guides a prospective sponsor through the design and approval process. City officials across the US are now utilizing the manual to craft their own parklet programs. It will be interesting to compare the range of legal and regulatory frameworks used to create parklet programs across the globe as the current legal definitions of "temporary" and "permanent" present regulatory obstacles to many temporary projects.

The parklet program was originally conceived of as a temporary step toward a more permanent project such as bulb-outs or widened sidewalks. Parklets have now become a novel open-space type, a semi-permanent occupation of the parking lane and an expansion of the public realm. The program has, however, raised some important questions. Public funding for civic infrastructure has been on the decline in the US since 1970. Parklets are a tactical move to create more open space in cities. Parklets also rely on public–private partnerships; on the one hand, this reliance represents greater public participation in shaping a small part of the commons, but, on the other, it is a substitute for greater public investment in the public realm.

To create a parklet, the city government issues a permit for the occupation of the public right-of-way, and the project sponsor finances the design, construction, and maintenance of the space. This works well when the project sponsor has a generous approach, creating a space that is welcoming to the public and truly provides a public amenity. Parklets fail when the project sponsor sees their parklet solely as an instrument for their own business to profit. The best parklets are doing both; they enhance the public realm and boost revenue for the project sponsor.

The other drawback to parklets as public–private partnerships is that they are unequally distributed throughout the city. Only those residents and business owners who are savvy enough and armed with sufficient resources to design, build, and maintain a mini-park are able to benefit from the program. Of the 40 or so parklets that have been created in San Francisco to date, only a few have been created in San Francisco's lower-income neighborhoods. In fact, in the particular corner of the Mission district that I live in, the local business association—which primarily represents Latino business owners—has blocked the approval of several parklets in the neighborhood because they associate parklets with gentrification.

Interim Use to Early Activation Plans

Our understanding of interim use is strongly informed by Florian Haydn and Robert Temel's seminal work on the subject, *Temporary Urban Spaces: Concepts for the Use of City Spaces* (2006). In the book, interim use is defined as "anchoring an alternative use alongside a dominant prescribed program" (Haydn and Temel 2006: 11). In 2010, the *San Francisco Chronicle* featured a series of articles by John King documenting the recent economic downturn in the US and the subsequent surge of interim-use activities. With capital markets for real estate investment and construction frozen, both the public and private sector sought alternatives to the traditional land development paradigm. Some interesting projects resulted in San Francisco's Hayes Valley neighborhood.

Following the removal of the Central Artery Freeway, which was damaged as a result of the Loma Prieta earthquake in 1998, the City of San Francisco conducted a multi-year planning process to develop a master plan for the neighborhood. The freeway was demolished and rebuilt as a surface arterial; commercial developments and affordable housing were planned for the parcels that were left vacant. Soon after the plan was released and made public, the country went into the Great Recession. The development plans for the vacant parcels in the neighborhood ground to a halt. In response to pressure from the politically savvy Hayes Valley Neighborhood Association, the Mayor's Office of Economic Redevelopment released a Request for Proposals for temporary uses for the vacant lots.

Architect Douglas Burnham from Oakland-based architecture firm Envelope A&D responded to the call for temporary projects. His plan for a two-to-five-year installation would renovate shipping containers for commercial and cultural uses. The so-called Proxy is now a temporary two-block project that creates a continuously changing environment of food, art, culture, and retail intended to incubate small businesses and provide new amenities for neighborhood residents (Figure 11.4). The current iteration of the site houses a coffee shop, an ice cream vendor, a beer garden, and a clothing boutique. Burnham refers to the project as a *content machine*:

> The project is tied to the pace of contemporary culture, where content is constantly changing on our computers, televisions, and mobile devices. Here events, retail spaces,

art, and food offerings will be in a constant state of change, with content being curated and occupying the multiple frames (or spaces) that the temporary structures create.

(San Francisco Magazine *with Jennie Nunn 2012: 4*)

One of the possible long-term impacts of the Proxy project is in incubating new businesses. Several of the businesses that occupied the shipping container commercial spaces in Proxy would not otherwise have been able to afford ground-floor retail space in the Hayes Valley neighborhood. In the case of Smitten Ice Cream, the company was able to build a following as part of the Proxy experiment. It is possible that Smitten may be one of the commercial establishments that leases the new retail space when the long-term plans for the parcels move forward. Having used their time in the temporary project to grow their business and to build their reputation with customers, Smitten and other local start-up businesses have developed both social and economic capital that they can utilize in the next phase of the site's development. The concepts of incubating programs and building social capital are terms that are used by agents within both the public and private sector development community who are increasingly using the tactic of interim use as part of a long-term site development strategy.

For another set of parcels nearby, Rebar worked with a coalition of urban farming organizations and a homeless services non-profit organization named Project Homeless Connect to develop interim-use urban farms in the neighborhood that proved to be extraordinarily popular with city residents. The Hayes Valley Farm project was a popular and successful project that engaged thousands of people by providing urban agriculture education and space for community gathering.

FIGURE 11.4 Proxy Beer Garden by Envelope A&D.

These interim uses in Hayes Valley emerged out of a period of economic scarcity, and out of the lack of financing for development as a result of frozen credit markets. Now that capital markets have returned to health, development is moving forward on many sites. In early 2012, the San Francisco Planning and Urban Research group (SPUR) convened a panel discussion entitled "The End of Temporary," in which the panel organizer Ben Grant wisely anticipated the debate around the role of temporary projects as their time comes to an end.

After three successful years, the Hayes Valley Farm recently closed the gates on its temporary urban farm project. Despite its success, the urban farmers were ultimately unable to contest the long-term development plans for the site, and therefore were unable to address the more fundamental issues of land tenure affecting the professional farming community. Due to the farmers' agreement to vacate the land at the agreed-upon time, the City of San Francisco—which has recently appointed an urban agriculture coordinator—has identified other City-owned sites for the farmers to utilize. The legacy of the farm, however, lives on. Soil that was created on site during the farm's three-year tenure was donated to urban gardens throughout the city. Seeds, plants, and other garden materials were similarly disbursed. Thousands of young people, who received urban agriculture training, are now working on other projects throughout the city. As a result of organizing by the San Francisco Urban Agriculture Alliance (SFUAA), the City of San Francisco passed an urban agriculture ordinance in 2012 allowing commercial food production on urban sites under an acre in size (SFUAA 2012). Understanding that temporary vacancy is part of the city's ecology, City technocrats have embraced interim-use projects as a way to fulfill unmet needs in a neighborhood and counteract the effects of the boom and bust cycles of real estate development.

The 5M Project

In October 2007, the Hearst Corporation, which owns the *San Francisco Chronicle* building and campus, a 4.5-acre property in San Francisco's Market district, chose Forest City, a national urban development company, to redevelop a mixed-use project at Fifth and Mission Street. As a result of the economic downturn, Forest City did not immediately pursue a more traditional development proposal. It used the half-empty *Chronicle* building to cultivate a local sense of community with an experimental mix of arts, culture, and entrepreneurial tenants who would inform the long-term plans for the building's development.

Instead of designing and entitling a building and then looking for a tenant to fill it, the developer created a community of tenants and then imagined a new place for them. Alexa Arena, Forest City's vice president in San Francisco, conceived the project as a way to build social capital by incubating a diverse mix of non-traditional users on the site. Arena conducted some research on the unmet needs in the San Francisco commercial development market and discovered that there was a disconnect between the office space that San Francisco has—mostly high-rise office towers—and the type of open, creative work environment that many of the fast-growing technology companies in the Bay Area's technology and innovation sector seek.

Arena and her partners at 5M curated a mix of arts, technology, and co-working tenants that now includes: Intersection for the Arts, San Francisco's oldest arts organization; The Hub, a business incubator and co-working space; and TechShop, a member-based do-it-yourself workshop. The project is designed to create a loose community of people working in the "creative economy," while creating public spaces that invite people to interact with each other. According to Arena, "maximizing social value and maximizing business value can be very much in tandem, and the best in urban development does that" (Baker 2011).

Forest City recently unveiled its plans for developing the four-acre site, which forms a border between a low-income stretch of the South of Market neighborhood to the southwest and the wealthier blocks devoted to conventions and shopping to the northeast. When complete, the project will feature two high-rises—one residential, one commercial—along with six smaller buildings, including the *Chronicle* office. The entire site will hold roughly 1.3 million square feet of commercial space and 700 market-rate-housing units. Some of the existing tenants, who are occupying buildings that will be demolished as part of the plan, have been promised space in the new development.

The genesis for the 5M project emerged out of a period of scarcity and a reluctance on the part of the private developer to pursue a design and entitlement process in the midst of a serious economic downturn. As a result of this willingness to experiment, the project has created a dynamic mix of tenants, fulfilled unmet needs for a new type of office space and working environment, catalyzed the creation of numerous new businesses, and built up a sense of community in the neighborhood years before construction of the new development begins. The 5M project has generated social capital within the neighborhood. Furthermore, the developer will be able to capture that social capital as real estate equity when the time comes to lease or sell desirable commercial and residential spaces. Based upon the success of the 5M project, Forest City is pursuing a similar approach with Pier 70, another multi-acre, multi-year development project in San Francisco along the eastern waterfront.

Adopting the tactic of interim use, Forest City has laid the groundwork for a new approach to real estate development that seeks to cultivate life before the city, to create a social network, and to generate social capital prior to the creation of brick-and-mortar physical infrastructure. However, it remains to be seen what occurs once the development plans move forward on the site, given the diverse mix of users that currently makes 5M so vibrant and desirable. Certainly, one possible outcome is that the arts organizations that are currently benefitting from the developer-subsidized space will no longer be able to afford rents in the new neighborhood and may be forced to relocate. In a pattern that is all too familiar, the very forces that created the social capital around the project and site may disappear. According to Arena, however, there will be ongoing commitment to arts, culture, diversity, and inclusion among diverse neighborhood residents.

The Right to Invest in Your City

One of the more interesting trends in urban development in the last several years is the advent of crowdfunding for public infrastructure and crowd equity in real estate developments. Based upon the success of the crowdfunding platform Kickstarter, a group of young urbanists in Helsinki began developing the concept for Brickstarter, a peer-to-peer platform that applies the model of crowdsourcing and crowdfunding to the built environment.

The concept of Brickstarter is to "take advantage of social media and mobile apps in order to create a more articulate, more responsive, and more representative platform for citizens and institutions to work together" (Boyer and Hill 2013: 4). Citing the current cumbersome interface between citizens and institutions, the goal of Brickstarter is to use the tools and media that people now use to orchestrate their everyday lives to better engage the city building technocracy (Boyer and Hill 2013).

The project's authors consider it neither as a top-down nor as a bottom-up tool:

> Citizens are now more eager than ever to play a part in local decision-making. Promising initiatives are popping up around the world, each exploring the potential of crowd-sourced or crowd-funded approaches to shared spaces, services and public infrastructure. Yet bottom-up is only half the story. Brickstarter sits between bottom-up and top-down, connecting the needs and desires of the community with the resources and representation of institutions. Brickstarter has a user-centered perspective, working with communities and government to help smooth institutional processes and permits, and prototype participative governance.
>
> *(Ibid.: 4)*

The project's founders have recently published a compilation of their writing on the concept and now, in true open-source fashion, invite the public to take ownership of the blueprint of the project and make it a reality.

On a recent trip to Copenhagen, I met with Kristian Koreman of ZUS Architects, who, in a public lecture organized by Bettina Lamm, described a fantastic real-world example of crowdfunded public infrastructure: a network of public walkways spanning the city of Rotterdam's auto-centric, modernist central business district (Figures 11.5 and 11.6). The Luchtsingel is a bridge that is intended to reconnect the Hofplein area with the northern districts of Rotterdam by allowing pedestrians to avoid the hectic traffic below. Rotterdam has long been struggling with a city center split in half by heavy traffic and few ways of accessing shopping and recreational areas. Having very limited means to invest in infrastructure, ZUS, whose office occupies a repurposed commercial building, pursued a crowdfunding approach to finance the project (ArchDaily 2013).

The idea of a footbridge in this area originated in the Central District Master Plan. However, the master plan originally scheduled for the bridge to be realized over the next 30 years, which was too long a wait for the city's current residents. The premise of ZUS's campaign was, the more you donate, the longer the bridge. Following a successful crowd-funding campaign, ZUS is building the Luchtsingel decades ahead of schedule (ArchDaily 2013).

In addition to crowdsourcing ideas for the city and crowdfunding public infrastructure, another game-changing trend in user-generated urbanism is the crowd equity platform,

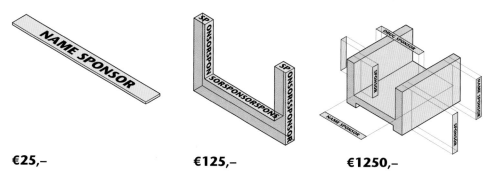

€25,–   €125,–   €1250,–

FIGURE 11.5 Diagram of crowdfunding framework for the Luchtsingel.

FIGURE 11.6 The Luchtsingel.

being developed, for example, by groups like Fundrise, which harness the power of peer networks in real estate development. According to Fundrise founder Benjamin Miller, crowdfunding for real estate investment is "[A] radical transformation of urban planning, of development, of investment, of local government. What the Internet has already achieved disrupting commerce, media and communication . . . is about to do to finance, remaking the very places where we live" (Badger 2012).

While crowdfunding is certainly not a new phenomenon (the base of the Statue of Liberty was financed through crowdsourced funding), the advent of internet-based platforms which streamline the process and enable connection among a broad network of peers makes the more recent iteration of this phenomenon powerfully transformative. In terms of user-generated urbanism, these platforms are the most interesting when they enable micro-investors to participate in existing planned developments and to shape the content of future proposed developments.

Historically, urban areas were financed and built by local people investing in their own neighborhoods. It is only a relatively recent phenomenon in which real estate investment is restricted to "accredited" investors (typically those with a net worth of $1 million or more). As a result, recent generations of real estate development have been financed by distant private equity backers, who see a real estate deal as an investment vehicle. This type of real estate development has tended to finance generic "cookie-cutter projects and strip malls anchored by chain stores—hardly what the community may want or need" (Cortese 2013).

The JOBS Act, signed into law by President Obama on April 5, 2012, enables equity-based crowdfunding when it is conducted by a licensed broker-dealer or via a funding portal registered with the U.S. Securities and Exchange Commission (SEC). By allowing the public to invest in an asset class that has traditionally been the exclusive domain of wealthy investors and private equity firms, crowd equity platforms like Fundrise are transforming the way real estate projects are built and who profits from them (ibid.).

However, as with many internet-based and peer network instruments for participation, there is unequal access to the tool. You might be precluded from participating in a crowd-funding or crowd equity project if, say, you are an immigrant, live in a place where you do not speak the language, or are in an income bracket that precludes you from participating.

While the current crowdsource platforms have been successful in financing some unique and interesting projects, the method has not been tested vis-à-vis necessary but less attractive neighborhood amenities such as drug treatment centers, homeless shelters, or other places designed for the public good. Nevertheless, it is certain that the democratization of finance has the potential to disrupt the current financial investment system that is controlled by a powerful class of multinational corporations and wealthy real estate investors. In the absence of public financing for civic infrastructure, crowd platforms, powered by peer networks operating within a framework established by strategic entities like Fundrise and Brickstarter, have enormous potential. They enable urban residents to help their cities achieve the goals of livability and social justice.

The Right to the City

Henri Lefebvre's concept of the "right to the city" is captured by the notion of the *oeuvre*: a life-enhancing environment produced by creative and collective participation. According to Margaret Crawford's evaluation of Lefebvre's work, citizenship was conceived as including all urban inhabitants and conferred two central rights: the rights to participation and appropriation. Participation allows urban inhabitants to access and influence decisions that produce urban space. Appropriation includes the right to access, occupy, and use space, and create new space that meets peoples' needs (Crawford 2011).

Lefebvre's concept, as interpreted by David Harvey, can be summarized as the democratic right to control the surplus:

> If exerting the right to the city means gaining "greater democratic control over the production and utilization of the surplus" and while throughout capitalist history some of the surplus value has been taxed and in social democratic phases the proportion at the state's disposal rose significantly, the neoliberal project over the last thirty years has been oriented towards privatizing that control . . . [T]he right to the city is restricted to a small political and economic elite who are in a position to shape cities more and more after their own desires.
>
> *(Harvey 2008)*

Evaluating PARK(ing) and parklets against these two concepts of the "right to the city"— democratic control over the surplus versus the *oeuvre*, a life-enhancing environment produced by creative and collective participation—it is clear that PARK(ing) is a powerful expression of the *oeuvre*. Created as a guerilla art installation by a group of young designers, then shared as an open-source design intervention, the power of PARK(ing) is not in Rebar's original conception of the piece regarding sampling and remixing or occupying a niche, but rather in its ability to inspire and harness global public participation and to introduce "a type of urban politics that recognizes that shaping the urban realm should (solely) not be the prerogative of technocrats, bureaucrats, and generally those who make a living out of city shaping, be they architects, planners, consultants, or politicians" (Plyushteva 2011: 42).

The diversity of interpretations of the parklet concept certainly represents greater public participation and appropriation in shaping the urban environment. However, due to their nature as public–private partnerships, parklets do not necessarily represent a greater democratic control over the surplus. With the scarcity of public financing for new open space, it is all the City Government can do to allocate the staff resources and manpower to oversee the parklet program. Parklets are a tactical approach to expanding the public realm being used by the City Government in response to scarce public resources. Tactical projects in the US in general are a response to the steady decline in public funding for civic space. In an era where we refuse to tax ourselves for public projects and direct much of our "surplus" towards military spending, artists, activists, and now guerilla bureaucrats who value the idea of a generous public realm take matters into their own hands to fix the problem.

In the private sector, Alexa Arena and Forest City have pioneered the utilization of interim use in the US as part of a long-term development strategy. The 5M project is now one of many development projects underway that are incorporating interim uses as a "Phase 0" intended to cultivate vibrancy, test spatial ideas, and incubate programs. We think this represents an evolution of a novel process of development that we call "iterative placemaking." As these projects are currently underway and are years away from breaking ground on brick-and-mortar development, it is too soon to tell if this novel process will result in a different outcome than a more traditional land development approach. If, as described in 5M's literature, there will be ongoing commitment to arts, culture, diversity, and inclusion among diverse neighborhood residents, then the project may actually embody the spirit of the "right to the city" relative to participation and appropriation—at least for the duration of the interim-use activities. Our hope is that 5M and other iterative placemaking projects will result in a more diverse social ecology, greater investment in public spaces, and opportunities for multiple tiers of economic actors that would represent Harvey's "democratic control of the surplus."

Crowdfunding and crowd equity projects like the Luchtsingel are examples of peer network solutions beginning to disrupt and displace centralized, hierarchical models of development financing. These instruments engage both dimensions of the "right to the city"—both participation and appropriation—allowing people, through the crowdsourcing platform, to determine what amenities they want in their communities and, through the mechanism of micro-investment, to circumvent Harvey's notion of the right to the city as democratic control of the surplus by engaging city residents as direct consumers and producers of the environments they inhabit. Will crowdfunding platforms ever be able to deliver large-scale and complex public infrastructure elements like public transit? The peer network advocate would say that supporting and enhancing systems like private car sharing could obviate the need for a separate public sector-financed transit system. However, as with the parklet program, it is possible that the benefits would tend to be unequally distributed in favour of the young, white, and digitally savvy.

Conclusion

A new model for city making is emerging with the tactical temporary intervention. Interim uses, iterative placemaking, and crowdfunding by strategic planning entities are all creating new instruments for flexible urban environments. "User-generated urbanism" is an attempt to synthesize the strategic and tactical dimensions of city planning, of centralized hierarchies and distributed peer-to-peer networks. It acknowledges that top-down actors provide critical structure and stability and that peer networks contribute equally important aspects such as adaptability and resilience. Using a people-centered approach, strategic entities—rather than creating a city for urban residents to consume—could offer up a content platform that urban residents can shape according to their own desires, thus giving urban residents the freedom to build the city they inhabit.

Evaluating user-generated urbanism against the ideals of the right to the city—participation, appropriation, and democratic control of the surplus—it seems very clear that user-generated urbanism enhances the *oeuvre*. Of the projects described above, all of them enhance public participation and allow for the appropriation of spaces to meet people's needs. What is less clear, however, is whether this practice has the power to contest the powerful economic forces of neoliberal capitalism and the increasing trends of privatization, income inequality, and unsustainable growth. Crowd equity seems to hold the most promise in that regard. It is also important to acknowledge that while many of the processes of forming a city may be beyond our control, having a sense of agency and realizing possibilities are crucial to our well-being.

It seems likely that in a decade from now, when peer networks and crowd platforms are commonplace, these emerging trends may no longer be called tactical urbanism, DIY urbanism, or user-generated urbanism. They will be called, simply, urbanism, or the way we make cities *now*. In a recent conversation on the power of peer networks and public participation with Dan Parham, creator of Neighborland, he noted that while projects like PARK(ing) Day, parklets, and Neighborland certainly rely on the power of the peer network, they also rely on the benevolent vision of the project's founder. PARK(ing) Day was an exploitation of a legal loophole regarding the short-term lease of a metered parking space. This legal loophole could have been easily exploited for private gain or for illicit purposes, which would have changed the character of the entire project. Over the last decade, one of the things that has emerged out of our reflection on PARK(ing) Day is how much the project is an expression of an intrinsic set of values that we share about the commons, public space, and a fundamental belief in human generosity. It does not matter whether you are a bureaucrat working in a public institution using tactical urbanism, or a private developer exploring the potential of interim use, or an urban activist hacking public space. What is truly important is that we share a similar set of values about democracy, justice, and social equity. The way in which we design, build, and inhabit cities is likely to continually evolve over time. The fundamental values that we share, hopefully, will not.

References

ArchDaily (2013, March 19). *Luchtsingel/ZUS + Hofbogen BV.* [Online]. Available: www.archdaily.com/346241/luchtsingel-zus-hofbogen-bv/.html [January 10, 2014].

Badger, E. (2012, November 19). The real estate deal that could change the future of everything. *The Atlantic Cities Place Matters.* [Online]. Available: www.citylab.com/work/2012/11/real-estate-deal-could-change-future-everything/3897/ [January 10, 2014].

Baker, D. R. (2011, November 18). Hearst plans major development around *Chronicle*. *San Francisco Chronicle.* [Online]. Available: www.sfgate.com/news/article/Hearst-plans-major-development-around-Chronicle-2289133.php [January 10, 2014].

Boyer, B. and Hill, D. (2013). *Brickstarter.* [Online]. www.brickstarter.org/Brickstarter.pdf [January 10, 2014].

Chen, D. and Grynbaum, M. (2011, June 26). Pilot label lets mayor's projects skip city review. *The New York Times*. [Online]. Available: www.nytimes.com/2011/06/27/nyregion/bloomberg-pilot-programs-avoid-red-tape-and-public-review.html [January 10, 2014].

City of San Francisco Planning Department (SFPD) (2010). *Pavement to Parks Program*. [Online]. Available: http://sfpavementtoparks.sfplanning.org/ [January 10, 2014].

Cortese, A. (2013, May 14). Washington projects invite the small local investor. *The New York Times*. [Online]. Available: www.nytimes.com/2013/05/15/realestate/commercial/washington-projects-invite-the-small-local-investor.html [January 10, 2014].

Crawford, M. (2011). Rethinking "rights", rethinking "cities": a response to David Harvey's "The right to the city." In Begg, Z. and Stickells, L. (eds), *The Right to the City*. Sydney: Tin Sheds Gallery, 33–37. [Online]. Available: http://emergencity.net/wp-content/uploads/2013/03/Tinsheds_catalogue_23MarchFINAL1.pdf [June 23, 2014].

Groth, P. and Bressi, T. (1997). *Understanding Ordinary Landscapes*. New Haven, CT: Yale University Press.

Harvey, D. (2008). The right to the city. *New Left Review*, 53, September–October, 23–40. [Online]. Available: http://newleftreview.org/II/53/david-harvey-the-right-to-the-city [January 10, 2014].

Haydn, F. and Temel, R. (eds) (2006). *Temporary Urban Spaces: Concepts for the use of city spaces*. Basel: Birkhäuser.

Plyushteva, A. (2011). Rescuing the right to the city. In Begg, Z. and Stickells, L. (eds), *The Right to the City*. Sydney: Tin Sheds Gallery, 42–45. [Online]. Available: http://emergencity.net/wp-content/uploads/2013/03/Tinsheds_catalogue_23MarchFINAL1.pdf [June 23, 2014].

Rebar Group (2009). *The PARK(ing) Day Manual*. San Francisco, CA: Rebar Group. [Online]. Available: http://parkingday.org/src/Parking_Day_Manual_Consecutive.pdf [July 4, 2014].

San Francisco Magazine with Jennie Nunn (2012). Interview: Douglas Burnham. *San Francisco Magazine*. [Online]. Available: www.mayorsinnovation.org/pdf/interviews.pdf [June 22, 2014].

San Francisco Planning Department (2013). *The San Francisco Parklet Manual*. San Francisco, CA: San Francisco Planning Department. [Online]. Available: http://pavementtoparks.sfplanning.org/docs/SF_P2P_Parklet_Manual_1.0_FULL.pdf [June 22, 2014].

San Francisco Urban Agriculture Alliance (SFUAA) (2012). *San Francisco Urban Agriculture Alliance*. [Online]. Available: www.sfuaa.org [January 10, 2014].

12

OPEN SOURCE CITY

Laura Kozak

Everyday conversations about how we interact with space—the pursuit of a new place to live, the satisfaction of rearranging the furniture or planting a garden, the process of renovating, fear of neighborhood change—reveal an intuitive understanding of how and where we exert control over the built environment, and where that control ends. In *The Structure of the Ordinary*, N. J. Habraken posits that the impulse to hang a picture on a wall or to reorganize the furniture is not essentially different from the motivation to rebuild an entire neighborhood, but rather that these actions all stem from the motivation to exert control over a space, or "live configuration," of the built environment, albeit at different scales (1998: 18–19).

A city is not a single live configuration, with a clear individual agent that exerts control over the built environment; a city is a complex assemblage of many configurations, and many agents vying for control. Government, industry, and citizens all play a role in the evolving production of the city; each group participates in a collaborative and competitive process to control elements at a variety of scales. For example, home-owners maintain their residences, making decisions about the materials and aesthetics of their homes' façades. Zoning, building codes, and sometimes heritage restrictions may supercede the home-owner's level of control, dictating the parameters within which that individual's decisions must fall. In a democracy, control ultimately loops back to the people, providing voters with an opportunity to decide who is in charge of rule-making and, in some cases, what the rules are (Kozak 2012).

One way of understanding the role of ordinary citizens in the production of the city is to separate the professional and non-professional contributions to the process, that is, contributions from those whose jobs are concerned with city making—planners, trades-people, architects, civil engineers—versus those whose contributions are made outside the context of a vocation. The role of this second group, the non-professionals, is important not just because they make up of the majority of a city's people, but also because the wisdom of a city's "organic intellectuals" is an abundant and valuable resource. This includes idiosyncratic, site-specific, on-the-ground knowledge; techniques and strategies imported from elsewhere; and knowledge from other eras or areas of practice. Some of the non-professionals most directly engaged in the production of space include DIY enthusiasts, gardeners, and tinkerers; those engaged in renovations and repairs; and neighborhood advocates and activists. Their contributions are what make a city interesting and unique, providing a genuine character and sense of identity and place. Without them, the city is at risk of becoming generic, monotonous, placeless.

Shifts in the approach to city making in North America have limited the agency of these individuals to make meaningful contributions to the built environment, creating an imbalance in professional and non-professional collaboration and jeopardizing the benefits of bottom-up, emergent ideas. These shifts, essentially roadblocks that limit non-professionals from making both material-based and abstract contributions to city making processes, include:

• the prolific development of high-density residential building typologies, which reduces access to garages, basements, and backyards—spaces where DIY building and other activities of "making" typically occur;
• a general "scaling-up" of city projects, in terms of size, cost, and the complexity of permitting and rezoning processes;
• a decline in access to tools and equipment through cooperatives, educational institutions, and industry.

This chapter investigates a possible model by which to encourage and give agency to this group to make contributions to the built environment. Borrowing from a range of precedent models, it explores a theoretical proposal for Vancouver, BC that brings together material production with abstract engagement, using three symbiotic tactics:

1   an educational model that attempts to help demystify city permitting and rezoning processes to the general public;
2   a facility that gives community members access to tools, materials, and workshop space;
3   a program that brings together a diverse cast of professionals and non-professionals into the same space, initiating two-way dialogue and networking.

Philosophically, the proposal adopts ideas promoted in open source theory, introduced in texts such as Eric Raymond's 1997 *The Cathedral and the Bazaar* and the writings of Pekka Himanen, Linus Torvalds, and Manuel Castells in *The Hacker Ethic* (2001), and applies them to approaches to enacting change in the city. The term "open source" originated in the 1990s as a software development strategy in which source code was made openly accessible, and self-identifying contributors could participate in the development, critique, and "debugging" of a program. Values in open source theory include sharing and collaboration amongst a community of contributors; the use of a hands-on approach; and an emergent, decentralized process for generating and critiquing ideas.

This chapter uses these as metaphorical principles on which to build the relationship between professionals (planners, architects, builders, engineers, and policy-makers) and the public in the production of the urban environment, adopting the process that occurs in the development of open source code. Mimicking a relationship between leadership or expertise and a broader group "reporting bugs," this project champions the idea that the general public can and should be involved in the critique of the built environment, as well as participating in some portion of the actual production of that environment. It does not ignore the need for professional expertise, specialized fields, or top-down planning: rather, it seeks to contribute to an equilibrium, where top-down and bottom-up approaches of contributing to the city are active (Kozak 2012).

Vancouver

Vancouver, BC is speculatively explored as a prospective region for this proposal. Although some conditions and approaches to urbanism are particular to Vancouver, many qualities are typical of exploding global cities.

Vancouver is globally lauded by urbanists, tourists, and residents alike for its spectacular geographical backdrop, its high-density urbanity, and its youthful and leisurely demeanor (Punter 2003: xiv). With an international reputation as an innovative, green-thinking, and liberal safe-haven, the city only recently dropped, in 2012, from its number one spot on the *Economist*'s Intelligence Unit's global "Liveability Ranking" (2012). Often cited for its high standard of urban design, the "Vancouver model" has been studied and exported around the world, most literally in the development of the Dubai Marina, a full-scale replica of Vancouver's False Creek seawall and its podium-tower building typology, in the United Arab Emirates (Boddy 2004: 18).

This "branding" of the city is not incidental, but rather economically and politically strategic, helping to drive tourism and investment in the region. By positioning itself as a place of "outstanding opportunity for outdoor adventure [with] the sophisticated amenities of a world-class city" (Tourism BC 2012) and "an innovation incubator—a place where new ideas, products and services are born" (Vancouver Economic Commission 2012), Vancouver has access to a global market for the wealthy elite, bringing an influx of foreign capital and immigration to the region, both of which have boosted the city's population and economy. Land values, currently among the highest in the world (Ladurantaye 2012), have soared, creating an extremely expensive real estate market and making it profitable to develop the high-density building typologies that have come to be associated with Vancouver's downtown landscape.

In striving to build its image as a world-class city, Vancouver has prioritized political and economic strategies that contribute to that image, including intensifying residential densification; stimulating rapid, large-scale development of new buildings; dismantling industrial production and manufacturing in the city; and increasing the use of regulatory control over the built environment. If stimulating a productive economy is the primary goal, there are numerous metrics that show how this "brand-scaping" has proven effective: immigration accounts for a large portion of the region's population growth, tourism makes up 8 percent of the overall economy, and the city attracts a wealthy elite with a high-end real estate market (Vancouver Economic Commission 2012). However, these strategies also have the effect of diminishing the agency of the individual to play an effective role in shaping the city, limiting opportunities to make both physical contributions to the built environment and abstract contributions to policy and planning.

The speed and scope of residential densification, particularly in Vancouver's downtown core, cannot be underestimated. Between 1971 and 2011, the residential population down-town jumped from 1,380 to 30,129, contributing in large part to a city where 62 percent of residents live in units other than single-family dwellings, like apartments, townhouses, and

FIGURE 12.1 The Vancouver skyline along the north shore of False Creek.

condominiums (Statistics Canada 2011). Residential development took place primarily in Yaletown and Downtown South, with podium-tower typologies replacing decommissioned industry along False Creek. These developments are typically primarily made up of small apartments (under 500 square feet), several street-level town homes, and a few larger penthouse suites.

Residential towers place limitations on individuality in a couple of ways. Aesthetically, they are unified configurations, designed to look cohesive from the exterior: symbols of order and control. Often strata councils impose rules about the type of window coverings a resident may use, place restrictions on hanging laundry or storing items on balconies, and present no opportunity for an individual to make any changes to a building's exterior. Concrete and steel towers (most buildings in Vancouver taller than six stories) present technical barriers to reconfiguring space too: structural systems cannot be dismantled or altered on the small scale, the way light-frame wood constructions can be; individuals cannot attach heavy items to concrete-backed drywall, making the hanging of shelves or even pictures difficult; there is no option to change the size, location, or proportion of windows. Finally, these typologies make it difficult for residents to make anything material-based, providing very little space to spread out, make noise, produce dust, or store tools.

The development of so many towers in Vancouver is part of a larger trend of the "scaling-up" of development in the city in general. The use of discretionary zoning (as opposed to administrative zoning), guided by the recommendations of Vancouver's Urban Design Panel and City Planning department, is intended to create a higher standard of urban design (Punter 2003: 14). It gives the city the authority to manage the "big picture" of the urban environment and to allow for case-by-case analysis of rezoning and development applications (curtailing the one-rule-fits-all principle of administrative zoning, which is consistent but certainly has its problems too). Comprehensive Development zoning and density bonusing favor developers and professionals with large amounts of upfront capital and the expertise to navigate the process of rezoning negotiations. Although an argument can be made for it, the use of discretionary zoning complicates the process of applying for a permit or rezoning for a layperson, as the city maintains the authority for the Director of Planning to override the rules as set out in zoning or policy, presenting individuals with increased barriers when undertaking renovations, business development, or building projects. These shifts in development and urban design strategies in Vancouver have occurred in tandem with a general decline of sites where individuals learn about, encounter, or work with materials and tools. Since the 1980s, the city's high schools have largely dismantled shop classes and vocational training (Crawford 2009: 11–13), in favor of technology-based and digital media training. To date, the Vancouver School Board has continued to offer some shop classes to the general public (about five or six woodworking and welding classes) through the Continuing and Adult Education Programs (BC Ministry of Education 2010: 24–27). The demand for the classes does exist—the Roundhouse Community Arts & Recreation Centre, the only Community Centre to offer woodshop access, runs dozens of woodworking classes each year, and provides open woodworking access to individuals for an hourly fee (Roundhouse Community Arts & Recreation Centre 2012: 43–44).

The rezoning of much of Vancouver, coupled with soaring real estate prices, has meant the departure of much of the city's light-industrial and manufacturing industry for cheaper, less restrictive land in the surrounding municipalities. Yaletown and False Creek are the two most extreme examples of the conversion of industrial land to residential property. Although currently being held as industrial land, many of the lots in the False Creek Flats and along the north shore of the Fraser River, in Marpole, are now vacant or unproductive. Even Granville Island, which was developed to showcase both artisanal and industrial production in the city, has become largely focused on artist retail and cottage industry, save for a few remaining industries, such as Ocean Cement. Although manufacturing still makes up for about 7 percent of jobs in the lower mainland region (Business Council of British Columbia 2012: 2), the relocation of these industries away from the urban core has meant that, in Vancouver, we are not exposed to this type of production on a daily basis. When taken together, the gap in materials-based educational opportunities coupled with the decline in everyday encounters with production contributes to a culture in which making things is not on our mind.

Employing the Open Source Model

So, how do we restore balance between what the professionals are doing and what the rest of us can do? This proposal learns from three existing models to find innovative ways to knit together professional and non-professional activities: a Vancouver-based bike repair shop with an innovative workshop model; a used building material supply center in Portland, OR; and a non-profit organization that promotes civic engagement in Brooklyn, NY.

Our Community Bikes, Vancouver, BC

Vancouver-based bike repair shop Our Community Bikes (OCB), among others, offers bike and bike parts sales, bike repair lessons (on an individual, drop-in basis or in formal group lessons), and access to tools and workshop space. For a nominal hourly fee, you can take your bike in to OCB to use specialized tools in a workshop space, access four levels of assistance (do it all yourself, ask staff an occasional question, have a staff member with you to teach and instruct you, or simply drop off your bike for service), and purchase new or used bike parts and tools (OCB 2012).

There are a number of advantages to this model, the most important and relevant of which is that it attracts a variety of customer groups, from leisure cyclists and commuters with little or no bike maintenance knowledge to highly knowledgeable cyclists needing simply to access specialized tools or work space. The shop acts as a venue for both formal and informal learning: formal learning occurs when customers register for a class or pay for staff assistance; informal learning occurs when those of differing skill levels are working side by side.

The ReBuilding Center, Portland, OR

The ReBuilding Center is a massive used building material supply store operated by Our United Villages, a not-for-profit organization in Portland, OR. With a primary mandate to "strengthen the environmental, economic, and social fabric of local communities," the ReBuilding Center employs 30 staff and upwards of 2,000 volunteers each year, who run the 50,000-square-foot material warehouse, process eight tons of materials each day (all of which gets diverted from a landfill for reuse), and receive over 300 daily visitors.

Salvaged materials available for sale include doors and windows, recertified lumber, siding, shingles, hardware, fixtures, and steel. The materials are sold at 10–50 percent of the cost of their new equivalent, creating a financial incentive for customers to visit the center and to purchase used materials instead of new. Material sales do not provide the ReBuilding Center with a source of revenue; revenue in their model is generated from a for-profit arm that provides deconstruction services at market rate. This gives the ReBuilding Center enough funding to cover staffing costs, operate their facility seven days a week and maintain a fleet of vans and trucks for moving materials around.[1]

The ReBuilding Center thrives on its capacity to attract citizens with a wide variety of skill sets, diverse socio-economic backgrounds, and a range of reasons for coming to the Center. There are always lots of jobs for volunteers to do: some that require minimal training, and others that demand expertise. The nature of working with materials is satisfying and productive, and volunteers gain knowledge through the process of working alongside staff.

The Center for Urban Pedagogy, Brooklyn, NY

The Center for Urban Pedagogy (CUP) is a non-profit organization in Brooklyn, NY that "collaborates with designers, educators, advocates, students, and communities to make educational tools that demystify complex policy and planning issues" (CUP 2012). Municipal governments generally take on the role of providing access to information about civic policy and planning issues, and there are few programs that operate independently or at arm's reach from the government or educational institutions. Providing education and access to information about cities in ways that make sense to a broader public and in an independent forum are essential factors in creating a population that is critical and effective in driving urban change.

One example of a project CUP has undertaken is called "Know Your Lines." Through CUP's Making Policy Public program, a design team called We Have Photoshop collaborated with the Brennan Center for Justice to produce a fold-out brochure that explains redistricting (the process of changing electoral boundaries) in clear and simple terms. This document, available as a free download or as printed copy for $8, is intended to help community groups and advocates in understanding the redistricting process, how it may affect them, and how to intervene to change this process (ibid.).

The strategies adopted by the Center for Urban Pedagogy to broaden the accessibility of policy and planning matters provide a valuable precedent for the Tool Shop, particularly in the way that they engage a variety of professionals, designers, citizens, and youth to create a growing collection of resources. Projects produced by CUP provide an example of the type of teaching and work that will be undertaken in the Tool Shop's classroom.

City Tool Shop

Borrowing elements from each precedent, the City Tool Shop is a theoretical proposal for a facility to help provide increased opportunity for individuals to learn about the city, to access tools and materials, and to collaborate with professionals working in sectors including construction, planning, and architecture.

Overview

A City Tool Shop (henceforth Shop) incorporates a publicly accessible workshop space, building materials depot, and classroom space. The aim of a Shop is to foster the opportunity for public participation in the production of the urban environment by providing programming on topics that might include home repair and construction, community visioning, mapping, civic policy, zoning, by-laws, and other city-related issues.

Operating on a membership basis, Shop members would have the opportunity to purchase and work with used materials, access tools and shop space, and take workshops or short courses taught by industry professionals. The Shop situates materials-based learning and abstract learning close together, connecting them visually and pedagogically and mimicking the larger-scale means by which the city gets produced. The three symbiotic programmatic and spatial elements (warehouse, fabrication space, and classroom) are highly programmed and designed for intensive use.

The primary objectives of the proposed Shop are:

- to process salvaged building materials for reuse, thereby diverting this material from landfill sites and reducing demands to transport new and waste material;
- to teach the public practical and affordable ways of repairing, designing, and building and to cultivate the development of resourcefulness with materials and skills-based knowledge through accessible tools and work areas, affordable materials, and vocational training;
- to foster cross-disciplinary communication, networking, and knowledge-sharing between professional and non-professional communities.

This proposal explores Metro Vancouver as the catchment area for a Shop, a region with a population of 2.3 million people, of whom approximately 84 percent are over the age of 15 (Statistics Canada 2011). Within this area, as is typical for an urban area of this size, there are a number of changing conditions that contribute to the demand for a facility of this nature:

- *Residential densification*: Vancouver's well-documented move towards residential densification in recent decades, led through policies such as "Living First" (2000) and "Eco-Density" (2010), has contributed to a city where 62 percent of residents live in apartments, condominiums, and town houses (Statistics Canada 2011). These smaller, denser dwelling units do not often include garages, basements, or outdoor spaces where messy, noisy, or dusty work with materials can take place. Providing an accessible, urban space for this type of work to take place is a major opportunity.

- *A deficit of shop access*: Though a number of studios and wood shops do exist in Metro Vancouver, there are barriers to their accessibility, which include affordability, a lack of training opportunities, and lengthy wait times. Most of the existing shops are private or cooperative, requiring individuals to make a long-term financial investment in tools and the lease of space. The Roundhouse Community Arts & Recreation Centre is one of the only facilities that offer affordable, open shop time.

- *A surplus of waste construction materials*: Construction and demolition materials make up approximately 22 percent of Metro Vancouver's landfill waste (City of Vancouver 2012). Of these, approximately 75 percent are reusable (depending on building typology and deconstruction technique); facilitating salvaging operations can divert a large portion of solid waste from the landfill and mitigate transportation costs (both environmental and financial), while also keeping valuable material resources within the city.

- *The increasing complexity of regulations*: In the last 100 years, cities in general, and Vancouver in particular, have seen an enormous surge of regulations and controls on the formation of the built environment, through building codes, by-laws, zoning, and historical preservation movements. As the language and bureaucracy increases in complexity, members of the general public—lay people—face increasing barriers in navigating these processes.

- *A gap in ways to learn about the city*: Although Vancouver has a well-developed culture of leading professionals, recognized scholars, and academic programs in fields of planning, architecture, urban studies, and construction, there are extremely limited opportunities that extend this type of learning to the general public through adult and continuing education programs. These types of programs exist in abundance in other cities; in Vancouver, there is an educational gap.

- *City policy that aligns with these values*: Current priorities at the municipal and regional level place high priority on waste diversion and reduction in transit emissions, through guidelines such as Vancouver's "Greenest City 2020" (City of Vancouver 2010). By providing an uptake system for waste materials, thereby also reducing the need to transport them, the proposal contributes to a larger, regional vision.

Shop Users

A diversity of appeal is fundamental in order to meet the Shop's aim to foster the building of new networks of interdisciplinary individuals. Therefore, the target audience includes a number of distinct groups: DIY enthusiasts seeking a venue to work; home-owners and renters with a desire to repair or renovate; neighbors, advocates, and activists; and practicing trades-workers.

Members will have a participatory mentality; they will want to be directly involved in the selection of materials, the production of an object, the use of a tool, or the conversation about their neighborhood. Some will have experience working with their hands and simply want to access space to do so; others will be beginners looking for more learning support.

Member needs will fall into one or more of the following three types:

1   *Access to tools and facilities*: Members will be seeking access to hand and power tools and workshop facilities suitable for dusty and noisy projects.
2   *Instruction and facilitation*: Members will seek both hands-on and dialogue-based learning from skilled instructors.
3   *Materials*: Members will be seeking access to hand and power tools, space to work on materials-based projects, and a source of inexpensive materials to work with.

Facilities and Services

Each of the three facilities that make up the Shop would provide different elements of physical infrastructure—such as space, tools, and materials—and services, including instruction, cutting services, and project consultation services, to support its mandate.

The material-processing warehouse is a space where waste building materials, such as lumber, hardware, windows, and fixtures, obtained through donations and deconstruction, could be separated, sorted, and made available for sale at a fraction of the cost of new material.

A fabrication and assembly area would allow students and community members to work with these materials, accessing space for the kind of work that is difficult or impossible in smaller, urban dwelling units, such as condominiums and apartments. An assembly area allows people to make noise, produce dust, and access stationary power tools in a safe work environment with supervision, ventilation, and proper equipment. This area includes a full service woodworking shop, equipped with stationary power tools like table saws, circular saws, drill presses, sanders, planers, and joiners. Ear protection, a ventilation system, a full-time technician, and regular shop safety demonstrations all contribute to a safe work environment.

Learning and knowledge exchange are central to the project, in both informal and formal ways, and a large amount of flexible classroom space provides a venue for workshops, talks, events, and "short courses." These workshops both support the materials-based learning in the assembly area (for example, basic shop safety and tool use) and provide broader learning about the city. A continuing education model could be used as the delivery structure for these workshops and courses, with low-barrier prerequisites and a fee-for-registration system.

The Shop is also intended to be a venue for community charrettes, public lectures, screenings, dialogues, and social events. It is essential that the space be heavily programmed, and in such a way to encourage constant opportunity for proximal contact—both formal and informal—between the professional community that drives the development of the built environment (planners, politicians, developers, designers, and trades-workers) and the public community (students, parents, senior citizens, activists, historians, and enthusiasts). In essence, this proximal contact replicates the relationships that exist in the city as a whole; the Shop concentrates this contact around the focused topic of city making itself. The Shop must be vibrant, both visually and programmatically; the production of maps, models, and community plans, the exchange and deconstruction of building materials, talks by visiting scholars and professionals, and a rich array of short courses will all contribute to this liveliness.

Outcomes

The core intention for the proposed Shop is to increase opportunity for regular people to engage in small-scale construction, material salvaging, repair, and learning about the city. By providing access to space, tools, equipment, affordable classes, and public programming, the Shop endeavors to strengthen bottom-up, emergent approaches to city making, including home renovation, repair, small-scale construction, and community-based planning. It aims to increase the opportunity for non-professionals to encounter and understand the work of professionals by providing programming that will bring these groups together around focused topics of urbanism.

By facilitating and supporting the work of individuals and groups engaged in these types of activities, the Shop will contribute to a number of long-term outcomes, including:

- a public that is better equipped to navigate permitting and rezoning application processes; more aware and engaged in neighborhood visioning and rezoning; and more enabled to critique the work of planners, architects, urban designers, and engineers;
- a process by which individuals may refurbish and reuse building materials;
- an increased comprehension amongst the general population of the BC Building Code and construction safety concerns, including safe use of tools;
- an increased number of individuals engaged in small-scale construction and building repair, contributing to a diversity of maintenance strategies and vernacular aesthetics;
- a decrease in financial and administrative barriers for individuals, community groups, organizations, and businesses undertaking small-scale construction or renovation;
- a forum and framework in which the public may propose, collaborate, and undertake new projects related to the city, such as the creation of a new community garden, a neighborhood composting facility, or the installation of street furniture.

Although the scope of this paper has been to envision a Shop in Vancouver, BC, the project could be enacted in a number of globalizing cities where similar conditions occur. Conversely, radial expansion of the proposal could also potentially take place through a number of satellite locations in the region, presenting an opportunity to build on the assets and resources developed by an initial, flagship location, while also tailoring programming and curriculum to municipality-specific needs, such as variation in permitting processes. Satellite locations could possibly take the form of mobile units, such as trucks, or small "branch" locations, maintaining a relationship and sharing resources with the flagship (Figure 12.2). Libraries could serve as a precedent model for the relationship between a central location, branches, and mobile services. Regional expansion or application elsewhere presents an area of inquiry left to be explored.

In keeping with the spirit of open source, this proposal imagines enabling a set of opportunities for Vancouver's people to participate in the production of their city in an emergent, incremental, and democratic way. It champions exchange and sharing amongst a community made up of professionals and non-professionals, and facilitates access to the tools, information, and materials needed to contribute to the built environment at a variety of

FIGURE 12.2 Metro Vancouver, showing an expanding satellite scenario for the Shop.

scales. Adopting principles employed by open source coders, the proposal envisions the values and operational framework of a Shop, while avoiding the impulse to predetermine all of the results. That said, it aims to cultivate a more participatory type of urban citizen, well equipped with the knowledge and resources to enact diverse and idiosyncratic ideas about how the city takes shape.

Notes

1   This information was provided in an interview conducted by Laura Kozak with Shane Endicott, Executive Director at the ReBuilding Center on December 6, 2010 in Portland, OR.

References

BC Ministry of Education (2010). *Ministry of Education 2009/10 Summary of Key Information*. Victoria, BC: BC Ministry of Education Information Department. [Online]. Available: www.bced.gov.bc.ca/reporting/docs/ski.pdf [March 3, 2012].

Boddy, T. (2004). New urbanism: "the Vancouver model." *Places*, 16(2), 14–21. [Online]. Available: http://places.designobserver.com/feature/new-urbanism—the-vancouver-model——-speaking-of-places/647/ [December 8, 2011].

Business Council of British Columbia (2012). Manufacturing: an important but overlooked industry in the lower mainland. *Policy Perspectives*, 19(1), 1–6. [Online]. Available: www.bcbc.com/content/209/PPv19n1.pdf [March 4, 2012].

Center for Urban Pedagogy (CUP) (2012). *About CUP* and *Know Your Lines*. Brooklyn, NY: Center for Urban Pedagogy. [Online]. Available: http://welcometocup.org/ [March 23, 2012].

City of Vancouver (2010). *Greenest City 2020*. Vancouver, BC: City of Vancouver. [Online]. Available: http://vancouver.ca/greenestcity/ [February 9, 2012].

City of Vancouver (2012). *Advanced Permitting for Deconstruction*. Vancouver, BC: City of Vancouver. [Online]. Available: http://vancouver.ca/files/cov/report-GC2020-implementation-20121016.pdf [March 24, 2012].

Crawford, M. (2009). *Shop Class as Soulcraft: An inquiry into the value of work*. New York: Penguin.

Economist Intelligence Unit (2012, August). *The Liveability Ranking and Overview*. [Online]. Available: www.eiu.com/public/topical_report.aspx?campaignid=Liveability2012 [August 11, 2013].

Habraken, N. J. (1998). *The Structure of the Ordinary: Form and control in the built environment*. Cambridge, MA: MIT Press.

Himanen, P. (2001). *The Hacker Ethic*. New York: Random House.

Kozak, L. (2012). *Open Source City: A proposal for a City Tool Shop*. Vancouver, BC: University of British Columbia. [Online]. Available: https://circle.ubc.ca/handle/2429/43238 [August 18, 2013].

Ladurantaye, S. (2012, January 23). Vancouver among world's "least affordable" housing markets. *The Globe and Mail*. [Online]. Available: www.theglobeandmail.com/report-on-business/economy/housing/vancouver-among-worlds-least-affordable-housing-markets/article1360121/ [March 24, 2012].

Our Community Bikes (OCB) (2012). *How OCB Works: Our Community Bikes*. Vancouver, BC: Pedal Energy Development Alternatives. [Online]. Available: http://pedalpower.org/our-community-bikes/ [February 17, 2012].

Punter, J. (2003). *The Vancouver Achievement: Urban planning and design*. Vancouver, BC: UBC Press.

Raymond, E. (1999). *The Cathedral and the Bazaar: Musings on Linux and open source by an accidental revolutionary*. Sebastapol, CA: O'Reilly Media.

Roundhouse Community Arts & Recreation Centre (2012). *Roundhouse Spring/Summer 2012 Program Guide*. Vancouver, BC: Vancouver Board of Parks and Recreation. [Online]. Available: http://roundhouse.ca/about-us/media/ [March 3, 2012].

Statistics Canada (2011). Vancouver, British Columbia (code 933) and British Columbia census profile (code 59). In *2011 Census*. Statistics Canada Catalogue no. 98-316-XWE. Ottawa, ON: Statistics Canada. [Online]. Available: www12.statcan.gc.ca/census-recensement/2011/as-sa/fogs-spg/Facts-cma-eng.cfm?LANG=Eng&GC=933 [February 23, 2012].

Tourism BC (2012). *Super, Natural British Columbia, Canada*. Vancouver, BC: Tourism BC. [Online]. Available: www.hellobc.com/vancouver.aspx [March 24, 2012].

Vancouver Economic Commission (2012). *Economic Profile*. Vancouver, BC: Vancouver Economic Commission. [Online]. Available: www.vancouvereconomic.com/page/economic-profile [March 24, 2012].

13

THE KIBERA PUBLIC SPACE PROJECT

Participation, Integration, and Networked Change

Chelina Odbert and Joseph Mulligan

We are now an urban planet. For the first time in history, more people are living in cities than in rural areas (UNFPA 2007). By 2050, it is expected that 70 percent of the world's population will be urban, with the majority of the growth in urban population taking place in the Global South (UN-Habitat 2009: xxii). However, cities have been and will continue to be unprepared to accommodate these newcomers: the formal sector will not build affordable, appropriate houses and infrastructure quickly enough; the economy will fail to create sufficient jobs; and governments will lack resources to enable social progress (UNFPA 2007). One in every three new urban dwellers will live in a slum. In sub-Saharan Africa, that number is three in every four (ibid.).

In the coming years, there will be "few greater challenges to widespread planetary health and security than the vast proliferation of nonformal settlements" (Beardsley and Werthmann 2008: 34). At the same time, the informal nature of urbanization creates an opportunity. Informal settlements, without the slum conditions, can offer unique models of urban density, environmentally efficient living, and connection to culture and community. Kounkuey Design Initiative (KDI) views slums not as catchments of waste and poverty but as spaces of renewal, entrepreneurship, and activism—as well as critical components in the reshaping of cities.

Since 2006, KDI—a multidisciplinary, non-profit design practice—has been working to generate radical alternatives to slum conditions caused by rapid urbanization. The initiative began with a simple question: why do slum conditions persist given significant investments and upgrading efforts? The journey towards a response started with a closer examination of the past.

Slum Improvement

Since the 1950s, urbanization has reached unprecedented rates, particularly in the global south. As slums rapidly expanded, the predominant approach to slums by most governments was one of negligence; policy-makers assumed that slums would ultimately disappear as economic development took hold (UN-Habitat 2003). In the late 1970s and early 1980s, it became clear that slums were not going away and many governments began to pressure slum communities to relocate. In the worst cases, this led to the forced eviction of slum dwellers. Relocated or evicted residents typically ended up in locations on the urban peripheries with no access to infrastructure, services, or transport—greatly compromising their ability to move out of poverty (ibid.). During the same period, the World Bank began to adopt and advocate a more evolved approach. Influenced by the activist architect John Turner, the Bank began to promote self-help and upgrading policies which aimed to provide basic municipal infrastructure, secure tenure, and access to credit, to allow slum dwellers to finance and construct their own dwelling units (ibid.). As laudable as these goals were, they were difficult to implement, largely resulting in abandoned projects with minimal infrastructure (ibid.). The mid-1980s to the mid-1990s brought the "enabling approach" (ibid.), rooted in the notion that effective decision making about economic, social, and physical development should be taken at the local level, rather than left to the state. Like the self-help approach, the "enabling approach" sought to give some agency to slum dwellers. In the end, neither approach proved sufficient in building capacity and creating true ownership (ibid.).

Studying the successes and failures of these various approaches offers some important lessons:

- Some approaches have incorporated stakeholder consultation and engagement, but residents have rarely been given true agency in the decision-making process. This has often led to lack of trust between different actors.
- The needs of residents have generally been oversimplified. Interventions have focused on housing or infrastructure without consideration for the broader social and economic needs of low-income communities, resulting in lopsided development.
- Efforts at the large scale have often disenfranchised people on the ground, but small-scale efforts have typically been isolated, and as a result have not led to broader and longer-term impacts.

Within these lessons, KDI found opportunities for innovation, and from these we derived an approach to slum improvement based on three key strategies: "multi-stakeholder participation," "sectoral integration," and "networked change."

In the context of KDI's approach, we define "multi-stakeholder participation" as an open, transparent, and iterative design process that harnesses a community's social, political, and economic capital and know-how, while involving the technical knowledge of design professionals, the political will of local government, and the investment capacity of the private sector. A successful project requires the full and active participation of residents, from conception through implementation and into long-term operation.

"Sectoral integration" is the combination of physical, social, and economic strategies in a single intervention (DFID 1999; Rossiter 2000; Syagga 2001). An integrated slum improvement project has layered elements of housing, recreation, sanitation, water access, and small business all on one site—each working to reinforce the other—in contrast to, for example, the sole provision of improved housing. Design is our entry point, but by necessity an integrated intervention expands beyond the design of structures and landscapes to include the design of programs, enterprises, processes, and organizational structures—all created with a multidisciplinary team with expertise in each area of intervention.

Participation and integration pave the way for bringing about "networked change." Networked change describes KDI's approach to addressing macro-scale issues, such as watershed improvement or poverty alleviation, through a network of micro-interventions. In the context of KDI's work in Kenya, neighborhood-scale projects improve physical and social conditions in corners of the vast slum by reclaiming small "leftover" waste spaces. However, these small spaces are envisioned from the outset as components of a future network through strategic selection and coordination of project sites. A network of residents and institutional collaborators grows in tandem with the physical network and builds new economies, social safety nets, and political capital at the scale of the site, settlement, and beyond.

These pillars of practice are not novel. Experienced practitioners and development research findings often point to long-term engagement, resident participation, and social development as the critical components in successful urban transformation projects. However, as William Cobbett of The Cities Alliance points out, successful implementation rarely follows suit:

> [F]ew projects make adequate provisions for all three [components], and an almost exclusive focus on infrastructure and housing is still the norm. As a result, the effects and sustainability of slum upgrading projects are frequently jeopardised.
>
> *(The Cities Alliance 2008: 4)*

Engaging these three strategies in a genuine and thorough way is not easy; it is a complex and lengthy undertaking, requiring intense coordination, patience, and engagement in the realities of the social, economic, and political context.

As a case study of this three-pronged approach, we offer KDI's Kibera Public Space Project in Nairobi, Kenya. Since 2006, KDI has partnered with six communities in Kibera, Nairobi's largest slum, to reclaim and transform waste areas into Productive Public Spaces.

Though the specific elements of each site and the priority needs of each community vary, all Productive Public Spaces embody six key outcomes that work in coordination to ensure the social, economic, and environmental sustainability of the projects. A Productive Public Space:

1   transforms an environmental liability into usable public space;
2   is authored and operated by its end-users collaborating with outside groups;
3   integrates income-generating and socially empowering uses;
4   adds value to a space without alienating the original community;
5   meets expressed community priorities and links to larger improvement efforts; and
6   uses strong design concepts to create beautiful places.

A closer look at the current network of Productive Public Spaces that make up the Kibera Public Space Project serves to illustrate KDI's emphasis on integrated, participatory, and networked slum improvement. After seven years of linked, small-scale interventions, the positive, larger-scale impacts of the growing network are beginning to emerge (Figure 13.1).

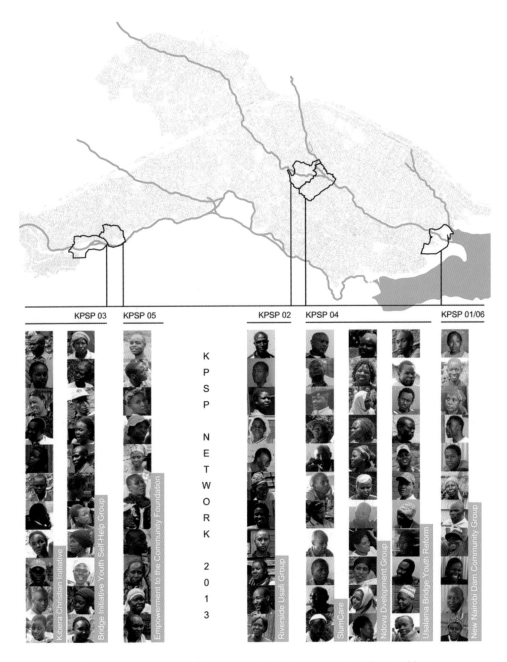

KPSP 03   KPSP 05   KPSP 02   KPSP 04   KPSP 01/06

K P S P   N E T W O R K   2 0 1 3

Kibera Christian Initiative

Bridge Initiative Youth Self-Help Group

Empowerment to the Community Foundation

Riverside Usafi Group

SlumCare

Ndovu Dvelopment Group

Usalama Bridge Youth Reform

New Nairobi Dam Community Group

FIGURE 13.1 The existing network of Productive Public Spaces in the Kibera Public Space Project.

The Kibera Public Space Project: A Case Study

Nairobi, Kenya's capital city, has over three million inhabitants. Approximately two million of those inhabitants live in one of 200 slums (UN-Habitat 2006; Binacchi 2010). Kibera is the largest slum in Nairobi, if not Africa, and is infamous for its scale, location, history, and degraded conditions.

In 1911, Kibera (Nubian for "forest") was designated as a temporary residential settlement for Sudanese veterans who served in the British army. The land was granted to those who had served more than 12 years (Binacchi 2010). Since then, rapid population growth has expanded the urban population of Nairobi, but investments in housing and infrastructure have not kept up with the growing population. Situated just seven kilometers south-west of the city center, Kibera has absorbed a large fraction of this migrant population, for whom it has evolved into a long-term housing solution.

Kibera comprises 12 "villages" that are home to more than 11 tribes (UN-Habitat 2007: 24) with population estimates varying from 170,000 inhabitants, according to the 2009 Kenyan National Census (KNBS 2010), to 600,000 to one million inhabitants, as stated by UN-Habitat (UN-Habitat 2007: 24). Yet Kibera occupies little more than 220 hectares, two-thirds the size of New York City's Central Park, with most people living in single-story dwellings. Density in some areas reaches 49,000 people per square kilometer (UN-Habitat 2006; UN-Habitat 2007).

Limited governmental capacity and lack of higher-level political will have restricted the city's ability to respond to residents' needs, resulting in poor quality of life. The majority of land is government-owned; residents are merely renters of unpermitted housing structures (Binacchi 2010). Narrow dirt alleyways, often navigable only by foot, weave between dense structures and are wholly impassable during high rains. Formal waste management is non-existent, and dumping occurs in nearly all open space, including the many tributaries to the Ngong River that run through the settlement to the Nairobi Dam. Improved toilets—approximately one per 75 residents—are only available in fee-based, shared sanitation centers (ibid.). Access to water is almost entirely provided by private, illegal connections or metered water points, where it is sold at higher prices than those paid by middle- and upper-income households elsewhere in Nairobi (UN-Habitat 2006). Paying for these services is not easy, as 70 percent of households in Kibera live on less than US$1 a day (ibid.).

These manifestations of poverty have made Kibera the poster child of slums and attracted a flood of improvement projects from governmental and non-governmental actors, none of which have successfully led to systemic change. Despite large monetary and social investments—approximately 700 NGOs spend about $23 million a year on projects (Bodewes 2005)—slum improvement programs continue to suffer from fundamental flaws. Missing is a genuine commitment to tapping local knowledge, consideration of elements beyond housing, and coordination, resulting in mistrust between residents and implementing partners (Syagga 2001).

KDI recognizes that poverty in Kibera involves a complex set of interconnected problems—financial, environmental, physical, political, and social—but also acknowledges Kibera's assets. For residents of Kibera, the informal sector is a key resource for income generation. Small businesses are set up in makeshift kiosks along nearly every street within the settlement. Residents sell produce, household staples, and second-hand clothing, or operate services such as barbershops, hot food stalls, and bars. Entrepreneurship and innovation are requirements of daily life. Indeed, evidence of both attributes is strong; 65 percent of those working in the informal sector run their own businesses (Bodewes 2005) and any piece of clothing, electronics, or ironwork can be fixed, adjusted, or replicated at a fraction of the cost of the same service in the formal city. Importantly, community networks thrive; one in every two residents is an active member of a community group (Binacchi 2010). This ability to survive and adapt is potentially transformative when channeled through initiatives with a long-term perspective and engagement.

The Kibera Public Space Project was launched to meet the challenges present in the settlement by tapping into this potential. In 2013, the project produced six networked, neighborhood-scale Productive Public Space sites in Kibera, referred to as KPSP 01–06 (Figure 13.2). The sites occupy leftover spaces along the Ngong River and its tributaries and offer a new meaning to "shared" spaces and amenities in the settlement. The following sections explore the Kibera Public Space Project through consideration of the three underlying strategies described earlier: multi-stakeholder participation, sectoral integration, and networked change.

Multi-Stakeholder Participation

KDI believes that successful urban environments must be shaped and sustained by the people who live in them. Experience has shown that residents often understand the complexities of the issues they face far better than any outsider, and have in many cases already identified viable solutions. Hence the KDI process starts with participation.

Participation comprises five overlapping phases within the KDI Productive Public Space process: request for proposals, stakeholder alignment, planning and design, implementation, and operations (Figure 13.3).

The process begins with an open and transparent "Request for Proposals" that is advertised across Kibera. All applicants are invited to visit Productive Public Space projects already in operation and to attend briefings on project selection criteria, and then to complete a formal application. Once proposals have been received and reviewed, there is a public announcement of finalists. KDI then conducts interviews and visits the proposed sites before selecting a community partner. Selection criteria prioritize group capacity, strength of vision, inclusivity, and physical and political site viability. A prerequisite of partnering is an agreement from the community partner to provide a percentage of the construction cost of the project (usually five percent), in a combination of cash and labor. This process of engagement and exchange can take a significant amount of time—in the case of KPSP 05, it took 12 months—but is critical to project success and longevity.

KDI recognizes the importance of engaging multiple stakeholders, beyond the immediate residents, whose interests must be acknowledged and mobilized in the delivery of the project; we call this process "stakeholder alignment." From the outset, KDI and the community partner work with the chieftaincy—local government representatives in Kibera—to understand the opportunities and constraints for a particular site. Permissions are formalized through a Memorandum of Understanding that is agreed to and signed by residents, traditional hierarchies, and local and district government.

Once the community partner is in place, the local leaders are in support, and the site is secure, the planning and design phase begins. Over the course of several months, KDI's

BEFORE   AFTER

KPSP 02

KPSP 03

KPSP 04

KPSP 05

FIGURE 13.2 KPSP sites before and after construction.

FIGURE 13.3 The five overlapping phases of participation in the Productive Public Space process.

community facilitators—comprised almost entirely of Kibera residents, some of whom were part of KDI's earliest projects—take the community through a series of iterative workshops that move from collecting broad aspirations to creating a detailed master plan of infrastructure, program, and management.

In initial workshops, visioning activities are conducted using various media—interviews, mapping, modeling, and photography—to give residents a new lens for interpreting their own landscape. These activities help communities move from utopian ideas to a realistic, collective articulation of their needs, and establish space for creative ideas to emerge. Together, the community and facilitators propose and then prioritize physical and programmatic solutions through a democratic, iterative process. Constraints of space and budget are incorporated into the decision-making process via a series of applied exercises: surveying, footprinting, costing, and business planning. Throughout the process, the community partner retains authority over the selection of project components and the allocation of the macro-level budget. The result is a schematic plan for the site that resolves community needs, is feasible under the set budget, and includes residents in the ongoing process of delivery.

To help move this schematic vision into reality, technical and design inputs are drawn from KDI's staff of designers (including architects, engineers, and planners) and community development professionals, and from a network of volunteers from partner organizations in Kenya, the US, and Europe. Designers assist the partner to understand, develop, visualize, and quantify the details of the project. Community development professionals support the partner in developing business plans for proposed enterprises early in the process so that design can respond to program. The outputs of both of these processes are brought together in a workshop setting—often using 3D visualization—to facilitate discussion, inform decisions, and inspire engagement and excitement.

Once there is consensus, the process moves into the implementation phase. As construction begins, local residents are centrally involved in delivery, with the majority of the unskilled labor coming from those living immediately adjacent to the site. Skilled labor is sourced from the neighborhood when possible or from the wider Kibera area.

Stakeholder alignment continues and extends beyond the confines of the site, village, and settlement boundary. KDI and our community partners often work closely with municipal agencies to connect the sites to larger-scale infrastructural and governmental systems. For example, at all current sites, KDI and our community partners have sought technical and material support from Nairobi Water and Sewerage Company to establish formal water and sewer connections.

In order to successfully begin operations, an effective structure for managing the programs on site and maintaining the physical facilities is needed. KDI works closely with the community partner's elected leaders from an early stage to develop a representative management committee. KDI helps members identify any skills lacking among them, and then tailors a training curriculum to fill those gaps. Courses offered include accounting, conflict resolution, and internet training.

After a site is fully operational, the project is formally inaugurated and handed over to the management committee and wider community. KDI then shifts from being a facilitator to an advisor and monitors the community partner for a minimum of one year to ensure the physical and financial sustainability of the project is intact. When appropriate, KDI exits.

The overall result is an end product designed by multiple authors and critics all acting within the same landscape, and a community partner who has taken ownership of the space and gone on to influence development in the wider community. Evidence of this gradual evolution is present at KPSP 01, KDI's first project, which now has five full years of independent operations. During this time, the community has established several new businesses on site, without assistance from KDI. The same pattern is emerging with the community partner at KPSP 02 that, after three years of operations, is independently implementing a new phase of site development to double the capacity of its water-vending business. The creation of a sound, autonomous, and capable community organization is perhaps the greatest developmental outcome of the Productive Public Space process; it maximizes the impact of the intervention and paves the way for influence and impact beyond the boundaries of the site.

Sectoral Integration

The Kibera Public Space Project aims to simultaneously attend to people, place, and economy—essential ingredients for a thriving community. Design interventions are layered with physical and environmental improvements, social empowerment initiatives, and economic opportunities. Each project element is carefully considered as part of the whole. In practice, this requires the design and development of processes, systems, and social structures, in addition to buildings and landscapes (Figure 13.4).

KPSP 01 is an example of how the integrated design and programming of a public space can deliver multiple outcomes. KPSP 01 lies at the border of the villages of Soweto East and Silanga at the south-eastern tip of the settlement, immediately adjacent to a small but highly polluted river that passes through the whole of Kibera before draining into the Nairobi Dam. Frequently flooded, the site had been deemed unfit for construction and used as a dumping ground for human and solid waste. The result was an isolated, crime-ridden backwater that posed a major social and environmental safety hazard for residents. This once-shunned garbage dump is now a Productive Public Space, which is managed independently by the New Nairobi Dam Community (NNDC) Group, KDI's community partner. The members of the NNDC Group represent 50 households living in the immediate area. The site was designed to meet the expressed priorities of the residents, namely: flood protection, improved sanitation, opportunities for idle youth, and income generation. The Productive Public Space currently serves between 1,000 and 2,000 beneficiaries per week. Because of the dramatic visual contrast between the site before and after the intervention, it is easy to categorize the Productive Public Space as a predominantly physical project. However, this underestimates the importance of the paired environmental, social, and economic elements, which have together revealed the latent assets of the site and community.

The first step in the process was to reclaim and remediate the site to make it viable for physical development. A community-wide clean-up cleared the area and simultaneously created momentum and focus for the project. Next, to control flooding, the community constructed a simple stone and wire-mesh gabion system along a 200-meter section of the riverbank. A small pedestrian bridge across the river made the area more readily accessible to the village of Soweto East. To remediate the polluted soils and restore the natural environment, the community partner undertook an intensive program of soil rotation and tree planting; the result is one of the only grass-covered, tree-filled spaces in Kibera. More recently, the large-scale planting of bamboo seedlings has served to further control erosion on the riverbanks, as well as to provide a future business and resource for crafts and construction.

PRODUCTIVE PUBLIC SPACE: INTEGRATED INTERVENTION

PHYSICAL	PHYSICAL + SOCIAL	PHYSICAL + SOCIAL + ECONOMIC
① Bridge	① Bridge	① Bridge
② Multi-Purpose Hall	② Multi-Purpose Hall	② Multi-Purpose Hall
③ Playground	③ Playground	③ Playground
④ Office	④ Office	④ Office
⑤ Garden + Greenhouse	⑤ Garden + Greenhouse	⑤ Garden + Greenhouse
⑥ Sundries Kiosk	⑥ Sundries Kiosk	⑥ Sundries Kiosk
⑦ Park	⑦ Park	⑦ Park
⑧ Access Road	⑧ Access Road	⑧ Access Road
	② School	② School
	② Church	② Church
	④ Management Training	④ Management Training
	④ Skills Training	④ Skills Training
	②⑧ Community Programming	②⑧ Community Programming
		④⑧ Savings and Loan Program
		④② Basket-Weaving Cooperative
		⑤⑥ Vegetable Business
		⑤⑥ Compost Farm
		② Community Hall Rental
		② Water Tap

FIGURE 13.4 The integration of physical, social, and economic interventions at KPSP 01.

As the form of the site began to emerge, residents and KDI mapped the natural assets of the area and explored how to utilize those resources. This investigation revealed opportunities to make use of the water hyacinth that covers the nearby dam, the organic waste prevalent in the area, and the rainwater flooding the site; all of these were previously considered nuisances. As part of our programmatic design and through our training and micro-loan program, KDI enabled the community to convert these natural resources into economic opportunities, resulting in a thriving basket-weaving cooperative called Kiki Women Weavers, a compost business called Grow Kenya, and a water tap run by the NNDC Group that sells harvested rainwater as well as piped, city water.

Once the site was reclaimed and buildable, KDI and the residents began to build landscapes, structures, and facilities, based on the collective vision developed in the design workshops. The physical site now includes: a playground built from recycled materials; a park with benches, chess tables, and an amphitheater; a water tap; laundry facilities; an NNDC Group office; a garden and greenhouse; a compost farm; security lights; a sundries kiosk; and a flexible, multi-purpose community center. The center has movable interior partitions and retractable façade panels, allowing for a variety of configurations and uses. The roof of the community center funnels rainwater into one of the NNDC Group's 10,000-liter tanks, while the back walls double as adjustable shelves that are used by the women's cooperative for drying the water hyacinth.

These predominantly physical interventions visibly build circulation, sanitation, safety, and recreation infrastructure. However, these spaces go beyond the visible to make possible the social and economic programs that ultimately improve quality of life and make the project sustainable. For example, the strategic placement of the bridge has opened up a new circulation route, allowing residents from across Kibera to save 30 minutes per day in commuting time. The two communities around KPSP 01, though only 100 meters apart, were socially fragmented because of the impassible river between them; the bridge has increased both their physical and social mobility. For example, women previously operated one savings group in Silanga and another in Soweto East; now, they have formed a single group with a larger pool of money and increased borrowing power. The community center is rented to a local school and vocational training college during the week and to a church, other community groups, and training seminars on the weekends—providing not only a source of income but also opportunities for personal development. The community garden and greenhouse improve residents' health by increasing access to fresh fruits and vegetables as well as generating additional revenue. The playground, reportedly the first of its kind in Kibera, provides hundreds of children with a safe place to play and encourages physical activity. Along with the park and amphitheater, all of these spaces have built social cohesion in the area by giving thousands of people an inspiring place to organize, learn, and enjoy their leisure time.

The economic components of the project also fund the ongoing maintenance and development of the site. A small portion of the revenue from businesses on site is directed into an account overseen by the NNDC Group and used to pay for security, repairs, and a caretaker, and also to fund future capital projects. This is an essential feature and theme replicated in all KPSP projects; Productive Public Spaces are financially self-sustaining through revenue from economic activity on site, which is made possible by the physical infrastructure created.

The success of KPSP 01 in the local environment is measurable both qualitatively and quantitatively. Its larger impact is its ability to demonstrate a replicable process for creating a network of spaces through the settlement.

With the benefits of experience, reputation, and momentum from the success of KPSP 01, KDI went on to partner with new communities to replicate the process. KPSP 02 (started 2009), 03 (started 2011), 04 and 05 (started 2012), and 06 (started 2013) also combine environmental, social, and economic development strategies, but have very different physical and programmatic manifestations, based on the specific locational, societal, and political contexts of each site.

KPSP 02 is a more dense and constrained space upstream of KPSP 01, where a number of latrines drained directly into the watercourse. KDI and the community partner constructed a city-connected, pay-for-use water and sanitation center to replace these latrines, a playground, and business kiosks. KPSP 03 is on the banks of a major river system in an area of steep topography and therefore focuses on drainage infrastructure, and hosts programs including a small school, a community center, a poultry farm, a garden, a water kiosk, and a playground. KPSP 04 provides recreational and income-generating spaces for the youth groups who previously idled in the area, while integrating new childcare and sanitation enterprises to diversify the users of the space. KPSP 05 capitalizes on its location on a major thoroughfare to provide services to locals and passersby, including a resting place, pharmacy, movie hall, toilet facility, spring-fed laundry area, and children's zone. Finally, KPSP 06 brings a decentralized sanitation center to an area where a gravity sewerage connection was physically impossible, and introduces a solid waste incinerator that provides hot water for showers and a stove for the new café-restaurant.

The development of multiple Productive Public Spaces in Kibera, all with their own challenges and successes, has shown how the twin strategies of participation and integration can be complimentary and mutually reinforcing. At every site, the active participation of residents has been the critical factor in the sustainability of the projects, while the integration of multiple sectors and disciplines has enabled diverse development outcomes. The relatively small scale of the individual sites has made it possible to explore an intensely participatory and multi-faceted solution. At the same time, the emergent potential of this approach is beginning to show as the interconnectedness of the individual projects starts to "trickle up" to larger-scale impacts.

Networked Change

City and slum are inextricably linked. KDI recognizes the imperative to address the environmental, economic, and social challenges of informal settlements in order to create more resilient cities and regional systems. One small-scale community project, no matter how nuanced or layered, cannot, on its own, solve problems that expand beyond the neighborhood. At the same time, large-scale, top-down initiatives are politically challenging and not grounded in a community's priorities, and thus may fail to meet the real needs at a local scale. KDI's strategy is not only to develop successful small-scale projects, but also to leverage these discrete improvements by creating a network of people, institutions, and physical systems that work together, to extend reach and impact beyond individual sites to the settlement, city, and region (Figure 13.5).

The Kibera Public Space Project has mobilized a network of Kibera residents with increased resilience and capacity to effect change. These residents recognize that with ownership of a Productive Public Space comes the responsibility to share the knowledge gained through the project process. The community partners from early KPSP projects have become central to the delivery of training and capacity building to subsequent community partners. For example, community members at KPSP 02 who were trained as brick-makers have since trained brick-making teams at KPSP 03, KPSP 05, and KPSP 06. The weaving and beading cooperatives from KPSP 01, KPSP 02, and KPSP 03 have cross-trained one another on specific skills and have recently joined forces to create one, large cooperative with increased buying and marketing power. The KPSP 02 community partner, the first to be trained on operating a sanitation center, has trained KPSP 04, KPSP 05, and KPSP 06 on how to effectively manage their own facilities.

FIGURE 13.5 KDI's vision of networked change in Kibera.

This human network also takes more organic forms. Whenever there is a community clean-up, or a design workshop for a new site, members of the other sites will come to participate, even if it means an hour's walk across the settlement. Community mobilization events become reunions for KPSP communities. More importantly, they have developed into opportunities for the informal exchange of institutional knowledge on the Productive Public Space process and experience: the challenges and the opportunities.

This strong, internal, human network has begun to influence change across the settlement. Residents and community partners have developed organizational and leadership skills through the delivery of these complex projects, which have proven to be transferrable to other change-making roles outside of the Kibera Public Space Project. Many of the KPSP partners are now called upon to advise other community-based organizations, NGOs, and governmental entities operating in the settlement and around the city. This growing network of empowered, engaged, and able people has the potential to deliver future projects on its own, but also to organize, collaborate, and campaign for change around other issues facing Kibera's residents, as they advocate for inclusion and acceptance within the formal city.

The Kibera Public Space Project has created a network of institutions that have a role in project delivery. These institutions all have mandates to deliver services to Kibera and include local government, municipal agencies, and national ministries. Through the Productive Public Space process, community members interact constructively with institutions (often for the first time) and, in doing so, establish a direct relationship with power. The community partners are subsequently in a better position to understand the mandate, capacity, and constraints of each institutional collaborator. Processes such as securing a permit for city water, which were previously opaque and difficult to traverse, become navigable for residents. Simultaneously, the institutions begin to better understand the realities facing their constituents. Ultimately, these interactions and collaborations allow both sides to more willingly, efficiently, and effectively demand and deliver services in the future, without the need for external facilitators like KDI.

Beyond the settlement, the Kibera Public Space Project has influenced the attitudes and approaches of these institutional actors, each of which has the responsibility to effect positive environmental, economic, and social change in the wider city and region. We are beginning to see material changes in strategy and approach around land-use planning through our affiliation with Nairobi City Council and UN-Habitat, and in water and sanitation practices at multiple scales through our joint projects with Nairobi City Water and Sewerage Company. As KDI starts to engage with other NGOs, governmental agencies, concessionaires, and multilateral bodies working on slum issues, the goal is always to connect the lessons of our on-the-ground experience and the voice of community know-how to these larger institutional levels to create networked and relevant change.

Finally, the Kibera Public Space Project has built a growing, physical network of amenities and infrastructure. Like the communities and institutions in the network, the collective strength of the Productive Public Spaces is greater than that of any one site alone. By design, the Productive Public Spaces reclaim strategic points along the polluted Kibera watercourses to form a "spine" of missing community assets that, piece by piece, begins to remediate the settlement and the watercourses. The projects have provided thousands of people with access to clean water and safe and affordable sanitation. They have also demonstrated how to grow municipal water and sanitation infrastructure where feasible, and how to pursue decentralized solutions when necessary. To tackle one of the most intractable problems, solid waste, KDI has worked with youth groups at each site to connect their local waste collection services (which currently dump in the rivers) to city waste management and/or to new waste incineration technologies being introduced at KPSP 06.

The implications of this network of remediated spaces along the watercourses extend beyond the settlement. Though the land area of Kibera is relatively small compared to the overall Nairobi river basin, the settlement has a disproportionate impact on water quality (the levels of organic pollution downstream of Kibera are equivalent to those of raw sewage). A proliferation of these Productive Public Space interventions would not only remediate the Kibera watercourses, but have a significant impact on water and environmental quality in the rest of the watershed.

As the physical network grows with KPSP 07, KPSP 08, KPSP 09, and beyond, so will the human and institutional networks—creating a more resilient and capable Kibera, a more aware and engaged administrative base, and a ripple of physical, economic, and social development opportunities.

Conclusion

KDI believes that the active participation of multiple stakeholders in the creation of integrated projects is a vehicle through which latent energies and possibilities can be harnessed and brought to bear on the city's most vexing conditions. Public spaces in slums are not a luxury; rather, they can be places of tremendous opportunity for civic growth and a means to address multiple dimensions of poverty. The Kibera Public Space Project and the process that guides it have been a testing ground for this premise. We believe that Productive Public Spaces can innovate beyond the usual shortcomings of slum improvement projects and offer an alternative future for slums and urban centers writ large. We hope the work offers evidence that with a slight shift in approach—a framework based on three simple strategies of participation, integration, and networking—we can create financially feasible plans for slum improvement and urban development that are less socially disruptive, more socially empowering, and robust enough to stand up to the urban realities of growing cities like Nairobi.

As a practice, we see our work in Kibera not in terms of success or failure, but in terms of new insights gained for improving the informal city. The process we discuss here is not static but dynamic; each roadblock we have faced has forced us to find new alternatives, and, in doing so, has taught us something valuable about how to improve our model.

Designing integrated projects is a complicated process; it might seem easier, cheaper, and faster to simply build structures and landscapes. Crafting systems to support the structures has been the real challenge for our practice, and in turn where we have needed to adapt and innovate the most—whether that means adjusting the process, budget, and framework of a project, or being flexible enough to navigate the delicate path between being right and being effective.

As our practice grows and we expand our approach to other communities—whether in Haiti, California, or elsewhere—KDI is committed to the artful design of both structures and systems that improve people's quality of life. It may not be the smoothest or most straightforward path, but we firmly believe it is the most enduring.

References

Beardsley, J. and Werthmann, C. (2008). Improving informal settlements: ideas from Latin America. *Harvard Design Magazine*, 28, Spring/Summer, 31–34.

Binacchi, M. (2010). *Slums and Shelter Policies in Kenya: The case of Kibera, Soweto East slum upgrading project*. Saarbrücken: Lambert Academic Publishing.

Bodewes, C. (2005). *Parish Transformation in Urban Slums: Voices of Kibera, Kenya*. Nairobi: Paulines Publications Africa.

The Cities Alliance (2008). *Alagados: The story of integrated slum upgrading in Salvador Brazil*. Washington, DC: The Cities Alliance.

Department for International Development (DFID) (1999). *Sustainable Livelihoods Guidance Sheets*. London: Department for International Development.

Kenya National Bureau of Statistics (KNBS) (2010). *Kenya 2009 Population and Housing Census*.

Rossiter, J. (2000). *Comparison of Single Sector, Multisector and Integrated Urban Development Projects and Their Impact on the Livelihoods of the Urban Poor*. London: Department for International Development.

Syagga, P. (2001). *Integrated, Multi-Sectoral and Sectoral Urban Development Initiatives in Kenya*. London: Department for International Development.

UNFPA (2007). *State of World Population 2007: Unleashing the potential of urban growth*. New York: United Nations Populations Fund.

UN-Habitat (2003). *Global Report on Human Settlements: The challenge of slums*. Oxford: Earthscan Publications Ltd.

UN-Habitat (2006). *Nairobi Urban Sector Profile*. Nairobi: United Nations Human Settlements Programme.

UN-Habitat (2007). *UN-Habitat and the Kenya Slum Upgrading Programme*. Nairobi: United Nations Human Settlements Programme.

UN-Habitat (2009). *Global Report on Human Settlements: Planning sustainable cities*. Oxford: Earthscan Publications Ltd.

INSTIGATING

Designers and planners have the potential to instigate profound change in cities. And yet, bound by the economics and intricacies of practice and mired in technocratic and institutionalized approaches to urban development, we seldom pursue this potential to its fullest. The world's most pressing problems—climate change, rapid urbanization, water scarcity, and social inequity—remain too big, too remote, and too time-consuming for most of us to engage in a meaningful way. Even when we do engage these issues, we tend to remain detached.

To instigate, designers and planners must think critically and creatively and we must inspire action. We must posit provocative ideas in response to pressing issues and pursue the realization of these ideas through advocacy and implementation. In some cases, instigation can take place within conventional frameworks. Designers and planners can work to modify regulations and pursue innovative projects that stretch established norms. In other cases, we must step beyond the bounds of conventional practice. We must engage urban citizens in our work and pursue strategies that enable these citizens to shape the cities in which they live. We must rally against environmental ignorance and degradation. Complex and non-linear, such internal and external processes have the potential to feed off and inform one another, leading to a more inclusive and dynamic interface between urban citizens, urban governance, and urban form.

The chapters of this section instigate. They demand engagement in the process of city making. From the work of Urban-Think Tank in the slums of Caracas to the Informal Urban Communities Initiative of Lima and the reSITE Initiative in Prague, these programs pursue deep community-driven, civic-minded forms of urban development that demand attention and force reflection.

14

FORGET ABOUT UTOPIA

Alfredo Brillembourg and Hubert Klumpner
With assistance from Alice Hertzog and Alexis Kalagas

Urbanization in the Global South

The center of gravity is shifting to the cities of the South, moving definitively below the equator. This shift is creating a new political and social equator—a messy, snaking line defined not by latitude, but by the global distribution of wealth. It skirts around neighborhoods, creating pockets of unimaginable affluence in Rio de Janeiro and zones of unexpected deprivation in Athens. South of this equator, urban communities are growing faster than ever anticipated, in the process posing challenges we are struggling to comprehend and address.

Our work as architects, researchers, and activists at Urban-Think Tank and ETH Zürich is deeply embedded in the cities of the Global South. Beginning in Caracas, we have observed and drawn inspiration from the incredible resilience of squatter communities, and the potential *barrios* offer as viable housing solutions—disconnected from public services, but often defined by supportive social networks, an acute sense of place, and useful proximity to employment opportunities. Working in Venezuela, we have learned to jump through hoops and crawl through loopholes, partnering with local communities and transnational firms alike to implement social design projects focused on achieving sustainable quality-of-life improvements for the urban poor.

Indeed, we believe that the cities of the South are the best training ground for the next generation of architects and urban designers. Artist Joaquin Torres García, the Uruguayan father of South American constructivism, once asserted:

> I have said School of the South; because in reality, our north is the South. There must not be north, for us, except in opposition to our South. Therefore we now turn the map upside down, and then we have a true idea of our position, and not as the rest of the world wishes.
>
> (*García 1984: 193*)

We adhere to this position as we embrace these chaotic and vibrant cities, marveling at their imperfect disorder. Yet, while people living amidst conditions of everyday urban scarcity

FIGURE 14.1 Paraisópolis is the second largest *favela* in Sao Paulo, and borders Morumbi, one of the city's wealthiest neighborhoods.

frequently demonstrate an innate capacity to use the limited resources found within their reach, the failure of urban governance and resource distribution denies them spatial justice through programs that address short-term conditions, but fall short on developing strategic responses to long-term needs.

In cities like Caracas, São Paulo, and Mumbai, observers continue to ineffectively comprehend and predict the pace of urbanization. By 2025, there will be three times more city dwellers in China than in the United States, and India's urban population will be twice as large again. As economist Edward Glaeser (2011) has argued persuasively, cities are the answer to, not the cause of, many of the challenges afflicting human beings as a species. Cities are the greatest human construct, and, like civilization, an intellectual work in progress, the result of human capacity for reason, imagination, and innovation. In concentrating people, resources, information, capital, and goods, cities offer the most efficient environment to build effective systems of service provision, housing, and energy supply. Agglomeration comes with clear benefits when urban-based consumption or production has flow-on effects to all city dwellers by expanding employment opportunities and allowing for increased investments in education or health services. It is in the hope of accessing these benefits that people continue to flock to cities worldwide.

Yet, while we reject alarmist, apocalyptic imagery of Third World urbanization out of control, the tale of the unbounded mega-city has become only too familiar. Though global urban growth actually peaked in the 1950s, setting the tone—alongside the new car culture—for how modern cityscapes would evolve, in developing countries this breakneck pace stretched into the 1980s, deluging cities largely ill-equipped to absorb millions of fresh

FIGURE 14.2 A resident of the Caracas *barrio* of San Agustin clears land on a hillside above the city.

arrivals in a rationally planned way. Metropolitan giants from Mexico City to Dhaka, Jakarta to Lagos, are demonstrating the limits of whirlwind expansion, in the process dominating current urban discourse with their oversized predicaments. They have become victims of their own success.

In these mega-cities, rapid urbanization has not given way to the core infrastructural developments that support a truly functioning urban system in antecedents like Tokyo and New York. Whether as a result of dysfunctional urban governance or simply a lack of adequate resources, water supply, waste removal, and transport have been introduced as an ad hoc afterthought, leaving inhabitants to cobble together their own off-the-grid solutions. These infrastructural oversights further support the social and economic inequalities built into the evolving geography of the contemporary city. In particular, mega-cities embody a cautionary tipping point, where the advantages of living, working, and producing amidst an intense concentration of humanity are outweighed by the attendant congestion, pollution, poverty, and insecurity. In such settings, urban form and architecture often spatializes and materializes uneven development, establishing dynamics that feed back into the complex system of the city, further fragmenting, segregating, and depriving the urban poor.

What You Call a Slum, I Call My Home

Key to understanding this tipping point are the squatter communities of the Global South. It has now passed into the realm of cliché to note how humanity has entered a new phase of urbanization, with over 50 percent of the world's population living in cities. More importantly, since 1970 the growth of informal settlements in the developing world has outpaced urbanization. Over 30 percent of the global urban population now lives in slums, *barrios*, shantytowns, *favelas*, *kampongs*, or *bidonvilles* (choose your nomenclature)—at the literal and figurative fringes of "formal" society. Characterized by self-built structures often located on occupied land, these sites inevitably deal out a range of negative externalities to their inhabitants, who are most likely to be found perched precariously on steep mountain slopes prone to landslides, spread vulnerably across flood plains, or left to deal with the "not in my backyard" risks of highly toxic activities nearby. Overall, the geography of informal settlements inflicts heavy burdens on everyday life that can only be overcome by the resilient tactics of their inhabitants.

At Urban-Think Tank, we strive not only to work with slum dwellers to develop useful strategic interventions, but also to reframe how informal settlements are perceived in the eyes of decision-makers. We have shown that it is possible to improve the lives of *barrio* dwellers significantly by introducing flexible and adaptable physical and social infrastructure designed with particular contexts in mind. Furthermore, in academic discourse it is now recognized that informal urbanism is a dominant force providing access to the city for many new arrivals.

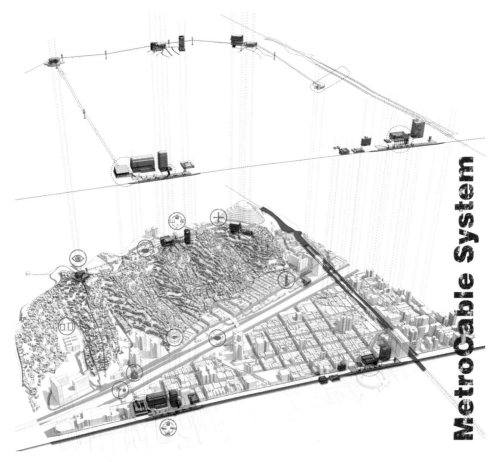

FIGURE 14.3 Urban-Think Tank's design for the Metro Cable in Caracas was informed by an extensive community consultation process giving a voice to residents of San Agustin.

The informal and formal inform each other, establishing the informal city as a dynamic entity that cannot simply be equated with poor, illegal, or marginal neighborhoods. In this regard, urban informality becomes a coherent mode of life, an organizing urban logic, "a process of structuration that constitutes the rules of the game, determining the nature of transactions between individuals and institutions within institutions" (AlSayyad and Roy 2004: 5).

Far from being irredeemable failures in housing policy and city governance, informal settlement areas represent potentially vital opportunities, from whose successes we can learn and whose failures we can seek to mitigate. Slums hold the promise of extraordinary design innovation; scarcity and adversity breed ingenuity and resilience. And where nothing exists, everything is possible. Despite this progress, our discipline is still confronted with the bare facts that we have been largely unsuccessful at transferring this appreciation of the positive qualities of urban informality to the upper spheres of urban governance. City leaders continue to overlook the realities of informal settlements. Even the most informed politicians fall prey to the idea that they will improve the lives of slum dwellers by demolishing their shacks and eliminating communities. Approaches involving large-scale, rapid change—the razing of slums; population relocation; infusions of capital for major, transformative public works—have typically failed, because dynamic, complex urban systems can only absorb so much change before reacting in unforeseen ways.

Such widescreen approaches fail too from a reversal of the forest-and-trees perspective; governments, and the planners and designers they enlist, cannot see the trees—the individuals who occupy this vast informal world and the homes they have devised for themselves—from the forest, the distant bird's-eye view of the city grid. This position is far from prudent, as mega-cities have demonstrated across time and space that they are incapable of meeting the most basic housing needs of the urban poor without dense networks of informal settlements. Constructing the millions of units required to re-house slum dwellers is a Herculean task—a feat no industry or government will meet. And even where governments have achieved admirable—though incomplete—results, such as in South Africa's post-apartheid Reconstruction and Development Program, delivery has been dwarfed by the enormous scale of need, and residents have often been forced into a trade-off. Most newly built formal settlements offer more robust built structures, but are inevitably located in peripheral zones. This displacement threatens the fragile livelihoods residents have carved out over time. As well as designing for the *barrio*, part of our task is convincing decision-makers that the informal city *is* part of the solution.

Slum dwellers are smart and informed. They know how to best manage their resources, how to recycle and reuse, and when it is feasible or not to upgrade. And yet residents of informal settlements have been kept at a distance from political decision-making processes as they relate to the planning of vast metropolitan areas. Engagement with community groups is rare, as are cases of truly participatory design that move beyond informative workshops or co-option of community leaders when self-developed modes of collective organization do exist. Indeed, agency has rarely been entrusted to those with the most to contribute—to those who have a proven record in upgrading space incrementally, based on the availability of financial, material, and social resources. The condition—and urban legacy—of cities in the Global South demands a more imaginative approach to contemporary governance and a longer-term strategy. While an already daunting task, the situation is not helped by multiple layers of decision-making that obstruct and hinder even as officials rush to catch up with developments on the ground.

FIGURE 14.4 Urban-Think Tank's Grotao music school and community center for Paraisópolis became the focus of a community campaign when local decision-makers threatened to derail the project.

This lack of representation represents a major barrier to progress in informal urban areas. In some instances, slum dwellers are not allowed to vote due to persistent notions of citizenship linked to official tenure systems. On the southern tip of Rourkela, India, for instance, over 30,000 people are not authorized to participate in municipal polls because the government has failed to identify them either as rural or urban dwellers. Residents can only vote in parliamentary elections under national law. In many other informal settlements across the globe, the lack of a registered address prevents residents from being able to exercise political rights. Crucially, a vote can hold power with respect to development in informal environments just as much as it does in relation to education or healthcare reform in the formal city. Political representation would go some way to ensuring that often low-priority urban issues like housing and employment for the urban poor gain traction in the realm of high-level policy discussions.

Informal communities have achieved incremental success over time in applying collective strategies to address their lack of representation and exclusion from decision-making processes directly impacting their lives. Slum Dwellers International (SDI), for example, is a network comprised of community-based organizations in 33 countries that launched in 1996 as a global platform to sponsor local initiatives providing alternatives to evictions and improving urban development agendas. The network aims to link communities from locations that have developed successful mobilization, advocacy, and problem-solving strategies, advancing the agenda of "pro-poor cities." Through its achievements to date, SDI reveals how informal communities can participate in formal institutions and structures to better promote their own interests and voice concerns through meaningful policy dialogue.

At the same time, when it comes to urban policy in the cities of the South, this status quo has led us to reconsider our professional role as architects and urban designers. It is not enough to deliver projects if there is no mediation between city dwellers and city governance. Successful projects need the energy of bottom-up, grassroots organizations, but they must also be connected to top-down agencies, institutions, and processes to achieve deeper impacts. Over time, we have found ourselves in a position where we are able to contribute to this more promising state of affairs. Our practice began as a stand in the Venezuelan *barrio* of Petare, and in the last 15 years we have become convinced that the patchwork slopes of that teeming capital represent the global urban norm rather than exception. Yet today, we find ourselves on the other side of the fence, holding a leadership position at one of Europe's premier technical institutions. We live and work in one of the world's most affluent countries, home to numerous international agencies and development groups—a far cry from our home city, Caracas. While our network still includes community organizers from Bangkok to Cape Town, our increasing access to a more closed world of international decision-makers has provided us with opportunities to place the need for new tactics to intervene in the informal city firmly on the agenda.

The Emerging and Sustainable Cities Initiative

In 2011, we came across such an opportunity. A brief encounter with the Inter-American Development Bank (IDB) opened the door to more substantive collaboration, in a context where the programs involved held the promise of operating on an entirely different scale to our previous projects. We were invited to participate in the Emerging and Sustainable Cities Initiative, providing technical assistance for a network of second-tier cities in Latin America and the Caribbean. We were drawn to this challenge because urbanization is now occurring much more rapidly in second-tier cities than in capitals or mega-cities, where the rate of growth has already peaked. Similarly, these cities have the possibility of following a different path, and avoiding some common pitfalls. Instead of representing remedies, emerging cities provide the valuable opportunity to anticipate future growth and environmental solutions. As Marcotullio suggests: "environmental challenges in developing cities are occurring sooner (at lower levels of income), rising faster . . . and emerging more simultaneously (as sets of problems) than previously experienced by developed cities" (2007: 46).

In China, there are now over 170 cities with populations exceeding one million residents, most of which have not yet registered in the global gaze. These cities are seen as promising investments. In fact, they have become opportunities, and, if managed correctly, there is no reason why second-tier cities could not provide the benefits of the mega-city—in terms of products and services—while avoiding the inconvenience of negative externalities. For Urban-Think Tank, the possibility of participating in the Emerging and Sustainable Cities Initiative is an opportunity to call attention to the significance and role of informal settlements in such places.

We began our work with the IDB in the oil city of Port of Spain, Trinidad and Tobago, where we had been asked to design urban projects in response to a set of predefined priorities that used a traffic light system to identify the most pressing issues. While many were reasonable, such as improving water supply and drainage, or cultural preservation, few were mapped onto specific neighborhoods or districts in the city, and none focused on informal settlements. We started by identifying through interviews and fieldwork which areas were most affected by environmental issues, engaging with all levels of local governance and community groups, and using our position as outsiders to the city to question current priorities. This, alongside our urban analysis, led us to a dry river that divided the highly segregated city, with slums on one side and the formal city on the other. Following a series of field missions involving community workshops and consultations with residents, we redesigned the site as a linear park, with social hubs on both sides. In doing so, our methodology identified an issue that had not previously featured in the IDB's funding program despite the evidence and testimonies of local stakeholders. Furthermore, although the linear park is still at a design stage, our mediation between these groups has led the city and IDB to appropriate the proposal and consider it worthy of funding.

Encouraged by this initial experience, we subsequently continued our work with the IDB in Mar del Plata, a coastal city south of Buenos Aires. The affluent location is an ocean resort for the capital's well-heeled residents, and doubles in size over the holiday period, growing to 1.3 million inhabitants. In this context, the mayor took the bold decision to relocate the municipal town hall from a colonial building by the water to a low-income neighborhood six kilometers away in the north-east of the city, home to many of Mar del Plata's poorest residents. In relocating such a public building, the administration sought to catalyze upgrading in the area, providing facilities for local residents without access to paved roads, water, or public services, and allowing the neighborhood to gain visibility and prominence

FIGURE 14.5 A community workshop convened by the authors at the East Dry River in Port of Spain, Trinidad and Tobago.

within the broader city. To accompany this initiative, we designed a civic center that would function as far more than an administrative space. The building is completely open on the ground floor, providing sports facilities (including skating, football, and swimming) as well as a restaurant and auditorium. Our pre-design is now in the hands of the municipality, which is developing it further in conjunction with local experts. In the meantime, we are now expanding our collaboration with the IDB to the Colombian port city of Barranquilla.

In Colombia, a quarter of the population lives in informal settlements and two-thirds of houses were built without a construction permit. The opening of the Panama Canal in 1919 marked the beginning of Barranquilla's decline. Informal neighborhoods grew rapidly, however, over the course of a long and vicious armed conflict, as large numbers of *desplazados* (internally displaced refugees) sought shelter and security on the edge of major cities. After years of decay, the city of Barranquilla is nonetheless experiencing a revival, following an overhaul of local finances and public policy, and an infusion of international development assistance. At the city's bicentenary in 2013, President Juan Manuel Santos declared that Barranquilla was a city at the "right place at the right time." Barranquilla has opened its markets to overseas trade, combining a *zona franca* (a free zone adjoining the port that permits the duty-free entry of foreign goods intended for re-export) with concessions to multinationals, and leveraging the activity generated by free-trade agreements with the United States and the European Union.

We see here an opportunity to influence decision-makers and urban planners on the diverse options available to them—and, if possible, steer part of this new-found wealth towards the development of local infrastructure that will benefit the most impoverished neighborhoods in the city. Over the course of the next few years, we will design a social facility and public space for Barranquilla, which we believe will allow it to continue its

FIGURE 14.6 For the Mar del Plata proposal, the existing city hall was shifted to a marginalized area and transformed into a civic center to benefit local residents.

growth in a more sustainable and equitable fashion. Our methodology remains similar to the work in Trinidad and Tobago, in that we have mapped pre-identified sustainability challenges to the realities of the city, while also identifying pre-existing local projects and initiatives that at times remain unnoticed by multilateral donor programs. Once again, as mediators, we are bringing together the different layers of decision-making in the city, from the IDB to residents, drawing on the varied expertise and resources of these diverse actors. The involvement of local practitioners, academics, and urban practitioners is also key to our methodology, as these figures are often only too aware of the challenges that have been left unaddressed by a successive series of investment programs. Indeed, in framing our intervention within an academic setting, we intend to create a space for discussion and debate surrounding urban investment programs that moves outside of the boardroom and into the context of the *barrio*.

In Barranquilla, building on initial suggestions from local stakeholders, we decided to draw upon the influence of Carnival, one of the key events bringing together members of the population from different social strata. Carnival can be read as a moment of diversity and tolerance where people from all walks of life appropriate the city. With a lack of facilities and buildings for cultural activities in the *barrios* to provide low-income communities with new opportunities, we have been asked by the municipality to help design a vocational arts school. Aside from addressing this cultural gap, the facility will allow local inhabitants to transform their skills into a livelihood, as well as encourage reintegration into the education system. Much like the dry river project in Trinidad and Tobago, the concept has emerged from close observation of the conditions in the city and dialogue with local stakeholders and decision-makers, which we hope in the long term will result in a strong and relevant design proposal.

FIGURE 14.7 A school-based cultural program integrating music, art, and theater to train low-income inhabitants in the south of Barranquilla, Colombia.

Finding Common Ground

As we combine forces with a development bank in the hopes of improving quality of life in the informal settlements of Latin America, we are mindful of the large-scale reforms and damaging interventions driven in the past by multilateral actors, none of which resulted in more workable, broadly applicable, or equitable city models than the one that has produced the asymmetries so visible in the cities of the South. At the same time, the kind of approach we have advocated is worlds away from the outdated notion of broad-brush urban renewal. Rather than erasing what already exists, we are using our new position to interact forcefully—but productively—with policy-makers and administrators in order to confront the realities of the future in emerging second-tier cities. We believe it is our responsibility to identify common ground between the diverse players defining and shaping the long-term urban fabric of cities like Barranquilla. Sharing knowledge, expertise, and advice—but also, more importantly, capitalizing on our unique position at the juncture of informal and formal urban communities—to bridge bottom-up and top-down processes, we aspire to participate collectively in the creation of more equitable and sustainable cities.

References

AlSayyad, N. and Roy, A. (2004). Urban informality: crossing borders. In Roy, A. and AlSayyad, N. (eds), *Urban Informality: Transnational perspectives from the Middle East, Latin America, and South Asia*. Oxford: Lexington Books, 1–6.

García, J. T. (1984). *Universalismo Constructivo*. Madrid: Alianza Editorial.

Glaeser, E. (2011). *Triumph of the City: How our greatest invention makes us richer, smarter, greener, healthier, and happier*. New York: Penguin Press.

Marcotullio, P. J. (2007). Variations of urban environmental transitions: the experiences of rapidly developing Asia-Pacific cities. In Marcotullio, P. J. and McGranahan, G. (eds), *Scaling Urban Environmental Challenges: From local to global and back*. London: Earthscan, 45–68.

15

THE INFORMAL URBAN COMMUNITIES INITIATIVE

Lomas de Zapallal, Lima, Peru

Benjamin Spencer, Susan Bolton, and Jorge Alarcon

At present, an estimated 863 million people—approximately one out of every three people in the cities of the developing world—live in informal urban settlements, also known as slums. By the year 2050, this number could reach three billion, more than a third of the world's total population (UN 2013a; UN 2013b). Stigmatized and marginalized, slum dwellers are often voiceless in the politics of urban development. They lack access to water, sanitation, structurally sound housing, and public space. They endure overcrowding, chronic unemployment, poverty, and disease. They face the constant threat of natural disaster and eviction from untitled land. Despite these hardships, slum dwellers demonstrate remarkable fortitude. Carrying out their lives in an environment of scarcity, they survive and even flourish. Step by step, they improve the quality of their homes and forge tightly networked communities (Spencer 2009). They build high-density neighborhoods with few environmental externalities, intimate scale, and an accretive, organic beauty seldom found in formal urban precincts (Figure 15.1). Slums are difficult places to live, but they are not ghettoes of despair. While their residents face enormous challenges, they are far from impotent victims.

As urban designers and planners, we have an ethical responsibility and professional capacity to reduce the environmental impacts of cities and to prioritize the needs and futures of the urban poor. Working in solidarity with slum dwellers, leveraging their knowledge and capacities, and building upon existing processes of informal development, we have the opportunity to effect significant improvements in the quality of built environments and the development of ecological resilience in slums. In doing so, we stand to learn how to better promote environmental regeneration, citizen engagement, and social equity in cities around the globe.

This chapter describes the Informal Urban Communities Initiative and its approach to design in slum communities. Based in Lomas de Zapallal, an urban slum in northern Lima, Peru, the initiative integrates design activism, interdisciplinary research, and design education. It celebrates and builds upon the unique vitality and incremental nature of informal urban development and examines how we can enable the urban poor to effect positive social and environmental change in their own communities. Through speculative

FIGURE 15.1 The Eliseo Collazos neighborhood in Lomas de Zapallal, Lima, Peru.

design, on-site intervention, and long-term project assessment, the initiative tests the hypothesis that multifunctional design solutions, distributed infrastructure, and close collaboration with poor urban communities offer a compelling alternative to top-down and technocratic approaches to slum upgrading.

Slums and Centralized Infrastructure

Slums have existed for as long as people have lived in cities. However, the growth of slums over the past 60 years is unprecedented. Never before have so many people lived in conditions of urban poverty and physical deprivation. The reasons for slum growth vary depending on time and context, and range from civil conflict to natural disaster. However, in general terms, it is attributable to "structural violence"—a form of violence lacking direct actors where social structures and institutions deprive people of their basic needs (Galtung 1969). Since World War II, the global economy has become increasingly networked, and political and financial capital has concentrated in cities (Davis 2006). At the same time, a lack of investment in rural populations, the industrialization of agriculture, and the commodification of land in the service of corporate interests have eroded rural livelihoods. Faced with few opportunities at home and drawn by the promise of a better life in the city, more than 70 million rural immigrants relocate to cities each year (Neuwirth 2005). More often than not, upon arrival their hardships are repositioned but continue unabated.

As the growth of slums has accelerated during the second half of the twentieth century, municipal governments have struggled to find ways to respond (UN-Habitat 2003). In some cases, slums have been allowed to grow and expand. In others, governments have taken aggressive action aimed at slum eradication. Even today, informal urban settlements are often leveled and residents are left to fend for themselves (Amnesty International 2013). This approach undermines vital social networks, often dislocates slum dwellers from their places of work, and perpetuates conditions of urban poverty.

In other cases, governments have chosen to relocate slum dwellers to tenement blocks. These tenement blocks are often as bad as or worse than slums, as their infrastructure deteriorates quickly due to poor planning and construction and/or as a result of the constraints placed on residents' ability to exercise control over their own living environments (UN-Habitat 2003). As self-help housing proponent, John F. C. Turner states:

> It is only when people have sufficient choices and are free to make their own decisions as to where they shall live, in what kind of dwelling, and with what form of tenure that a sufficient variety can evolve. And it is only when people exercise their necessary freedoms that the planning and building or the improvement, management and maintenance of homes and neighborhoods can become vehicles for community building.
>
> *(Turner 1988: 15)*

Where informal urban settlements occupy seismically unstable, polluted, flood-prone, or landslide-prone sites, slum resettlement is often the only responsible option (UN-Habitat 2003). However, where environmental conditions permit, *in situ* renovation of informal urban settlements, known as slum upgrading, represents the preferred approach. It allows residents to remain in their homes, close to their social networks and, in some cases, close to their workplaces. Typical slum-upgrading projects adopt a government-supported, self-help housing paradigm that provides residents with basic infrastructure, grants them tenure on the land they occupy, and encourages them to improve their dwellings.

Although typical slum upgrading decentralizes the provision of housing, it retains a heavy reliance on centralized infrastructure or the provision of services through large-scale, centrally administered institutions, systems, and technologies. This implies a bias towards housing as a vehicle for progressive action and reflects a broader historical tendency to construe cities in architectural terms (Waldheim 2006). Centralized infrastructure remains relatively axiomatic and escapes critique.

In recent decades, the concept of landscape urbanism has promoted the idea that landscape represents a more appropriate starting point for the analysis and creation of cities than architecture (ibid.). Expanding upon this foundation, ecological urbanism promotes a systems-based approach to urban design, the integration of social and ecological agendas, and dynamic, landscape-centric alternatives to traditional infrastructure systems (Mostafavi and Doherty 2010).

Ecological urbanism remains largely speculative and its inclusivity limits its depth, especially with respect to issues of social equity. However, by calling for a more diverse, distributed, and unpredictable approach to urbanism and, in particular, by acknowledging the potential of bottom-up approaches for the generation of urban environments, it does provide an alternative lens through which we can assess and respond to the challenges of informal urban development. It supports the critical examination of slum upgrading based upon the paradigm of centralized infrastructure and elicits the question of how we might adapt the lessons of "self-help housing" to community-controlled infrastructural landscapes.

Centralized infrastructure contributes to structural violence in several respects. First, as it relies on one system to provide services to large populations, it is capital intensive (Spencer et al. 2010). It cannot be implemented in a piecemeal fashion as its constituent parts cease to function when disconnected from the larger system. Even modest infrastructural interventions in slum communities require significant investment and many developing cities lack the resources and/or the political will to implement them. The technocratic, top-down management of centralized infrastructure represents an additional constraint. Multiple layers of bureaucracy complicate project implementation and the path from permission to project completion can be years in the making. Even those projects that survive the permitting process can wither when elections bring new political parties with new agendas into power. Despite repeated election promises, slum dwellers often go decades without basic services. Writ large, this means that slum-upgrading projects cannot keep pace with the expansion of slums worldwide. Despite the enormous efforts of the United Nations and a decrease in the relative proportion of urban populations living in the slums over the past decade, the absolute number of slum dwellers continues to increase (UN 2013a).

The top-down implementation of slum upgrading not only limits its reach, but also constrains its depth and quality. Standardized approaches to the construction of public amenities and the provision of services lead to generic outcomes and compromise the diversity and richness often found in informal settlements. Millions of dollars that might have otherwise been spent on the holistic improvement of the public realm are buried beneath the ground in support of engineering-focused solutions (Garrido-Lecca 2010). Often limited, the participation of community members is overwhelmed by the complexities of the bureaucratic process and they become passive bystanders rather than active contributors to the development of their own neighborhoods. This, in turn, weakens community initiative, externalizes ownership, and undermines investment in sustainable local action (Kumar 2002). Without active community support and engagement, projects implemented by external actors often falter and ultimately fail. Financial resources go primarily towards the salaries of engineers and administrators. An opportunity for capacity building and community empowerment becomes an exercise in service provision alone. The rich get richer and the poor get pipes.

The shortcomings of traditional slum upgrading are further compounded by centralized infrastructure's contribution to environmental degradation across multiple scales. The Urban Environmental Transition hypothesis argues that as communities become more affluent, they externalize their environmental burdens (McGranahan 2007). In impoverished cities, environmental degradation remains localized and has a direct impact on human health and living conditions. Poor sanitation, for example, pollutes drinking water supplies that contribute to gastrointestinal disease, malnutrition, and death, especially amongst young children living in slums (WHO and UN-Habitat 2010).

In addition to dealing with localized environmental degradation and associated health issues, resource-poor communities are usually those most affected by the externalities of middle-income and affluent communities (Costello et al. 2009). They often reside along rivers downstream from sewage outfalls, downwind of poorly regulated factories, and on polluted post-industrial sites. Changing climatic conditions increase the vulnerability of rural populations to crop failure, spur urban migration, and increase the density of already overcrowded, precarious urban settlements. More extreme weather patterns increase risk of landslide and flooding in the often precarious sites occupied by informal settlements.

Although they provide immediate human health benefits, centralized infrastructure systems facilitate urban environmental transitions and, ultimately, transfer environmental burdens to the urban poor (Boeston et al. 2007). Buried underground, they transport water, energy, and wastes to and from distant sites. In doing so, they export the social and ecological impacts of localized consumption and reinforce an "out of sight, out of mind" mentality. Slum upgrading based on the paradigm of centralized infrastructure is thus short-sighted and ultimately self-defeating. This approach solves the immediate environmental and health issues of one impoverished community by transferring pollution to another community either directly downstream, a few miles away, or somewhere on the other side of the world. Further, centralized infrastructure is inherently inflexible and limited in its potential to respond to shifting conditions. As global environmental change accelerates, our ability to adapt to fluctuations in weather and climate, and to ongoing human migration, is paramount.

The Informal Urban Communities Initiative (IUCI)

Building upon the critique above, the Informal Urban Communities Initiative offers an alternative, community-based approach to slum upgrading that espouses decentralized, flexible, and adaptive infrastructural development. The IUCI's five primary tenets are as follows:

1   close collaboration with poor urban communities and participatory processes that honor local knowledge, resources, and capacity and enable community members to become agents of change;
2   multi-scalar approaches to community design that integrate small-scale interventions, adaptable long-term planning, community imperatives, and professional expertise;
3   ecologically responsive, distributed infrastructure strategies and networks that improve human well-being (e.g. health, income, social capital) while reducing external environmental burdens;
4   synthetic and multifunctional design solutions that engage culturally contingent aesthetics and enhance the public realm;
5   the integration of creative speculation, concrete intervention, monitoring and evaluation, and ongoing adaption in response to project outcomes.

In support of these goals, the IUCI is activated through two interdependent activities: (1) the University of Washington-based Landscape Architecture Design Activism Studio and (2) the participatory planning, design, construction, and assessment of distributed infrastructure and public spaces on-site in the slum community, Lomas de Zapallal (LdZ), Lima, Peru (Figure 15.2).

Lomas de Zapallal

Lomas de Zapallal (LdZ) is an informal urban community in the district of Puente Piedra on the northern outskirts of Lima. Established in the mid-1990s, LdZ is home to almost 30,000 people and growing. Most LdZ residents live in poverty and those residing in its newer neighborhoods have no land tenure. They occupy precariously steep slopes and lack household water connections and improved sanitation.

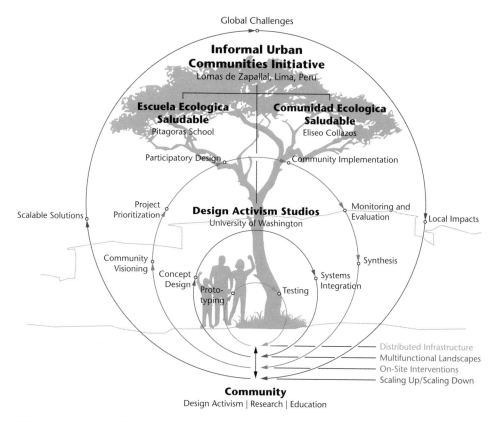

Global Challenges

**Informal Urban
Communities Initiative**
Lomas de Zapallal, Lima, Peru

**Escuela Ecologica
Saludable**
Pitagoras School

**Comunidad Ecologica
Saludable**
Eliseo Collazos

Participatory Design

Community Implementation

Project
Prioritization

Design Activism Studios
University of Washington

Monitoring and
Evaluation

Scalable Solutions

Local Impacts

Community
Visioning

Concept
Design

Proto-
typing

Testing

Systems
Integration

Synthesis

Distributed Infrastructure
Multifunctional Landscapes
On-Site Interventions
Scaling Up/Scaling Down

Community
Design Activism | Research | Education

FIGURE 15.2 Diagram illustrating the organization and dynamics of the IUCI.

Lima receives little more than 1 cm of precipitation per year and green space—at close to 2 m^2 per capita—is less than a third of the 9 m^2 per capita minimum recommended by the WHO (UN-Habitat 2012; Murphy 2013). In LdZ, this number is likely less than 0.5 m^2 per capita. There are very few street trees and, although many neighborhoods have lots set aside for parks, the vast majority of these lots remain undeveloped. Some individual households maintain small gardens and a few grow food. However, urban agriculture is not practiced widely and food options that are both nutritious and affordable are limited.

As with most cities worldwide, Lima's approach to slum upgrading relies heavily upon centralized infrastructure. For example, beginning in 2006, President Alan Garcia's *Agua Para Todos* (Water for All) program relied exclusively on centralized networks to extend water and sanitation networks into Lima's slum communities (Garrido-Lecca 2010). Similarly, many of the city's investments in green space in informal settlements focus on large-scale, centrally administered, pay-to-enter district parks (SERPAR 2014). As the climate shifts and temperatures increase, the low-elevation glaciers that supply much of Lima's water are expected to melt completely within a relatively short period of time (Painter 2007). At the same time, the city's population is expected to increase significantly (Castro et al. 2011). Even if the city is able to extend water and sanitation networks to all of its residents, there is no guarantee that these networks would function (i.e., provide water) on a consistent basis.

While water is scarce, a thick blanket of fog covers LdZ for up to nine months of the year and has potential as an untapped water resource. Similarly, some of LdZ's residents have knowledge of plant cultivation. This represents an untapped resource as well.

University of Washington Design Activism Studio

The Design Activism Studio is conducted during the winter term in the University of Washington's Department of Landscape Architecture. It focuses on design interventions in LdZ. Enrollment consists primarily of landscape architecture students; however, the class also involves students and faculty members in architecture, urban planning, environmental sciences, engineering, and the health sciences.

Many landscape design studios follow a trajectory from large-scale analysis to site-specific design. Details, material exploration, and technical experimentation come at the end of this process and receive relatively little attention (if any at all) (Spencer et al. 2014a). This studio process parallels traditional professional practice and the institutionalized execution of landscape projects wherein initial large-scale contextual, programmatic, and site analysis is followed by conceptual and schematic design, design development, permitting, and construction documentation. While this approach prepares students to work in formal contexts, it is inconsistent with the dynamics of slum communities. By asking students to think big *before* they think small, it disregards the bottom-up process of slum development and ultimately reinforces the structural biases of top-down implementation outlined above.

In contrast, the UW Design Activism Studio emphasizes interdependent and *concurrent*, "emergent," and "convergent" design processes.

"Emergence" is defined as unpredictable and complex behavior that arises out of the relatively simple interactions of individual elements without the influence of a single coordinating authority or "brain" (Hamdi 2004). Slime molds with the ability to search for food are a classic example of emergence. Individual cells communicate with one another and self-organize. Their independent actions aggregate, ultimately providing for the collective sustenance of the organism as a whole (Johnson 2002). In many respects, slums exhibit similar emergent behavior.

Emergent design engages slum communities at the scale of individual, household, or small community group. Incremental infrastructural interventions that capitalize on existing community assets and that community members can implement on their own operate at a cellular level to improve the living conditions and well-being. Just as products such as smartphones have gained popularity worldwide, when emergent interventions strike a chord, they have the potential to propagate virally, independent of external impetus, and to exert a positive influence on the aggregate dynamics of slum communities at larger scales. Emergent design is intended to forge a closer correspondence between infrastructural technology and informal urban processes. Rather than attempting to orchestrate systems, it responds to the dynamics of existing systems and intervenes within them.

Emergent design can operate independently. However, ideally, it forms part of a convergent design process, which further incorporates participatory planning and systems integration at the scale of the neighborhood. Designers work with communities to establish a collective vision that informs small-scale interventions and influences their emergent outcomes. By continually revisiting and revising approaches to small-scale intervention and revising this vision in response to emergent outcomes, individual action and collective goals become increasingly congruent. Independent interventions become increasingly networked. Lessons learned on one project inform projects that follow and the potential pitfalls of emergent design, as characterized by "the tragedy of the commons," for example, can be averted. Emergent behavior becomes more intentional, planning becomes contingent, and their outcomes "converge."

Convergence also characterizes the relationship between designers and community members. By establishing long-term relationships and an extended dialogue, designers gain insight into community dynamics, priorities, and knowledge while community members gain insight into the processes and potential of design thinking. Community and design expertise "converge" upon mutually inspiring solutions.

The UW Design Activism Studio pursues learning objectives that strengthen students' emergent and convergent design skills. They include:

1   establishing broad foundational knowledge about urban slum development and the systems and processes that shape informal urban settlements;
2   establishing contextually specific knowledge of sites and systems operating within Lima and LdZ;
3   strengthening skills in the iterative design, hands-on prototyping, and testing of infrastructural technologies that respond to the social, economic, and environmental conditions of LdZ;
4   introducing skills in cross-cultural participatory design;
5   developing skills in multi-scalar and interdisciplinary synthesis, site design, and systems integration;
6   developing the discipline of critical evaluation, the ability to learn from both success and failure, and the ability to adapt to unforeseen circumstances and outcomes.

Introductory lectures, readings, and discussions (Primary Learning Objectives 1 and 2) draw upon multiple disciplines and attempt to illustrate both the complexity of and an urgent need to confront the challenges of informal urban development. They provide students with broad foundational knowledge of the history, scope, and causes of urbanization and slum development worldwide, the potential impacts of climate change on vulnerable urban communities, urban infrastructural systems, and participatory design methodologies. They also introduce students to the specific context and conditions of Lima and LdZ.

Subsequent assignments build upon this foundation, focusing on prototyping, multi-scalar/interdisciplinary synthesis, site design, and systems integration. They include Slum Toys, Site Systems, Incremental Interventions, and Integrated Landscapes.

Slum Toys

Slum Toys (Primary Learning Objectives 2 and 3) is a short introductory assignment that challenges students to design an easy-to-construct toy using recycled or low-cost materials. Students engage their preliminary knowledge of the context and conditions of LdZ, gain insights into the integration of multiple objectives in a coherent design, and practice iterative hands-on prototyping.

Site Systems

Site Systems (Primary Learning Objectives 2 and 5) focuses on multi-scalar systems-based site analysis. It asks students to map and analyze the complex urban systems that intersect, overlap, and interact at Lima's regional, metropolitan, and neighborhood scales. Students research and synthesize socio-political, environmental, and infrastructural themes such as the history of Lima, climate, and food. The assignment helps students understand how issues that affect LdZ residents on a daily basis relate to the broader contexts of Lima and Peru, gives them a better understanding of site conditions in LdZ, and contextualizes subsequent design exploration.

Incremental Interventions

Incremental Interventions (Primary Learning Objectives 3, 4, 5, and 6) emphasizes the concept of emergent design and focuses on the design, construction, and testing of small-scale, low-cost, ecologically responsive interventions in community infrastructure. After an initial meeting with community members via Skype, the assignment asks students to respond to community priorities, assess the opportunities and constraints of LdZ, and develop prototypes that are appropriate to LdZ's cultural and economic context. It challenges them to develop innovative approaches to community infrastructure with viral potential, that "out-perform," "out-shine," and "leap-frog" more traditional approaches.

Prototyping is a central tenet of the assignment and reflects the hands-on and iterative nature of informal urban development. Construction in informal settlements is an ongoing process without a fixed end point and projects in slums rarely unfold according to a fixed schedule. Slum dwellers build according to their means, improving their dwellings as their families grow or as their wealth increases. Prototyping mirrors this process in many respects. Building, testing, and building again, sometimes starting from scratch, not only leads to incremental improvements in prototype performance, but also helps students develop construction skills, the ability to adapt to the unexpected, and the resolve to see projects through. Testing of prototype performance informs the iterative process and serves as a means of verifying and communicating prototype function.

Integrated Landscapes

Integrated Landscapes (Primary Learning Objectives 4, 5, and 6) promotes the concept of "landscape as infrastructure." The assignment focuses on the design of public space and, in conjunction with Incremental Interventions, engages the concept of convergent design. Students are challenged to design multifunctional landscapes that respond to community priorities, provide practical benefits, and enhance the spatial and aesthetic quality of the public realm. Designs are often focused on improving health, fostering ecological resilience, and generating income in LdZ. Temporal evolution is a key component of design development and students are encouraged not only to articulate designs as initially implemented but also to speculate on how they might evolve, expand, or contract over time.

Prototype and site design take place concurrently. Students are encouraged to work with each other to coordinate prototype designs as part of multifunctional, community-scaled infrastructure networks and to integrate these networks into their landscape design proposals. As the design process unfolds, detail and site-scale interventions "converge" both in terms of their conceptual consistency and their speculative co-evolution (Figures 15.3 and 15.4).[1]

FIGURE 15.3 As part of the Incremental Interventions and Integrated Landscapes assignments in 2012, students developed a modular container gardening system. They integrated these gardens into a series of stairways that provided access to homes perched precariously on the steep slopes of one of LdZ's neighborhoods. At first no more than a simple stair and a dispersed scattering of the gardens at individual households, the design grew over time and co-opted other prototypes such as a greywater recycling system. Stairways eventually reached across the full breadth of the neighborhood and incorporated broad landings for public gathering, street trees, and other amenities.

On-Site in LdZ

The second component of the IUCI takes place on-site in LdZ and emphasizes community-based action. Each summer (winter in Lima), students, professors, and professionals representing multiple disciplines from the University of Washington, the Universidad Nacional de San Marcos, Architects Without Borders, and Engineers Without Borders travel to LdZ and spend between four and ten weeks working in the community. During their time on-site, they engage in activities including participatory analysis and design, the implementation of built projects in collaboration with community members, and the assessment of project impacts. Over the past four years, efforts have focused on two programs:

1   the *Escuela Ecológica Saludable* (EES) program based at the Pitágoras School, a combined primary and secondary school in LdZ;
2   the *Comunidad Ecológica Saludable* (CES) program based in Eliseo Collazos (EC), one of LdZ's newest and poorest neighborhoods.

EES projects completed to date include a park, a stairway/terraced garden, and a classroom. CES projects include a pilot fog collection project and 29 household gardens.

While there is not a one-to-one correspondence between the Design Activism Studio and on-site activities, the two are closely related. Projects undertaken in the studio respond to community-identified priorities. Similarly, projects undertaken on-site build upon and draw inspiration from ideas generated during the studio. On-site activities further the learning objectives initiated during the studio by grounding them in real-world circumstances. In

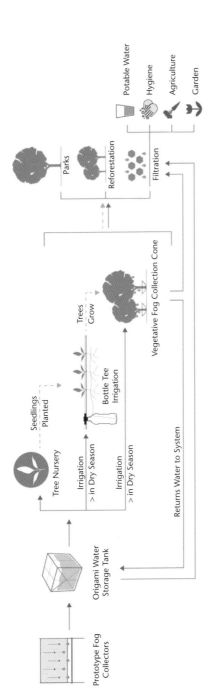

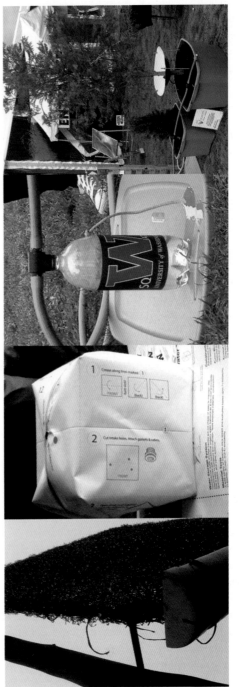

FIGURE 15.4 In 2013, students developed a series of prototypes related to alternative water supply, storage, and use. Prototypes included innovative fog collection materials, a low-cost origami water storage tank, and subsurface wick irrigation utilizing soda bottles. Each prototype could be deployed independently or as part of a fog collection system. Students integrated the fog collection system into designs for a public park and ecological restoration in the hills beyond LdZ.

some respects, the studio acts as a "dress rehearsal" for on-site projects and many students participate in both.

Like the UW Design Activism Studio, on-site activities take a critical view of the top-down implementation of centralized infrastructure and espouse emergent and convergent approaches to design. Participatory planning and design workshops, community-driven project implementation, and Participatory Impact Assessment (PIA) represent some of the IUCI's primary *modus operandi*.

As a means of illustration, the planning, design, and implementation of the CES household garden project are summarized below.

Gardens, Green Space, and Health

Numerous studies have documented the health benefits of vegetated landscapes in urban contexts. They range from reduced respiratory disease, to reduced heat-related morbidity, to improvements in physical fitness and social capital. Regular contact with nature can also reduce stress and mental fatigue (De Sousa 2006; Van den Berg et al. 2007; Nurse et al. 2010; Spencer et al. 2014b). Other studies have documented urban agriculture's positive impacts in impoverished urban households. It diversifies diet, lessens exposure to volatile food prices, improves nutrition (especially in children, women, and the elderly), generates income, and increases the time that mothers have available to raise their children (Maxwell et al. 1998; Zezza and Taciottie 2010).

The CES household garden project attempted to bring these benefits to residents of EC. During inaugural participatory workshops held in 2011, community members drew maps depicting their vision for the community and identified their development priorities. Retaining walls to stabilize the community's precariously steep terrain, improved water access, and "green areas" were at the top of their list. Based upon these priorities, the IUCI team collaborated with community leaders to initiate the CES household garden project in July 2013 (Figure 15.5). The project consisted of:

- a baseline assessment of community health and well-being;
- participatory design, construction, and cultivation of gardens by individual households; and
- follow-up assessments of community health and well-being.

Twenty-nine of EC's 90 households volunteered to participate in the project. It began with a household health questionnaire, a baseline Participatory Impact Assessment and focus group interviews. Efforts then turned to garden design. During an initial workshop (Workshop 1), participants drew the gardens they wanted to build at their houses and chose elements, materials, and plants they hoped to include in their designs. Based upon this information, the design team developed a low-cost modular garden kit that included:

- precast concrete water utility risers repurposed as modular planters and wicking beds;
- walls and paths constructed with local stone;
- prefabricated wooden fences, trellises, and arbors; and
- various types of vegetation.

FIGURE 15.5 Household garden design, construction, and cultivation workshops.

The team then devised a modeling exercise using to-scale components of various sizes and colors that represented different elements of the garden modules. During Workshop 2, participants modeled their gardens in 3D using these components. The following week, IUCI team members visited households with photographs of their models and spoke with participants to further refine and make adjustments to their designs where necessary to accommodate site conditions.

During Workshop 3, participants indicated their specific plant choices and quantities. The IUCI team and a community volunteer with construction experience then demonstrated construction techniques for the various modular components. Over the course of the next two weeks, materials for garden construction were delivered to site and participants constructed the hardscape elements of their gardens. Many participants committed large amounts of time and their own financial resources to garden construction. They also took ownership of the design process, continuing to modify their designs during construction and personalizing the kit-of-parts system proposed by the IUCI team.

Workshop 4 focused on garden planting, cultivation, maintenance, and journaling. Sessions were taught by a local NGO with extensive experience in urban agriculture and a resident of LdZ with a garden and a worm-composting system at her house. A garden manual, later distributed to all project participants, served as a reference during instruction. Following the completion of instruction, participants picked up soil and plants. Over the next several days, they prepared their planting beds and planted their trees, shrubs, flowers, vegetables, and herbs.

The IUCI team confronted a number of challenges during the design and implementation process that are important to note. First, most of the residents of EC work six days a week and only had one free day to participate in the project. Taking this limitation into account and adjusting the work plan accordingly was critical. Unfortunately, work and other life constraints did still prevent some households from participating. Second, initial enrollment in the program was limited due to the skepticism of some community members that the project would actually take place. Once the project was underway, the opposite was true and more community members wanted to participate than it was possible to accommodate. Establishing and clearly communicating criteria for project participation (such as workshop attendance) were important strategies in managing expectations and avoiding potential discontent. Finally, along similar lines, the ordinary challenges of any design activity are often magnified when working across cultures and disciplines. Although the project team worked well together throughout most of the project, disagreements stemming from differences in cultural and disciplinary perspective did arise. Open communication and pre-agreed-upon roles can minimize the potential for such conflict.

In total, project design and implementation unfolded over a six-week period with a materials budget of under US$6,000. The gardens have transformed many of EC's houses. Although they were constructed by individual families, almost all of them are streetside and contribute to a shared public realm. The variety of garden configurations, colors, and plants builds upon and enriches the informal, accretive beauty of the community and reinforces its unique identity (Figures 15.6 and 15.7).

At the time of writing, garden journals, resident interviews, and visual inspection indicate that most of the gardens are producing multiple forms of vegetation and food. Residents of EC are both taking care of and benefitting from them as sources of mental well-being, nutrition, and income. Initial assessments also suggest the project's emergent potential. Many participant households have expanded their gardens and a few households not enrolled in the program have constructed their own gardens (Figure 15.8). In addition, a group of

FIGURE 15.6 House in Eliseo Collazos before and after household garden implementation.

FIGURE 15.7 Street in Eliseo Collazos after household garden implementation.

FIGURE 15.8 Flowers and produce grown in household gardens.

community members is planning to purchase a large number of precast water utility risers to construct retaining walls—an outcome postulated but unanticipated by IUCI team members.

Follow-up qualitative and quantitative well-being assessments are scheduled. This ongoing monitoring and evaluation is critical. It will help the IUCI team improve upon their work as they pursue the integration of a community-operated fog collection system, additional green space interventions, and other future projects.

Although long-term project evolution and impacts remain to be seen, initial outcomes provide an indication of the effectiveness of the IUCI's emergent/convergent approach. By thoughtfully assessing community priorities at the scale of the neighborhood, pursuing accessible small-scale interventions at the scale of the household, designing in close collaboration with community members, and relying on the community members themselves as the drivers of garden implementation, the CES household garden project acknowledged and built upon emergent community development processes and ensured that community members were invested in its success. Synthesis of local and professional expertise and knowledge helped reduce project costs, expedited project execution, and strengthened the capacity of EC's residents to effect positive change in their own neighborhood. While waiting for municipal authorities to construct distant district parks, the families of EC have improved access to food and flowers today and at their doorstep.

Conclusion

Design is, by definition, a political act. In deciding what to design, how to design, and, perhaps most importantly, who to design for and with, we take a stance relative to systems of power that shape society and the environment. As we become increasingly aware of exploitation and inequities in cities, it is crucial that we reassess our values and pursue practice accordingly; in order to create change, we must do our best to live and act it. In doing so, it is important that we recognize that change does not spring forth in full form. It starts out small and grows. It requires compromise, persistence, and sensitivity to the challenges of cross-cultural and interdisciplinary collaboration.

By engaging in critical inquiry, questioning the premises of education and practice, taking grounded action in partnership with resource-poor communities, assessing the outcomes of these actions, and sharing the lessons we learn across multi-dimensional networks, the process and products of our work have the potential to expand virally and exponentially. The principles upon which they are founded have the potential to transcend the design professions and influence social, political, and economic processes at multiple scales—to foster the simultaneous distribution of technology and power, strengthen democratic processes at the local scale, forge a more intimate dialogue between citizen and state, and transform structural violence into structural enablement. Our actions and our ideas breathe new life into cities on a daily basis. As we recreate them over and over again, the cities of today have the potential to emerge and converge to become equitable, ecologically responsive cities of tomorrow.

Acknowledgements

The authors would like to thank the following organizations for their contributions to the IUCI: Pitagoras School administrators and teachers; APAFA Parents' Association; residents of the Eliseo Collazos neighborhood; COPASED; FORPRODES; Fundacion San Marcos; University of Washington Department of Landscape Architecture, School of Environmental and Forest Sciences, School of Nursing, Department of Global Health, College of the Environment, Global Health and Environment Fellows; Architects Without Borders—Seattle; Engineers Without Borders–Service Corps; R. Hunter Simpson Foundation; Suenos Peru; University of Washington Royalty Research Fund; US Environmental Protection Agency; Fogarty International Scholars Program; GOHealth Fellowship Program; Landscape Architecture Foundation Olmsted Scholars Program; National Defense Science; and Engineering Graduate Fellowship.

Many thanks to all of the students involved in the SQWater project; the Gardens, Green Space, and Health project; Design Activism Studios; International Exploration Seminars; and other independent study. Thank you as well to the many faculty, staff, and professionals who have participated in Design Activism Studios as lecturers and reviewers and who have helped to organize or participated in International Exploration Seminars. The authors would like to extend particular thanks to the following individuals for their contributions to the development of the IUCI: Joachim Voss, University of Washington School of Nursing; Joe Zunt, University of Washington Department of Global Health; Leann Andrews, University of Washington College of Built Environments; Gayna Nakajo, University of Washington Department of Landscape Architecture; and Shara Feld, University of Washington Department of Civil and Environmental Engineering.

Note

1   Shara Feld, Daniel Hoffman, Daniel Ramirez, Sunni Wissmer, Corey Dolbeare, Brooke Alford, Betsy Anderson, Leann Andrews, Kevin Bogle, Erica Bush, Peter Cromwell, Ginger Daniel, Vera Eve Giampietro, Orona Hai, Taj Hanson, Shu-Kuei Hsu, Cayce James, Kaie Kuldkepp, Jordan Lewis, Yu-Ting Lin, Gayna Nakajo, Jonathan Pagan, Hillary Pritchett, Angelica Rockquemore, Michael Schwindeller, Philip Syvertsen, Malda Takieddine, Hsien Ai Wang, Kei Sing Yiu, and Winnie Kuo, 2013 SQWater project.

References

Amnesty International (2013). *We Are Like Rubbish in this Country*. London: Amnesty International Ltd.

Boeston, K., Kolsky, P., and Hunt, C. (2007). Improving urban water and sanitation services: health, access and boundaries. In Marcotullio, P. J. and McGranahan, G. (eds), *Scaling Urban Environmental Challenges: From local to global and back*. London: Earthscan, 106–131.

Castro, C., Merzthal, G., and van Veenhuizen, R. (2011). The potential for treated wastewater use in Lima. In Butterworth, J., McIntyre, P., and da Silva Wells, C. (eds) *SWITCH in the City: Putting urban water management to the test*. The Hague: IRC International Water and Sanitation Centre, 68–83. [Online]. Available: www.switchurbanwater.eu/outputs/pdfs/SWITCH_in_the_City.pdf [July 2, 2014].

Costello, A., Abbas M., Allen A., Ball, S., Bell, S., Bellamy, R., Friel, S., Groce, N., Johnson, A., Kett, M., Lee, M., Levy, C., Maslin, M., McCoy, D., McGuire, D., Napier, D., Pagel, C., Patel, J., Antonio, J., de Oliveira, P., Redclift, N., Rees, H., Rogger, D., Scott, J., Stephenson, J., Twigg, J., Wolff, J., and Patterson, C. (2009). Managing the health effects of climate change. *The Lancet*, 373(9676), 1693–1733.

Davis, M. (2006). *Planet of Slums*. London: Verso.

De Sousa, C. A. (2006). Unearthing the benefits of brownfield to green space projects: an examination of project use and quality of life impacts. *Local Environment*, 11(5), 577–600.

Galtung, J. (1969). Violence, peace and peace research. *Journal of Peace Research*, 6(3), 167–191.

Garrido-Lecca, H. (2010). *Inversion en agua y sanamiento como respuesta a la exclusión en el Peru: gestación, puesta en marcha y lecciones de Programa Agua Para Todos (PAPT)*. Santiago, Chile: UN.

Hamdi, N. (2004). *Small Change: About the art of practice and the limits of planning in cities*. London: Earthscan.

Johnson, S. (2002). *Emergence: The connected lives of ants, brains, cities, and software*. New York: Scribner.

Kumar, S. (2002). *Methods for Community Participation: A complete guide for practitioners*. London: Practical Action Publishing.

McGranahan, G. (2007). Urban transitions and the spatial displacement of environmental burdens. In Marcotullio, P. J. and McGranahan, G. (eds), *Scaling Urban Environmental Challenges: From local to global and back*. London: Earthscan, 18–44.

Maxwell, D., Levin, C., and Csete, J. (1998). Does urban agriculture help prevent malnutrition? Evidence from Kampala. *Food Policy*, 23(5), 411–424.

Mostafavi, M. and Doherty, G. (2010). Why ecological urbanism? Why now? In Mostafavi, M. and Doherty, G. (eds), *Ecological Urbanism*. Baden: Lars Müller Publishers, 12–55.

Murphy, A. (2013, December 24). What's a walk in the park worth in Peru? *The Christian Science Monitor*. [Online]. Available: www.csmonitor.com/World/Americas/2013/1224/What-s-a-walk-in-the-park-worth-in-Peru [January 8, 2014].

Neuwirth, R. (2005). *Shadow Cities: A billion squatters in a new urban world*. New York: Routledge.

Nurse, J., Basher, D., Bone, A., and Bird, W. (2010). An ecological approach to promoting population mental health and well-being: a response to the challenge of climate change. *Perspectives in Public Health*, 130(1), 27–33.

Painter, J. (2007). *Deglaciation in the Andean Region*. UNDP Human Development Report 2007/2008. New York: UN Development Programme. [Online]. Available: http://hdr.undp.org/sites/default/files/painter_james.pdf [July 9, 2014].

Servicio de Parques de Lima (SERPAR) (2014). *Proyectos y Obras*. [Online]. Available: www.serpar.gob.pe/obras-entregadas/ [January 8, 2014].

Spencer, B. (2009). Upgrading slum upgrading. *Column 5*, 23, 64–69.

Spencer, B. (2010). Design, ecology and health in Lomas de Zapallal. In Carsjens, G. J. (ed.), *Landscape Legacy: Landscape architecture and planning between art and science: Council of Educators in Landscape Architecture and International Study Group on Multiple Uses of Land Conference Proceedings*. Maastricht: Council of Educators in Landscape Architecture and International Study Group on Multiple Uses of Land, 56.

Spencer, B., Bolton, S., and Feld, S. (2014a). SQWater: Design pedagogy for slum cities. In Li, M. H., and Kim, H. W. (eds), *Layers: Landscape, city and community: Council of Educators in Landscape Architecture, Conference Proceedings*. Baltimore, MD: Council of Educators in Landscape Architecture, 54.

Spencer, B., Bolton, S., Voss, J., Alarcon, J., Andrews, L., Feld, S., Ravindran, R., Salazar, F., Alford, B., and Nakajo, G. (2014b). Gardens and health in Eliseo Collazos. In Carney, J. A, and Cheramie, K. (eds), *EDRA 45, Building With Change: Proceedings of the 45th Annual Conference of the Environmental Design Research Association*. New Orleans, LA: Environmental Design Research Association, 311.

Turner, J. F. C. (1988). An introductory perspective. In Turner, B. (ed.), *Community Building: A third world case book*. London: Building Community Books, 13–16.

UN-Habitat (2003). *The Challenge of Slums: Global report on human settlements 2003*. London: Earthscan.

UN-Habitat (2012). *Urban Planning for City Leaders*. Nairobi: UN-Habitat.

UN (2013a). *The Millennium Development Goals Report*. New York: UN.

UN (2013b). *World Economic and Social Survey 2013: Sustainable development challenges*. New York: UN.

Van den Berg, A., Hartig, E. T., and Staats, H. (2007). Preference for nature in urbanized societies: stress, restoration, and the pursuit of sustainability. *Journal of Social Issues*, 63(1), 79–96.

Waldheim, C. (2006). Landscape as urbanism. In Waldheim, C. (ed.), *The Landscape Urbanism Reader*. New York: Princeton Architectural Press, 37–53.

World Health Organization (WHO) and UN-Habitat (2010). *Hidden Cities: Unmasking and overcoming health inequities in urban settings*. Kobe: WHO and UN-Habitat.

Zezza, A. and Taciottie, L. (2010). Urban agriculture, poverty and food security: empirical evidence from a sample of developing countries. *Food Policy*, 35(4), 265–273.

16

SHIFTING LANDSCAPE

reTHINKING Central and Eastern European Cities

Martin Joseph Barry

A dramatically new approach is required if we are to bring a human-centered perspective to designing livable and breathable cities around the world in the coming century. Landscape architects are in the midst of stealing the director's chair on this global project while we are keenly aware that "it is always too early, or too late, to talk about the cities of the future" (Bhabha 2009). While the cities of Central and Eastern Europe are far from the microphone of urbanism and future cities discussions, the region is ripe with new ideas and new perspectives on bringing contemporary urban discourse and participatory design to bear on a complicated past, replete with medieval buildings and a post-communist/pre-modern mindset. reSITE in Prague is an initiative that is currently testing the limits of collaboration and design discussion, building on other bottom-up movements that have been swelling in the region since the onset of the Great Recession.

Cities around the world are growing at the rate of about one million people per week. If you are reading this chapter, you are likely to know that by 2030, half of the world's population will live in cities, with 2.7 billion more people living in the world than do at this moment (EIU 2013). Over the next century, cities will continue to be centers of economic growth, innovation, and habitation for the world's most productive people. The reason: proximity matters. Good ideas and innovation are born in environments where people can exchange ideas and share information. According to the *Economist* Intelligence Unit, the cities of North America and Western Europe are and will continue to be the most innovative and competitive in the world until at least 2025 (ibid.). For several years, the science community has studied climate change and sea-level rise as a global and urban risk while the design community has researched best practices for future cities to withstand this risk, now commonly referred to as resiliency. Trademarked ecological solutions abound from "Oystertecture" to "sponge parks."[1] While ecological urbanism[2] is part and parcel of a design strategy for dense, urban, breathable environments, it is fair to say that a new kind of practice needs to be developed to deal with a growing urban population and a growing need to find resiliency—both ecological and community—for our cities. As a guiding framework, ecological landscape infrastructure is not the answer; nor is a dated model of public space design. A balanced environment needs a multifaceted design think-do tank that can respond artfully, scientifically, and gracefully to create urban space where serendipity and innovation proliferate. The urbane landscape architects among us have surmised that public space and urban landscape give urban citizens juxtaposition. "Cities are juxtaposition machines," as Michael Sorkin describes (2009: 8).

Not long ago, the architecture and planning community contended that flashy, multi-dimensional cultural buildings were the drivers of cultural vibrancy and neighborhood development with subsequent investment in the public realm. This is still the case in many developing countries, and may still play a positive role (if it ever did in our developing country). However, in a recent study directed by the Architectural League of New York, *Success Looks Different Now: Design and Cultural Vitality in Lower Manhattan*, author Raymond Gastil (2013) contends that iconic public space is the main driver of vitality in Manhattan and cities that can build dramatic civic space are the new "it" cities. "Well-designed, heavily used public space is already both symbol and embodiment of New York's cultural vibrancy," argues Gastil (2013: Recommendations and Conclusions).

Theorists and critics such as Michael Sorkin and Michael Kimmelman have also criticized the focus on the social and economic merit of individual buildings in our cityscape. Both Sorkin and Kimmelman claim that we should refocus our attention on civic and public sites. In the end, people come to cities to make their lives better. "They want to eat, meet, and make love so we should focus on the places where those connections happen—in streets and

FIGURE 16.1 The EDGE Waterfront, Brooklyn, New York, by W Architecture and Landscape Architecture.

squares" (Rogers 2012). The point is that our focus should be on the spaces in between the buildings.

To the delight of landscape architects and urbanists, attention has turned to urban landscape as the savior of livability in the modern city. The construction of iconic public space is now the symbol of a cool city, as city planner Gastil (2013) contends. Rightfully, buildings have become secondary in the discussion of city making because it is the space between that creates serendipity, connection, and innovation. If we set the urban stage to catalyze these moments, we will enrich the bones of breathing cities because the "capillaries of democracy" are in public space where theater happens, where chance encounters and surprise are interlinked to enhance the urban condition (Coles 2005: 23).[3]

Central and Eastern European (CEE) Cities

Central and Eastern European (CEE) cities, far from the focus of international planning and architecture circles yet geographically close to their counterparts in Western Europe, are struggling to overcome 40 years of communist-era planning and 20 years of rampant (and often corrupt) market-driven development to become more modern and livable.

Igor Kovacevic, a Bosnian architect and urbanist practicing and teaching in Prague, points to what he calls the "twin decades" as a basis of understanding why CEE cities like Prague have experienced a disconnect with their Western European neighbors:

> In central Europe we speak about twin decades in urbanism and city development. The twin decades are a cycle in our generation in Central Europe where everything started from zero. Urbanism is a perfect example of starting from zero. After the [Velvet] Revolution, urbanism became almost a taboo because it was politically incorrect to propose big ideas about what will happen in the future where the predominant architects and urban planners believed that free market would solve everything. So, we had this twin decade, let's say until 2008/9, when everyone finally understood that the free market economy and neo-liberal ideology would not save the world.
>
> *(Kovacevic 2013)*

The transition from communism to the free market was essentially a shift from one limiting, dogmatic ideology to another. Nowhere are the effects of ideology-driven policies more visible than in a city's physical environment. The close-mindedness of the architectural elite in cities like Prague has delayed the shift in urbanism praxis, limiting the ability to move a modern, collaborative discourse forward. This has left CEE cities struggling to incorporate new ideas in planning, which focus on urban-scale sustainability, iconic public spaces, resiliency, and livable, human-scaled environments.

Of 120 cities ranked in the *Economist* Intelligence Unit report (2013), Prague ranked 54. This middle-of-the-road placing suits the contemporary Czech condition quite well. As the popular young critic and public figure (and Czech national) Adam Gebrian points out, the Czech and Slovak national creed is "nothing ventured, nothing lost" (2011: 34).

While CEE cities are not experiencing the massive growth seen in the developing world, they still share concerns and solutions that the rest of the developed and developing world deal with. Transportation, democracy, equity, private and public development, sustainability, transparency, quality governance, real estate finance, and improving public participation are

FIGURE 16.2 Prague, Czech Republic.

all areas of urbanism that require study and improvement in these cities. Prague, the seventh richest city in the European Union (measured by GDP per capita), is a city that is geographically west of Vienna yet almost universally considered Eastern Europe by those who live outside of the Czech Republic. Yet, no one would consider Vienna as part of Eastern Europe. Why? Prague is geographically in the center of Europe with strategic connections to the west and east. It is ranked number eight in terms of "city branding" by the City Mayors Foundation (2008). When considering architecture, urbanism, and planning, part of the answer lies in the fact that the Czech Republic has closed its eyes when confronted with contemporary models of urbanism from abroad, especially since gaining independence after the Velvet Revolution of 1989 when the free-market ideology began its reign. Nigel Atkins, the Paris- and Prague-based developer and urban planning professor at the Sorbonne, stimulated discussion at reSITE Conference 2013 with his critique of Czech architects and politicians. Atkins—in a moment of near-exasperation—exclaimed that "the problem with Czechs is that they are at once self-conscious and self-righteous," meaning that Czech politicians, architects, and urbanists will never admit that they need international advice because they think that they have all of the best answers already, regardless of training or awareness of established and tested international norms.

Transitioning from the first to second era of the twin decades, forward-thinking cities and universities around the world began focusing on public space and public landscapes in cities while Czech faculties, developers, and municipalities struggled to balance a former communist bloc, top-down planning (often facilitated by architects), and a city management model with progressive market models. When I asked Kovacevic what the biggest roadblocks have been, the answer was simple:

> Things which have gone wrong are done under an umbrella of corruption. I hope that normal inhabitants of the city will lead the fight against corruption. The question is not about "what Prague is doing right" but rather what Prague citizens are doing well. I think that finally we have a generation that cares about public interest and civic good. That is the biggest advantage of Prague in this moment. Only if political stupidity or intolerance will not destroy it.
>
> *(Kovacevic 2013)*

This closed mindset has produced a dangerous knowledge void relative to urban planning and development. Most of this seems to be driven by fear of change in pedagogy and practice. When considering landscape architecture, a profession that has recently provided leadership on large-scale urban projects around the world, CEE has not embraced the change, particularly with regard to engaging landscape architects and other allied disciplines in the design process. Prominent architects reveal that they have a desire to integrate innovative landscape architects into their teams, as is common in other countries, but the consensus is that the local talent pool is ill-trained for urban works. In the Czech Republic, there is limited acceptance of foreign teams working in the country because municipalities are unaware of norms in neighboring countries, and the local architects are unwilling to share a piece of the pie.

Moreover, there is a lack of public discourse in CEE urbanism and planning. In the Czech Republic, community groups are seldom included or interested in development discussions. This is at least in part due to a communist past, where communal demonstrations and participation in government activities was frowned upon—unless, of course, groups were showing their support for the Party. Cultural norms are also different in Prague than in my hometown, New York, where community groups have had large influence over public–private works since the Jane Jacobs-inspired activism in the 1960s. Slavic people tend to be shy, or passive, as Adam Gebrian pointed out to me in a recent interview. Thus, there is little discourse about the public realm *in* the public realm. Last, the political and architectural elite do not think that planning is a topic that the public should comment on. Prominent Czech professors have told me that urban planning, architecture, and development are not topics that should be discussed with the public.

"Public health depends on the freedom of public discourse. A society that cannot speak to itself is a society in crisis. Public space provides a physical context for this discourse" (Kimmelmann 2012). We frequently fail, even in the United States, to carry out healthy public discourse with a civic good in mind. This is the case in the Czech Republic, and in CEE at large. While public criticism of certain municipal projects in Prague has encouraged a rethinking of specific infrastructure expenditures in the city, public discourse about architecture, landscape, urbanism, and planning in general is surprisingly scarce. There are over 50 civil societies that claim to focus on public space in Prague, a city of 1.3 million people, but there is a surprising lack of collaboration among these groups, with virtually none forming coalitions to influence positive change, until very recently. However, there is an emerging hunger for more information and more discussion about what is happening in Prague and in international city development on the whole, particularly in the public realm where Prague has been the overlooked middle child of city development over the last several decades.

FIGURE 16.3 Vltava River waterfront, Prague, Czech Republic.

As described by Maria Topolcanska, public space suffers from a sacred cow syndrome in the CEE region:

> Usually the sacred cow of public space occurs in two variants: scraggly, unnoticed and without stimuli (where it is a leftover of large spatial urban gestures) or a fat, commercially manipulated 'public good' (decorated with the gifts of the new capitalist economy, tourist attractions or Christmas markets). In both cases, this sacred urban animal is unhealthy and kept on the chain of prejudice.
>
> *(Topolcanska 2011: 70)*

She goes on to describe how keeping public space sacred only allows us to know that the "public" still exists and has a right to demonstrate or use it. Yet, the label "public space" gives it a stigma rather than releasing it to be rethought and repurposed for a modern society. It is easy to spot both the commercialized squares and the dilapidated ones in any of these cities. At reSITE Conference 2013, Adrian Benepe, former Commissioner of Parks for the City of New York, described Prague's public spaces as having inherent beauty but noted that graffiti on buildings and walls highlights the lack of maintenance, complacency, and general dereliction.

Contemporary education and the practice of landscape architecture in the Czech Republic—and CEE in general—is largely limited to garden and romantic park design with strong roots in the Beaux Arts garden tradition. Landscape architects are rarely integrated into design teams for large urban projects while planners, architects, engineers, and clients typically define a minimal role for them when they are included. Planners are more often than not architects who studied "architecture and urbanism," a building-centric pedagogy that focuses on buildings as icons and tools for urban development, a very outdated model of urban planning. In both eras of the twin decades, rather than focusing on increasing density in underutilized areas of the city, the municipality has been incentivizing development in the outer districts, far from public transport hubs and mostly reliant on the automobile in a salute to postwar America, even in a city whose public transport network is seen as one of the finest in Europe. The new flats on the outskirts are dismal semi-urban environments, unrelated to the magnificent architectural, economic, and cultural legacy of Prague, not to mention the greenfields that the developments have commandeered.

In order to facilitate a suburban expansion, Prague embarked on one of the largest urban motorway expansions in Europe with the Blanka Tunnel project. Blanka, started in 2007 and now 80 percent complete, has cost 1.4 billion euro. Blanka provided an incentive for Czech civil societies to criticize the expenditure. We now know that the best way for cities to reduce their carbon footprint and be "green" is to limit car usage and to build up, not out. Rather than making money available to incentivize more density and create more affordable housing closer to the historic center, the city is actively investing enormous sums in more roads and other projects that result in less density. Not only does this send the wrong message to the world, but also it misses an opportunity to define sustainable development in the region. If the city was paying attention to urban trends around the world, the funding could have been used on a plethora of projects aimed at improving the waterfront, public space, and sustainable mobility in Prague and other Czech cities.

As Enrique Peñalosa, the former Mayor of Bogotá and a prominent urban thinker, pointed out at reSITE Conference 2013 in Prague, "An advanced city is not a place where the poor move about in cars, rather it's where even the rich use public transportation." Peñalosa went on to add, "If we can design a successful city for children, we will have a successful city for all people" (Peñalosa 2013) Peñalosa is right; it is our moral obligation to integrate landscape and sustainable mobility as a free democratic right in cities while connecting with and bringing the public into the process.

Emergent Urbanisms in Central Europe

An incremental and tactical approach is required to aggregate the necessary data while overcoming many of the existing hurdles of bringing diverse and opposing groups together to solve pressing urban problems such as overlooked public space and investment on the riverfronts. Part and parcel of a design strategy for rebranding dense urban environments in the region will be to define the next kind of design practice for our century. As stated in the introduction, a new kind of practice needs to be developed to deal with a growing urban population and cities interested in change but not ill-equipped to realize it.

So, what has been happening in recent years to change the situation? There are new alternatives to the status quo and several emerging students, designers, and academics are engaging urban landscape issues that are shifting the design discourse in Prague, Bratislava, Brno, and other cities in the region. Sustainable urbanism is beginning to seep into political and academic circles at conferences such as reSITE Conference and Urban Interventions and at the first private international college of architecture in Prague, the newly established Architectural Institute in Prague (ARCHIP). ARCHIP, which is in the midst of its second semester, is interested in the intersection of architecture, urban design, and landscape architecture, which is a ground-breaking endeavor.

In 2008, Igor Kovacevic and an organization he founded with Yvette Vasourkova, CCEA, launched the project Urbanity: Twenty Years Later, where they put together seven capitals of Central Europe: Prague, Budapest, Bratislava, Berlin, Vienna, Ljubljana, and Warsaw. Under the auspices of six mayors, "we developed new approaches in the urban planning in the CE capitals. Seven universities and academies joined the project and we published a book about the findings" (Kovacevic 2013). A crucial change in ideology was noticed when "we started to speak with urban planners and architects in public forums, asking them to share their knowledge and experience. I must say that Prague was the hardest one to start serious debate with people teaching at university."

Urban Interventions

> We are tired of the fact that people don't shout when they should shout, that they look down when they should look all around; we do not like the fact that too many of our friends want to leave our city. Resignation is a disease of our latitudes and generation.
>
> *(Vallo and Sadovsky 2011: 19)*

One of the most notable projects that focused on the urban landscape was an open-call exhibition, blog, lecture series, documentary film, and subsequent publication called Urban Interventions. Two enterprising young architects from Bratislava named Matus Vallo and Oliver Sadovsky devised the project, very simply, to solicit ideas for their city. They wanted to provoke their friends in architecture to think about the neglected urban environments in

Bratislava. The project was so popular that the Czech cities Prague and Brno started their own Urban Interventions. By 2011, when it was all over, 255 architects had spent over 9,800 hours creating and submitting ideas that were worth 186,900 euro in design fees for their cities (Vallo 2011). In the inaugural open call in Bratislava, 36 teams proposed 49 interventions for their city. Two years later in Prague, 60 teams submitted 81 interventions. In Brno, 60 architects submitted 193 interventions in the 2011 call or re-installation as it was named. The ideas ranged from lightweight foldable chairs for street musicians to dramatic transformations of the waterfronts.

In 2013, I spoke with the co-founder of Urban Interventions, Matus Vallo, and he explained the reasons behind launching the now internationally popular project:

> The Urban Interventions project was implemented in 2008 as a response to the catastrophic situation not only within the corporeality of our public premises, which were, of course, neglected and, in fact, beyond the city's interests but also to the way in which city officials faced the problem. The [project's] concern was also to change public opinion regarding architects as individuals who just make profit of often non-ethical developers' actions that destroy cities.
>
> *(Vallo 2013)*

The seed of Urban Interventions took root when Vallo noticed a narrow sidewalk on his girlfriend's street. He doubted that the city would ever take seriously his idea of adding a pedestrian path because politics and city development in Bratislava are not set up to listen to citizen complaints and ideas for their public realm. For Vallo, the premise of the initiative was as much about the time that architects spend doing this work for free—as advocacy—as it was about the propositions themselves. Vallo put "unsolicited architecture" and "pro bono architecture" in the context of the Great Recession and noted that the world of private finance and development, in which many generations of architects worked before him, was effectively over. He illustrated that politicians and decision-makers in the region rarely put public interest or public architectural opinion at the center of their urban development decisions:

> With Urban Interventions, we have probed a world where a municipal official still holds unusual power and the entanglement of legislative acts still gives him great opportunities; however, they are not always making the right decisions to regulate urban growth, but rather as a means of obtaining personal favors.
>
> *(Ibid.)*

The fact of the matter is that even in a modern age of more access to information and pressure from the European Union, large urban development projects still lose up to 30 percent of project budgets to corruption. Staggering as it may be, the numbers climb higher when you travel further east.

The ideas call was interesting in that it was the first time anyone had organized professionals to propose ideas for their cities in the region. It investigated the risk that architects needed to take to imagine such grand projects. "Would they wait for the phone to ring"? as John Peterson states in the foreword (Peterson 2011: 12). Contrary to when the phone rings with a developer on the other end, no one here was offered a fee. No participant had the promise of project realization. In fact, 90 percent of respondents in Bratislava answered "No" when asked by the organizers if they thought their project would be built. This was a leap of faith and commitment to one's city. Realized projects, in this case, would be an achievement; however, "the collective power of these projects may lie in their ability to fuel the belief of everyday people that cities are not immutable and that they have the ability and right to rearrange the furniture" (Peterson 2011: 12). The reality is that the projects jumpstarted a dead conversation about the collective urban realm in these cities. They unleashed the potential and imagination of hundreds of places in the cities. The designers did not bother to ask, "Who will pay for this?" or "How will it be received by the public?" The goals of the initiative were simple: advocate for the place and see if the idea sticks; see if politicians and decision-makers notice. In Bratislava, the first installment, the project was a direct criticism of the inaction of public officials while in Brno, the last, the mayor approached the organizers and became the lead partner. In Prague, over 28,000 people came to see the exhibition. The projects stuck.

Urban Interventions sought to leapfrog over the shyness of citizens and develop a new kind of urban stewardship by promoting and advocating for new kinds of urban public space. Unsolicited architecture sought to visualize a new platform for dialog about the cities' public spaces. This speaks to some of the reasons why the reticence of local citizens is now being usurped by cool, accessible platforms for young architects to be heard.

From a foreigner's perspective, the projects have great merit but fail only in their ability to be implemented and the respondents' understanding of comprehensive city design. As Vallo told me, nearly all participants were trained architects. Nearly no respondents were

FIGURE 16.4 The Green Square project is not only the cheapest method but also simultaneously the most visible attempt to change the atmosphere under the bridge, and to highlight the dysfunctional environment that everyone accepts out of habit.

urban planners, urban designers, or landscape architects, so the responses tended to be more object- or bobble-oriented than a systematic rethinking of the urban fabric. It was easy for municipal leaders and cultural figures to view the projects through the lens of art interventions or temporary installations to "spruce up" the public realm. In other words, many of the projects lacked economic backbone or redevelopment potential. This simply points to the fact that there is no higher-level education that focuses on the kind of collaboration and cross-disciplinary rigor between architects, engineers, landscape architects, economists, real estate specialists, and ecologists to propose and make truly sustainable and modern cityscapes, yet the architects still want to engage in this type of discourse. Vallo says that if they had the opportunity to rethink the project, they "would make it open to other professions and limit the proposals in a stricter format. We would perhaps offer two categories: vision and more real projects" (Vallo 2013). Urban Interventions was a great success in that it catalyzed a significant conversation about rethinking the "sacred cow" in three geographically, economically, and culturally significant cities in the region. Since 2011, seven other towns and cities have adopted the project in the former Czechoslovakia, which, as Vallo contends, is a testament the project's success.

reSITE

Building on the interest of public space and underutilized waterfronts that had been brewing for several years in Prague, I spent one year as Fulbright Scholar studying the existing urbanism framework and discourse. I found that there was immense hunger to learn how the public realm was designed elsewhere and how collaborative processes yielded smarter urban projects. After several months investigating the issues, I founded a non-profit organization and put together a team to raise awareness and foster long-term change that centered on more transparency, international input, and quality in governance. reSITE, a think tank and collaborative urban platform based in Prague, is setting the stage for a new kind of urban activism and urban design. reSITE acts as a catalyst for social action and innovative leadership—an international platform to exchange ideas about making cities more livable, resilient, and competitive. For the first time in the region, reSITE is merging the fields of science, design, finance, policy, and activism to promote balanced and innovative urban models to rethink public space, waterfronts, and mobility. Our international and diverse group is focusing our efforts in the CEE region that, as mentioned earlier, is often neglected in contemporary architecture, urbanism, and landscape discourse. Why? To stimulate social action for sustainable urban design and therefore cooler cities. reSITE stands for public space. The now internationally recognized platform is focused on urban issues that can help make cities in the region become cooler places to live, work, and play.

Since its launch in December 2011, reSITE has mobilized thousands of people at public events, free festivals, and three major international conferences in Prague. The events focus on asking questions and providing solutions for politicians, citizens, and investors to think about growth while weaving in a complex past. reSITE represents the future, as the prominent journalist Jan Machacek (2013) contended in his weekly column in the widely distributed *Respekt Magazine* after attending the 2013 conference. The energy surrounding the events has inspired businesses and a young generation to rally around our message partly because of the inspiring nature of the events and a mix of a young, educated, and energetic audience balanced by the more subdued presence of hardened politicians, architects, and investors.

FIGURE 16.5 Rosy (the Ballerina) at reSITE Festival 2012 in Prague.

FIGURE 16.6 reSITE Möbius Pavilion 2013 in Prague.

The themes that reSITE embodies—architecture, landscape, politics, finance, planning, and democracy—all meet when one thinks of cities and urban design. However, this multi-disciplinary mix is very unique—even strange—in the Czech Republic. We are often asked why we have merged so many topics into two-day conferences, and why we will not focus on one particular facet of city-building. Simply put, cities are not built of individual pieces; they are complex organisms built at the intersections of cultures, disciplines, and dynamic economies. Groups cannot address urban planning and urban design in an international and thoughtful way without merging disciplines and instigating discussion. Moreover, the public needs to be involved; hence the open admission policy of the conference and the popular, free public events and workshops that reSITE organizes.

In 2012, after five months of organization and two months of public notice, we attracted over 30 partners, were successful in a kickstarter.com fundraising campaign, and organized a major international conference and festival. At the inaugural reSITE Conference (2012), many of the world's top architecture, NGO, real estate finance, planning, landscape architecture, and urbanism experts convened in Prague to debate the state of the art and propose changes to the status quo. Speakers such as Craig Dykers (Snøhetta), Reinier de Graaf (OMA), Jan Gehl (Gehl Architects), Janette Sadik-Khan (City of New York), and Alex Washburn (City of New York) debated with locals Jakub Cigler, Igor Marko, Adam Gebrian, Nigel Atkins, Igor Kovacevic, and business leaders Paul Koch and Radek Spicar. Inspiring urban projects from Moscow, Paris, New York, Prague, London, Amsterdam, Copenhagen, Hamburg, and other world-class cities exhibited how effective municipal leaders and financiers commissioned leading architects to improve their cities not just for today, but for the next generation. Young people, business leaders, and the media greeted the six-day festival with tremendous enthusiasm.

In June 2013, reSITE organized the second annual conference at DOX Centre for Contemporary Art. Over 550 delegates from 20 countries attended the two-day event and 48 speakers from 19 countries contributed to the discussion. Since the conference, reSITE has formed closer ties with the City of Prague due to a very favorable review by politicians, deputies, investors, and journalists at the conference. While we understand that the political situation will continue to be unstable, we know that there are future leaders who will answer the challenges of demanding business leaders and that, most importantly, there is an energized and aware electorate that is pushing for a bottom-up, Jane Jacobs-type of approach, evidenced by like-minded projects such as Urban Interventions, *Zazit Mesto Jinak* (Experience the City Differently), and CCEA's Urbanity.

reSITE works with over 58 partners—large and small—across a spectrum of influential cultural, business, political, and community spheres. These organizations and businesses understand the need to infuse quality architecture, urbanism, and discussion about planning in their cities. We have negotiated a multi-year sponsorship from the largest private equity firm in the region, Penta Investments, the first sponsorship of its kind for the company. This partnership is evidence alone that we are finally bridging the gap between corporate interests and civic virtues, a relationship that has been strained for two decades.

Speakers like Greg Lindsay (*Fast Company Magazine*) talked about innovation and smarter work environments at reSITE Conference 2013, while Alex Washburn addressed finance, zoning, and sustainable, bottom-up/top-down urban planning perspectives. Adrian Benepe (former Commissioner of Parks for the City of New York) talked about the need for more resilient design, private–public partnerships, and Mayor Bloomberg's goal of having a park within a ten-minute walk of every New Yorker. The conference highlighted European expertise by having Kees Christiaanese (KCAP) discuss urban planning in the Netherlands while Winy Maas (MVRDV) talked about merging the past with the future in an innovative way that stimulates controversial discussions about the cities he works in. The tremendously popular Enrique Peñalosa, former Mayor of Bogotá, brought a room of over 450 to their feet, with thundering applause for his critique of democracy and his observations in the city of Prague. A special panel of experts Gines Garrido, Vladimir Sitta (Terragram), and Barbara Wilks (W Architecture and Landscape Architecture) debated resiliency, flooding, and waterfront investment ideas with local officials Tomas Ctibor and Pavla Melkova from the newly established Prague Office for Public Space at the City Development Authority (URM). For two years in a row, the question that has endured after dozens of presentations and debates has been: "Why can't we do this here?"

The reality is that cities like Prague are uniquely positioned, geographically and historically, to be very competitive and livable cities. Speaking of competitiveness, there is no correlation between the size of a city and how competitive it is. Cities of all sizes can be competitive. For example, Zürich, with a population of 1.4 million people, is in the top ten most competitive cities in the world (EIU 2013). reSITE is utilizing this kind of data and analysis to make the argument for public and private investment in the public realm, which we know will help attract and retain young, talented people in CEE cities.

reSITE aims to be a symbol of informed awareness. In its second year, the organization is already a leading expert voice in the region about internationally significant urban planning and development. It is also important to note that we are the only organization discussing landscape architecture as an internationally viable and emerging design profession. In order to be fresh yet regionally relevant, the program mixes fresh local energy with iconic, international expertise that can catalyze social awareness and citizen participation. We hold the deep belief that Prague and other cities can evolve to become uniquely modern metropolises. Our outreach and awareness bridge is helping encourage politicians to make better decisions for the future of their cities.

The energy created by events like ours represents a new generation of thinkers and doers in Central Europe. reSITE has become popular addressing the reticence of citizens partly because we are addressing the issue of modernization. This is exciting to a young population that is looking past the tired post-communist narrative to inspire a new vision of the city that will be led by a new generation unburdened with the inefficiencies of the past.

We have addressed these issues in a fresh, transparent format in order to pull formerly shy citizens out of their shells. In 2012, we commissioned raumlaborberlin to install a 150-person, inflatable, transparent bubble in the center of Prague. Named Rosy (the Ballerina), the bubble served as a venue for films, performances, discussions, urban games, and workshops. In 2013, we commissioned a young architecture studio to design and build a timber pavilion with students at ARCHIP: the Möbius Pavilion. It was installed for four days at Charles Square, again in Prague. In both cases, the pavilions became a literal manifestation of our mission, a tool for rethinking the urban environment. The workshops and free events we have hosted over the last two years at the pavilions have encouraged people to re-engage and re-imagine their public space by learning to draw or game it, and by teaching them about the merits of collaboration. This has helped people connect with each other and the public space, which we hope has encouraged them to engage significant issues with peers and politicians.

Over the next five years, reSITE will remain committed to exploring the real economic, social, and ecological value that international and sustainable urban design adds to cities. Moving forward, the group will hold closed-door conferences during the year in order to form working groups to build consensus on new legislation and new priorities to innovate and regenerate CEE cities. We will continue to hold a major international conference in Prague, while working to expand our reach in the region. As part of this expansion, we are forming a graduate program focused on cities at an internationally recognized graduate institute of economics. We are also in the midst of designing the future reSITE pavilion, dPAV, in partnership with the world-renowned structural designer and artist Cecil Balmond. This pavilion will be the product of a two-year project, which commenced with an international workshop competition and will conclude with the construction of a state-of-the-art, open-air mobile pavilion that we will install in cities across the region as reSITE Festival expands.

In Central and Eastern Europe, there has been overwhelmingly positive media attention focused on the international scope, professionalism, and complexity of reSITE. We have been approached by and are currently working with organizations in Krakow, Katowice, Bratislava, Belgrade, Berlin, and Budapest to bring our events to those urban centers.

Initiatives such as Urbanity, Urban Interventions, and reSITE are restating how designers, communities, financiers, and politicians are shaping their urban environments. By highlighting design proposals that are accessible, transparent, and human-centered, attention will continue to shift to these types of projects and strategies in the region. reSITE, in particular, will continue to be driven by collaboration among diverse voices and will aim to catalyze more of the public to care for their city, to work on "unsolicited architecture," and

FIGURE 16.7 dPAV Pavilion winning entry.

to make politicians more aware of their options by working with international experts. reSITE is helping to create an entirely new market for diverse design and planning professionals who wish to be involved in city making in the region. The initiative is about making urban design cool and accessible and ultimately about making cities more livable, resilient, and competitive in the region. With the ball rolling toward modernization, reSITE and other ground-breaking initiatives are slowly chipping away at the formerly closed institution of city-building, ushering in a sense of collaboration and urgency while helping young professionals understand how to push for and adapt to change.

Notes

1   Kate Orff/SCAPE (2010) proposed the idea of "Oystertecture" as an active oyster culture that engages issues of rising tides, community participation, and water quality for the Museum of Modern Art exhibition titled *Rising Currents*. Susannah Drake/dlandstudio (2008) proposed the trademarked "sponge parks" to collect storm-water run-off on dead-end streets along the Gowanus Canal in Brooklyn, New York.
2   Ecological urbanism was the subject of a conference at the Harvard Graduate School of Design (2009) and a subsequent publication (2010). Ecological urbanism "considers the city with multiple instruments and with a worldview that is fluid in scale and interdisciplinary focus. Design provides the synthetic key to connect ecology with an urbanism that is not in contradiction with its environment. The book is part of an ongoing series of research projects at the GSD that explore alternative and radical approaches between ecology and architecture, landscape architecture, planning, and urbanism."
3   Coles refers to the churches, community centers, cafés, and streets of Durham in this light.

References

Bhabha, H. (2009, April 3). Keynote address: Rem Koolhaas in conversation with Homi Bhabha. *Ecological Urbanism: Alternative and sustainable cities of the future.*

City Mayors Foundation (2008, August 28). Paris, London and Barcelona are Europe's top city brands. *City Mayors Foundation.* [Online]. Available: www.citymayors.com/marketing/city-brands.html [July 9, 2014].

Coles, R. (2005). *Beyond Gated Politics: Reflections for the possibilities of democracy.* Minneapolis, MN: University of Minnesota Press.

Economist Intelligence Unit (EIU) (2013). *Hot Spots 2025: Benchmarking the future competitiveness of cities.* [Online]. Available: www.citigroup.com/citi/citiforcities/pdfs/hotspots2025.pdf [January 1, 2013].

Gastil, R. (2013). *Success Looks Different Now: Design and cultural vitality in lower Manhattan.* New York: The Architectural League of New York. [Online]. Available: http://archleague.org/2013/06/success-looks-different-now/ [June 1, 2013].

Gebrian, A. (2011). Can a city be changed quickly? Can demand be stimulated? In Vallo, M. and Sadovsky, O. (eds), *Urban Interventions.* Bratislava: Slovart Publishing, 34–36.

Kimmelmann, M. (2012, March 6). Public space and public consciousness. In *For the Public Good* (lecture series). Barnard College, New York.

Kovacevic, I. (2013). Unpublished interview with author.

Machecek, J. (2013, June 21). Nejlepši je za name (It is best for us). *Respekt Magazine.* Available: http://respekt.ihned.cz/index.php?p=R00000_d&article[id]=60112250&article[what]=resite&article[sklonuj]=on [July 7, 2014].

Mostafavi, M. and Doherty, G. (eds) (2010). *Ecological Urbanism.* Baden, Switzerland: Lars Müller Publishers.

Peñalosa, E. (2013, June 21). reSITE 2013 keynote speech. reSITE 2013 Metropolis Central: Infinite Resources, June 20–21, Prague, Czech Republic.

Peterson, J. (2011). Foreword. In Vallo, M. and Sadovsky, O. (eds), *Urban Interventions*. Bratislava: Slovart Publishing, 10–12.

Rogers, R. (2012, December). Discussion panel: Richard Rogers and Richard Sennett. Urban Age conference *Electric City*, London.

Sorkin, M. (2009). *Twenty Minutes in Manhattan*. London: Reaktion Books.

Topolcanska, M. (2011). Stop wasting urban area. In Vallo, M. and Sadovsky, O. (eds), *Urban Interventions*. Bratislava: Slovart Publishing, 70–80.

Vallo, M. (2013). Unpublished interview with author.

Vallo, M. and Sadovsky, O. (eds) (2011). *Urban Interventions*. Bratislava: Slovart Publishing. Bilingual edition.

ENDURING

How can our cities and communities adapt to ongoing changes in our political and atmospheric systems? How can our present actions lead to the long-term well-being of our cities and regions? As cities, communities, and ecosystems face calamities of ever-increasing scale and intensity, the resilience of the natural and built environments represents one of the most pressing challenges of our time. The present city does not stand still. The actions that we take *now* matter *now* and *later*.

Endurance is the ability to persist and prosper. It requires the capacity to adapt and regenerate in response to change, and to emerge from disturbance with function and direction. It is a dynamic predicated upon the presupposition of evolution. As the culminating section of this book, Enduring represents both an outcome—the consilience of the programs, actions, and processes that have been explored in earlier sections—and a provocation—an invitation to embrace change as an inherent characteristic of cities and a call for the ongoing interrogation of rote approaches to urban design.

Enduring cities learn from the past, live in the present, and look ahead to the future. They cultivate diversity, anticipate adversity, and acknowledge the interdependence of human and ecological systems. They situate, ground, perform, distribute, instigate, and endure. Endurance argues for neither the bromide of utopia nor the complacency of resignation. It requires us to come to terms with the present character of urban places, processes, and people, to bridge spatial, temporal, and disciplinary boundaries, and to imagine, think, and act in pursuit of ecological, equitable urban futures—now.

The chapters in this section explore how changing conceptions of the "city as nature" shape resiliency and generate new directions for endurance. The section concludes with a methodological articulation challenging positivist tendencies toward single-source responses in the production of urban nature. Together, these chapters outline a more nuanced and powerful resiliency that is about enduring now and in the future.

17

CITY SINK—SINKING CITIES

Or: How I Learned to Stop Worrying about the Carbon Cycle and Love Climate-Adaptive Design and Planning[1]

Denise Hoffman Brandt

City Sink: Carbon Storage Infrastructure for our Built Environment was an investigation into tactics for reducing the scale of climate change triggered by disruption of the carbon cycle by increasing the "sink" (non-atmospheric carbon storage) capacity within the urban landscape (Hoffman Brandt 2013). To say I "stopped worrying" about the carbon cycle is perhaps an overstatement. Writing this chapter was used as an opportunity to step back and reconsider urban carbon sink planning and design in light of a more fatalistic prioritization of climate change adaptation over preventive measures after Hurricane Sandy hit New York City in October 2012. *City Sink* was an optimistic call for city and suburban transformation across a spectrum of time-scales, from immediate sink in biomass to long-term—and slow—carbon sink in soil. The objective was to enhance the popular idea of the city as an urban ecosystem through building public awareness of the carbon cycle and not just emission control. This more nuanced understanding of the city as an ecosystem could increase the actionable intelligence of citizens as participants in processes of global climate change.

City Sink was framed by three key assertions. First, in order to act, planners and designers will have to overcome a normative assumption of their capacity to exert authority over urban landscapes. In place of that assumption, practitioners must seek to engage indeterminate processes that are not, ultimately, controllable. Carbon-cycle-based climate change is a complex scenario requiring action. However, beyond the clarity of its basic mechanisms, there is much indeterminacy in its projected effects in any specific location over time. This is problematic from a traditional planning standpoint. For example, it is not clear where the scale and rate of temperature and precipitation changes will result in a significant shift in food production capacity. How specific plants will respond to a shifting cocktail of atmospheric gases is also unknown. Could higher atmospheric carbon levels *naturally* increase sink to offset emissions? It is not possible to establish clear protocols with measurable metrics for remediation in such a dynamic scenario.

Second, this approach prioritizes the design of robust relationships within the urban ecosystem. Considering urban planning and design through the lens of ecological system cycling offers the potential to sync city making with environmental processes and non-human biotic systems. Reducing climate change to an *energy* issue obscures the inextricable relationships between human settlement practices and the carbon cycle. For example, prior to global industrialization, disruption of sink processes through land practices associated with urbanization (such as deforestation and tilling) was a significant contributor to rising atmospheric carbon levels (Ryan et al. 2010).[2] Concrete is currently the second most consumed substance on earth after water, and producing a ton of cement generates approximately a ton of CO_2 (Rubenstein 2012). By 2000, emissions due to concrete production had increased to over five percent of total emissions. Globally, homogeneous construction practices increasingly contribute to climate cycle disruption.

Third, and perhaps most importantly, to overcome lingering ambivalence toward human influence in environmental systems, the city itself, in the form of the everyday landscape (not just parks), should make legible the inextricable mesh of relationships between humans and *nature*.[3] Callendar's (1938) ground-breaking analysis of carbon data going back to 1880 and Keeling's equally unknown upward "curve" of atmospheric carbon data since 1958 reveal the longevity of scientific awareness of the linkages between carbon emissions and climate (Roston 2010). After 80 years, substantive planning and policy change to mitigate carbon cycle disruption remains elusive. The aforementioned indeterminacy and complexity of carbon cycling sustains political factions that balk at palliative action. There are plenty of openings for alternative theories of causation to create doubt within citizens already somewhat confused by the scientific rhetoric. Those doubts are reinforced by a perceived temporal discord wherein short-term expectations supersede understanding of the long time horizons required for some environmental processes to manifest—as in: "the planet can't be warming because we had a really cold winter."

I am concerned that with the rush to put a band-aid on New York City's coastline, there has been little acknowledgement that the wound was self-inflicted. The behaviors that instigated Hurricane Sandy are likely to continue unabated. Data from the *Global Carbon Budget 2012* (Global Carbon Project 2012) indicate that "large and sustained mitigation" will be required to keep temperature change below 2 °C, and current greenhouse gas emissions remain at the higher end of levels used in all Intergovernmental Panel on Climate Change (IPCC) model scenarios (ibid.). Ecologically viable urban adaptation to a changing climate will require more than reflexively rebuilding vulnerable neighborhoods, or even abandoning vulnerable areas. It will mandate a cultural re-imagining of the city as a dynamic ecological entity.

My optimism that a popular will can prevail to mitigate carbon cycle disruption dissipates when I observe the seemingly omnipotent forces of the coal/petroleum corporate complex. So, finding tactics for adapting cities to the many effects, both chronic (for example, seasonal flooding) and dramatically episodic (for example, superstorms), of higher global temperatures has reached parity with the original emphasis on mitigation strategies that framed *City Sink*. In other words, in a context where acting to prevent catastrophe was dominant in the discourse, my approach leveraged that energy. Now that preparing for the future climate transformation has taken over the public imagination, alliance with that mission seems essential. For both, the strategic agenda for the physical city is the same: to recover debilitated urban environmental system processes.

A Stronger, More Resilient New York (henceforth "SIRR"), published by the city's Special Initiative on Rebuilding and Resiliency in June 2013, was the primary frame of reference for the following reflections on applying the ideas in *City Sink* to adaptive planning and design (NYC 2013). That report is an impressive achievement from several standpoints, not least of which is the clarity of the explication of the effects of Hurricane Sandy on New York City. I think it is important to see the SIRR as a first step in an iterative recovery and adaptation planning process, and the following thoughts are intended to contribute to that ongoing discourse.

On Time

> Ecosystems are not readily defined by spatial criteria. Ecosystems are more easily conceived as a set of interlinked, differently scaled processes that may be diffuse in space, but easily defined in turnover time . . . Ecosystems can be seen more powerfully as sequences of events rather than things in a place.
>
> *(Allen and Hoekstra 1992, cited in Callicott 2002: 101)*

Gasification of fossil fuels creates a disruption not so much in space—where it is largely invisible—but in time. What took thousands of years to sink is emitted instantaneously into the atmosphere where it remains for 2,000 to 20,000 years. The need to make legible the temporal scope of the carbon cycle—and other earth systems—led me to contend that urban landscapes must convey time-spans from the instantaneous to the epochal. Positioning design to reveal the transformation of processes redirects practitioners to see their medium as operative verbs as opposed to nouns, things that are inert in a place.

Two tactics explored in *City Sink* to achieve this were:

1 establishing scenarios for biotic processes in the public realm to play out completely (rather than being cleaned up or truncated by maintenance regimes);
2 systemically aligning urban land-use and real estate cycles to the time-spans of carbon cycle processes.

Acting on both of these tactics would result in a much more dynamic experience of plant–soil systems in the urban environment than we have presently (Figure 17.1). Activating even short-term openings in the city fabric as temporary biomass sinks would generate a continually shifting patchwork of planted lots, many of them in neighborhoods that have little *green* space.[4]

City Sink proposed to reveal the full temporal scope and variable time-frames of environmental processes within the context of everyday experience to counter the perception that cities are not *nature* and to build actionable environmental intelligence.[5] As straightforward as this objective seems, it carries with it a substantive alteration in the normative approach to urban landscape planning and design. Precepts for "designing with nature" reliant on the idea that biotic systems are measurable, orderable, and tend toward a stable "climax" condition (the trajectory of which could be stewarded by humans for mutual benefit) were fervently articulated by Ian McHarg (1969). McHarg's mission to sustain ecosystems by minimizing anthropogenic disturbance through fixing rules for sustainable planning—rules based on an assumption of humanity's "unique and important role" and an ethical mandate to facilitate a deterministic natural order—has been carried forward by countless practitioners. This outdated, dichotomous ecological theory remains manifest in the production of predictive plans for unpredictable socio-environmental systems.

In order to plan within a context of indeterminate landscape capacities, the *City Sink* proposal established time-lines for activating urban parcels with carbon storage functionality based on land-use time-frames (Figure 17.2). For example, parcels with latent carbon sink

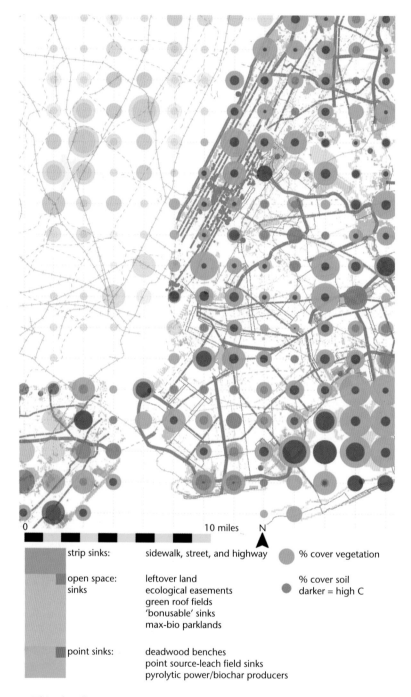

strip sinks: sidewalk, street, and highway   % cover vegetation

open space: leftover land   % cover soil
sinks   ecological easements   darker = high C
                       green roof fields
                       'bonusable' sinks
                       max-bio parklands

point sinks: deadwood benches
                       point source-leach field sinks
                       pyrolytic power/biochar producers

FIGURE 17.1 This plot illustrates the systemic infrastructure proposed in *City Sink* with an overlay of the projected increased relative levels of stored carbon in biomass and soil resulting from the new carbon sinks. What the static map does not convey is the seasonal expansion and contraction of the biomass quantities in the overlay, the spatially shifting sink sites as they are activated and deactivated with land-use change, and the constancy of the long-term sinks—forest and wetland—in areas with long-term land-use stability.

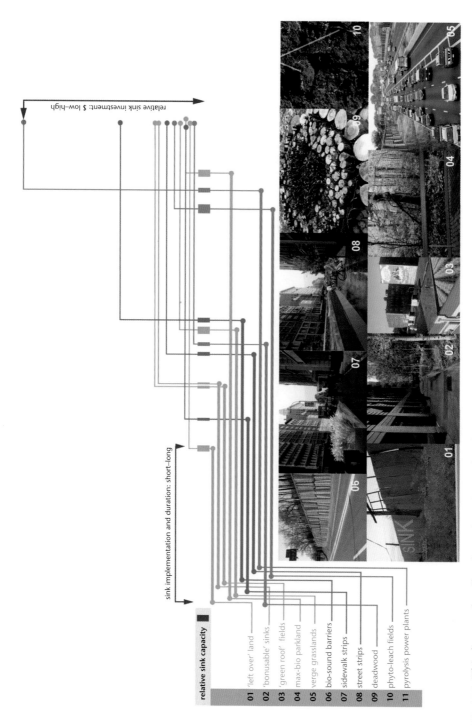

relative sink investment: $ low–high

sink implementation and duration: short–long

relative sink capacity

01 'left over' land
02 'bonusable' sinks
03 'green roof' fields
04 max-bio parkland
05 verge grasslands
06 bio-sound barriers
07 sidewalk strips
08 street strips
09 deadwood
10 phyto-leach fields
11 pyrolysis power plants

FIGURE 17.2 This diagram describes the various *City Sink* carbon storage apparatus: orange field installations, blue strip installations, and pink "point" sites in terms of their implementation time-frames, relative sink capacities, and relative implementation. These capacities were factored into a matrix of urban land-use types to outline a strategy for sink planning that can be adapted to variable and dynamic socio-environmental conditions.

capacity in dynamic real estate zones (areas with a potential property turnover of less than five years) could be activated with seasonal biomass cycling. Lots expected to be vacant longer (such as rights-of-way and brownfields) could be used for longer-term carbon sink processes that would contribute to soil carbon levels; or they could be activated with initiatives that contribute to civic and economic enterprises, such as nurseries growing urban-adapted plant material or phytoremediation test plots.

A more comprehensive syncing of socio-environmental process time-frames with projected climate change phenomena would have given the SIRR more credibility as a strategic plan for the whole city. The report attempted to parse an unfolding scenario, with chronic and episodic effects, based on a predicted (yet in reality unpredictable) scale of spatial impact. Matrices for each infrastructural sector inadequately distinguished between "gradual" effects of climate change (sea level rise, increased precipitation, and higher temperature averages) and "extreme events" (storm surges, heavy downpours, heat waves, and high winds). In nearly all cases, the "gradual" hazards associated with climate change were assessed to have minor to moderate risks over extensive time periods. Yet there are already many neighborhoods where existing precipitation and regular high tides are a source of persistent flooding that has begun to chronically undermine community stability.[6]

Destructive forces recurring with persistence in time can have, overall, as devastating an effect on communities as singular catastrophic events. The SIRR prioritizes coastal hazard events over the continuous and long-term degradation of processes such as seepage, low-level floods, brown-outs, black-outs, heat waves, and winter storm destruction that are affecting—and will continue to affect—areas of the city that are not necessarily on a shore-line. As a tacit policy, discounting the chronically debilitating conditions associated with climate change creates a burden on owners and renters who will have to continually adapt to the challenges of backed-up storm sewers, a rising water table, wind damage, and transit disruption among other stressors. The continuation of this policy will force many of New York's citizens to adapt to climate change at the domestic scale—without support from the city—reinforcing environmental injustice by entrenching people in neighborhoods with higher costs of domestic maintenance and suppressed property values.

On Indeterminacy

The emergence of theories relative to dynamic systems has altered fundamental practices in many disciplines directly related to urban planning and design. In weather forecasting, the introduction of alternate variables into calculations—to account for inherent uncertainty—has transformed deterministic predictions into probabilistic forecasting (Silver 2012: 120). That evolution reflects the transformation of the "fundamental organizing concepts in twentieth-century ecology" that occurred in the mid-1980s, the time period in which ecological theory shifted from "the balance of nature to the flux of nature" (Callicott 2002: 95). Idealization of a state of *natural* equilibrium within ecosystems and amongst biotic communities was supplanted by recognition that ecosystems are a continuously dynamic milieu wherein disturbance is normative. Biotic communities adapt, or not.

Still, the majority of planners and designers remain driven to produce an ideal condition of control over environmental systems and non-human biotic processes. Urban landscapes designed to have a static ornamental character in perpetuity—with change limited to managed growth of plant material—fulfill that objective. The underlying message of the view, an unnatural stability, coerces citizens to lose sight of the foundational condition of their ecosystem in exchange for an illusory peace of mind in the face of social and environmental forces beyond their control. More "natural" urban landscapes that are temporary, ad hoc, evolving in unexpected ways, and even dying, are hard to fit into the cities we seem to have inadvertently planned and designed *without* nature. Suffice it to say that the SIRR did not break new ground in this area.

On Planning to Build Robust Relationships to Support Ecosystem Processes

Despite the preponderance of theoretical writing on heterogeneity and dynamic urbanism, the standard operating procedures of city-planning remain to mandate spatial order, to communicate security, and to promote economic growth. Strategic plans that accommodate a multiplicity of possible agendas and potential formal outcomes are a very recent evolution in practice. Their outreach strategies reflect the emergence of trans-disciplinary planning teams, in that they often seek to connect with community members and institutions that are not typically cast into the planning process. Public outreach is taken out of the meeting room and into the streets to connect with inhabitants disassociated from existing political hierarchies (Interboro Partners 2009; Detroit Works Project 2013).

Loading the planning and design process with multi-faceted agendas—top-down, bottom-up, and everything in between—asserts that city making is more appropriately an act of orchestration than of fixing in space. To devise the sink landscape, *City Sink* orchestrated diverse scientific, economic, and design perspectives within a spectrum of land-use scenarios. Sinks had to perform environmentally by fixing carbon, and socially by adapting and contributing to local community habits of living. They also had to be financially viable and reasonably self-sustaining. The importance of leveraging a broad array of community and institutional forces beyond the typical cast of players was articulated in the technological, financial, and regulatory structures invoked.

Despite its pragmatic, incremental propositions, *City Sink* could be seen as idealistic. Timely, concerted, trans-disciplinary action assumes that the authority of the usual cast of characters—and their typical modes of operation—can be circumvented. Setting new performance criteria for urban infrastructures will require re-imagining not only the physical apparatus, but also the structuring authorities that determine city systems. The entities establishing priorities and parameters for transformation shape the outcome—so new projected outcomes will entail making new public and private sector partnerships.

In the rush to move forward post-Sandy, the SIRR team referred almost exclusively to the existing cast of city service providers, regulators, and trade organizations for guidance. This was a lost opportunity to initiate new partnerships to meet the heretofore unknown yet increasingly urgent challenges of climate change. For example, in the SIRR's proposal for "Utilities," of the 23 strategies outlined, all but three of them mandated participation of the normative cast of players: "utilities and regulators," "industry partners," "government and private sector partners" and the like. Voices who could speak to alternative modes of production, distribution, finance, and policy-making for new energy systems, but who were unaffiliated with the regional standard operators, were marginalized in the discourse. This undermined any potential to establish new parameters for future urban performance. The report sustains the status quo because the team did not take on the challenge of considering structural transformation of the relationships between institutional leadership roles. For example, the SIRR tipped its hat to micro-grid and other renewable, distributed energy systems, but did not mandate change because of the fear of undermining the viability of centralized utilities that will not prosper in a shift to decentralized systems and alternative fuel sourcing. This issue could have at least been laid out clearly as one that will require hard decisions for future resolution.

The role of public outreach should be reconsidered and expanded in future recovery planning. Instead of organizing public outreach to gather new knowledge from citizens for use in determining strategic action, the SIRR public engagement process was formatted as "briefings." SIRR meetings required pre-registration and were described as support for an in-progress report that would "address . . . how we rebuild New York City to be more resilient in the wake of Sandy" (NYC 2013). The mode of outreach established a forum for policy-makers to *inform* the community of their situation and then to hear *feedback* specifically framed around those ideas. The SIRR website notes that over 1,000 people "were directly briefed about SIRR." This is in contrast to the 150,000 citizens who participated over two years with the Detroit Works Project. The *Detroit Future City: 2012 Strategic Framework Plan* incorporated "Civic Engagement" as an ongoing social infrastructure (it warranted its own chapter in the book) that should be leveraged throughout research, planning, and implementation (Detroit Works Project 2013). Building long-term civic relationships and using feedback loops to reflect community input were highlighted as critical to the evolution of the strategies for future Detroit. Efforts like this should be incorporated into shaping future New York as well.

On Systemic Scope versus "Bigness"

The two key challenges for any proposal for boosting both terrestrial carbon storage and public awareness of carbon cycle processes are:

1   achieving substantive carbon offset capacity;
2   achieving legibility of the sink system.

I deemed the most effective action to meet the necessary scalar operations within the confines of the existing city would be to manifest the sinks as a city-wide infrastructural system. This allowed sink apparatus to pervade the city by latching onto existing infrastructure networks to insinuate overlapping functions into tight spaces. Sink capacity was proposed as an aggregate sum of the performance of many adaptive, multi-form structures: highway sound barriers, "soft" storm water management infrastructure, productive plantations, pyrolitic power plants, and septic remediation wetlands.

Finding equivalence between landscape and infrastructure has relevance for developing new infrastructures to adapt cities to sea level rise, increased storms or tidal surges, and other looming, city-debilitating processes associated with a projected global temperature increase. Both infrastructure and landscape can be understood as constructions that sustain socio-environmental processes. Landscape architecture[7] is currently the only design/planning discipline that foregrounds an understanding of environmental system processes, which will be essential to reinventing our cities with an understanding that they are *nature*. This approach would, of course, have implications for landscape policy-making.

In *City Sink*, "ecological easements" were devised as a mechanism to establish usufruct agreements between municipalities and property owners similar to "hard" utility easements. These compacts would benefit both parties and support the overlay of "soft," environmental process-based, public utility performance on private land. *City Sink* examined the easements' potential in the context of residential neighborhood storm water management (Figure 17.3). High-biomass drainage swales running along property lines were proposed to intercept run-off before it entered the street catch-basins. In this case, carbon sink was an indirect benefit of the direct enhancement to the existing, overloaded storm water management system. Such easements could be a valuable tactic to mitigate frequent, low-level flooding associated with projected increases in precipitation rates. This could eliminate the costs of monumental mechanical upgrades that incidentally use vast amounts of electricity to process storm water prior to release into streams.

Monumental marine barriers can trigger indirect, unintended negative socio-environmental impacts. Because of their size, they invariably but differentially affect many contiguous socio-environmental systems. For that reason, it was a relief to hear fairly early in the public discourse of a pull-back on the part of the local and regional leadership from proposals for big estuarine barrier walls and gates. These expensive barriers would have necessitated extensive shoreline alterations to protect property and coastal systems on the "outside" of them. Those structures in turn would have had incalculable costs and effects on regional marine hydrology and coastal habitats.

FIGURE 17.3 Bio-swales to collect run-off from yards before entering the street, with permeable pavement in the residential roadway, were proposed as an alternative to expansion of the energy-intensive sewage treatment facility for Glen Cove on Long Island. The current storm water system is not adequate to handle the run-off from Long Island's sprawling development, and there is no money available to upgrade the system. Systematizing ecological easements present a low-cost mechanism to manage storm water and reduce energy usage.

Recognizing the ramifications of big moves reflects an evolution in urban systems planning. The format of the first section of the SIRR—an array of tactics organized by infrastructure sector—had the potential to be a kit-of-parts from which to build context-specific plans over time. Instead, the proposals for immediate action in the second half of the report were predictive rather than conditional, framed as the single, *right* solution for action with no explication of weighing alternative approaches. This rush to present a viable future for damaged neighborhoods is understandable, but the opportunity to develop a clear criteria-based method for using the tools in the first half of the report was lost.

On Balkanization

The SIRR presents tactical solutions to the challenges of climate change without acknowledging the systemic practices that instigated the disruptive phenomena in the first place. With the exception of a few references to increasing energy efficiency, there is no critique of the relationship between New York City's energy sourcing or the environmental impact of common construction practices, nor is there any consideration for building carbon sink capacity to reduce the city's carbon footprint. The report presents the city as an island unto itself, dissociated from the national and global challenges that climate change presents. It is as if the city were somehow at a still place outside the causal scope of the complex interweave of human and environmental forces that the report seeks to mitigate (Figure 17.4).

Constructing the future city is to build human habitat. Habitat-building requires conceptualization of the operating systems of the organism, not simply classification of geospatial phenomena. Environmental process trajectories are variably scaled and contingent on an array of processes acted on by multivalent forces that have reciprocal influence on each other. Traditional planning practices establish artificial boundaries (for manageability and cost efficiency, and based on arbitrary corporate or municipal divides) that squelch robust landscape relationships by disregarding the scope of interrelated socio-environmental processes in time and space.

To counteract these balkanizing influences, future SIRR reports could take more advantage of a growing confluence in New York City agency interrelationships. In recent years, the city's agencies have begun to coordinate projects to take advantage of overlapping performance capacities in the urban landscape. The New York City Department of Parks & Recreation Green Infrastructure program is one example. Parkland (in New York City that generally means any area with plants) takes on storm water management and traffic control functions in the form of Greenstreets plantings. Here, one agency's park is another agency's storm water retention area. What if those areas were also a source of renewable bio-fuel and a resource for a school learning lab? All of these capacities can only be fulfilled if designers and planners can look across bureaucratic, political, and physiographic lines to design with multi-scalar, socio-environmental processes playing out at variable rates.

On Common Sense and Metrics

Open land, *vacant* lots, *abandoned* sites, and brownfields—all terms that imply latent unrealized social-use potential—should be revalued to account for existing environmental process capacities that contribute directly and indirectly to human ecologies. Re-visioning

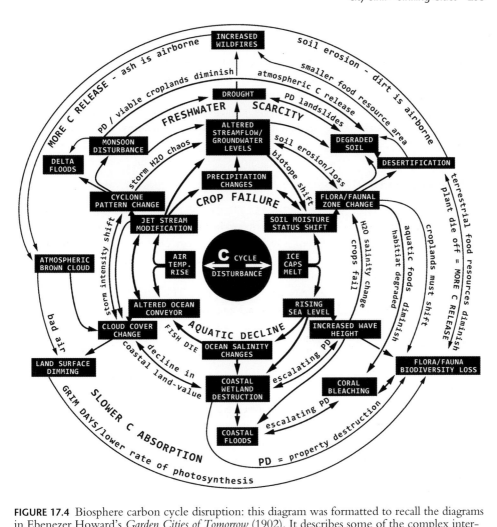

FIGURE 17.4 Biosphere carbon cycle disruption: this diagram was formatted to recall the diagrams in Ebenezer Howard's *Garden Cities of Tomorrow* (1902). It describes some of the complex inter-relationships between human and environmental systems triggered by, and reciprocally escalating, global climate change.

urban landscape in an expanded field, as not just park but rather as a constructed city-sustaining socio-environmental system—an infrastructure—challenges the current criteria for valuing urban landscape performance.

In America, land that is perceived as unproductive is considered to be wasted. The land—and by extension the landowner—is not achieving its "highest and best use." This extends even to situations where there is a clear, high degree of local cultural or environmental attachment to the place but where no direct social benefit is discernible. Production of pollinator habitat, run-off retention, carbon sink in biomass accumulation, and soil building are just a few of the critical operations of urban open space that could be perceived as valuable if indirect benefits were to be factored into urban land assessment. Valuing indirect environmental or cultural benefits would add additional overlays of significance to be factored into land assessment outside of capital markets.

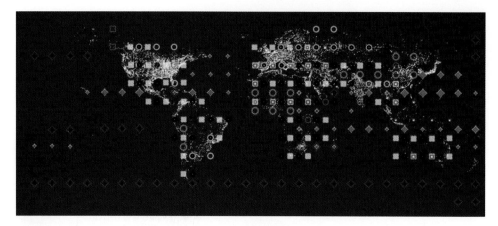

FIGURE 17.5 Still from an animation describing evolving global territorial ecologies. The changing map illustrates the operational context of twenty-first-century urbanism as defined by the various hazards associated with climate change. The hazard icons reference in their form the Louis Vuitton's "Monogram" canvas pattern. The economic system that gives the "LV" motif a wide cultural meaning is as unintelligible at a human scale as the global environmental processes the icons represent. Within the time-frames of individuals and community associations, both systems are characterized by dramatic, compelling incidents, while the forces that relate them systemically remain hidden. Their time-scales surpass easy apprehension. To design for ecological viability, we must act as agents within these larger forces, be they the compulsions of economic hegemony or the seemingly limitless contingencies of myriad environmental systems.

For example, we know carbon sink, as a process, is particularly valuable as high atmospheric carbon levels threaten global climate stability. The observation that Eastern Forest regrowth was a measurable offset to escalating atmospheric carbon levels associated with industrialization establishes a meaningful paradigm for action. It is no great intellectual leap to assume that boosting biomass carbon storage is a good thing. So while we wait for scientists to explore the intricacies of which type of plant offers optimal sink capacity, or what quantity of a specific type of plant would be required to sink a designated amount of CO_2, why are we not radically transforming our cities with massive new plantings using common sense?

The SIRR offers no overarching standard of achievement beyond reducing "expected losses in the 2050s by up to 25 percent, or more than \$22 billion" as stated in the foreword by Mayor Bloomberg (NYC 2013). The SIRR's call to build a stronger, more resilient city rests on constructing the apparatus to limit future economic losses due to climate change phenomena. It is sensible to seek to avert economic destabilization; but should that be the sole criterion for success? Is there no other actionable value system that could inform the development of a more satisfying future vision for remaking the city?

On an Expanded Idea of Material Integrity

Material integrity tends to refer to the *wholeness* of a material component in relation to its potential for break-up and performance failure. If the scope of landscape performance is expanded beyond human placemaking and aesthetic styling, designers are unburdened of the task of modeling ever more refined forms to reflect a progressive advancement of cultural refinement. Practices would shift toward exploring diverse material capacities rather than seeking to fit within a recognizable formal style. This approach is more appropriate to instrumental sites that have physical performance requirements that must be formally negotiated through complex, multi-layered design parametrics. The ensuing landscapes would defy stylistic categorization. It is in that interstice—the moment of haziness where one cannot quite make out what they are experiencing[8]—that I believe lays landscape's capacity to convey the complexity of human and environmental forces that shape the urban ecosystem.

Our current material products and practices contribute significantly to global CO_2 release into the atmosphere. Recovery planning has to take in the big picture and curtail the environmentally destructive practices that instigated the stressor scenario in the first place. *City Sink* asserted that low material production costs (in terms of carbon footprint) equal high ecosystem value. Reconsidering material lifecycle criteria can also achieve hard-to-calculate, indirect economic benefits by activating new markets. This thinking runs counter to typical project cost calculations that stress long-lasting material life-span and short-term cost savings in products and construction. Shifting values will require enhanced research into deep production systems, including material-sourcing practices, production process leakage, and costs associated with transfer and distribution practices, as well as buried implementation costs. Code adjustments to address this issue should be considered in future planning discourse.

On Drawing a Line in the Sand

In June 2013, the state of New Jersey's release of a commercial soundtrack, boasting that they are "stronger than the storm," coincided with the release of *A Stronger, More Resilient New York*. This type of punchy rhetoric is playing across the Northeast in opposition to what is now referred to as *retreat*. The idea that a political entity should not necessarily stand its ground against an encroaching ocean is not radical. It was first broached as New York State policy in February 2013, when Governor Cuomo proposed a $400 million plan to buy out homes in flood-prone areas, have them demolished, and restrict future building in those areas in perpetuity. The generally well-received plan aimed to use not only FEMA funds to purchase homes in disaster-stricken areas, but also earmarked HUD money to expand the program (Kaplan 2013).

Somewhere in the intervening months between February and June 2013, the legislative winds shifted, and reconsidering the footprint of cities became un-American. There has been little positive discussion about reformatting the city, or relocating communities. Those options have instead been framed as retreat, as pulling back—a form of surrender, an apparent act of cowardice when juxtaposed with the claims of strength. It is notable that while Governor Christie of New Jersey did not rule out a buy-out plan, there was no funding set aside in the first $1.8 billion Block Grant the state received.

Words matter. There are two very powerful ideas of American landscape at play here:

1   the principle of "highest and best use," generally meaning the use that generates the greatest direct, short-term benefits in terms of economic development (to understand the positioning of the SIRR, it is useful to know that it was spearheaded by the President of the New York City Economic Development Corporation); and

2   the matter of contesting the right of the individual to retain unfettered control over their own property, even if that is potentially dangerous for them or costly to the greater community.

City Sink confronted these dysfunctional ideations head on by asserting the need to assign value to indirect, long-term systemic benefits that might outweigh direct short-term benefits, and by seeking to merge public and private agendas through policy initiatives such as usufruct. These strategies are actionable within a dynamic milieu. The assumption that a city can draw a line in the sand against an encroaching ocean is absurd. Planners will have to weigh myriad existing urban scenarios and devise new ones to negotiate unique local conditions. Now, more than ever, an updated popular understanding of ecology will be essential for good governance and the viability of future cities. The discourse of *City Sink* should be amped up and, given the tenor of the times, boiled down to a slogan: "We are the storm; together we can build cities that weather better, and that better weather!"

Concluding Thoughts

Learning to stop worrying about the carbon cycle and to love climate-adaptive urban design and planning is in some respects a semantic game. The mission and even some of the methods attached to carbon cycle planning are in many aspects indistinguishable from what will be required of cities to reconcile their policy and practice to a changing climate. There is a critical difference in the positioning associated with the current level of discourse. Carbon cycle planning as described in *City Sink* aims to impart a complex, nuanced understanding of urban ecosystems to a public overwhelmed by the politicization of climate discourse. Climate-adaptive design, as presented in reports like the SIRR, seeks to reassure the public that there are straightforward, economically productive solutions to the problem of climate change. Whether or not the proposals in the plan will be successful—or even achievable—remains to be seen. The pressing question is: will the SIRR instigate an essential discourse on the city as nature across the socio-economic spectrum of New York's citizens? This exchange must be a precursor to the realization of any plan. If that happens, it will be, as they say "the bomb"; and I look forward to being a voice in a crowd.

Notes

1   The reference is to the movie *Dr Strangelove or: How I Learned to Stop Worrying and Love the Bomb* (1964), written by Stanley Kubrick and Terry Southern.
2   "Between 1850 and 2000, global land-use change resulted in the release of 156,000 teragrams of carbon to the atmosphere, mostly from deforestation. This amount is equivalent to 21.9 years of global fossil fuel CO_2 emissions at the 2003 level" (Ryan et al. 2010: 6). See also: C. Le Quéré et al. (2012: 1110).
3   For a survey of the scope of climate awareness in America, see Leiserowitz and Smith (2010). The study identified areas of awareness and gaps between expert and public knowledge of climate change across diverse demographic groups.
4   See the Hunts Point case study in Hoffman Brandt (2013: 76–83).
5   With regard to the seminal research of Hungerford and Volk (1990), *City Sink* aligns with their idea of the need to build "sensitivity," a key process in operationalizing environmental awareness that cannot be taught in a classroom.
6   For an example of one Queens neighborhood seriously affected by tidal flooding on a regular basis, see Gregory (2013). For a vivid description of regular sewage overflows in the Gowanus

neighborhood of Brooklyn in 2010 (after it was listed as a Superfund Site in March of that year), see Navarro (2010).

7 I include in this a number of evolving design-disciplinary gray areas described with semantic qualifiers such as landscape urbanism, green urbanism, and ecological urbanism that offer tantalizing potential to expand trans-disciplinary approaches to design that prioritize engaging all aspects of socio-environmental systems. Unfortunately, the tendency thus far has been to stake special claim to ideological territory and retain the autonomy of the various disciplines through opposition to other positions in the discourse. I suggest a more complex and variable approach to the design of the human ecosystem that would necessitate the syncopated skills of many disciplines—not even just design.

8 I think here of Joseph Conrad's allusion to the process of absorbing understanding, deeply and indirectly, in *Heart of Darkness*: "the meaning of an episode . . . not inside like a kernel but outside, enveloping the tale which brought it out only as a glow brings out a haze" (1969: 7).

References

Callendar, G. S. (1938). The artificial production of carbon dioxide and its influence on temperature. *Quarterly Journal of the Royal Meteorological Society*, 64(1), 223–240, doi: 10.1002/qj.49706427503.

Callicott, J. B. (2002). From the balance of nature to the flux of nature. In Knight, R. and Reidel, S. (eds), *Aldo Leopold and the Ecological Conscience*. Oxford: Oxford University Press, 90–105.

Conrad, J. (1969 [1899]). *Heart of Darkness and the Secret Sharer*. New York: Bantam Critical Edition.

Detroit Works Project (2013). *Detroit Future City: 2012 Detroit Strategic Framework Plan*. Detroit, MI: Inland Press.

Global Carbon Project (2012). *Global Carbon Budget 2012*. [Online]. Available: www.globalcarbon project.org/carbonbudget/12/presentation.htm [July 7, 2013].

Gregory, K. (2013, July 9). Where streets flood with the tide, a debate over city aid. *The New York Times*. [Online]. Available: http://www.nytimes.com/2013/07/10/nyregion/debate-over-cost-and-practicality-of-protecting-part-of-queens-coast.html [July 4, 2014].

Hoffman Brandt, D. (2013). *City Sink: Carbon storage infrastructure for our built environment*. China: Oscar Riera Ojeda Publishers Limited.

Howard, E. (1902). *Garden Cities of Tomorrow*. London: S. Sonnenschein & Co., Ltd.

Hungerford, H. and Volk, T. (1990). Changing learner behavior through environmental education. *Journal of Environmental Education*, 21(3), 8–22.

Interboro Partners (2009). *Northern Fairmount Neighborhood Redevelopment Plan for Newark, New Jersey*. [Online]. Available: www.interboropartners.net/2009/west-market-area-neighborhood-redevelopment-plan/ [November 22, 2013].

Kaplan, T. (2013, February 3). Cuomo seeking home buyouts in flood zones. *The New York Times*. [Online]. Available: www.nytimes.com/2013/02/04/nyregion/cuomo-seeking-home-buyouts-in-flood-zones.html [July 9, 2013].

Leiserowitz, A. and Smith, N. (2010). *Knowledge of Climate Change Across Global Warming's Six Americas*. New Haven, CT: Yale University Project on Climate Change Communication. [Online]. Available: http://environment.yale.edu/climate/files/Knowledge_Across_Six_Americas.pdf [August 11, 2011].

Le Quéré, C. et al. (2012). The global carbon budget 1959–2011. *Earth System Science Data Discussion Paper*, 5, 1107–1157. [Online]. Available: www.earth-syst-sci-data-discuss.net/5/1107/2012/essdd-5-1107-2012.html [July 7, 2013].

McHarg, I. (1995 [1969]). *Design with Nature: 25th anniversary edition*. London: Wiley.

Navarro, M. (2010, September 29). Sewage overflow in New York? Believe it. *The New York Times*. [Online]. Available: http://green.blogs.nytimes.com/2010/09/29/sewage-overflow-in-new-york-believe-it/ [July 4, 2014].

New York City Special Initiative on Rebuilding and Resiliency (NYC) (2013). *A Stronger, More Resilient New York*. [Online]. Available: www.nyc.gov/html/sirr/html/report/report.shtml [June 3, 2013].

Roston, E. (2010, April 16). The Climate Post: why isn't the Keeling Curve more famous? *Grist*. [Online]. Available: http://grist.org/article/the-climate-post-why-isnt-the-keeling-curve-more-famous/ [July 7, 2013].

Rubenstein, M. (2012, May 9). Emissions from the cement industry. *State of the Planet: Blogs from the Earth Institute.* [Online]. Available: http://blogs.ei.columbia.edu/2012/05/09/emissions-from-the-cement-industry/ [July 9, 2013].

Ryan, M. et al. (2010). A synthesis of the science on forests and carbon for U.S. forests. *Issues in Ecology,* Report No. 13. [Online]. Available: www.esa.org/science_resources/issues/FileEnglish/issue13.pdf [July 4, 2014].

Silver, N. (2012). *The Signal and the Noise.* New York: Penguin Press.

18

[GU]GROWING URBANISM

An Evolutionary Urban Ecology in Cascadia

Gundula Proksch, Joshua Brevoort, and Lisa Chun

Imagine a city in which nature and urban form are indistinguishable. Food grows in perma-culture gardens where people live and work; tidelands re-emerge in industrial zones, allowing rivers to return to their meandering past; and twentieth-century infrastructure is replaced by biologically engineered soft systems that generate increasingly complex eco-systems. The beginnings of Growing Urbanism flourish amid the monuments of a bygone industrial era.

Entering the Anthropocene, humans have become a geophysical force with the power to transform the earth's ecosystems (Wilson 2006). Cities are an expression of this trans-formation and the engines fueling it. The technologies from which they are constructed have come to define and mediate the relationship between humans and nature (Benjamin and Demetz 1986; Williams 2010). Growing Urbanism is a vision for a new urban ecology that explores the intersection of humans, nature, and technology, and imagines how the holistic reconceptualization of their relationship might assist cities to become living ecosystems composed of biological urban structures. This vision rejects the conceptuali-zation of humans and nature as separate entities, and attempts to generate a collective awareness of interconnected environmental systems. Influenced by the conditions in Seattle and the Pacific Northwest (generally known as the bioregion of Cascadia), this ecological approach to urbanism is rooted in place. Yet, it has the potential to grow and to transform urban futures globally.

Seattle as Site

The *Dkh^w'Duw'Absh* or Duwamish were the first people to inhabit the lush area between the Cascade Range and Olympic Mountains that is now home to Seattle. According to oral history, their ancestors witnessed geologic and tectonic events that left the Puget Sound region scarred by glaciation, recurrent earthquakes, and spewing volcanoes produced by the Cascadia subduction zone (Troost and Booth 2008). The temperate climate's rich abundance of plants and animals engendered a sophisticated, seasonally associated hunter-gatherer society dating back to the sixth century AD (Speer 2004). By the time the first European settlers

FIGURE 18.1 Growing Urbanism in Seattle: high-rise buildings in the Dense City overlook the re-emerging tidal marshlands in the Tidal City and Elliott Bay, the Water City.

arrived in 1851 (less than 165 years ago), the Duwamish had actively manipulated the environment in which they lived and established 17 villages around Elliott Bay.

Seattle, as it exists today, was founded as a lumber and port city with an economy based on the Pacific Northwest's wealth of natural resources. Western settlers started exploiting local resources in a series of boom cycles involving logging, gold rush, shipbuilding, and aviation industries. From the end of the 1800s into the 1960s, these growth-oriented resource-intensive industries transformed the natural environment through human interventions, including re-grading hills, filling bays, dredging harbors, cutting new waterways, and constructing interstate highways. These changes degraded ecosystems and created a sharp demarcation between natural ecologies and built environments. The advancement of industrial and economic expansion served as the driving force behind these interventions and society embraced the domination of nature with technology without understanding the costs of an extractive and consumption-driven culture.

During the first oil crisis in the 1970s, the trajectory of constant economic growth and production became increasingly subject to criticism and widespread acknowledgment of an environmental crisis spurred the development of the ecological movement. Amid these changes, Ernest Callenbach published *Ecotopia* (1975). In this novel, Northern California, Oregon, and Washington State secede from the United States to create a "stable-state" ecosystem whose citizens strive for balance between themselves and the environment. Members of this "ecotopian" society adopt technology selectively, so as to preserve human health and sanity, and promote social and ecological well-being. The book is primarily a statement against consumerism and materialism (Hilton 2007). It offers a vivid illustration of an ecologically sound urban environment and lifestyle, reflecting the dream of an alternative future held by many movements of the 1970s (Buhle 2001).

While Callenbach's vision for a secessionist movement has not become reality, many of his aspirations have taken root in urban life in the Pacific Northwest and Seattle has gained

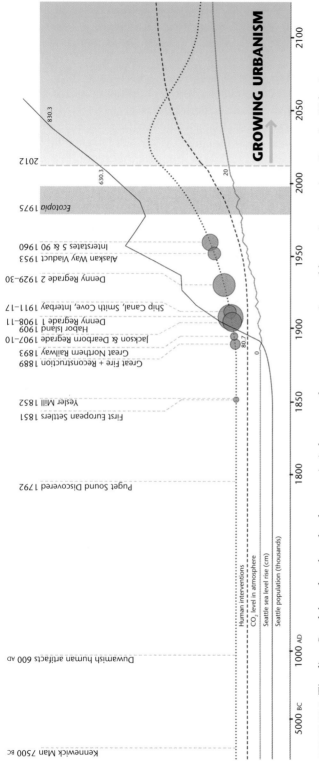

FIGURE 18.2 Timeline: Seattle's early urban development is tied to natural resource extraction and human intervention. Growing Urbanism proposes an alternative future.

a reputation for its counterculture and environmental activism. Organizations like Seattle Tilth and P-Patch community gardens as well as composting and recycling programs began advocating for an increased awareness of food and urban agriculture as tools to transform the city (Sander 2010). These early projects were successful in inaugurating Seattle's leading role in urban ecology and sustainability. Today, several Seattle-based organizations, including the Bullitt Foundation, Sightline, and the International Living Future Institute have become influential advocates for the natural environment, responsible human activities, and resilient communities. Many of their efforts focus on establishing metrics to gauge the environmental impact of human activities and taking steps to minimize urban ecological footprints. Growing Urbanism builds upon these efforts, while at the same time rethinking and moving beyond metrics-driven methodologies and goals.

Seeds

Thirty-five years after Callenbach proposed the first "ecotopia" for the Pacific Northwest, Growing Urbanism envisions a future city in which natural systems not only re-emerge but also become an inseparable part of the urban fabric, and the nebulous boundaries between nature and cityscape blur. This vision for a new ecological urbanism is based on three premises.

1   The dichotomy between nature and humanity is false. Building upon conceptual foundations such as William Cronon's "second nature," or nature constructed by humans, it posits that there is neither pristine nature nor isolated human creation (Cronon 1991). Growing Urbanism reconnects the city with the natural environment by acknowledging their shared geological and ecological histories and patterns. It promotes their fusion within enhanced ecosystems of greater diversity and density.

2   Technology constitutes the predominant interface between humanity and the environment. Natural systems and organisms not only provide invaluable inspirations for technological design, they can also become technologies themselves (Russell 2010). Growing Urbanism promotes the seamless integration of natural systems into the built environment through the development of soft systems and technologies including living buildings and urban agricultural landscapes.

3   A new understanding of the site, or the city itself, in its past and current state, is required. Kristina Hill writes about a new ecological perspective on sites in "Shifting Sites" (2005). Hill advocates a non-deterministic approach to landscapes based on non-equilibrium theories in geology, geography, and ecology. She describes a shift away from bounded place to a more abstract definition of boundaries, which support various forms of energy flow. In a similar conceptual shift, Growing Urbanism imagines the city evolving into an increasingly dynamic and adaptive entity, which relies on the interplay between urban components in constant exchange. Boundaries no longer separate; they allow selective permeability. Urban zones—each of which carries a unique ecological, geological, social, and economic signature—contribute to the city's overall self-sustenance and reduce reliance on outside resources and support. The city evolves into a complex ecological system, wherein each zone supports—and is supported by—the city as a whole. This integration is further augmented by innovative urban information systems and the evolution of an ecological economy.

Soft Systems

Growing Urbanism eschews conventional approaches to urban design and the deployment of hard infrastructures in favor of a flexible, soft systems approach. Soft systems address the complexity and dynamic nature of contemporary cities and transform the role that architecture, infrastructure, and technology play in urban environments (Bhatia and Sheppard 2012). They do not follow a grand master plan. Rather, they direct change through small interventions that set complex forces into motion and non-deterministic approaches without preset final outcomes. Just as ecosystems develop resilience over time, soft systems evolve quasi-evolutionarily in response to context. Nature and city, biological and technical systems develop together.

Soft systems are characterized primarily by qualities that emerge from the interactions of their parts rather than by their parts alone (Kwinter 1993). They require the acceptance of a certain amount of uncertainty and messiness. Growing Urbanism embraces these subnatures. For example, it treats waste streams, which are often stigmatized and hidden from view, as an asset necessary to close resource and energy cycles (Gissen 2009).

Along closely related lines, Growing Urbanism avoids static and isolated technologies that are designed to handle single tasks. It re-imagines centralized infrastructures that supply and process water, power, and waste as softer and increasingly fine-grained elements knit seamlessly into neighborhoods. Technologies that incorporate natural processes—such as green infrastructure, living machines, smart networks, and synthetic biology—facilitate self-reliance through greater adaptability and redundancy. Like nature, they solve multiple problems simultaneously and make the city more resilient.

Living Buildings

The integration of biological systems into both new construction and the existing urban fabric represents one example of a Growing Urbanism soft system or technology. Buildings become regenerative, self-sufficient organisms that increase the density and diversity while managing the resources of the core city.

Living buildings are quickly moving from science fiction to reality as digital fabrication becomes increasingly sophisticated and begins to incorporate biological processes. Gramazio & Kohler Architekten in Zürich, Switzerland, for example, have deployed digital fabrication to optimize structural, mechanical, and thermal properties of systems (Gramazio and Kohler 2007). Generative design driven by parametrics calculates multi-agent systems and responds with additive or subtractive modes of fabrication and assembly. Research institutes and architects have recently demonstrated that technologies like advanced 3D printing and computer numerical control (CNC) fabrication can be applied at a building scale (Loughborough University 2013; *Dezeen* 2013). Other researchers, most notably Skylar Tibbits at MIT, have made advancements in self-assembling matter through the use of modular robotics systems. Synthetic biologists, who engineer new biological systems or re-engineer existing ones, have been able to generate the first self-replicating synthetic bacterial cell (J. Craig Venter Institute 2013).

Although technologies to fabricate and replicate biology at larger scales do not yet exist, Growing Urbanism assumes that it will eventually be possible to construct with synthetic, living materials that help mitigate the current depletion of environmental resources. For

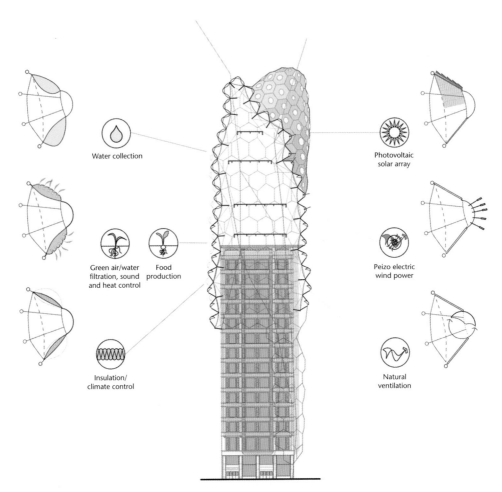

FIGURE 18.3 Self-regulating building systems: the proposed building skins are active, cell-like membranes, which adopt different functions, primarily water collection, food production, insulation, energy production, and natural ventilation.

example, it proposes building skins as active, cell-like membranes that mediate light, air, water, energy, and waste. Growing Urbanism speculates that boundaries between natural systems and machines will eventually disappear entirely as biological fabrication will produce self-regulating, self-repairing, and self-replicating built environments (Lipson and Pollack 2000).

Urban Agricultural Landscapes

Urban agricultural landscapes are another example of a Growing Urbanism soft system. Following the principles of permaculture (an integrated approach to design that has been widely adopted in its birthplace of Australia), food production is modeled on relationships found in natural ecologies. It recycles nutrients and spreads throughout the city to create sustainable human environments (Mars 2003; Coyne and Knutzen 2008). Growing Urbanism

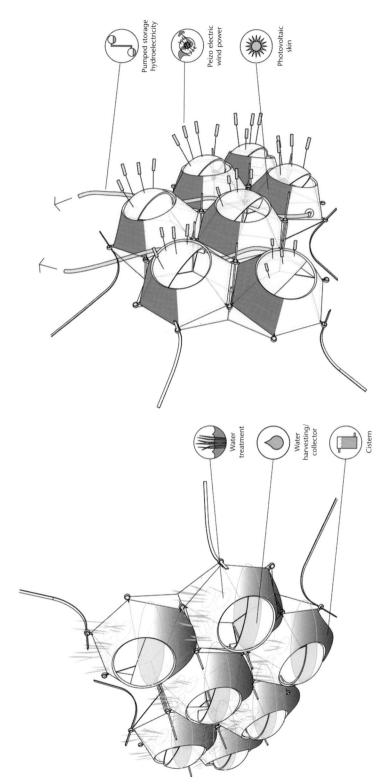

Pumped storage hydroelectricity

Peizo electric wind power

Photovoltaic skin

Water treatment

Water harvesting/ collector

Cistern

FIGURE 18.4 Building cells: the building system can specialize in water collection and treatment (on the left) and energy harvesting (on the right).

FIGURE 18.5 Urban agricultural landscapes: permaculture flourishes on vacant transportation infrastructure and on public land.

proposes that vacant transportation infrastructure and other leftover places provide space for the growth of low-maintenance food forests. The use of vacant public land for urban agricultural operations is encouraged through municipal land-use policy changes and edible landscapes become public (Ackerman 2012). Breaking with conventional Western owner-ship structures, these landscapes require shared stewardship and allow for unrestricted harvest by all residents. Seattle is currently testing this approach to urban farming. Drawing upon strong community support and outreach efforts, its Beacon Food Forest will soon grow edible plants for park visitors on seven acres of public land (Mellinger 2012).

Re-Emerging Symbiosis

At a larger scale, Growing Urbanism focuses on the urban core of Seattle, once home to the Duwamish and the place of the city's original settlement. Three important topographical features and urban zones meet here:

1   the Dense City, or Downtown and the historic Pioneer Square area built on bedrock;
2   the Tidal City, or the former mudflats south of Downtown transfigured over time, which housed large industry and stadia; and
3   the Water City, which encompassed the water's edge and Elliot Bay.

These urban districts evolve from political entities, municipal districts, and economic zones into distinct ecosystems with permeable boundaries, fostering biodiversity and strengthening habitat within city limits. Wildlife and indigenous vegetation return to the urban core.

FIGURE 18.6 Dense City: a previously piped, urban stream emerges from the railway tunnel in downtown Seattle.

Growing Urbanism establishes interconnected water, energy, waste, and nutrient cycles by recognizing and capitalizing on the distinct characteristics and resources of the three urban districts. The excess or waste products of one district become a resource for another, creating complex interchanges of healthy symbiosis. Tidal and wind power from the Water City serve users in the Dense City, and support aquaponic cultures in the Tidal City. The Tidal City acts as a nursery for the Water City and feeds the Dense City; energy provided in the form of food to the Dense City returns as fertilizer to the other parts of the city. Complex resource loops nest and recur at the scale of the district, neighborhood, and block. Buildings develop internal, net-zero systems for managing resources and waste.

The first steps towards such a web have already been taken. Based on the Energy Independence and Security Act of 2007, the Department of Energy monitors the deployment of smart-grid technology in the US nationwide. Smart grids for electricity rely not only on the improving ability to connect distributed generation, storage, and renewable resources, they also build on a long history of automation and information technology utilized by electricity utilities (US Department of Energy 2009). More recently, water and waste services have started to adopt similar networked systems. For example, advanced water

FIGURE 18.7 Tidal City: the rich ecology of a tidal estuary re-emerges south of downtown Seattle.

utilities use software that integrate remote meter reading, water quality sensors, GIS data, and models that detect faults, jams, or leaks so as to create more sustainable supply systems.

Information Systems

Big data and the ability to process it will change the way urban environments function and how people perceive them. Cities are full of sensors for data collection; people carrying handheld devices generate data constantly by calling, making purchases, mapping, searching, and socializing online (Arup/RIBA 2013). Growing Urbanism explores how the hard city can be supplemented by the parallel, mainly invisible city of data flows (Manaugh 2012). Information is analyzed, mapped, and used to predict urban behaviors and enhance our understanding of the relationship between humans and the urban environment (Dirks and Keeling 2009).

Data has two functions:

1   augmenting the user's experiences by adding insights to day-to-day activities through interactive, visual overlays; and
2   regulating the interactions between a multitude of existing, complex systems.

In addition to data such as demographic information, retail tracking, and consumer profiling, the possibilities of collective information technology are expanding rapidly. Crowd-sourced solutions to problems, new economic models like Kickstarter, and social networks such as Facebook and Twitter are just the beginnings of constantly changing information landscapes. Architects and planners are only now starting to appreciate and work with this wealth of

FIGURE 18.8 Water City: alternative energy harvesting and marine seafood gardens prosper along the waterfront and in Elliott Bay.

information. Their increasing interest in it will have a profound effect on the physical city. Information strengthens connections between humans and emergent urban biologies, and encourages adaptive behaviors within the larger environment. It is essential to the creation of a novel, environmentally sound city.

Ecological Economy

Environmental capitalism adds natural capital to labor, land, goods, and finances as a criteria used in the evaluation of economic health. It accounts for the true cost of all natural resources used in production and distribution and, in contrast to current standard economic methods, quantifies the goods and services provided by natural systems (Russell 2010). It allows for broad-based participation by all citizens and encourages reinvestment of proceeds within communities. Building upon this foundation, Growing Urbanism assumes that as cities become richer ecosystems, their economies will undergo a paradigm shift. Traditional economic models will evolve in step with the physical transformation of the city. New systems will promote regenerative flows of resources and collective distribution of dividends including food, energy, water, and other amenities.

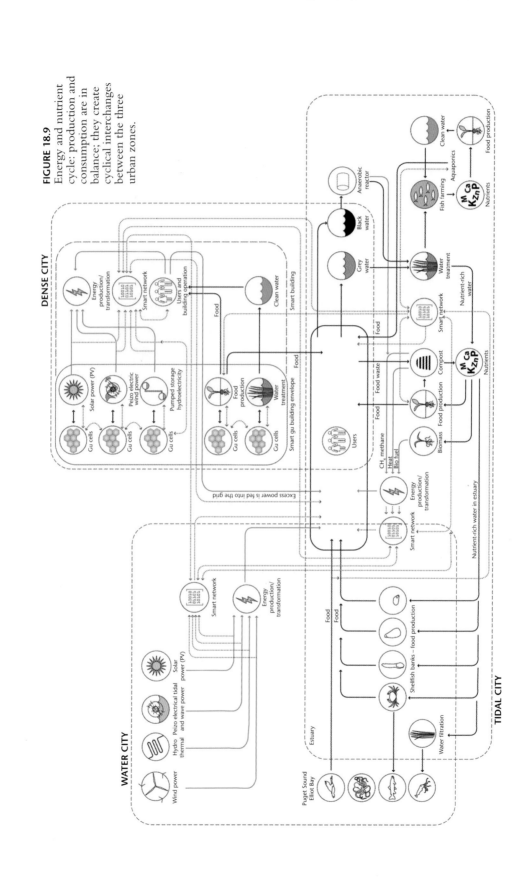

FIGURE 18.9
Energy and nutrient cycle: production and consumption are in balance; they create cyclical interchanges between the three urban zones.

FIGURE 18.10 Visual data overlay: in an interactive, visual overlay, the user receives additional information about the surrounding site, shown here while looking at a self-regulating building in downtown Seattle.

Propagation

Natural resources and their potential are location specific. Elliott Bay and its adjacent estuary, for example, are unique to Seattle. They fed the Duwamish for millennia and could potentially feed a large population again. Growing Urbanism honors the idiosyncrasies of every ecosystem and contends that cities can only become thriving ecological environments when they acknowledge their local natural context. At the same time, Growing Urbanism's principles have broad implications and Growing Urbanism is intended to expand both in terms of its generative methods and beyond its origins in the Pacific Northwest. As it expands, Growing Urbanism will adapt to each new location, function at the local level, and enhance the unique assets and character of place.

Conclusion

Thirty-five years ago, Ernest Callenbach envisioned a world in which citizens strive for balance between themselves and the environment. In doing so, he planted the seeds of an ecological movement that has slowly taken root. Growing Urbanism represents the metamorphosis of this vision. By rethinking cities as the synthesis of the natural and built environments, rejecting predetermined, static, metrics-driven practices, and promoting an organic, holistic approach to urban development, it shifts the idea of the ecological city from one of balance and restraint to one of complex and networked symbiosis. Soft systems replace traditional approaches to infrastructure and the emergent technologies of the present give birth to biologically generative offspring. The seeds that Growing Urbanism plants today may well take root, evolve, and grow. Thirty-five years in the future, Growing Urbanism may flourish amid the monuments of a bygone industrial era.

Acknowledgments

The visualizations of Growing Urbanism were initially developed for the Living City Design Competition sponsored by the International Living Building Institute in partnership with The National Trust for Historic Preservation. In April 2011 Growing Urbanism was awarded the Images that Provoke award. We express our appreciation to our collaborators Mac Lamphere, Cameron Hall, and Lauren McCunney, who contributed to the project.

References

Ackerman, K. (2012). Urban agriculture: opportunities and constraints. In Zeman, F. (ed.), *Metropolitan Sustainability: Understanding and improving the urban environment*. Cambridge: Woodhead Publishing Limited, 118–146.

Arup/RIBA (2013). *Designing with Data: Shaping our future cities*. Palo Alto: Issuu, Inc. [Online]. Available: www.architecture.com/TheRIBA/AboutUs/InfluencingPolicy/Designingwithdata.aspx #.UrDaR_RDt8E [July 11, 2013].

Benjamin, W. and Demetz, P. (1986). *Reflections: Essays, aphorisms, autobiographical writings*. New York: Harcourt Brace Jovanovich.

Bhatia, N. and Sheppard, L. (eds) (2012). *Goes Soft: Bracket 2*. Barcelona: Actar.

Buhle, P. (2001). Ecotopia. *Capitalism, Nature, Socialism*, 12(3), 149–153.

Callenbach, E. (1975). *Ecotopia: The notebooks and reports of William Weston*. Berkeley, CA: Banyan Tree Books.

Coyne, K. and Knutzen, E. (2008). *The Urban Homestead: Your guide to self-sufficient living in the heart of the city*. Los Angeles, CA: Process Media.

Cronon, W. (1991). *Nature's Metropolis: Chicago and the Great West*. New York: Norton.

Dezeen (2013, January 20). Dutch architects to use 3D printer to build a house. *Dezeen*. [Online]. Available: http://www.dezeen.com/2013/01/20/dutch-architects-to-use-3d-printer-to-build-a-house/ [July 11, 2013].

Dirks, S. and Keeling, M. (2009). *A Vision of Smarter Cities: How cities can lead the way into a prosperous and sustainable future*. Somers, NY: IBM Global Business Services. [Online]. Available: http://public.dhe.ibm.com/common/ssi/ecm/en/gbe03227usen/GBE03227USEN.PDF [July 15, 2013].

Gissen, D. (2009). *Subnature: Architecture's other environments*. New York: Princeton Architectural Press.

Gramazio, F. and Kohler, M. (2007). *1:1 Architecture and Digital Fabrication*. Baden: Lars Müller.

Hill, K. (2005). Shifting sites. In Burns, C. J. and Kahn, A. (eds), *Site Matters*. New York and London: Routledge, 131–155.

Hilton, M. (2007). Consumers and the State since the Second World War. *The Annals of the American Academy of Political and Social Science*, 611(1), 66–81.

J. Craig Venter Institute (2013). *First Self-Replicating Synthetic Bacterial Cell*. [Online]. Available: www.jcvi.org/cms/research/projects/first-self-replicating-synthetic-bacterial-cell/overview/ [July 11, 2013].

Kwinter, S. (1993). Soft systems. In Boigen, B. (ed.), *Culture Lab*. New York: Princeton Architectural Press, 207–228.

Lipson, H. and Pollack, J. B. (2000). Automatic design and manufacture of robotic lifeforms. *Nature*, 406, 974–978. [Online]. Available: http://creativemachines.cornell.edu/papers/Nature00_Lipson.pdf [July 15, 2013].

Loughborough University (2013). *3D Concrete Printing: An innovative construction process*. [Online]. Available: www.buildfreeform.com/ [July 11, 2013].

Manaugh, G. (2012). Soft serve space. In Bhatia, N. and Sheppard, L. (eds), *Goes Soft: Bracket 2*. Barcelona, Actar, 10–16.

Mars, R. (2003). *The Basics of Permaculture Design*. East Meon, Hampshire, UK: Permanent Living.

Mellinger, R. (2012, February 16). Nation's largest food forest takes root on Beacon Hill. *Crosscut*. [Online]. Available: http://crosscut.com/2012/02/16/agriculture/21892/Nations-largest-public-Food-Forest-takes-root-on-B/ [July 11, 2013].

Russell, E. (2010). Can organisms be technology? In Reuss, M. and Cutcliffe, S. H. (eds), *The Illusory Boundary: Environment and technology in history*. Charlottesville, VA: University of Virginia Press, 249–262.

Sander, J. C. (2010). *Seattle and the Roots of Urban Sustainability*. Pittsburgh, PA: University of Pittsburgh Press.

Speer, T. R. (2004). Dkhʷ'Duw'Absh from Dkhʷ'Duw'Absh, "People of the Inside." *Duwamish Tribe*. [Online]. Available: www.duwamishtribe.org/culture.html [July 9, 2013].

Troost, K. G. and Booth, D. B. (2008). Geology of Seattle and the Seattle area. *Washington Reviews, Engineering Geology*, 20, 1–36. [Online]. Available: http://reg.gsapubs.org/content/20/1 [July 9 2013].

US Department of Energy (2009). *Smart Grid System Report*. Washington, DC: US Department of Energy. [Online]. Available: http://energy.gov/oe/downloads/2009-smart-grid-system-report-july-2009 [July 2, 2014].

Williams, J. C. (2010). Understanding the place of humans in nature. In Reuss, M. and Cutcliffe, S. H. (eds), *The Illusory Boundary: Environment and technology in history*. Charlottesville, VA: University of Virginia Press, 10–25.

Wilson, E. O. (2006). *The Creation: An appeal to save life on Earth*. New York: Norton.

19

PATHWAYS OF URBAN NATURE

Diversity in the Greening of the Twenty-First-Century City

Andrew Karvonen

Nature is a central component of the twenty-first-century city. Beyond parks and open spaces, urban nature is implicated in strategies of economic development, climate change mitigation and adaptation, public art, biodiversity enhancement, local food production, health and livability, social justice, community identity, and more.[1] This "pluralization" of urban nature has come about in the last four decades as a result of the mainstreaming of environmental protection activities; the proliferation of knowledge about how natural systems support and maintain cities; a wide range of innovative and inspiring projects, policies, and technologies that feature urban nature; and a gradual shift away from cultural perceptions that nature and cities are diametrically opposed. Greening activities continue to be undertaken by environmentalists and community activists, but also by a broader array of stakeholders including private development interests, natural scientists, artists, social justice advocates, and others. The broadening of the urban greening agenda to incorporate a wide variety of actors and strategies is a welcome development, but it can result in confusion due to a cacophony of voices and ideas on how and why we green cities. How can we make sense of the multiple ways that nature is being reworked in today's cities?

The aim of this chapter is to propose a "pathways" approach to interpreting the multiple ways that urban nature is being realized today. The notion of pathways has been used by a wide variety of scholars in the social sciences and the design disciplines to deal with the multiplicity of ways that sustainable development and design has been conceptualized and acted upon in a variety of contexts. Pathways are useful for identifying key actors and their perceptions of improved urban futures with an emphasis on the means by which they frame and enact their particular visions in specific social and physical contexts. Pathways serve as a heuristic tool to structure and assess the various approaches to urban greening that are shaped by particular cultural and political pressures. I begin the chapter by defining the theoretical underpinnings and intentions of the pathways approach. I then use three vignettes of urban nature projects in Manchester, England, to demonstrate how the pathways perspective can be used to reflect upon and scrutinize urban green activities. I conclude by arguing that the greening of cities not only involves the introduction and rearrangement of nature in the city, but also has implications for how human societies are governed. In this way, we can understand the greening of cities as a deeply political process of reinventing the relations between humans and their physical surroundings.

The Pathways Approach to Urban Development

The pathways approach has been developed over the past two decades by scholars in architecture, planning, geography, sociology, anthropology, political science, and environmental studies to challenge positivist tendencies towards a single definition of sustainable development. Inspired by post-colonial, feminist, and post-structural critiques of modernity, these authors share a belief that sustainable development involves a plurality of logics and practices rather than one ideal approach. The notion of pathways rejects the predefined norms and universal assumptions that underpin the majority of theoretical and empirical work on sustainable development and instead embraces the pursuit of sustainability as discursive, contested, and multiple. With respect to cities, the pathways approach has been used to interpret urban development and planning processes (Haughton 1997; Guy and Marvin 1999, 2000; Pinderhughes 2004, 2008), architecture (Guy and Farmer 2000, 2001; Farmer and Guy 2002; Guy and Moore 2005, 2007), energy (Marvin et al. 1999; Guy 2004, 2006; Rydin et al. 2013), food (Allen et al. 2003), transport (Evans et al. 2001), social movements (Gottlieb 2001; Hess 2007), and environmental politics (Taylor 2000; Jamison 2001; Moore 2007; Leach et al. 2010). Hess argues that pathways "make it possible to avoid drawing premature boundaries when confronted with the fluidity of goals and repertoires of action" (2007: 4), and Guy and Marvin add that pathways are helpful in "the recognition that a wide diversity of sustainable urban futures are likely to coexist within a single city" (2001: 31).

By recognizing diversity as a condition to be analyzed rather than suppressed, the pathways approach interprets sustainability as an inherently discursive notion. Leach and colleagues argue that "a pathways approach aims to uncover diversity, broaden out the debate and open up possibilities for ways forward" (2010: 168). Such a perspective can be used to identify coalitions of actors and shared development agendas as well as expose the frictions and tensions between different conceptions of "the good city," "the green city," and "the sustainable city." It highlights that there are a range of possible options or potential trajectories that might be pursued via a selected suite of technologies, policies, and strategies. Pathways reveal the contrasting visions and aspirations of various stakeholders in achieving more sustainable urban conditions and serve to widen the debate on sustainability by considering how different interests are represented or overlooked in specific activities. The approach encourages us to consider why an activity was undertaken, who was included in it and who was excluded from decision-making processes, and how new conditions were realized. It shifts the emphasis of sustainable development away from idealized solutions and towards the processes of defining problems, negotiating interests, formulating and undertaking actions, and assessing the outcomes.

At the same time, the pathways approach does not suggest that the multiple perspectives on urban nature and sustainability are equal. Instead, it provides a framework to unpack embedded political, cultural, and social assumptions. Pathways are useful for making sense of the messy processes of sustainable development in particular times and places. In this way, the approach provides a heuristic device or conceptual window that is more flexible and fluid than traditional models of sustainable development (Guy 2012). There is an understanding that pathways are not mutually exclusive or static; instead, they represent a range of options that overlap and interact. The pathways approach encourages a comparative sensibility among theorists, policy-makers, practitioners, and the general public (Jamison 2001). The purpose of identifying pathways is not to identify the best or most effective route to a singular future but to recognize the multiplicity of ways that interventions in cities could produce different urban futures. As Leach and colleagues conclude, "a pathways approach thus offers a way to overcome the kinds of simplifications that have limited options and stultified debate about sustainable development" (2010: 168).

With respect to urban nature, the pathways approach provides conceptual guideposts to follow when analyzing how greening projects or agendas are being interpreted and acted upon. The approach reinforces the idea that "there is no singular nature as such, only natures. And such natures are historically, geographically, and socially constituted" (Macnaghten and Urry 1998: 15). To understand this diversity, it is helpful to situate and unpack the various interpretations and motivations of the actors involved beyond ecological and aesthetic interpretations to understand the social, cultural, and political implications. Likewise, it opens up the greening of cities to more than environmentalist agendas to embrace multiple modes of interpretation and intervention. Pathways shift the gaze of urban nature practitioners and researchers from products—green roofs, community gardens, rainwater-harvesting policies, restored waterways, and so on—to the messy and contested processes that constitute urban development (Guy and Marvin 2000, 2001). In this way, the pathways approach situates urban nature in particular social and physical contexts and highlights the centrality of place in the ecologizing of cities.

Urban Nature Pathways in Manchester

To illustrate the multiplicity of contemporary urban nature projects today and to show how the pathways perspective can be used to interpret them, I briefly summarize three urban nature projects in Manchester, England. Manchester has an international reputation as "the first industrial city," and its rapid development in the nineteenth century was one of the earliest and most vibrant examples of the promise and pitfalls of industrial economic development. The rapid rise in Manchester's global economic trade activities was accompanied by increasingly polluted and unhealthy living conditions for the lower and working classes in the city, serving as an early example of the tensions between international flows of capital and quality of life for local residents (Platt 2005). In short, Manchester serves as a quintessential example of the "unsustainable" urban conditions that proliferated in the Global North in the twentieth century. Today, Manchester is often touted as the "second city" of England, with a strong emphasis on international business and creative culture (Peck and Ward 2002; Williams 2003; Hebbert 2010; Hatherley 2011), but, like many cities in northern England, it continues to reflect its early industrial legacy with a lack of green space in the urban core and a large number of derelict buildings and empty sites.

In the following sections, I describe three projects in Manchester that are aimed at greening the city in different ways. My intention is not to frame these projects as exemplars of urban nature that can and should be replicated around the world; nor am I am arguing that these projects will rescue Manchester from its industrial past. Instead, the projects serve to illustrate a few of the innovative ways that urban nature is being interpreted for and applied to particular physical and social conditions. Each project embodies implicit and explicit assumptions about desirable future conditions for Manchester and constitutes new forms of socio-material organization to realize those futures. By considering the motivations of stakeholders and the methods of organization and action, we can derive more general lessons about what nature can potentially achieve in contemporary cities.

The Manchester Garden City initiative

In 2010, employees at international design firm BDP initiated a program to address the lack of green space in the city center. They realized that through voluntary efforts and the application of their collective landscape and urban design expertise, they could realize a more livable urban environment for workers and residents. The Manchester Garden City initiative was conceived with a clear and understandable brand complemented by a handful of simple design proposals to create temporary and permanent niches of urban agriculture, biodiversity, and recreation in the city center (CityCo 2013). The volunteers at BDP reached out to CityCo, a non-profit membership organization of city center employers, to generate funding, materials, and volunteers for the construction and maintenance of their proposed projects. The program appealed to CityCo's mission to support and enhance the local economy of Manchester through physical interventions. As a result, a coalition of design and economic development interests was born. In May 2011, the Manchester Garden City initiative completed its first project in the Piccadilly Basin neighborhood consisting of a wall of wildflowers to serve as an aesthetic partition between a public canal path and an adjacent parking lot (Figure 19.1). The wall served double duty as a home for insects and native plants, enhancing the biodiversity of the city center. Subsequent projects included an urban orchard, pocket parks, children's play areas, and temporary spaces for events. A volunteer stated, "Manchester, being the first industrial city in the world, there's always been a lack of green spaces. So I think that anything that introduces more green spaces, more places to relax in a nicer environment and increase the biodiversity, is a great idea" (BBC News 2011).

The Manchester Garden City initiative follows an "urban acupuncture" strategy (Sim 2009; Villagomez 2010) to green the city by completing small projects in interstitial spaces. The projects are attractive to the design and business communities because they can be

FIGURE 19.1 Volunteers help to plant the first Manchester Garden City initiative canal-side scheme in Piccadilly Basin.

undertaken with relative ease and lack of disruption. Their aim is to create a beautiful and bio-diverse city through collaborative activities between property owners, businesses, employees, and residents in the marginal spaces of the city center. The initiative encourages corporate citizenship by allowing property owners to take collective responsibility for enhancing and maintaining their surroundings while providing city center workers and residents with an improved public realm. In short, it encourages Mancunians in the city center to be deliberative and active neighbors by pursuing complementary goals of quality of life and social cohesion. This can be described as a "business/community pathway" that involves landscape design, corporate social responsibility, and community development.

Sow Sew

A second urban nature project in Manchester takes a markedly different approach. In 2010, designers Rob Thomas and Chris Wilkins won a design competition for public art in the New Islington area of East Manchester (Thomas Wilkins Design 2013). This area of the city was the original site of mills and warehouses that supported the industrial economy of the city and served as the heart of "Cottonopolis" from the mid-nineteenth to the mid-twentieth centuries. After World War II, the neighborhoods in East Manchester withered as industry and employment left, leaving a patchy urban landscape of crumbling mills, derelict housing, and empty lots (Grant 2010). Thomas and Wilkins' Sow Sew project recognized an opportunity in the downturn of the property development cycle to temporarily grow flax on vacant land (Figure 19.2). Flax is a hearty plant that can grow in less than ideal conditions and requires little maintenance beyond weeding. As an organic and local alternative to

FIGURE 19.2 Volunteers harvest flax for the Sow Sew project in East Manchester.

cotton, flax has advantages of lower environmental impacts due to the use of fertilizers and pesticides as well as transportation impacts of importing foreign materials into England (MERCi 2013).

The project was spearheaded by a local non-profit organization, the Manchester Environmental Research Centre initiative (MERCi), with the aim of reviving local industrial production in a more sustainable manner (Mallett 2011). The first crop of flax was harvested in 2011 and then processed, dyed, and donated to local artists to create clothing, bags, banners, and other items under the label of "Made in Manchester." This process has since been repeated on other vacant lots in East Manchester to build a long-term local culture of raw material production and artistic design.

The Sow Sew project builds upon contemporary ideas of temporary use to create a productive landscape in derelict or overlooked spaces (Urban Catalyst 2003, 2007; Haydn and Temel 2006; Andres 2013). There is an understanding that these open spaces will most likely be developed in the coming years, but in the meantime they can be used to promote economic, cultural, and ecological goals. The project taps into the temporal rhythms of urban change—economically with respect to the property development cycle and ecologically with respect to the seasonal growing and harvesting of flax. Moreover, the creation of industrial production creates a new identity for East Manchester that resonates with the historical activities in the area. A key element to the project is the intermediary role that MERCi plays in connecting the various stakeholders including the landowner, growers, processors, and artists. The project can be described as an "industry/art pathway" because it provides a basis for a new local economy to emerge that is based on sustainable natural resource production and local skilled workers.

Biospheric Project

A third urban nature project in Manchester is actually located just a short walk across the River Irwell in neighboring Salford. The Biospheric Project was initiated in 2010 and involves a partnership between Manchester Metropolitan University, Queens University Belfast, Salford City Council, and the Manchester International Festival. Initiated by urban ecologist and "eco-preneur" Vincent Walsh, the project is a combination of scientific laboratory, urban farm, and social experiment (Arden 2013; Biospheric Project 2013). The project is housed in an empty printworks building and includes a plethora of horticultural experiments including a wormery, aquaponics, vertical gardens, mushroom growing, and roof gardens (Figure 19.3). Scientists and volunteers are conducting a wide range of studies to provide proof of concept for the latest ideas about industrial ecology, closed-loop systems, and regenerative design (Lyle 1994) and to develop strategies to scale up and roll out these ideas to other locales.

Beyond scientific experiments, the Biospheric Project aims to support local residents in buying and eventually growing their own food. The experiments are large enough to supplement the project's local food store (78 Steps) and home delivery service (Whole Box) and to provide residents with ready access to local, healthy food. The social mission of the Biospheric Project is directly related to its location in a severely deprived neighborhood. The project received £300,000 of funding from the local government to improve public health through the promotion of better eating habits. Walsh's aim is "to develop an action-led research laboratory in an area of urban deprivation where it is really needed, because the

FIGURE 19.3 Visitors explore the roof garden at the Biospheric Project, an industrial building in a low-income area of Salford.

access to food on this estate is so poor" (Rawsthorn 2013). This approach mirrors the Sanitary City movement of the mid- to late nineteenth century when sanitarians applied the latest scientific findings to alleviate conditions of urban poverty (Melosi 2000; Pincetl 2010). Rather than water, wastewater, and air, the emphasis of the Biospheric Project is on food and nutrition through community outreach and engagement. The project serves as a "living lab" of innovation by pushing the boundaries of what nature can do from a horticultural as well as a social standpoint. It can be described as a "science/public health pathway" that recognizes synergies between horticultural innovation and the alleviation of poverty.

These three projects are well-known examples of urban nature in Manchester today. They are inspired by a wide range of ideas for how the city can leverage its existing social and material infrastructure to green the city in different ways. The Manchester Garden City initiative exploits niches in the highly built-up city center, Sow Sew targets vacant land as a temporary opportunity for growing, and the Biospheric Project re-imagines an abandoned industrial building to promote scientific experiments and improved public health. The projects tap into different networks of stakeholders to complement and expand upon the conventional work of the local government to introduce green and blue infrastructure to the city. Traditional environmental and community groups are joined by the private sector, artistic and cultural groups, public health advocates, and others, demonstrating how urban nature can encompass a wide range of motivations and strategies.

Table 19.1 provides a summary of the above three examples to compare and contrast the motivations and strategies of each pathway. The Manchester Garden City initiative creates new relationships between companies that are situated in the city center and residents who

TABLE 19.1 Three pathways of urban nature in Manchester, England.

	Manchester Garden City initiative	Sow Sew project	Biospheric Project
Pathway	Business/community	Industry/art	Science/public health
Contextual opportunity	Interstitial spaces	Vacant land	Vacant building
Drivers	Convivial urban environments	Natural resources and skills	Food production and social equity
Role of nature	Beauty and biodiversity	Historical reminder and natural resource	Food production and public health
Key actor	Corporate citizen	Skilled artist	Natural scientist
Aims	Placemaking and community building	Revival of local economy and support of artist community	Production of scientific findings and social learning

call the city center home, the Sow Sew project brings together horticulturalists with local artists to create new industrial products, and the Biospheric Project involves academic researchers and volunteers who are testing new ideas about urban agriculture and then using this knowledge to improve the public health of the surrounding deprived community. This comparison shows how contextual conditions drive each project and how the stakeholders interpret nature in various ways to achieve their desired goals.

These projects are not intended to encompass all urban nature activities in Manchester; indeed, there are numerous other pathways that involve regulatory innovation, artistic expression, cultural capital, local agriculture, and so on. Furthermore, these pathways are not autonomous; they overlap and combine to form distinctive, context-bound approaches to urban nature. For example, the notion of ecological science is common to all of the above projects, although its role is most prominent in the Biospheric Project. Likewise, the idea of "community" is strong in all three examples, although what constitutes community varies across each project. And all of the projects build upon the existing conditions in Manchester; they are bottom-up, context-specific, and place-bound (Moore and Karvonen 2008), although they do take inspiration and ideas from projects in England as well as around the world. The projects are all relatively new and it is unclear if they will thrive and grow in the long term or fade away as new projects and initiatives emerge. If nothing else, they serve as inspiration for others interested in creating better urban conditions in Manchester and elsewhere.

Greening the Twenty-First-Century City

The pathways approach to urban nature is useful for making sense of the multiple ways that nature is being interpreted and enacted in cities today. It shifts the focus away from idealized, universal notions of urban nature to emphasize the physical and social contexts that are being reoriented to realize change. Once we understand that nature is not something outside of cities or restricted to the work of environmentalists and community groups, we can begin to understand urban greening activities as social, cultural, and political interventions. Manchester's urban nature projects are context-specific and build upon the industrial past of the city and its historic development that is largely built up and devoid of green space. These projects bring together unique groups of urban stakeholders around specific ideas about how to green the city. In this way, they create "working landscapes" that simultaneously celebrate the past while producing new conditions (Cannovò 2007). Looking across these examples, several lessons emerge that can be useful for urban greening projects in other locales.

First, urban nature projects frequently involve collaboration between complementary and strategic stakeholders. By expanding the notion of nature beyond aesthetic and ecological ideas, a variety of public-, private-, and third-sector partners come together to work side by side on a particular project. Reflecting on the pathways approach, Guy and Marvin note that "new and sometimes unlikely partnerships may be formed in the pursuit of alternative urban futures" (1999: 272). Agyeman and colleagues refer to this as "joined-up sustainability" (Agyeman et al. 2003; Agyeman 2005), a trans-disciplinary perspective that trespasses across conventional conceptual boundaries to realize synergies between related agendas. This suggests that urban greening is ultimately about building relations, both socially and materially (Gandy 2002; Karvonen 2011; Karvonen and Yocom 2011).

A second lesson of urban greening from the Manchester projects is the need for brokerage and intermediation. Gottlieb celebrates those activities "where movements and agendas emerge and coalesce" (2001: 232), but this requires individuals and organizations to identify commonalities and nurture relations between potential collaborators. The Manchester projects were possible because the participants embraced a collaborative attitude and were guided by intermediaries who could look across all of the agendas and identify commonalities (Brand and Karvonen 2007; Karvonen and Brand 2009, 2013; Guy et al. 2011). The emphasis on partnerships and more open visions of "the green city" suggests the need for advocates of urban nature to be flexible and pragmatic in their activities. Identifying windows of opportunity becomes more important than realizing idealized models of urban nature.

A third lesson from the Manchester projects is the need for a clear narrative to describe such projects. With the multitude of actors and agendas participating in these projects, it was essential for each to be able to convey the aims of the project succinctly and accurately. As Beauregard notes, "Stories are told not just to express understandings and intentions to listeners but also to reshape them" (2003: 68). Contemporary urban nature projects can be confusing and opaque to those who view nature through conventional lenses of recreation or ecological science. This suggests that a key challenge of ecologizing the city in the twenty-first century is to be able to tell a coherent story that can appeal to a wide range of stakeholders. The Manchester projects are cognizant of the importance of storytelling and have developed strong narratives that go beyond "green is good" to advertise the multiple ways that their projects benefit a range of urban stakeholders.

Ultimately, the pathways approach challenges all urban stakeholders—from residents and activists to policy-makers, practitioners, and private companies—to identify and develop strategies that resonate with their social and physical contexts. At its best, the greening of cities constitutes a new form of civic politics and new modes of citizenship (Dobson 2003; Light 2003; Hester 2006; Karvonen 2010, 2011; Karvonen and Yocom 2011), with multiple forms of urban nature fueling civic association and attachment to place (Hinchliffe et al.

2005; Hinchliffe and Whatmore 2006). Pathways are intended to reveal the motivations of various stakeholders, reflect on decision-making processes, negotiate compromise, and critically assess the results of all urban greening projects. It is through this process of reflection and communication about urban nature in cities that we can leverage its inherent diversity to realize more livable and resilient cities of the twenty-first century.

Note

1   For a range of contemporary perspectives on urban nature, see Johnson and Hill (2002), Heynen et al. (2006), Waldheim (2006), Benton-Short and Short (2008), Radovic (2009), Mostafavi (2010), and Stefanovic and Scharper (2012).

References

Agyeman, J. (2005). *Sustainable Communities and the Challenge of Environmental Justice*. New York: New York University Press.

Agyeman, J., Bullard, R. D., and Evans, B. (2003). Introduction: joined-up thinking: bringing together sustainability, environmental justice and equity. In Agyeman, J., Bullard, R. D., and Evans, B. (eds), *Just Sustainabilities: Development in an unequal world*. London: Earthscan, 1–16.

Allen, P., FitzSimmons, M., Goodman, M., and Warner, K. (2003). Shifting plates in the agrifood landscape: the tectonics of alternative food initiatives in California. *Journal of Rural Studies*, 19(1), 61–75.

Andres, L. (2013). Differential spaces, power hierarchy, and collaborative planning: a critique of the role of temporary uses in shaping and making places. *Urban Studies*, 50(4), 759–775.

Arden, C. (2013, March 1). Manchester International Festival: fruit and veg sprout from industrial past. *The Guardian*. [Online]. Available: www.theguardian.com/uk/the-northerner/2013/mar/01/manchester-salford-biosphere-international-festival [August 5, 2013].

BBC News (2011, April 6). Manchester's first Garden City project gets under way. *BBC News*. [Online]. Available: www.bbc.co.uk/news/uk-england-manchester-12984084 [August 5, 2013].

Beauregard, R. (2003). Democracy, storytelling, and the sustainable city. In Eckstein, B. and Throgmorton, J. (eds), *Story and Sustainability: Planning, practice, and the possibility for American cities*. Cambridge, MA: MIT Press, 65–77.

Benton-Short, L. and Short, J. R. (2008). *Cities and Nature*. New York: Routledge.

Biospheric Project (2013). *Biospheric Project Website*. [Online]. Available: http://biosphericproject.com [August 5, 2013].

Brand, R. and Karvonen, A. (2007). The ecosystem of expertise: complementary knowledges for sustainable development. *Sustainability: Science, Practice & Policy*, 3(1), 21–31.

Cannavò, P. F. (2007). *The Working Landscape: Founding, preservation, and the politics of place*. Cambridge, MA: MIT Press.

CityCo (2013). *Manchester Garden City Webpage*. [Online]. Available: http://cityco.com/initiative/manchester-garden-city/ [August 5, 2013].

Dobson, A. (2003). *Citizenship and the Environment*. New York: Oxford University Press.

Evans, R., Guy, S., and Marvin, S. (2001). Views of the city: multiple pathways to sustainable transport futures. *Local Environment*, 6(2), 121–133.

Farmer, G. and Guy, S. (2002). Conditional constructions: environmental discourses on natural ventilation. *International Journal of Environmental Technology and Management*, 2(1), 187–199.

Gandy, M. (2002). *Concrete and Clay: Reworking nature in New York City*. Cambridge, MA: MIT Press.

Gottlieb, R. (2001). *Environmentalism Unbound: Exploring new pathways for change*. Cambridge, MA: MIT Press.

Grant, L. (2010). *Reclaiming East Manchester: Ten years of resident-led regeneration*. Manchester: New Deal for Communities.

Guy, S. (2004). Consumption, energy, and the environment. *Encyclopedia of Energy*, 1, 687–696.

Guy, S. (2006). Designing urban knowledge: competing perspectives on energy and buildings. *Environment and Planning C*, 24(5), 645–659.

Guy, S. (2012). Introduction: whither "Earthly" architectures: constructing sustainability. In Crysler, C. G., Cairns, S., and Heynen, H. (eds), *The SAGE Handbook of Architectural Theory*. Thousand Oaks, CA: Sage, 555–572.

Guy, S. and Farmer, G. (2000). Contested constructions: the competing logics of green building and ethics. In Fox, W. (ed.), *Ethics and the Built Environment*. London: Routledge, 73–87.

Guy, S. and Farmer, G. (2001). Reinterpreting sustainable architecture: the place of technology. *Journal of Architectural Education*, 54(3), 140–148.

Guy, S. and Marvin, S. (1999). Understanding sustainable cities: competing urban futures. *European Urban and Regional Studies*, 6(3), 268–275.

Guy, S. and Marvin, S. (2000). Models and pathways: the diversity of sustainable urban futures. In Williams, K., Burton, E., and Jenks, M. (eds), *Achieving Sustainable Urban Form*. London: E&FN Spon, 9–18.

Guy, S. and Marvin, S. (2001). Constructing sustainable urban futures: from models to competing pathways. *Impact Assessment and Project Appraisal*, 19(2), 131–139.

Guy, S. and Moore, S. A. (eds) (2005). *Sustainable Architectures: Cultures and natures in Europe and North America*. New York: Routledge.

Guy, S. and Moore, S. A. (2007). Sustainable architecture and the pluralist imagination. *Journal of Architectural Education*, 60(4), 15–23.

Guy, S., Marvin, S., Medd, W., and Moss, T. (eds) (2011). *Shaping Urban Infrastructures: Intermediaries and the governance of socio-technical networks*. London: Earthscan.

Hatherley, O. (2011). *A Guide to the New Ruins of Great Britain*. London: Verso.

Haughton, G. (1997). Developing sustainable urban development models. *Cities*, 14(4), 189–195.

Haydn, F. and Temel, R. (eds) (2006). *Temporary Urban Spaces: Concepts for the use of city spaces*. Basel: Birkhäuser.

Hebbert, M. (2010). Manchester: making it happen. In Punter, J. (ed.), *Urban Design and the British Urban Renaissance*. New York: Routledge, 51–67.

Hess, D. J. (2007). *Alternative Pathways in Science and Industry: Activism, innovation, and the environment in an era of globalization*. Cambridge, MA: MIT Press.

Hester, R. T. (2006). *Design for Ecological Democracy*. Cambridge, MA: MIT Press.

Heynen, N., Kaika, M., and Swyngedouw, E. (eds) (2006). *In the Nature of Cities: Urban political ecology and the politics of urban metabolism*. New York: Routledge.

Hinchliffe, S. and Whatmore, S. (2006). Living cities: towards a politics of conviviality. *Science as Culture*, 15(2), 123–138.

Hinchliffe, S., Kearnes, M. B., Degen, M., and Whatmore, S. (2005). Urban wild things: a cosmopolitical experiment. *Environment and Planning D: Society and Space*, 23(5), 643–658.

Jamison, A. (2001). Science, technology and the quest for sustainable development. *Technology Analysis & Strategic Management*, 13(1), 9–22.

Johnson, B. R. and Hill, K. (2002). *Ecology and Design: Frameworks for learning*. Washington, DC: Island Press.

Karvonen, A. (2010). Metronatural™: inventing and reworking urban nature in Seattle. *Progress in Planning*, 74(4), 153–202.

Karvonen, A. (2011). *Politics of Urban Runoff: Nature, technology, and the sustainable city*. Cambridge, MA: MIT Press.

Karvonen, A. and Brand, R. (2009). Technical expertise, sustainability, and the politics of specialized knowledge. In Kütting, G. and Lipshutz, R. D. (eds), *Environmental Governance: Power and knowledge in a local-global world*. New York: Routledge, 38–59.

Karvonen, A. and Brand, R. (2013). Expertise: specialized knowledge in environmental politics and sustainability. In Harris, P. (ed.), *Routledge Handbook of Global Environmental Politics*. New York: Routledge, 215–230.

Karvonen, A. and Yocom, K. (2011). The civics of urban nature: enacting hybrid landscapes. *Environment and Planning A*, 43(6), 1305–1322.

Leach, M., Scoones, I., and Stirling, A. (2010). *Dynamic Sustainabilities: Technology, environment, social justice*. London: Earthscan.

Light, A. (2003). Urban ecological citizenship. *Journal of Social Philosophy*, 34(1), 44–63.

Lyle, J. T. (1994). *Regenerative Design for Sustainable Development*. New York: John Wiley & Sons.

Macnaghten, P. and Urry, J. (1998). *Contested Natures*. Thousand Oaks, CA: Sage Publications.

Mallett, L. (2011, July 22). State of flax. *Property Week*. [Online]. Available: www.propertyweek.com/news/news-by-region/north-west/state-of-flax/5021932.article [August 5, 2013].

Marvin, S., Chappells, H., and Guy, S. (1999). Pathways of smart metering development: shaping environmental innovation. *Computers, Environment and Urban Systems*, 23(2), 109–126.

Melosi, M. (2000). *The Sanitary City: Urban infrastructure in America from colonial times to the present*. Baltimore, MD: Johns Hopkins University Press.

MERCi (2013). *Sow Sew Project Website*. [Online]. Available: www.merci.org.uk/drupal/node/2538 [August 5, 2013].

Moore, S. A. (2007). *Alternative Routes to the Sustainable City: Austin, Curitiba, and Frankfurt*. Lanham, MD: Lexington Books.

Moore, S. A. and Karvonen, A. (2008). Sustainable design in context: STS and design thinking. *Science Studies*, 21(1), 29–46.

Mostafavi, M. (ed.) (2010). *Ecological Urbanism*. Baden: Lars Müller Publishers.

Peck, J. and Ward, K. (eds) (2002). *City of Revolution: Restructuring Manchester*. Manchester: University of Manchester Press.

Pincetl, S. (2010). From the sanitary city to the sustainable city: challenges to institutionalizing biogenic (nature's services) infrastructure. *Local Environment*, 15(1), 43–58.

Pinderhughes, R. (2004). *Alternative Urban Futures: Planning for sustainable development in cities throughout the world*. Lanham, MD: Rowman & Littlefield Publishers.

Pinderhughes, R. (2008). Alternative urban futures: designing urban infrastructures that prioritize human needs, are less damaging to the natural resource base, and produce less waste. In Heberle, L. C. and Opp, S. M. (eds), *Local Sustainable Urban Development in a Globalized World*. Aldershot: Ashgate, 9–18.

Platt, H. L. (2005). *Shock Cities: The environmental transformation and reform of Manchester and Chicago*. Chicago, IL: University of Chicago Press.

Radovic, D. (ed.) (2009). *Eco-Urbanity: Towards well-mannered built environments*. New York: Routledge.

Rawsthorn, A. (2013, June 30). Garden of Eden amid rubble. *New York Times*. [Online]. Available: www.nytimes.com/2013/07/01/arts/design/Biospheric-Project-salford-england.html [August 5, 2013].

Rydin, Y., Turcu, C., Guy, S., and Austin, P. (2013). Mapping the coevolution of urban energy systems: pathways of change. *Environment and Planning A*, 45(3), 634–649.

Sim, D. (2009). The sustainable city as a fine-grained city. In Radovic, D. (ed.), *Eco-Urbanity: Towards well-mannered built environments*. New York: Routledge, 47–62.

Stefanovic, I. L. and Scharper, S. B. (eds) (2012). *The Natural City: Re-envisioning the built environment*. Toronto: University of Toronto Press.

Taylor, D. (2000). The rise of the environmental justice paradigm: injustice framing and the social construction of environmental discourses. *American Behavioral Scientist*, 43(4), 508–580.

Thomas Wilkins Design (2013). *Sow Sew, Thomas Wilkins Design Website*. [Online]. Available: http://thomaswilkinsdesign.com/#!sowsew [August 5, 2013].

Urban Catalyst (2003). *Strategies for Temporary Uses: Potential for development of urban residual areas in European metropolises*. Berlin: Studio Urban Catalyst.

Urban Catalyst (2007). Patterns of the unplanned. In Franck, K. and Stevens, Q. (eds), *Loose Space: Possibility and diversity in urban life*. New York: Routledge, 271–288.

Villagomez, E. (2010). Claiming residual spaces in the heterogeneous city. In Hou, J. (ed.), *Insurgent Public Space: Guerrilla urbanism and the remaking of contemporary cities*. New York: Routledge, 81–95.

Waldheim, C. (ed.) (2006). *The Landscape Urbanism Reader*. New York: Princeton Architectural Press.

Williams, G. (2003). *The Enterprising City Centre: Manchester's development challenge*. London: Spon Press.

Afterword

20

CITIES AND SURVIVAL

Thomas Fisher

This book marks a watershed in our thinking about cities. Other books have dealt with the relationship of nature and the city and the connection between landscape architecture and urbanism. But I know of no other that weaves together ecology, anthropology, urban design, and social activism with anywhere near the complexity and nuance of the essays in this book, while looking at cities across the globe, ranging from the wealthiest communities of Silicon Valley or in the Roppongi district of Tokyo to some of the poorest slums on the planet in cities like Nairobi or Mumbai. The editors call this "Now Urbanism," defining it as a "critical and complex practice that is simultaneously local, regional, and global" and that "views city making as grounded in the imperfect, messy, yet rich reality of the present city and the everyday purposeful agency of its dwellers" (p. 7).

I also think the book represents how we think about urbanism from now on. I say that, in part, because Now Urbanism reflects a much larger shift that will have an enormous effect on life in both the developed and developing world. That shift involves moving away from the mechanistic, hierarchical view of reality that arose during the Enlightenment and that prevailed through much of the twentieth century, and moving toward an ecological, networked view of reality, in which the "web" has become not just a place to seek or send information, but also a metaphor for how we now see ourselves and the world around us.

We no longer envision the brain, for example, as a giant computer but instead as a neural network; we no longer see organizations as well-oiled machines but rather as social networks; and we no longer describe the natural world as a competitive struggle for survival but now as an integrated web of life. In an intellectual context in which ecology has become the reality, it makes perfect sense to see cities the same way. As the authors here demonstrate to great effect, an ecological framework for investigating urbanism opens up all kinds of new possibilities and enables us to see things in completely new ways.

The Ecology of Cities

In the older, hierarchical, mechanistic worldview, for example, officials either ignored slums at the bottom of the economic pyramid or wanted to eradicate them as some sort of urban malfunctioning. The newer, networked, ecological worldview turns that thinking on its head. We now see informal settlements, as Kounkuey Design Initiative (KDI) puts it, "not as catchments of waste and poverty, but as spaces of renewal, entrepreneurship, and activism—as well as critical components in the reshaping of cities" (p. 177).

As many of the essays in this book make clear, we have a tremendous amount to gain from the ingenuity, resilience, and determination of the residents of these settlements, and a terrific asset to work with, given the rich networks of human and social capital that these communities have to offer. Rather than ignore or eradicate slums, we need to go to them, learn from them, and work with their residents not only to improve the lives of the people living there, but also to draw from them strategies that we will need to apply to cities everywhere, increasingly faced with what slum dwellers have long figured out: how to do more with less—often much less.

Systems of Survival

As such, cities have become about survival—not just the survival of individuals and families trying to improve their lives, but also the survival of whole districts in the city and of cities and regions themselves, trying to meet the growing demands on urban budgets and infrastructure with shrinking tax revenues and resources. The old hierarchical, mechanistic way of running cities has, at least in part, created this condition. When those at the top of a hierarchy think they have the answers and when they believe that a city should work as if it were a machine, too much of the goodwill of the people of a place goes unused and too many of the best ideas of the residents of a city get overlooked. Likewise, when we see cities and the various groups within them engaged in a competitive struggle, we fail to see the myriad cooperative and mutually reinforcing relationships that actually exist there now.

Now Urbanism completely reframes that situation. From this perspective, cities do not have deficits, but incredible abundance, with far more capital—human capital, social capital, and natural capital—than they have yet to figure out how to tap. And survival does not involve a ruthless struggle among the fittest, but a creative, entrepreneurial opportunity of reinterpreting, re-imagining, and repurposing almost anything and everything. In a web-like world, cities thrive according to how well they help their residents build and sustain their networks of relationships, which requires not a lot of money, but a great deal of sensitivity to the wealth that these human interactions create and a willingness to move obstacles to that wealth formation out of the way.

Panarchy Predictions

Cities also hold the key to our survival as a species. That may sound like an odd statement, given our dominance over most other species and the apparent invincibility that our technology has provided us. However, as we know from ecology, the very moment one species in an ecosystem becomes so pervasive, it also becomes extremely vulnerable—an idea explored in the work of the ecologists Lance Gunderson and Buzz Holling (2001). Their theory of "panarchy" recognizes that ecosystems become susceptible to collapse when one species becomes too dominant, efficient, and reliant on other species—as humans have become on this planet.

That makes the question of how we organize and operate cities—the most complex human ecosystems—so crucially important. If we continue to conceive of cities as highly efficient, interconnected, resource-intensive systems and design and operate them as we have in the past hundred years, we will only push ourselves more rapidly to a collapse of the human ecosystem, as panarchy predicts. If we follow the pathways laid out in this book, however, we can begin to move in a very different and less vulnerable direction. This involves—as Benjamin Spencer, Susan Bolton, and Jorge Alarcon write in Chapter 15—an "emergent" or "bottom-up" design of "small-scale, low-cost, ecologically responsive interventions in community infrastructure" (p. 214), and it entails, as the book's editors write in the introduction, "selecting those interventions that suggest a path towards the increased health of coupled human and natural environments" (p. 7).

Urban Scaling Laws

This incremental, accessible, sustainable, and participatory approach to city-building also shows why scale matters. If our dominance as a species threatens our viability, then breaking down the scale of what we do has not only practical value, but also real survival value. That relates to the work of Geoffrey West and his colleagues at the Santa Fe Institute, which Jon Christensen discusses in Chapter 6 (West 1999). The biophysicists there have discovered a universal scaling law in nature in which the metabolism or energy used by an organism equals its mass to the ¾ power ($E=m^{¾}$). This holds true for all plants and animals, with one exception, as I will get to in a moment. And the ¾ power means that organisms are "sublinear," realizing a roughly 15 percent increase in efficiency as they increase in size.

As West's colleague Luis Bettencourt has also argued, and as Christensen notes, cities achieve these same efficiencies of scale as they grow larger, using less energy and using their infrastructure more efficiently. However, they also have a "superlinear" tendency to speed up the pace of life and the rate of innovation as they grow in size, which counters the tendency of large organisms to slow down as size increases (Bettencourt 2013). This also leads to an increasing rate of negative effects like crime, pollution, and disease that makes it essential—especially in an era of growing mega-cities—that we design the metropolis to minimize such undesirable impacts. To do that, we need to engage the talents of everyone including the poorest residents of a city, use the environmental services of a region as effectively as possible, and put in place as much green infrastructure as we can. In doing so, we can not only reduce crime, pollution, and disease, but also improve the quality of life of every urban resident and the habitat of other species in the process.

Human Outliers

This will also require, though, an adjustment in how we define quality of life. As West has observed, the universal scaling law of nature has one outlier: us. Because of technology, human beings now have the metabolism or energy use equivalent to that of a blue whale (Lehrer 2010). When we consider a world made up of over seven billion blue whales—over seven billion of us—no wonder we have stressed the planet's ecosystems, affected its climate, and over-consumed its resources. This makes the study of informal settlements of the sort we have seen in this book doubly important. We need to understand how people can lead their lives with so little not only for humanitarian reasons, but also because we will all need to learn how to do this—either by choice in order to avert a collapse or by necessity if or when the collapse occurs.

Cities, then, represent a survival strategy for our species. However, that strategy will work only if we maximize the involvement, ingenuity, and imagination of absolutely everyone in the city, since we never know who will have the best idea, the most creative insight, or the most ingenious solution to the challenges we face. This, in turn, makes poverty something we can no longer afford. Every person who does not have an opportunity to realize their potential reduces the opportunity of all of us to achieve the kind of innovation that can mean the difference between our surviving or not. The stakes are that high.

Urban Futures

This recalibration of what constitutes a good life would be hard enough without our also having to deal with two of the most momentous and unprecedented changes that our species has ever faced. The first involves dramatic demographic change: the rapid rise in the number of people now on the planet, having increased from two billion to over seven billion people over the span of a single human lifetime, and the equally rapid rise in the number of people now living in cities. As Chelina Odbert and Joseph Mulligan state at the start of Chapter 13, "For the first time in history, more people are living in cities than in rural areas. By 2050, it is expected that 70 percent of the world's population will be urban" (p. 177).

The second monumental shift we face involves climate change and its effects on the natural environment. As Denise Hoffman Brandt observes in Chapter 17, there exist both "'gradual' effects of climate change (sea level rise, increased precipitation, and higher temperature averages) and 'extreme events' (storm surges, heavy downpours, heat waves, and high winds)" (p. 248). These have all happened with greater frequency and force than even many in the scientific community anticipated. And all of them will disrupt the "envelope of regularity," as William Morrish puts it in Chapter 5—"the safe and supporting urban landscapes" we seek to create for ourselves even as "our acts have produced a wilder and more unpredictable nature, throwing past environmental rhythms out of sync" (p. 66).

Avoiding Extinction

How we deal with the intersection of those two trends—our rapidly growing and urbanizing human population with our rapidly changing and destabilizing climate—will determine whether we survive as a species or whether we join the myriad other species facing what Richard Leakey and Roger Lewin call the planet's "sixth extinction" event because of our fragmentation of habitat and the disruption of vital ecosystems (Leakey and Lewin 1996). We should not discount the possibility—nor ignore the paradox—of our succumbing to the very things that we have brought on others. Few species rely on so many other species as we do and the more we undercut their viability, the more we threaten ourselves.

The survival of the human species may seem like so remote a possibility or an event so far off into the future that most people might not think it worth worrying about. After all, we live in an era of "urban triumphalism" as Jon Christensen so succinctly describes—and so ably debunks—in Chapter 6, and we have at our disposal an unbelievable level of technological prowess. As Morrish observes in Chapter 5, "As a society, we are producing and capturing more data each day than has been seen by everyone since civilization began" (p. 73). However, the very urbanity and technology that insulate us from the threats to our existence also ironically create the conditions most likely to bring us down.

The Vulnerability of Cities

There is a third threat that I have outlined elsewhere (Fisher 2013): not climate change per se, but disease transfer. The real threat comes in our having created the most efficient disease transfer technology ever devised: transcontinental jet airplanes. A virulent influenza pandemic of the sort that epidemiologist Michael Osterholm sees as "immanent"—or worse, a hemorrhagic fever of the sort that we have no immunity against or ability to stop—can now quickly move around the globe, infecting people before they know it in a rapidly spreading infection that may ultimately affect every human being (Osterholm 2005).

The prospect of such a pandemic relates to this book in several ways. First, it seems likely that the deadliest viruses will arise because of poor sanitation and the ease of disease transfer from animals to humans in one of the world's informal settlements. As Spencer, Bolton, and Alarcon note in Chapter 15, "an estimated 863 million people—approximately one out of every three people in the cities of the developing world—live in informal urban settlements . . . By the year 2050, this number could reach three billion, more than a third of the world's total population" (p. 206). As those numbers increase, so do the chances of a zoonotic disease developing and spreading.

Second, the pandemic will travel to cities first; the larger the city and the busier its airport, the sooner it will arrive there and the earlier the infection, when we have the least capacity to fight the disease. At the same time, it will likely strike the wealthiest populations—they travel more than the poor—first, countering the illusion of those in the developed world who may think that they have the means to protect themselves from any such illness. "In the event of a major pandemic," writes Dr. Grattan Woodson, "healthcare services and especially hospital services will be rapidly overwhelmed. It is likely that the healthcare system will be the first societal institution to collapse" (Woodson 2005).

Third, the best way to stop a pandemic involves arresting it at its source and slowing its spread, all of which plays to the themes taken up in this book. We greatly reduce our chances of a new zoonotic disease arising by improving the living conditions and sanitary systems of the world's poor. Several chapters here make that point in various ways, ranging from the efforts of Spencer, Bolton, and Alarcon in developing "small-scale, low-cost, ecologically responsive . . . infrastructure" in an informal Peruvian settlement (Chapter 15), to the work of KDI in engaging multiple stakeholders in participatory, multi-sector efforts to create networks of public spaces in a Nairobi slum (Chapter 13). Given the danger that the diseases bred in these informal settlements present to the entire human population, the cost of upgrading global slums seems minor compared to the likelihood that those who have the most to invest will also be among the first to pay the price in not doing so.

Deep Engagement in Places

Reducing the possibility of a global pandemic may also come from limiting or at least slowing the mobility of those who would travel from one part of the world to another. Here, the analogy of cities as ecosystems, which appears in several chapters, has particular importance. In Chapter 7, Judith Stilgenbauer writes about the landscape ecologist Richard Forman, who views "the landscape as a mosaic consisting of a matrix, patches (as the basic units that evolve and fluctuate), and corridors forming networks" (p. 95). This idea of landscape, when applied to urban form, results in a very different kind of city than the highly vulnerable, globally connected, and environmentally unsustainable metropolises we have built over the last century. The remarkable localism of so much of the work discussed in this book makes that clear. When we conceive of cities as mosaics of ecosystem patches, then urban life and professional practice involves not recklessly jet-setting around the world, carrying invasive species and infectious viruses with us, but instead engaging deeply and over the long term in particular communities, as several contributors in this book have described in places as diverse as Lima, Mumbai, Nairobi, and Tijuana.

Moving Bytes, Not Bodies

In Chapter 5, Morrish also highlights the flip side to this localism: the global digital revolution and the "Internet of Things" that link us instantaneously around the world. Too often the digital revolution gets viewed, wrongly, as irrelevant or even hostile to the needs of impoverished communities, as something controlled by and mainly available to global elites. While true on the face of it, this waste stream of information also has the potential, as Morrish recognizes, to provide "an open 'know-how' platform of collective trust to help citizens build and maintain a civil society, and a sustainable city" (p. 76). It also suggests a future in which we will stop moving bodies so frequently and so rapidly around the world—threatening all of us in the process—and instead will increasingly move digital bytes of data that can empower people in their local communities with the information that they need to have agency over their lives, and that we all need if we are to fully leverage the human capital required to innovate our way out of the demographic and environmental double whammy we face as a species (Fisher 2014).

Survival through Cities

Cities have long served as places of opportunity, and the rapid urbanization going on around the world testifies to that. As Spencer, Bolton and Alarcon summarize in Chapter 15:

> Since World War II, the global economy has become increasingly networked, and political and financial capital has concentrated in cities. At the same time, a lack of investment in rural populations, the industrialization of agriculture, and the commodification of land in the service of corporate interests have eroded rural livelihoods. Faced with few opportunities at home and drawn by the promise of a better life in the city, more than 70 million rural immigrants relocate to cities each year. More often than not, upon arrival their hardships are repositioned but continue unabated.
>
> *(p. 207)*

That promise of a better life, though, clearly trumps the hardships that continue, since people keep flooding into cities globally.

Living Off the Waste Stream

The lure of the waste stream that Morrish writes about in Chapter 5 in all of its variety has a lot to do with the sense of so many people that, whatever their challenges, cities still offer a better chance of surviving and eventually thriving. As the journalist Katherine Boo conveys so powerfully in her book about the Annawadi slum near Mumbai airport, scavenging, recycling, repurposing, and disposing of the enormous waste stream of products, materials, and resources in the city represents opportunities that rural people rarely have, and so urbanization feeds on itself (Boo 2012). The more people in a city, the more waste, and the more waste, the more people move to the city. As Morrish writes, quoting William McDonough, "waste equals food," which remains almost literally true in the case of the residents of many informal settlements. They have a better chance at feeding themselves and their families by living off the waste stream than by trying to grow their food themselves.

In this sense, the human ecosystem operates no differently than any other. As one of the only species that generates waste that ends up not as food for others, but as garbage in landfills, we have a lot to learn from the more advanced species we share the planet with that have long established a balance among predator, prey, and scavenger. We may think of ourselves as predators, but before we become some viruses' prey, we need to greatly increase our scavenging. The residents of informal settlements understand what a scavenging economy entails and the ingenuity it involves.

The Economy of Cities

A scavenging economy may also help us address the paradox of value that Adam Smith put at the beginning of *The Wealth of Nations* (1909–1914) and that capitalism has yet to resolve. Smith asked why we value diamonds that have no use but do not value water without which we cannot live. A moral philosopher by training, Smith thought that the invisible hand of the marketplace would solve that paradox by enabling people to do well financially and do good ethically—and environmentally—at the same time. This has not happened yet. We still over-value diamonds and under-value water to the point where large segments of the human population do not have ready access to clean water—something that, as we have seen, jeopardizes us all because of its pandemic threat.

To resolve the paradox of value, we will need to rethink—or rather finally achieve what Smith had in mind—capitalism and begin to treasure the things essential to life (clean air, fresh water, diverse species, the human imagination) and price out of reach everything that threatens our survivability (pollution, poverty, and predatory behavior of all kinds). This will, in turn, require an inversion of social mores in which status accrues to those who need and consume the least rather than, as today, the other way around. We will one day—and soon, I hope—admire the residents of informal settlements for this reason, for we ignore them at our own peril.

The Third Industrial Revolution

In many ways, the global economy has begun to move in this direction, in what the economist Jeremy Rifkin has called "the Third Industrial Revolution" (Rifkin 2011). This revolution represents a shift away from the mass production and consumption that characterized the Second Industrial Revolution, ushered in by the assembly-line process, and toward an economy based on mass customization and micro-production, enabled by mobile digital devices and "big data."

As Rifkin describes this Third Industrial Revolution, it sounds remarkably similar to the vision of the future laid out in this book. He sees the world's economy moving from the "top-down organization of society . . . to distributed and collaborative relationships," from "fossil-fueled" industry to a "green industrial era," and from "hierarchical power" to "lateral power" (ibid.: 37). At the same time, this revolution undermines the old hierarchical, capital-intensive, and resource-demanding production methods of the second one by empowering ordinary people with extremely low-cost production methods, as Gundula Proksch, Joshua Brevoort, and Lisa Chun mention in Chapter 18.

The Informal Economy

This also alters our perception of informal economies, which, as a couple of contributors note in their chapters, have become major players in the economic activity in many countries, as much as 40 percent of the annual output in developing countries. Economists have tended to see this as a transitional phase as these countries become more developed and presumably move toward a larger formal economy (Elgin and Oztunali 2012). However, Rifkin's assessment of where the global economy is heading suggests that informal economic activity might grow not just in developing countries, but in the developed world as well, as design and production go virtual and increasingly are undertaken anywhere and anytime by almost anyone.

Here, too, the study of informal settlements and human ecosystems has much to offer. On the one hand, everyone with a cell phone now has access to a vast, global market, making it possible for people to overcome the limits on their activities that impoverished places have placed upon them. On the other hand, the virtual, fluid nature of living, working, and making things in the Third Industrial Revolution makes place, paradoxically, an ever more important concept. Innovation will increasingly depend upon our maximizing the inter-actions among diverse people and human activities, making dense, mixed-use, and mixed-income neighborhoods of the sort discussed in this book vital to economic development.

Place-Based Thinking

This paradox of place becoming increasingly important in a placeless economy suggests another transition key to our thriving in the future. With the waning of hierarchical, mechanistic ways of thinking and of the capital- and resource-intensive methods of the Second Industrial Revolution will come a change in how we understand and sort our knowledge about the world. We continue to convey information in linear ways, in the form of books and e-books; to teach it according to disciplines; and to store it in libraries—real and virtual—by sequential number and lettering systems on shelves.

Whatever advantages this way of storing and accessing knowledge has had in order for us to command and control the world around us, it has also enabled us to damage the world and ultimately to harm ourselves because we do not organize our understanding of the world as it is inherently organized: by place. We see the world topically and sequentially, while it occurs spatially and temporally. This suggests that a tool essential to landscape architecture and urban design, geographical information systems (GIS), will eventually become a major way—perhaps the dominant way—in which we will access information in the future. For most of our history, humanity has understood the environments in which we have lived in this way. We survived as a species because of our knowledge of particular places and all that they comprise, and we will thrive in the future if we can rediscover that ancient way of knowing.

Spatializing Knowledge

This place-based way of knowing also reinforces the social and economic changes mentioned above. We have come to put a premium on text-based literacy, which has left out large segments of the human population that we consider "illiterate," without always acknowledging that there exist many kinds of literacy—social literacy, cultural literacy, and environmental literacy among them. The great opportunity suggested in so many of the chapters in this book lies in our coming to understand and appreciate these other ways of knowing and to "read" the world in new ways through these other forms of communication.

Which leads to a final point. The temporalizing of knowledge has, through the agency of history, helped us understand the past and possibly comprehend how the present came to be, but rarely do we venture very far into the future. We call that science fiction or fantasy in order to set such future-oriented thinking apart from what we can reliably know about the world as it is or once was. And we tend to see such futurist work as somehow of lesser quality or validity than knowledge substantiated in the sciences, social sciences, and humanities.

However, spatial understanding has a different relationship to the future, as well as the past and present. Spatial knowledge recognizes place, rather than time, as the ultimate continuity in our lives. And while none of us can predict the future, we continually picture in our minds the future of places, projecting possible spatial arrangements based on what we see around us. The design disciplines do this all the time, using spatial means to imagine what could be, envisioning the future of a place, product, or environment, and depicting it visually for others to see.

And in that lies perhaps the most powerful message of this book. Design emerges here not as many have seen it in the past, as a somewhat superficial activity involving subjective opinion and aesthetic preference, but instead as something key to how we will empower communities and build our cities in more sustainable, equitable—and indeed, survivable— ways going forward. Rather than seeing future-oriented thinking as somehow science fiction or fantasy, design allows us to connect what we know about the world with what we want the world to be—not just Now Urbanism, but also the urbanism that we now need to create, with books such as this as our guide.

References

Bettencourt, L. (2013). The origins of scaling in cities. *Science*, 340, 1438–1441.

Boo, K. (2012). *Behind the Beautiful Forevers*. New York: Random House.

Elgin, C. and Oztunali, O. (2012, May 10). Shadow economies all around the world: model-based estimates. *Vox*. Centre for Economic Policy Research. [Online]. Available: www.voxeu.org/article/shadow-economies-around-world-model-based-estimates [July 9, 2014].

Fisher, T. (2013). *Designing to Avoid Disaster: The nature of fracture-critical design*. New York: Routledge.

Fisher, T. (2014, January 24). Architecture in the Third Industrial Revolution. *Architect*. [Online]. Available: www.architectmagazine.com/urban-design/architecture-and-the-third-industrial-revolution_o.aspx [July 9, 2014].

Gunderson, L. and Holling, C. (2001). *Panarchy: Understanding transformations in human and natural systems*. Washington, DC: Island Press.

Leakey, R. and Lewin, R. (1996). *The Sixth Extinction: Patterns of life and the future of humankind*. New York: Anchor Books.

Lehrer, J. (2010, December 17). A physicist solves the city. *New York Times Magazine*, 46.

Osterholm, M. (2005, July/August). Preparing for the next pandemic. *Foreign Affairs*. New York: Council on Foreign Relations, 24–37.

Rifkin, J. (2011). *The Third Industrial Revolution: How lateral power is transforming energy, the economy, and the world*. New York: Palgrave Macmillan.

Smith, A. (1909–1914). *The Wealth of Nations*. C. J. Bullock (ed.) Vol. X. The Harvard Classics. New York: P. F. Collier & Son; Book IV.

West, G. (1999). The origin of universal scaling laws in biology. *Physica A*, 263, 104–113.

Woodson, G. (2005). Preparing for the coming influenza pandemic. *The Druid Oaks Health Center*, Decatur, Georgia. [Online]. Available: http://crofsblogs.typepad.com/h5n1/files/ComingPandemic.pdf [July 2, 2014].

ILLUSTRATION CREDITS

1.1   Photograph by Jeffrey Hou
1.2   Photograph courtesy of Informal Urban Communities Initiative (IUCI) Team
2.1   Photographs by author
2.2   Drawings by author
2.3   Drawing by author
2.4   Photographs by author
2.5   Data gathered from various sources; map generated by author
2.6   Image courtesy of Wikimedia Commons; data from Mike Davis, Planet of Slums
3.1   Courtesy General Electric
3.2   Courtesy Stanford University Archives
3.3   Map by Michael Reilly
3.4   Photograph by author
3.5   Photograph by author
3.6   Photograph by author
4.1   Photograph by author
4.2   Courtesy of SWA Group-City of Irvine-Irvine Company
4.3   Courtesy of SWA Group-City of Irvine-Irvine Company
4.4   Illustration by author
4.5   Illustration by author
4.6   Photograph by author
4.7   Adapted from Orillard and Picon (2012)
4.8   Illustration by author
5.1   Diagram from Visual Thesaurus 3 software developed by Thinkmap, Inc
5.2   Chart courtesy of Lisa Graumilch, Robert Costanza, Will Steffen, Carole Crumley,
        John Dearing, Kathy Hibbard, Rik Leemans, Charles Redman, and David Schimel
5.3   Drawing by author
5.4   Drawing by author
5.5   Drawings by author, adapted from Figure 5.2

6.1   From Bettencourt and West (2010), image courtesy of Macmillan Publishers Ltd: *Nature*, copyright 2010

6.2   Photograph courtesy of Save the Bay

6.3   Photograph courtesy of Ed Bierman

6.4   Courtesy of Save the Bay

6.5   Courtesy of Save the Bay

6.6   From Denning, McDonald, and Christensen (2010), courtesy of authors

6.7   From City Nature (2013), courtesy of Stanford University Libraries

7.1   Photograph by author

7.2   Image courtesy of Rainer Schmidt Landscape Architecture

7.3   Photograph by author

7.4   Photograph by author

7.5   Image courtesy of author

8.1   Photograph by author

8.2(a) Photograph by author

8.2(b) Photograph by author

8.3   Photograph by author

8.4   Photograph by author

9.1   Photograph courtesy of Koichi Torimura

9.2   Photograph courtesy of Koichi Torimura

9.3   Photograph courtesy of ON Design

9.4   Photograph courtesy of Koichi Torimura

9.5   Photograph courtesy of Children of Farmers

10.1   Photograph by author

10.2   Photograph by author

10.3   Photograph by author

10.4   Photograph by author

10.5   Photograph by author

10.6   Photograph by author

10.7   Photograph by author

10.8   Photograph by author

11.1   Photograph courtesy of San Francisco Planning Department

11.2   Photograph by author

11.3   Photograph by Rebar Group, Inc

11.4   Photograph by author

11.5   Diagram by Luchtsingel Rotterdam by ZUS

11.6   Photograph by Luchtsingel Rotterdam by ZUS

12.1   Photograph by Thomas Quine

12.2   Map by author

13.1   Courtesy of Jessica Bremner, Kounkuey Design Initiative

13.2   Courtesy of Kounkuey Design Initiative

13.3   Courtesy of Kounkuey Design Initiative

13.4   Courtesy of Kounkuey Design Initiative

13.5   Diagram by Jack Campbell Clause, Kounkuey Design Initiative; base image by Schreibkraft

14.1   Photograph by Daniel Schwartz/U-TT & ETH

14.2	Photograph by Daniel Schwartz/U-TT & ETH
14.3	Image by U-TT
14.4	Image by U-TT/Brillembourg & Klumpner Chair of Architecture and Urban Design, ETH
14.5	Photograph by U-TT/Brillembourg & Klumpner Chair of Architecture and Urban Design, ETH
14.6	Image by U-TT/Brillembourg & Klumpner Chair of Architecture and Urban Design, ETH
14.7	Photograph by U-TT/Brillembourg & Klumpner Chair of Architecture and Urban Design, ETH
15.1	Photograph courtesy of the IUCI team
15.2	Diagram courtesy of the IUCI team
15.3	Illustrations by Jessica Michalak and Michael Ward, 2012 Design Activism Studio
15.4	Photographs and diagram courtesy of the IUCI team
15.5	Photographs courtesy of the IUCI team
15.6	Photographs courtesy of the IUCI team
15.7	Photograph courtesy of the IUCI team
15.8	Photographs courtesy of the IUCI team
16.1	Photograph courtesy of W Architecture and Landscape Architecture
16.2	Photograph by Rick Johnson
16.3	Photograph by Rick Johnson
16.4	Copyright © 2010 Pato Safko
16.5	Photograph courtesy of Mixed Grill Productions and reSITE
16.6	Photograph courtesy of reSITE
16.7	Photograph courtesy of reSITE
17.1	Map by author
17.2	Diagram and photographs by author
17.3	Image by author
17.4	Diagram by author
17.5	Map by author, animation by Andrew Zientek
18.1	Rendering by authors
18.2	Diagram by authors
18.3	Diagram by authors
18.4	Diagram by authors
18.5	Rendering by authors
18.6	Rendering by authors
18.7	Rendering by authors
18.8	Rendering by authors
18.9	Diagram by authors
18.10	Rendering by authors
19.1	Photograph by Karen Wright Photography and CityCo
19.2	Photograph by MERCi
19.3	Photograph by author

INDEX

Numbers in **bold** refer to illustrations.